D0071226

A
SHORT HISTORY
OF EUROPE
1600-1815

A
SHORT HISTORY
OF EUROPE
1600-1815
SEARCH FOR A
REASONABLE WORLD

LISA ROSNER
JOHN THEIBAULT

M.E. Sharpe

Armonk, New York
London, England

Copyright © 2000 by M. E. Sharpe, Inc.

All rights reserved. No part of this book may be reproduced in any form
without written permission from the publisher, M. E. Sharpe, Inc.,
80 Business Park Drive, Armonk, New York 10504.

Library of Congress Cataloging-in-Publication Data

Rosner, Lisa, 1958–
  A short history of Europe, 1600–1815 : search for a reasonable world / Lisa Rosner
and John Theibault.
      p. cm.
  Includes bibliographical references and index.
  ISBN 0-7656-0327-6 (alk. paper) – ISBN 0-7656-0328-4 (pbk. : alk. paper)
    1. Europe—History—17th century. 2. Europe—History—18th century.
    3. Europe—History—1789–1815. I. Theibault, John, 1957– II. Title.

D246.R57 2000
940.2–dc21   00-035751

Printed in the United States of America

The paper used in this publication meets the minimum requirements of
American National Standard for Information Sciences
Permanence of Paper for Printed Library Materials,
ANSI Z 39.48-1984.

BM (c)   10   9   8   7   6   5   4   3   2   1
BM (p)   10   9   8   7   6   5   4   3   2   1

Table of Contents

List of Illustrations

PHOTOS

Preface

This book is a general survey of European history from roughly 1600 to the end of the Napoleonic era in 1815. It is designed to fill a niche between the large, multi-authored, general textbooks created expressly for Western Civilization and World History courses and specialized thematic or chronological surveys usually presented only in upper division college courses. Our goal is to be engaging for students, by giving ample coverage of personalities and events, while integrating insights from the last generation's research on social and cultural history, including women's history.

No such survey can lay claim to comprehensive coverage of all topics worthy of consideration, nor is it always easy to find a balance between being reader-friendly and methodologically up-to-date. We hope that our occasional extended discussions of some topics will prove more valuable for giving the flavor of the era than would the addition of three or four more facts or events within the same space. We have divided the overall content into four large chronological blocs and included a timeline at the end of each chapter to refresh the understanding of key concepts and relationships of the era. Each chapter ends with a "profile" of a person, event, or institution that is connected to the theme of the chapter, but which would not ordinarily be mentioned in a survey. Finally, we have included an extensive bibliography with each chapter, to provide students and instructors with both the sources of our arguments and the most recent interpretations of controversial issues.

Acknowledgments

This book would not have been written if it had not been for Jonathan Zophy. We first began thinking about the book when one of us used Zophy's survey of the Renaissance and Reformation with great success in an undergraduate early modern European history class. We contacted Zophy to express our students' enthusiasm for his book, and he encouraged us to write our own. Since then, he has been a constant source of support for the project. He has read almost all of the chapters and has been generous in criticism. We do not claim to have written the same kind of book that Zophy would have written had he attempted the period from 1600 to 1815, but we hope that our work serves as a worthy complement to his earlier work.

Other scholars have been equally generous in their support of our work. We want to acknowledge Bill Bowman, Magdalena Sanchez, Bill Bearden, and Eithne Bearden for reading some or all of the manuscript with meticulous attention.

A
SHORT HISTORY
OF EUROPE
1600-1815

Chapter One

Introduction: Sad Stories of the Death of Kings

On a frosty January afternoon in 1649, Charles I, King of England, mounted a scaffold in a small square near Whitehall palace in London. For the previous three weeks he had been subjected to a public trial under the authority of the English Parliament and had been found guilty of being a "Tyrant, a Traitor, a Murderer, and a Public Enemy to the Commonwealth of England." The sentence for his crime was "death, by the severing of his head from his body." A crowd of spectators filled the square, the adjoining streets, and the roofs of the surrounding buildings. The king gave a short speech, audible only to those onstage; then he prayed and signaled to the executioner when his prayers were finished. His last word was "Remember!"; his executioner's last words to him, as he laid his head on the block, were "an' it please Your Majesty." At the signal, the executioner's axe fell and severed the head from the body. The crowd let out "such a groan," one observer reported, "as I never heard before, and desire I may never hear again."[1]

Nearly a century and a half later, on a cold, gray morning in January 1793, another king, Louis XVI of France, mounted a scaffold on the newly renamed Place de la Revolution in France. Like Charles, Louis had been put on public trial, in his case by the National Convention, and had been found guilty of treason against the French nation. At the signal, the guillotine blade fell and severed the head from the body. At first, there was silence. Then some voices in the crowd took up the chant of "Vive la République!" "Long Live the Republic."

These two stories of executed kings frame the chronological period covered in this survey of European history and highlight many of its themes. First, of course, they point out that monarchy, government by

1

kings, was the normal form of government in the era, and that much of the political history of the era must be written in terms of the successes and failures of kings. But the fates of Charles I and Louis XVI were distinctive, even given that fact. Monarchs had been killed before and since, defeated in battle, deposed by rivals for the throne, assassinated by enemies and madmen. But these executions were not the ordinary products of the often bloody history of the European monarchy, inflicted by other princes who wished to claim for themselves the thrones of England or France. Instead, they were carried out by men who considered themselves to be the true representatives of the nation, justified in bringing "their Sovereign lord to public trial" for treason against his own country. These two cases—the only two such executions in European history—demonstrate the struggles over political authority that dominated the era. By what right, wrote one of Charles's supporters on the eve of his trial, did Parliament presume to try the king? Under whose jurisdiction would he fall? Who would be his peers to pass judgment? "Never was such damnable doctrine vented before in the world . . . it being contrary to the law of Nature, the custom of Nations, and the sacred Scriptures."[2] There was similar outcry against the imprisonment of Louis XVI. Reacting to the news of the execution, the French minister Talleyrand commented, "Since the leaders of the Jacobins down to the most honest citizens defer to the head-cutters, there is today nothing but a chain of villainy and lies, of which the first link is lost in filth." But the supporters of Parliament and of the national assembly had their own political principles. In the trial against Charles I, the prosecutor said, they "pronounced sentence not only against one tyrant, but against tyranny itself."[3] And Robespierre, pronouncing sentence in turn against Louis XVI, wrote, "I do not recognize a humanity that massacres the people and pardons despots." How had such different, contradictory political principles evolved within each country? And could such opposing definitions of nation, and commonwealth, and body politic, of treason and tyranny, ever be reconciled?

While highlighting these questions that unite the period, the two executions also point up the changes that took place in the 150 years separating them. The conflict between Charles and his Parliament was religious as much as it was political: both the king and his executioners were sure that they were acting in accordance with God's will. By 1793 neither Louis nor the National Convention had the same conviction that God's hand was omnipresent in determining the fate of nations.

Louis XVI's own reflections on his dilemma did not focus on religion, but indicated that a king "ought to devote himself entirely to the happiness of his fellow citizens . . . that he cannot promote the happiness of the nation but by reigning according to the laws; yet at the same time that a King cannot enforce those laws and do the good his heart prompts unless he be possessed of the necessary authority." It is not that religion "declined" or became unimportant for large segments of the population (although certainly more people would have been willing to claim that in 1793 than in 1649); but the particular urgency with which religious issues fused with political issues in the early seventeenth century had indeed declined notably by the end of the eighteenth century. How that happened is one of the themes of this book.

Equally striking was the result of the executions on the constitution of their respective governments. For though Parliament, on the death of Charles I, proclaimed a republic (a state ruled not by a king, but by "the people"), it lasted only four years before it was replaced by a quasi-military governorship under the authority of Charles's sternest opponent, Oliver Cromwell. On Cromwell's death, only the restoration of the monarchy had widespread support, and Charles's son, Charles II, returned to assume the crown amidst nearly universal rejoicing. The king was dead, but Charles II was greeted with the traditional acclamation of "Long Live the King," and in later years the eleven-year period between the death of Charles I and the restoration of Charles II came to be considered no more than a temporary gap, an "interregnum" (between the reigns) in the otherwise unbroken royal succession. In contrast, the execution of Louis XVI very quickly came to be seen as the end of the old order, the destruction of the "ancien régime": "The king is dead," proclaimed the crowd who witnessed it; "Long Live the Republic." What had occurred in the intervening 150 years to make two such similar deaths be interpreted so differently? Why was the first seen as a minor interruption, a blip on the screen which otherwise registered a straight line, while the second was perceived as a political event of seismic proportions, a political earthquake well off the existing scale?

Other similarities and differences highlight additional themes of this text. The public trials and public executions, the pronouncements of the prosecutors and response of the crowd, all demonstrate the creation of a public sphere for public events, distinct from the purely private sphere of personal affairs. The execution of Charles I widened public debate to encompass a whole set of public discussions on the nature of government and on ownership of property. By the time of Louis's execution, the discussion had broadened to include the nature of mankind, the origin of governments, the authority of fathers over children, and the relationships between men and women. It had broadened, too, to encompass a much wider social spectrum. The members of the National Convention who presumed to put their king on trial in 1793 were only a fraction of the educated public who presumed to form their own opinions of the trial from books and newspapers, as the "crowd" witnessing the execution formed only a fraction of the population of the lower orders intent on entering the arena of political action. Both executions sparked radical as well as conservative responses, calls for overturning the existing order as well as appeals for preservation of tradition. Where did the division of public sphere and private life come from? Why did it seem so much harder to change the social than the political order? Why could a nation depose a king, as the political theorist Mary Wollstonecraft asked, and not redress the inequity in the education of brothers and sisters?

A final theme highlighted by the executions and discussed in this text is the ongoing competition for power among European nations. The execution of Charles I was a local affair, of little concern outside of his own kingdoms. In contrast, the execution of Louis XVI became part of an international conflict that involved much of Europe for the succeeding twelve years. The countries that we associate with Europe today— Britain, France, the Netherlands, Spain, the German states—had once been collections of sovereignties bound together primarily through their allegiances to the families who ruled them. By the end of the eighteenth century they had become nations, whose jurisdictions reached far beyond the borders of Europe to include what they called the New World as well as much of Asia and Africa. The ideas that shaped the execution of Louis XVI were spread around the globe together with the conflict it engendered. When France sneezes, wrote one commentator, the rest of the world catches cold. How could the execution of one man come to have such an impact? How did the European world become the world itself? And how could ideas and institutions, conceived in one part of the globe, shape and be shaped by their transplantation to new environments?

The Search for a Reasonable World

In this text, we will address these questions as we trace the history of Europe from the early seventeenth century through the early nineteenth.

Our interpretation will be based on the notion that the century and a half prior to 1600 had posed a number of intractable problems, for which competing solutions were put forward. We have called the process of finding solutions the "search for a reasonable world" because "reason" became a powerful idea for justifying many of the solutions, but also because at no time did it seem that the "search" had been completed. We will follow political developments to see how kingdoms became nations and government by lords became government by the state. We will trace the path of diplomatic history to see how Europe expanded to include the world and countries became Great Powers. We will examine intellectual history to see the pursuit of truth and certainty in philosophy, in science, and in political theory. We will follow the creation of the public sphere, the relegation of women to the merely private, and women's struggle against it; we will follow, too, the rise of commercial culture and the economic expansion that made it possible. We will analyze the calls for reform and revolution in the late eighteenth century and their culmination in the French Revolution and Napoleon.

Throughout, we will stress the contested nature of these developments. For though history textbooks are usually written when the struggles they record are over, it is important to remember that those struggles existed, that men and women living in the period 1600 to 1815 did not know, as we do, how the events they witnessed would turn out and could not, as we can, turn the page to find out what happened. Like us, they believed that there was often a right path and a wrong path in human events; they believed, too, that much depended on their choosing the right path; but most of all they believed, again like us, that the question of right and wrong was a contested one, that they faced opposition, and that they had to choose with no foreknowledge of the future. As we read the pages of their history, then, we must try to understand it as they did. If we cannot give them our knowledge of their future, let us give them our sympathetic attention.

About the Term "Early Modern"

Historians invented the term "early modern" to cover a large chronological gap. Most have argued that the "modern world" began around 1800, the time of the French and Industrial Revolutions, when mass politics and rapid economic change became widespread. The Middle Ages, on the other hand, ended some time before then—depending on one's tastes, around 1300, 1400, or 1500. What, then, to call the three to five centuries between the end of the Middle Ages and the beginnings of the modern era? Since historians generally noted that the period between 1400 and 1800 carried the seeds of what came later, they have tended to emphasize the connection between that period and the modern world with the designation "early modern."

That long period also can be divided into at least two chunks. The first part of the early modern era falls fairly easily under the labels "Renaissance and Reformation." These were the two great cultural and social movements that dissolved the medieval worldview. There are any number of surveys that cover that period. But by 1600, the impetus of Renaissance and Reformation was beginning to wane. There are no neat labels for the succeeding two hundred years. The seventeenth century has been called "The Age of Crisis" or the "Age of Absolutism," and the eighteenth, "The Enlightenment," but historians argue about the validity of these labels even as they use them. It is important to remember that, for the men and women of the period, their own lifetime was always "the modern world." Any labels we may give it are only for our own convenience.

Further Reading

Other works concerning roughly the same era:

Maurice Ashley, *The Golden Century: Europe 1598–1715* (New York, 1969)
Raymond Birn, *Crisis, Absolutism, Revolution: Europe 1648–1789* (Fort Worth, 1992)
Euan Cameron, ed., *Early Modern Europe* (Oxford, 1999)
William Doyle, *The Old European Order 1660–1800* (Oxford, 1992)
Philippe Erlanger, *The Age of Courts and Kings: Manners and Morals 1558–1715* (New York, 1967)
Peter Gay and R.K. Webb, *Modern Europe to 1815* (New York, 1973)
Thomas Munck, *Seventeenth Century Europe: State Conflict and the Social Order in Europe, 1598–1700* (Houndsmills, England, 1990)
D.H. Pennington, *Europe in the Seventeenth Century* 2nd ed. (London, 1989)
Geoffrey Treasure, *The Making of Modern Europe, 1648–1780* (London, 1970)
E.N. Williams, *The Ancien Régime in Europe* (London, 1970)

Part I

ca. 1600–1660

Chapter Two

The European World in 1600

Nowadays, students learn that Europe is a continent, and an aerial view of its landmass, extending from the Arctic in the north to the northern coast of the Mediterranean in the south, with the Iberian peninsula jutting out into the Atlantic Ocean in the west, seems clearly to define a single, united entity except on the eastern frontier, where the Ural mountains form an arbitrary barrier between Europe and Asia. But in fact the area known as Europe comprises two distinct geographical and climatic zones.

The southern zone is dominated by the Mediterranean, the "sea between the land." It is arid, warm, and sunny, with wine and olives its agricultural staples. From ancient times, the human population has clustered in the thin strip of land between the coast and the mountains just behind, making ships the most efficient form of transport among human settlements. Only the most reckless of navigators—smugglers, for instance, seeking to avoid tolls levied by seaport towns—tried to sail directly across the Mediterranean, for once a ship was out of sight of land it lost all its bearings and might circle around and around forever. The subterranean wrecks found by modern divers are testimony to the dangers involved. For the most part, people and goods crept along the shore, never moving too far from the landmarks necessary for navigation.

North of the Mediterranean zone lie the great mountain ranges of Europe, the Pyrenees, the Alps, and the Carpathians. Prior to the railroad they were effective barriers, for there are only a few overland routes through the Alps, and each required long days of travel. The mountains divide the south from the great northern plain which stretches from central Asia to the Atlantic. The northern climate is called maritime, characterized by moderate, gray winters and cool summers. It is a good climate for growing grain, which, together with timber, was its agricultural staple since the ancient period, when the Roman empire conquered much of the region extending to northern England. The most northern reaches of the modern continent of Europe extend up to the Arctic circle, where winters are long and summers brief, though beautiful.

The real highways of Europe are the waterways, and nearly every important city was located on a seacoast or a navigable river. The proximity of coastlines oriented all European countries toward the sea. Inland there are the great transnational rivers, such as the Rhine and the Danube. The importance of the rivers, especially for north-south trade, was exploited early on by the countries they went through: the Rhine, for example, had as many tolls as some modern highways.

By 1600, Europe's reach extended far beyond its continental borders. Christopher Columbus had led the way in exploring the western hemisphere; Vasco da Gama had done the same in the Far East. Already in 1494, Spain and Portugal had reached an agreement that effectively divided the world in half between them—with the Americas (except for a small chunk of South America in Brazil) consigned to Spain, while Africa and the Indian Ocean were consigned to Portugal. Naturally, the inhabitants of those regions were not asked for their participation in this division, but neither were England, France, the Netherlands, or Denmark, each of whom staked its own claims overseas in the course of the sixteenth century. In effect, by 1600, Europeans considered regions of the world extending from Brazil to Nova Scotia, the Spice Islands to Cape Town, to be part of "Europe."

The Renaissance

In 1600, these disparate geographical regions were united by the common history of their human inhabitants. Renaissance humanism, which had first developed in Italy in the 1300s and then spread steadily northwards, held that early modern Europeans were the direct heirs of the Greek and Latin culture of the ancient Roman empire, even though large sections of the northern plain had remained outside the direct influence of ancient Rome. That culture, considered by Europeans the most glorious the world had ever known, had been almost lost during the Middle Ages, the period extending from the fall of the western Roman Empire in 476 A.D. until the 1300s. It was the task of humanists to revive and recreate it, to give it a "new birth" (hence the term *Renaissance* or "rebirth"). In Italy, artists of the Renaissance tried visibly to recreate the ancient world: Filippo Brunelleschi (1377–1446) created the great Dome of Florence by studying ancient models.

Humanists wished to revive written texts of the ancients, as well as their artwork. In England, the dramatist and poet George Chapman (1559?–1634) translated the ancient Greek poet Homer into English for the first time, considering the epics *The Iliad* and *The Odyssey* works of history as much as literature. The process of reviving texts was aided by the invention of the printing press by Johann Gutenberg (ca. 1398–1468) in the 1450s. Soon the invention spread throughout Europe, with books being produced in the hundreds. The early modern bestsellers were generally religious books, including the Bible in Latin and in translation. But they were followed closely by newly translated editions of Greek and Roman authors such as Plato (ca. 429–347 B.C.E.) and Aristotle (384–322 B.C.E.), and, later, by modern writers like the Italian Dante Alighieri (1265–1321) and the French poet Pierre de Ronsard (1524–1585). The printing press spread Renaissance ideas and culture; it also spread vernacular languages as they went from speech, to paper, to print.

Despite the humanists' assumption of a common history for all of Europe, the spread of culture via the printing press could produce division as well. Europe was divided by many different languages. The romance languages came from the old Roman Latin, but by 1600 had split into the languages common today: French, Italian, Portuguese, Spanish, Romanian. The Germanic languages, from the ancient Germanic tribes of Europe, had split as well into German, English, Dutch, and the Scandinavian languages. The Slavic languages, from the natives of the Baltic countries, had divided into Russian, Polish, Czech, Bulgarian, Serbian, and many others. There were even some peoples who spoke languages that were completely unrelated to the three main divisions: Magyar, in Hungary; Finnish and Estonian in northern Scandinavia; and Basque in the Pyrenees. In this hodgepodge of tongues, Latin was the common language of scholarship, of law, of diplomacy, even of international trade, and for some learned men could become more familiar than the vernacular: "The Latin tongue is to me in a manner natural," according to one French writer: "I understand it better than the French," and when his father became suddenly ill, "I . . . uttered my first words in Latin."[1]

The Reformation

The printing press helped unite Europe by spreading the Renaissance, but it also helped divide the continent, even more effectively than the mountain ranges, by spreading religious Reformation. The medieval definition of Europe was "Western Christendom," the part of the world which acknowledged the religious authority of the Pope of St. Peter in Rome. It was distinct from both the Byzantine Empire (also known as Eastern Christendom) in the eastern Mediterranean and the Islamic empires controlling the southern Mediterranean and the modern Middle East.

The pope's authority was called *Catholic,* meaning "universal," and children born in western Christendom were automatically Christian, in the same way as children born in a modern country automatically become citizens of that country. One set of exceptions was Jews, who were sometimes allowed to live in peace and practice their religion under the protection of a ruler. They were not, however, considered truly part of "Western Christendom" and were subject to periodic persecution.

Within the unity of Christian Europe, though, there were also divisions: over the authority of the pope against kings and princes in the regulation of religion, over the correct interpretation of the Bible, over the value of celibacy of the priesthood, over the value of the monastic orders. Many thoughtful people were concerned, too, about the abuses of the church that popes and other church officials seemed incapable of stopping. High church positions, like bishoprics and archbishoprics, were sold or simply awarded to noblemen's sons who seemed to have little religious feeling. Popular belief was that few priests were capable of celibacy, and many were downright immoral. Some church practices, such as the sale of indulgences, seemed to imply that people could buy their way into heaven. These questions became more and more hotly contested in the wave of religious feeling that spread over Europe in the early 1500s. In 1517, a monk and professor of Holy Scripture, Martin Luther (1483–1546), posted a paper consisting of 95 theses (arguments) against the sale of indulgences and other notorious practices. His followers, and those of other reformers, such as the Swiss preacher Ulrich Zwingli (1484–1531) and the French lawyer Jean Calvin (1509–1564), became convinced that true Christianity required a reformed church, one that did not follow the authority of the pope. Their teachings became the basis of a broad social and cultural movement called the Reformation. Catholic reformers like the Spaniard Ignatius Loyola (1491–1556), founder of the Society of Jesus (Jesuits), responded with a reformed Christianity that still required obedience to the pope, but eliminated abuses. Those who did not accept the authority of the pope began to refer to his church as "Roman Catholic" or, more derisively, "papists" or "popery"; the Catholics, in turn, referred to their opponents as "Protestants."

Religious differences led to religious war. No one believed in religious toleration. Instead, one of the obligations of a ruler was to ensure that his or her subjects were in the right relationship with God. This was essential not only for the salvation of the subjects—and the ruler—but for maintenance of order within the principality. As one writer put it, "Religion and Law are to be patronized and upheld as the Pillars of a Kingdom."[2] European rulers therefore began to choose sides among the different religious reformers. They were swayed by pragmatic considerations as well. If they supported Protestant ideas opposing convents and monasteries, they had an excuse to shut them down and confiscate their lands. If they supported Catholic ideas, the pope would be a useful ally in diplomatic negotiation.

War broke out first in the German principalities in the 1540s, ending at the Peace of Augsburg in 1555. The settlement contained the clause that rulers could choose either the Catholic or Lutheran faith for their territory. It became known as *cuius regio eius religio*: literally "whose region, his the religion." In the same period King Henry VIII of England (1497–1547) reformed the church in England along Protestant lines, making the king, not the pope, the head of what became known as the Anglican church. In France, rivalry between Catholic and French Calvinist (Huguenot) nobles erupted into bloody civil war between 1562 and 1598. In the Netherlands, the spread of Calvinist ideas led to revolt against the rulers, the kings of Catholic Spain, from 1566 to 1609. In all areas, individuals who did not accept the legally imposed religion were subject to persecution and, in many cases, execution. "See the horrible impudence with which we toss back and forth arguments concerning God's will," lamented the French writer Michel Montaigne (1533–1592). "There is no hostility so fine as Christian hostility. Our zeal does marvels when it supports our inclination toward hatred, cruelty, ambition, avarice, slander, rebellion. On the contrary, toward kindness, gentleness, temperance . . . it neither runs nor flies."[3] But Montaigne's plea for temperance was unusual. Western Christendom—Europe—had once been united by faith. Most people assumed that it would have to be united by faith again, by means of the sword, and gun, if necessary

14

Europe in 1559 (Copyright: Hammond World Atlas Corporation, NJ, Lic. No. 12504)

A Tour of Europe in 1600

In 1591 Fynes Moryson, a twenty-five-year-old Englishman, set out on the first of several journeys around Europe that were to occupy his time for the next ten years. His aim was to provide a written account of the countries—the commonwealths, as he called them—of the principal part of the world. We can take his full and circumstantial writings as our guide, though we will omit some places on his itinerary and add others. Before we begin, though, we must fill in a few details Moryson and his readers would have taken for granted. Though he learned German, Italian, and French, he conversed with most of the people he met in Latin. That meant that most of the conversations he had were with the elite of educated men. He was a sharp observer, however, and though he spoke to few farmers or artisans, his curiosity did extend to features like agriculture, crafts, and even marriage and birthing customs.

A very few of the countries he visited were republics, governed by a body of men considered to be representative of the commonwealth, though "representation" was, by modern standards, very limited. Most countries were kingdoms, or dukedoms, or principalities, and they had a monarch, or sovereign lord, who could have a variety of titles, such as king, queen, duke, landgrave, prince. The prince to whom Niccolo Machiavelli (1469–1527) addressed his political treatise of that name was a sovereign lord over his territory, not the son of a king. A sovereign "lord" could be male or female: in 1591, King Henry IV of France (1553–1610) and Queen Elizabeth I of England (1533–1603) were both sole rulers of their kingdoms. Though rulers could seize territory, the most usual way for a monarch to acquire a kingdom was through inheritance, following the same inheritance law as everyone else in the kingdom. Royal marriages were thus enormously important in international diplomacy, for descendants of well-planned marriages could acquire vast territories. The kings of France acquired the wealthy territory of Brittany through marriage, which increased their domain substantially. By their marriage in 1469, Isabella of Castille (1451–1507) and Ferdinand of Aragon (1452–1516) united Spain; similar marriage strategies led to the rule of their grandson, Charles V (1500–1555), over territory stretching from the Netherlands to Austria to the Iberian Peninsula to Spanish territories in South America. Yet though disparate kingdoms might all have one sovereign lord, those kingdoms generally resisted the efforts of their lord to impose uniform administration and, especially, uniform religious practices. The struggle between rulers trying to centralize authority, and countries trying to maintain local customs and traditions, went on throughout the early modern period.

England

We can start our tour with Moryson's own England, which included the ancient Kingdom of Wales, conquered by the English crown in the Middle Ages. Ireland also belonged to the English crown. In 1542, Henry VIII declared himself "king" instead of just "lord" of Ireland. But practically speaking, for much of the sixteenth century Ireland remained independent. Only the immediate vicinity around Dublin, called "the Pale," was touched by the Reformation of the church in England under Henry VIII. As the English tried to exert more control in the course of the sixteenth century, they provoked resistance, culminating in a revolt in the 1590s that was brutally suppressed.

In 1600, the ruler of the English kingdoms was a queen, Elizabeth I, of the Tudor family. She was considered one of the greatest statesmen of her day, with a talent for choosing able ministers, and her long reign gave both political and religious stability to the country. Though the Anglican church established by Henry VIII was the only legal religion, Elizabeth preferred to fine, rather than execute, those who refused to attend the established church. As a Protestant ruler with ships able to challenge the naval power of the much stronger and wealthier kings of Catholic Spain, Elizabeth was seen as the champion of the Protestant cause in Europe. Moryson mentioned "the heroic virtues of Queen Elizabeth, her great actions in Christendom, and especially her prevailing against the Pope and king of Spain, her professed enemies." Unfortunately he did not give us his opinion of any of the writers for whom we now remember the Elizabethan Age, Christopher Marlowe (1564–1593), Edmund Spenser (ca. 1552–1599) and William Shakespeare (1564–1616) only mentioning that as there were "more plays in London than in all parts of the world I have seen, so do these players . . . excell all other in the world."[4]

Scotland, part of modern Great Britain, was a separate kingdom in 1600. Throughout the preceding 600 years it had often been allied with France against England, but since the Reformation the Church of Scotland had been Calvinist (Presbyterian), and it had turned away from Catholic France. The King of Scotland, James VI, was from the Stuart family; he was Elizabeth's closest male relative and generally expected to be her successor, since Elizabeth, in an unusual decision for the era, chose never to marry and thus had no direct successors.

France

Just as the English crown was about to pass to the Stuart family because the Tudor family produced no more heirs, so the French crown passed in 1589 from the Valois to the Bourbon family after the former died out. But that transition was even more fraught because it took place in the midst of a devastating civil war. The new king, Henry IV, only secured his succession when he renounced his Calvinist religion and declared himself ready to convert back to Catholicism in 1593. It took until 1598 for Henry to pacify the factions in the civil war. He then issued the Edict of Nantes, which gave freedom of worship to Huguenots as well as allowing them their own law courts and governance of important cities.

No royal edict could unify the entire country, however. French was the language of the king's realms and the central part of the country. But regions like Brittany, in the north, and Languedoc, in the south, still had their own languages, customs, and privileges. The Edict of Nantes left significant parts of western and southern France under the practical control of the Huguenots. Nor were all French-speaking regions incorporated into the French crown. Especially on its eastern border, the German Holy Roman Empire contained several French provinces.

Moryson was impressed, like most travelers, with the sheer agricultural wealth of the country. The French did not have much interest in navigation or commerce, he noted, "because they abound almost with all things for plentiful food and rich attire, and if they want any thing, strangers gladly bring it to them, and exchange it" for the commodities of wine, salt, linen cloths, and wheat, "which in that respect some call the lodestones (magnets) of France."[5] He noted, too, the many rivers that connected the wealthy cities and facilitated trade. Measured by population as well as agricultural resources, France was the wealthiest country in Europe.

Italy

Italy, home of the Renaissance, was one of the favorite destinations for most travelers. Even in 1600, long after Michelangelo, Moryson noted that, "for painting, sculpture, or carving in brass and stone, and for architecture, they have been of old and still are most skillful masters." Unlike France, Italy was not and never had been ruled by a single monarch. It consisted of a mixture of small and large principalities, all of whom, complained Moryson, "impose not only upon their subjects but upon all strangers passing through . . . very many tolls, customs, and like exactions. . . . The cities, towns, and new territories of petty princes are very frequent, so as a traveler passeth in any of them in one day's journey, and he cannot pass a town or a bridge, but he shall pay."[6]

The political landscape of Italy was complicated by the fact that the papacy itself ruled an extensive territory. Indeed, a frequent complaint of the era was that the pope was so preoccupied with his secular responsibilities as a territorial ruler that he neglected his spiritual duties to Christendom. He was deeply involved in the struggles between France and Spain for political predominance within Europe, which meant that he could be seen taking sides between the two most powerful Catholic states. The territories south of Rome were ruled by the king of Spain, who also had a great deal of influence over the city of Genoa, in the north, the birthplace of Christopher Columbus, who had sailed under the Spanish flag. The French, meanwhile, had a powerful ally in the dukes of Florence, the de Medici family, whose territory included the cities of Pisa and Siena, conquered in the fifteenth and sixteenth centuries.

The third major power within the Italian peninsula was the Republic of Venice, which had been famous (indeed infamous) since the Middle Ages for its wealth built on the monopoly of trade with the "Levant," the term Europeans used to refer to the Middle East under the rule of the Ottoman Turks. Venice was the preeminent naval power in the Mediterranean. It was one of the few territories in Europe not ruled by a prince, but was nevertheless widely sought after as an ally because of its wealth. Moryson was astute in noting that a balance of power existed among all the Italian rulers, with the "union of the Pope, the State of Venice, and the great Duke of Florence," as the greatest force for stability.

Spain and Portugal

The economic preeminence of the Italian city states, especially Venice, suffered a notable blow from the rise of the Atlantic trade beginning in the fifteenth century. The true pioneer in the Atlantic was Portugal, which, like France and England, saw its ruling house become extinct in the late sixteenth century and was incorporated into the Spanish crown in 1580. By that time, the Portuguese had established several bases along the African coast and forged trading connections as far as modern Indonesia. They also set up their South American colony, Brazil, as a source for raw materials. Already in the 1530s they had established sugar plantations and begun transporting Africans as slaves to work in them. The plantation system was to become the model for European economic dominance in the seventeenth century, but in the sixteenth century, Portugal undoubtedly profited much more from its Indian Ocean trade (which reached Europe via the Atlantic) than it did from Brazil.

The first country to profit from the Americas was Spain. Columbus's voyage of 1492 was just the start of a wave of voyages of exploration and conquest that left Spain in nominal control of most of the Caribbean and Central and South America by the end of the sixteenth century. Unlike the Portuguese, the Spanish actively settled many of the regions that they laid claim to. The massive transfer of plants and animals between the old world and the new is sometimes called the "Columbian Exchange," but in the sixteenth century, the most obvious "exchange" between the old world and the new was that large quantities of gold and silver were extracted from mines in Mexico and Bolivia and sent to Spain's main trading centers in Europe. Spain was a major power in European affairs for many reasons in the sixteenth century, but the treasure coming from the New World was perhaps the most important.

For all his roaming across Europe, Fynes Moryson never went to Spain. As an Englishman and Protestant, he would have immediately stood out as an enemy there. In all the religious tumults of the sixteenth century, Spain stood as a bedrock of defense of the Catholic faith. It was the place where Protestantism made the fewest converts and the crown wavered the least in its promotion of Catholicism. Thanks to the union of the territories of Aragon and Castile under Ferdinand and Isabella in 1469, virtually all Spanish-speaking territories were subject to the Spanish crown. The last outpost of Muslim rule had been driven from the Iberian peninsula in the same year that Columbus set sail. The crusading spirit that infused Spanish society shaped the strong Catholic identity. But like France, Spain possessed a number of different regional cultures and languages that hindered unity. Castile was the "heart" of Spain, but Aragon maintained its own identity and was never fully integrated into the Castilian system.

Throughout the sixteenth century, Spain's Catholic identity was backed by the most powerful armed forces in Europe. The Spanish army was the most technically advanced in Europe, while the fleet possessed the most modern fighting vessels. That army was in constant use during the reign of Philip II (1527–1598), the king who ruled over Spain at the height of its power. In 1588, just three years before Fynes Moryson set out on his journey, Spain had attempted to invade England with its powerful fleet, called the Armada. But compared with Spain's principal conflicts, with France and the Netherlands, the Armada was a sidelight. The strains of financing constant warfare proved to be too great for the Spanish crown, despite the constant influx of new gold and silver from the new world. Philip's grand designs were often thwarted by the fact that the money ran out and the crown was forced to declare bankruptcy.

The Netherlands

From the perspective of today, it can be hard to appreciate how much the fortunes of Europe in the later sixteenth century hinged on a conflict between the Spanish and the Dutch. In the early sixteenth century, the Netherlands consisted of seventeen provinces ruled by the Spanish Habsburgs. But in 1566 those provinces revolted to preserve both traditional custom and the Calvinist faith. Philip II could not tolerate either of these principles and so set about trying to reconquer the rebellious territories. Though Spain was Europe's most powerful country, the Netherlands were deceptively powerful as well. A substantial part of the wealth generated in the New World had flowed through the Netherlands, especially the port city of Antwerp. The Dutch were wealthy, stubborn, and well-connected with other powers. Thus, despite possessing the greatest army in Europe, the Spanish were only able to fight the Dutch to a draw. Neither side accomplished all of its goals, but the Spanish had to swallow the greater defeat. The original seventeen provinces were divided into two new states: the origins of modern Belgium and the Netherlands.

The northernmost seven declared their independence as the United Provinces in 1581. Each province was governed by a body called the Estates, which was dominated by wealthy merchants. A federal body, called the States General, managed the foreign affairs of the United Provinces. Delegates from the States General to each provincial Estate were called stadtholders. In 1600, the stadtholders were princes from the house of Orange and Nassau, sons of William of Orange (known as William the Silent) (1533–1584), who had led the revolt against Spanish rule.

The Low Countries, as they were sometimes called, had been a major center for international trade since the Middle Ages, and the United Provinces carried on that tradition in dominating overseas trade. The war with Spain, as Moryson astutely noted, had fallen particularly hard on the southern provinces, and the United Provinces benefited by extending their trade, drawing "the commodities of all nations to them, and fetch them from the very Indies, and in like sort they transport them to the remotest parts, where they yield most gain."[7] Amsterdam, in Holland, became the most important commercial center in Europe. The United Provinces were Calvinist, but became known as a haven for freedom of conscience. Holland, especially, became a center of the book trade, with Amsterdam, Leyden, Rotterdam, The Hague, and Utrecht as major publishing centers.

The ten southern provinces, including the wealthiest, Flanders, continued to be ruled by Spain. Most of the ringleaders of the original revolt had been from Flanders, but they all fled or were executed, so that the so-called Spanish Netherlands became a devoutly Catholic region. Flanders was as renowned as Italy for its skilled craftsmen, especially artists, and provided many of the most prominent artists for the Spanish court, such as Peter Paul Rubens (1577–1640). But economic competition between Spain and the Northern Netherlands continued in the seventeenth century, and the wealth of the great cities of Flanders—Ghent, Bruges, and Antwerp—was eclipsed by their northern neighbors.

The Holy Roman Empire

The situation of the Netherlands was complicated for yet another reason. While subject to the Spanish Habsburg crown, they were also part of another political structure, under the nominal rule of the other branch of the Habsburg family in Austria, called the Holy Roman Empire. The Holy Roman Empire consisted of hundreds of principalities in what is now Germany, Poland, the Netherlands, and Eastern Europe. Some, like Bavaria, were large and important principalities; some, like Hesse, were small. Some were independent city-states governed by a town council, like Strasburg on the Rhine, while others were called "ecclesiastical states," ruled by a bishop or archbishop. The office of emperor was formally an elected position, with seven of the principalities retaining, by long tradition, the privilege of voting; but in practice the powerful Habsburgs, territorial rulers of Austria and Hungary, had been elected for the preceding 150 years.

The emperor in 1600 was Rudolf II (1552–1612). Though himself a Catholic, he acceded to the settlement of the Peace of Augsburg, which allowed the ruler of each German principality to decide the religion of his or her own territory. The result was that the territories of the two most powerful rulers in the Empire, the Habsburgs of Austria and the dukes of Bavaria, as well as the territories ruled by bishops and archbishops, were Catholic. The rest of the principalities were either Lutheran or Calvinist. Formally, Calvinist worship was not permitted by the Peace of Augsburg, but, Moryson stated, when Emperor Rudolf tried to outlaw it, "his subjects . . . raised a tumult, which he was forced to repress by restoring freedom of conscience, they . . . protesting they would rather be subject to the Turk permitting them that freedom, than be vexed by a Christian prince for their conscience."[8] The Holy Roman Empire was, therefore, a curious hybrid. In one sense, the emperor was supposed to be first among all the kings of Europe. (The title came from the claim that the emperor was the successor to the ancient Roman empire and the empire of Charlemagne.) But his practical power was limited by the fact that each of the territories within the empire had its own ruler who did whatever he wanted and listened to the emperor only when it was in his own interest. And while the Holy Roman Empire was mostly German, there was a variety of other languages and cultures within it, like the Dutch and Bohemians, who complicated the picture still more.

Bohemia

The imperial court during the reign of Rudolf II was in the city of Prague, in the kingdom of Bohemia (the modern Czech Republic). For Moryson, Bohemia offered in microcosm the peculiarities of religious diversity within the Empire. "Generally in all the kingdom there was great confusion of Religion so as in the same city some were Calvinists, some Lutherans, some [other faiths] . . . some Papists (Catholic). . . . And as the Jews have a peculiar city at Prague, so they had freedom throughout all the kingdom. Yea the same confusion was in all villages, and even in most of the private families, among those who lived at one table, and rested in one bed together. For I have often seen servants wait upon their masters to the Church door, and there leave them to go to another church." Still, among German territories, the situation in Bohemia was unusual, since, Moryson said, "the subjects of diverse princes meet together at marts, and like public assemblies, whom I never observed to dispute seriously about religion, but only sometimes to pass many quips and jests one against the other." In south and central Germany, "where each absolute Prince allows but one religion in his dominion," Moryson wrote, Lutherans and Calvinists attack both Catholics, and each other, for "they will not hear other doctrine preached without tumult."[9]

Switzerland

Moryson might have made the same observation about the Swiss, yet another group that was nominally part of the Holy Roman Empire, but that had made itself essentially self-standing during the Middle Ages. Made up of small city-states, called cantons, nestled in the Alps, Switzerland was chiefly known as the provider of the best mercenary soldiers in Europe. Poor in agricultural resources, with few waterways to stimulate trade, the Swiss cantons contracted out regiments of foot soldiers to other monarchs. "The Swiss are by nature, education, and much more by reward, given to the military life," wrote Moryson, " for they are born in the high mountains called the Alps . . . apt to suffer labor, cold, hunger, and thirst." They were also, he noted, "lovers of liberty"[10] who had been helped by their geography to resist the Holy Roman Emperors during the Middle Ages. For most of the early modern era, the phrase "turning Swiss" was synonymous with popular rebellion. As one German nobleman complained, "Everyone wants to be free, just like the Swiss."[11]

The Swiss cantons were separately governed, usually by a council or other representative body. Some had remained Catholic, while others had adopted one or another of the Protestant faiths. Jean Calvin had been the minister of Geneva until his death, and in 1600 Geneva was still the center of Calvinist theology and education.

Denmark and Sweden

The Scandinavian countries of Sweden and Denmark had long been united socially and culturally, with languages so similar as to appear to be two dialects, and a nobility that freely intermarried. Politically, though, they had separated in the early sixteenth century, and divergent political interests sometimes led to conflicts between their rulers. The Kingdom of Denmark, including the territory of modern Norway, was ruled by King Christian IV (1577–1648). Moryson saw him on his trip to Denmark in 1593, describing him as "of a fair complexion and big set . . .

and they said he could speak the Dutch, French, and Italian tongues, and was delighted with shooting a musket, with music and with reading of histories, and spent two hours in the morning and as many after dinner at his book."[12] Denmark's main economic resource was its access to both the North and Baltic Seas. All ships who traded in the Baltic had to pass through the Danish sound and pay a toll. Throughout the sixteenth century Denmark challenged the commercial power of Hansa towns, northern German trading cities including Lubeck and Bremen. As a Lutheran principality under the Holy Roman Empire, though, it had more recently been forging alliances with other Protestant German territories. Like Shakespeare's Hamlet, Danish princes often studied at the University of Wittenberg, and the names of two of the characters in the play, Rosenkrantz and Guildenstern, are those of traditional noble families attached to the Danish court.

In 1600 the Kingdom of Sweden still looked more to the east than south towards central Europe, and included the territories of Finland, Estonia, and Livonia. In 1600 the King, Karl IX (1550–1611), of the Vasa family, had just wrested control from his nephew Sigismund, who was also King of Poland. The civil war had involved religious as well as dynastic issues, for Karl had, Moryson reported, "the suspected favor of the people, he being of the reformed religion," Lutheran, as was much of the country, while Sigismund had been "brought up by his mother in the Roman [Catholic] religion."[13] Though Karl IX openly courted the German Protestants, few heads of state in continental Europe concerned themselves over the Swedish dynastic struggle or gave Sweden the same importance as England or the Dutch as champions of the Protestant cause.

Poland

Part of the reason for Karl's failure to attract international respect was the fear of offending King Sigismund III (1566–1632), as he was known in Poland, for his Polish territories dominated the Baltic grain trade. When Moryson visited Poland, it was formally a republic, comprising the principalities of Poland and Lithuania. The representative body was the Sejm, which consisted of all nobles who cared to attend, and each noble, no matter what his economic status or political experience, had the right to veto any legislation. The motto of the Republic of Poland-Lithuania was "It is by unrule that Poland stands,"[14] and certainly the process worked well to prevent the centralization of royal authority over nobles that took place elsewhere in Europe. The Polish nobility—perhaps 1,300 of them at a time—elected their king at a great ceremony "near Cracow," wrote Moryson, "and lasts some six weeks, all the Gentlemen lying in tents like an army taking up some ten miles compass, and having a great tent for the general meetings."[15] Before taking office, the king was required to swear to the nobility's free right to elect the future king, to approve all declarations of war and imposition of taxes, and to resist the currently elected king if he tried to impose his own authority.

The decentralization of authority had the consequence that, though there was as little true religious tolerance in Poland as elsewhere in Europe, there was little religious fighting, for neither king nor noble had the authority to impose his religious beliefs on anyone else. Adherents to the Catholic Church were a dominant minority in the sixteenth century and grew steadily to a majority, but both Protestant denominations and Jews maintained their religious communities. The Confederation of Warsaw, a meeting of religious leaders in 1573, declared, "We swear to each other . . . that we who differ in matters of religion will keep the peace among ourselves, and neither shed blood on account of differences of Faith, or kinds of church, nor punish one another by confiscation of goods, deprivation of honor, imprisonment, or exile."[16]

Russia

On the frontiers of Europe were two large states that were partly European and partly not. Russia had been historically on the margins of Europe, because it had never been within the influence of the Roman church. Its faith was Eastern Orthodox Christianity, which, while Christian, was different enough from either Catholicism or Protestantism to arouse suspicions in both. Because of their faith, the Russians had been oriented towards Constantinople rather than the West. Their rulers adopted the title "czar" after Constantinople fell, thus assuming both the religious and political continuity of the eastern half of the Roman Empire.

The sixteenth century was a harsh time in Russia. From 1549 to 1584, the state was ruled by Ivan "the Terrible," who instituted a reign of terror against supposed political opponents. Ivan's policies had weakened the position of the Russian nobility, called the *boyars*, which perhaps prevented Russia from developing in the direction of noble anarchy that Poland did. But at his death, the boyars attempted to regain their preeminence and launched a period known as the "Time of Troubles," a civil war between various noble factions, which lasted until 1613. At that point, a new ruling family was selected, the Romanovs, who were to continue in power until 1917.

The Ottoman Empire

The other frontier of Europe was the southeast, which was dominated by the Ottoman Empire. The Ottoman Empire was at its greatest extent during Moryson's travels, when it included modern Turkey, Greece, Armenia, the Middle East, and North Africa. It had long been outside the boundaries of the European world, since its inhabitants were Muslim, not Christian, but it had also been at the forefront of European consciousness, because it controlled many of the key sites of the Christian tradition. To fight against the Turks had been something of a spiritual necessity ever since the Crusades, which began in the eleventh century. The last crusade had petered out by 1291, but fighting continued off and on throughout the sixteenth and seventeenth centuries. Furthermore, as Western Christendom itself was divided by religious differences, rulers sought allies from afar. Francis I of France sought help from the Sultan Suleyman in his wars against Charles V, Holy Roman Emperor. The Ottoman navy dominated the eastern Mediterranean until defeated at the battle of Lepanto in 1571, and word of the invading Ottoman armies could still frighten Europe until 1683, the last time they attempted to invade Vienna.

Moryson, like most Europeans, was fascinated by the great riches of this vast empire but repelled by the power of its sultans. Some of the riches were spiritual, for within the sultan's territories lay the city of Jerusalem, and there was "no place more worthy to be viewed in the whole world," Moryson thought, which "filled my mind prepared to devotion, with holy motions." Moryson could not but be impressed by the wealth of the chief cities, of Constantinople on the Straits of the Bosphorus; of Cairo, whose "rich traffic . . . yields exceeding great revenues" to the Sultan; of the famous city of Aleppo, "whither all the precious wares of the East are brought by great rivers and upon the backs of camels." He was appalled, though, by the absolute power of the sultan, for technically all inhabitants of the empire were his slaves, and Muslim nobles did not form part of the central government. Instead, children of Christian lands subject to the Sultan, called *devshirme,* or tribute children, were taken from their parents to be raised and educated at the court. The strongest became soldiers, called *janissaries*, in the sultan's armies, while those with most talent in government became his chief advisors, called *viziers*. One purpose of this system was to provide both an army and government administration based on talent, rather than birth. Another was to provide the sultan with government servants who owed their entire position, and thus their allegiance, solely to him, "so as when they come to age, they neither know their Country nor parents, nor kinsmen so much as by name."[17]

With the Ottoman Empire, and with Moryson's words, we will leave this tour of Europe at the turn of the seventeenth century. Future events will be the subject of later chapters.

Profile: The Dangers of Foreign Travel

Travelers with a ready supply of money did not find transportation difficult throughout Europe. Many, like Moryson, went with letters of introduction to ambassadors, or prominent merchants, or scholars from their own country, who would facilitate travel arrangements. By 1600 certain towns even had a well-developed tourist industry: the first guidebooks to Rome and Jerusalem date from the Middle Ages, and in Venice, Moryson tells us, inhabitants were as willing to show off their "paintings, carving in stone and brass, architecture, setting of jewels . . . and making of instruments" as visitors were to see them.

Still, there were dangers. Most gentlemen carried swords, and pikes and even muskets were common among those of lower social status. Religious arguments in a German principality, or insults to a nobleman in Poland, could provoke fights which might turn into full-scale riots. Several of the Italian principalities required men to give up all firearms on entering the territory, in the hopes of cutting down on violence. Moryson faced danger from being of the wrong religion in the wrong place. He had to be very circumspect in Rome, for if it became known that he was an English traveler he might be suspect as a spy and detained indefinitely by the Inquisition, the church court. Determined sightseer that he was, he sought the protection of an English cardinal, agreeing to attend Catholic service and dip his fingers in holy water to avoid suspicion, all to "view the antiquities of Rome." In the Ottoman Empire, his danger was more acute, for any Christian who struck or injured any Muslim was subject to imprisonment and execution. European travelers handled this danger by leaving all their weapons behind and hiring a janissary to protect them. Moryson was nearly attacked when visiting the famous mosque Hagia Sofia for standing too close to a Muslim nobleman, and one old woman, supposing him a slave, proposed to buy him. In both cases he was well looked after by his janissary, who had been recommended by the English ambassador and, presumably, was used to this sort of duty.

The worst dangers travelers faced, though, were accidents and disease. Shipwrecks were common, and so were fires. Moryson, like many travelers, took out an insurance policy on his own life before commencing his travels. His younger brother Henry, who traveled with him, did likewise, and sadly his family had to collect on it. Soon after leaving Aleppo, where they had been courteously entertained by the English consul, Henry Moryson became ill with a fever. There was no remedy beyond the patient's own constitution against infectious disease any time before the twentieth century, and the trip by camelback only made Henry worse. He died in his brother's arms, and Moryson was overcome with sorrow. He became ill himself and, for the first time, impatient for his travels to end. He returned to England in 1597. The itinerary of his travels was published, first in Latin, then in English, in 1617.

Important Dates

ca. 1300	Beginnings of Renaissance in Europe
1456	Development of movable type printing press
1469	Unification of the crowns of Spain
1492	Columbus's first voyage to the Americas
1517	Luther's 95 Theses begin Reformation
1519–1556	Reign of Charles V as Holy Roman Emperor and King of Spain
1534	Henry VIII begins Reformation in England
1549–1584	Reign of Ivan the Terrible in Russia
1555	Peace of Augsburg in Germany
1556–1598	Reign of Philip II in Spain
1558–1603	Reign of Elizabeth I in England
1562–1598	Wars of religion in France
1566–1609	Rebellion of the Netherlands against Spain
1571	Battle of Lepanto
1573	Confederation of Warsaw
1576–1612	Reign of Rudolf II as Holy Roman Emperor

1581	Northern United Provinces declare their independence from Spain
1584	Death of William of Orange
1584–1613	Time of Troubles in Russia
1587–1631	Reign of Sigismund III in Poland
1588	Spanish Armada against England
1588–1648	Reign of Christian IV in Denmark
1589–1610	Reign of Henry IV in France
1593–1606	Thirteen-year Turkish War
1616	Death of Shakespeare

Further Reading

Renaissance and Reformation surveys:

Thomas Bergin and Jennifer Speake, eds., *Encyclopedia of the Renaissance* (New York, 1987)
Euan Cameron, *The European Reformation* (Oxford, 1991)
William Estep, *Renaissance and Reformation* (Grand Rapids, MI, 1986)
John Hale, *The Civilization of Europe in the Renaissance* (London, 1984)
Hans J. Hillerbrand, ed., *Encyclopedia of the Reformation* 4 Vols. (Oxford, 1996)
Steven Ozment, *The Age of Reform 1250–1550* (New Haven, 1980)
Eugene Rice and Anthony Grafton, *The Foundations of Early Modern Europe 1460–1559* (New York, 1994)
Jonathan Zophy, *A Short History of Renaissance and Reformation Europe: Dances over Fire and Water* (Upper Saddle River, NJ, 1996)

Itinerary of Europe ca. 1600:

M.S. Anderson, *The Origins of the Modern State System, 1494–1618* (London, 1998)
Perry Anderson, *Lineages of the Absolutist State* (New York, 1974)
Richard Bonney, *The European Dynastic States 1494–1660* (Oxford, 1991)
Thomas A. Brady, Jr., Heiko Oberman, and James Tracy, eds., *Handbook of European History, 1400–1600* 2 vols. (Leiden, 1994–1995)
Thomas Ertmann, *Birth of the Leviathan: Building States and Regimes in Medieval and Early Modern Europe* (Cambridge, 1997)
V.G. Kiernan, *State and Society in Europe, 1550–1650* (Oxford, 1980)
Geoffrey Parker, *The Grand Strategy of Philip II* (New Haven, 1998)
Theodore K. Rabb, *The Struggle for Stability in Early Modern Europe* (Oxford, 1975)
Quentin Skinner, *The Foundations of Modern Political Thought* 2 vols. (Cambridge, 1980)
John Stoye, *English Travelers Abroad, 1604–1667* 2nd ed. (New Haven, 1989)
Wayne te Brake, *Shaping History: Ordinary People in European Politics, 1500–1700* (Berkeley, 1998)

Chapter Three

A Society of Localities

The problems of travel experienced by Fynes Moryson indicate why most Europeans rarely went beyond a fairly small distance from their homes. Frames of reference were intensely local. People's personal loyalty was to the village, town, or manor where they lived and the neighbors they knew there. Those localities often had completely different customs from localities a mere hundred miles away, in what we would now consider the same country. And yet, at the same time, there were common features to all of European society and the ways in which people imagined it.

The contemporary French writer Charles Loyseau explained this seeming paradox in the following way:

> There must be order in all things. . . . The world itself is so-named for that reason in Latin. . . . The inanimate creatures are all placed in it in accordance with their higher or lower degree of perfection. As for the animate creation, the heavenly intelligences have their hierarchical orders, which are changeless; and with regard to men, who are designated by God to rule over the other animate creatures of this world, though their order may be changeable and subject to vicissitudes . . . . it is the case that they cannot survive without order, for we should not be able to live together in a state of equality, but of necessity some must command and others obey. Those who command have many orders and ranks. . . . Thus, through these manifold divisions and subdivisions, out of many orders a general order is established . . . so that, in the end, by means of order, a number numberless achieves oneness.[1]

His point was that everything had its proper place and the overall sense of the world came from the way that all of the places fit together.

The many subdivisions of Europe and of the kinds of people that inhabited it were part of a common society. The word "order" turns up eight times in the quote, indicating how important the concept was for him. Equally important is the fact that Loyseau sees order as a natural state, derived from the orderly process God used in Creation. A German peasant expressed the same idea more pragmatically in a quotation he had inscribed above the door to his house: "The Lord's blessings will make you rich without effort if you remain steadfast and industrious in your station in life and do what you are told."[2]

Kinship and Inheritance

Throughout Europe, two social facts determined how an individual fit in this larger world order. The first was kinship, and the second was social status or estate. From the moment of birth—or even before—individuals were caught up in a web of kinship. All babies had to be baptized into a church; their fathers had to be named as well as their mothers; in many cases they had to have godparents who served as an extended family. One of the most important determinants of where someone would end up later in life was the circumstances of one's parents. Individuals carried within them obligations to their bloodlines, literally embodied in their blood. Social mobility was constrained partly by community pressure to conform to those obligations and partly by a practical barrier: children could not escape from the demands of parents unless they had some property of their own, and the easiest way to get property was to inherit it from parents. Thus, a child born to a peasant was likely to die a peasant; a child born to an urban artisan was likely to die an urban artisan.

Kinship or blood was closely tied to the issue of inheritance. Customs varied from one region to another, but there was a general understanding that direct descendants had rights to family property. Two practices predominated: primogeniture and partible inheritance. In primogeniture, the oldest son received the main property, while all other siblings had to make do with small allowances. In partible inheritance, the main property was divided evenly among heirs. Sometimes, one sibling would buy out the inheritance portion of the others in order to keep a farm intact, though he or she could fall into substantial debt in the process. But children did not only inherit their parents' assets, they also inherited their liabilities. Some properties came with extensive debts that could ruin the options for succeeding generations.

Family and Household

With the issue of ultimate inheritance looming, family life was often a tense affair. Peasants sometimes came to blows over the distribution of property in a will. The situation became even more tense because families represented the joining of two distinct lineages, that of the husband and that of the wife. Mortality rates were high in early modern Europe (and it was not at all unusual for women to die in childbirth), so remarriage was common. Children might have to compete for the inheritance with half and stepbrothers and sisters and their relatives, not just with brothers and sisters. In the German village of Ulfen, heirs of one peasant estate had to pay a fine "because they went against the official command to negotiate and chased the stepmother from the house before they had reached an agreement with her."[3] The plight of Cinderella with her evil stepmother and stepsisters would have resonated well with many peasants of the seventeenth century locked in their own disputes with relatives over the family's resources.

Though we may think today of the family as a straightforward kind of institution, it actually embodies two elements that were not always joined in early modern Europe. On the one hand, there is the family as a "descent group": all of those people related by blood. On the other, there is the family as a "co-resident group": all of those people living together in the same house, a household. It has been easier for historians to track households than descent groups, because most documents from the seventeenth century group people by households rather than by descent. It was not at all unusual for sons and daughters of some peasants to spend time as servants (really farmhands) in another household. And in the urban world, most sons of urban artisans spent much of their youth as apprentices and journeymen in someone else's shop. So a snapshot of a peasant household at any given moment might not include all of the children of the family because some would be residents elsewhere. On the other hand, it would include servants, who were children from someone else's family.

The seventeenth-century ideal of family life was really an ideal of household life. The household was viewed as a microcosm of society as a whole, and it had to have its order just as society had its order. It was a unit of production and consumption under the leadership of its head, the "housefather." Though it was understood that the housefather stood in a bloodline and had an obligation to maintain the family property to the best of his ability, there were few structural barriers to his absolute control over the property. In the seventeenth century, publishers produced books dedicated to showing housefathers how to run their estates most effectively. It was as a householder that the housefather was also a participant in the communal life of a village or town. He was expected to keep discipline within his house and was recognized as the official representative of everyone within the house.

It was also assumed that any effective household had to have more than just a housefather. It had to have a housemother too. Heads of households were supposed to be married in order to fit properly in society, and it was, in fact, quite rare for men who ran a farm or urban business to remain single for long. A wife, therefore, played the role of second in command in the house. She often made decisions for the house when her husband was absent. In some areas, her position within her husband's household was so taken for granted that, when her husband died, instead of being referred to as, say, Anna Schmidt, she would be referred to as Hans Schmidt's widow, Anna. But that also meant that widowhood was a moment of increasing power and responsibility for women. The widow could play the roles of both housemother and housefather. In many urban crafts, widows of artisans were sought out as wives by other artisans eager to establish a position for themselves in the town.

Thus, while the ideal may have been for the housefather to rule over his children and servants with the assistance of his supportive wife, there is plenty of evidence that the actual relations between children, servants, husbands, and wives could be contested, negotiated, even fought over. A popular satire of the era described the "Battle of the Pants" whereby women strove to usurp their husbands' authority. But also court cases are filled with evidence of fights, insults, and occasionally even divorces, which indicate the breakdowns and challenges to the ideal order.

One consequence of early modern assumptions about the connections between kinship and household was that a man's social position was determined by his relation to his father and other male heads of households, while a woman's social position was determined primarily by her relation to her husband and children. Adult men were simply assumed to be married with children. Adult women achieved social identity by being married and having children. In theory, all public interactions of the household were controlled by men, though in practice women had ways of participating in public.

The Three Estates

Medieval political thought had divided society into three groups, corresponding to three functions in society. The groups were called "orders" or "estates" and the social classification corresponded to political representation in political "estates." The French Estates General of 1484 summarized the medieval viewpoint as follows: "Everyone knows that the Commonweal is divided into members and estates: the clergy to pray for the others, to counsel, to exhort; the nobility to protect the others by arms; and the people to nourish and sustain the nobles and clergy with payments and produce."[4] Their mutual dependency was often expressed in the analogy that the clergy were the good shepherds, the nobles the good watchdogs, and the commons the good sheep. Different European languages adopted rhyming schemes that expressed that analogy: in Latin the three estates were the *Oratores*, *Bellatores*, and *Laboratores*; in German they were the *Lehrstand*, *Wehrstand*, and *Nährstand*. Another way of conceiving of the relationship was as a "Tree of Orders," with the farming peasant as the roots of the tree and the highest ranks of nobility at the top of the tree. According to writers like the Frenchman Claude de Seyssel, social harmony came from each member of each estate knowing his/her own place: "Thus each Estate remains within its limits— both because it is content and because it cannot do otherwise without great risk. By these means they all live in good order and accord, and especially in obedience to the king." Seyssel's image rather overstated the degree to which the different estates were content with their stations, but it did recognize how difficult social mobility from one estate to another would be.

Medieval writers placed the clergy first among the estates because they were closest to God. But the central "social fact" of the society of orders is the predominance of the second estate, the nobility. After all, the highest reaches of clergy hierarchy were almost always reserved for members of nobility, usually younger sons and daughters of regional nobles. Sons of kings and dukes became bishops and archbishops, sons of more ordinary nobles dominated the cathedral chapters and monasteries. So to understand the society of orders, the first thing we need to know is what it meant to be a nobleman. By the early seventeenth century, that definition was in flux. The basic image of the noble is the knight in shining armor. That was a leftover of the medieval worldview, but one that continued to exert a powerful influence on noble self-perception. Nobles themselves would have argued that their position in society came from their "service" to the crown. In theory, that service was as a fighter, thus the persistence of the image of the knight in armor and the fondness of the nobility for tournaments and duels. But in practice, more and more nobles exercised their service by being a regional power within the kingdom. Noble power was concentrated in the rural world through the control of land by hereditary succession. Thus, nobility was not defined so much by performing great deeds, but by having noble blood. Whoever could trace line of descent back farthest was most noble. In seventeenth-century France, for example, lots of families produced genealogies "proving" that a family had served under Charlemagne. There was lots of discussion in the era whether noble status was derived primarily from "merit" or from "birth."

If there had been any sociologists in the seventeenth century, they would have immediately noticed some problems with this "Society of Orders" as a system for social classification. The size of the first two estates was dramatically smaller than that of the third estate. In fact, around 90 percent of the European population belonged to the third estate. Also, there were tremendous differences in wealth and status of individuals within each of these estates. This was obvious in the third estate, where most of the wealthiest merchants in the great cities were technically "commoners," along with the poorest landless beggars. But it was no less true of the clergy and the nobility. The clergy in Catholic Europe ranged from poor, lowly rural parish priests and their support staff up to bishops, archbishops, and the pope, who were among the wealthiest and most powerful people in Europe. The nobility ranged from impoverished rural landholders scarcely richer than a peasant up to princes and kings. The gradations of status within orders were referred to as "ranks" or "degrees." Everyone knew that these ranks were powerful markers of status and that the elite of the third estate really had much more in common with the upper ranks of the nobility than it did with ordinary artisans of the towns. Likewise, the upper nobility had more in common with wealthy merchants, bankers, and lawyers than they did with their country-bumpkin noble compatriots.

Some contemporaries noticed the problems in the Society of Orders model. Claude de Seyssel proposed that the real distinction between noble and commoner was in their role in the "public" world (i.e., in politics) as opposed to the "private" world (i.e., in business). Nobles were obligated to serve their king above all else, while commoners were only supposed to obey their king and thus could focus on their own business. And, in fact, a number of public offices in France conferred automatic nobility on those that occupied them. A number of "commoners" achieved nobility by that route, thus moving from the "private" to the "public" world. According to Seyssel, there were five occupations in the private realm: the rich and landowners, university educated, honorable merchants and small office holders, artisans, and wage laborers. Thus, it was also possible for nobles to have parts of their lives that were private: the part devoted to running their lands.

A Society of Privileges

Nevertheless, there were things that defined and separated the three estates. One of the key principles of the social order in the era was the idea of "privilege." Privilege was viewed as a good thing. It was like a kind of inverse affirmative action: if you started out life in a powerful position, you deserved additional advantages. Once an individual or any group of individuals managed to get a privilege, they fought tenaciously to ensure that that privilege was never violated, because having the privilege conferred status. The most famous and widespread privilege for both the clergy and nobility was exemption from taxes. Kings always conferred with nobles if they needed to raise a tax, but the taxes themselves were to be paid by townspeople and peasants, not by nobles. Another privilege of the nobility was that certain offices in army and government were reserved for them. Nobles could be tried only by courts made up of other nobles and were almost always punished less severely than commoners, except for crimes that "proved" the lack of true nobility of the noble, such as perjury, fraud, or treason.

Along with these practical advantages from privilege came many symbolic advantages too. Most European countries had sumptuary laws, which regulated what kind of clothing people could wear. They forbade commoners to wear clothing that was as elegant as the clothing noblemen were allowed to wear. Only noblemen were permitted to carry a sword with them wherever they went. This privilege could be a practical advantage if the nobleman was offended by some insolence of a commoner. This could very well happen, for adhering to very strict and elaborate etiquette in how to address superiors was also part of the system of privilege. If a mere merchant called a high nobleman "mister" instead of "your excellence," it would have been considered perfectly appropriate for the nobleman to respond by thrashing the merchant with his sword.

But inherent in the notion of privilege was the obligation to fulfill the demands of status. Nobles were expected to live nobly or they could lose their noble status. According to the Laws of Castile: "if any nobleman falls into poverty and cannot maintain his noble status, he shall become a commoner, and all his children with him."[6] For a nobleman, fulfilling the obligations of status meant lavish display. Noble houses in the countryside developed from castles, designed primarily for defense, to elaborate palaces, designed to demonstrate the authority and taste of their owners. All of this cost a great deal of money. But at the same time, many avenues for making money were off limits to nobles. Nobles in most countries were forbidden to carry out a trade. There was even a stigma attached to very high level financial dealings as being beneath the station of a nobleman.

The obligation to adhere to status could also produce some bizarre behavior. For example, after a particularly fierce battle in the French Wars of Religion in 1562, a great noble was captured and brought to the commander of the opposing forces, also a great noble. The captured officer was treated in accordance with his rank. At the end of the evening, when it was time to go to sleep, alas, there was only one bed in the headquarters castle appropriate for a great noble. After a long series of offers and refusals ("you take the bed . . . no, you take it, I insist . . . no, you take it"), the only solution that preserved the dignity of both of their ranks was for the two to share the bed. So they did.

The Rural World

Superimposed on the distinctions between social orders was a different distinction: that between lord and subjects. Lords were both rulers and owners of land, from which we get the term "landlord," the "lord of the land." (Historians have adopted the term "seigneurialism," from the French term *seigneurie*, meaning a piece of property both owned and ruled by a lord, to describe this form of lordship over land.) It was understood that all land had to have an overlord, the ultimate owner of the land. This fact was one of the underlying bases of noble authority.

Though peasants acted as if they "owned" land, almost all of that land was actually owned by a member of the first or second estate. Some of the land owned by landlords was farmed directly in accordance with their wishes. This was their domain or manor. Nobles would usually hire stewards to look after the domain and would rely on it as the main source of their wealth. The rest of the landlord's land was farmed by peasants for their own benefit. The peasants were required to pay the lords (either with cash or "in kind," with grain, chickens, or other farm products) for their "usufruct," or right to use the land. Aside from that payment, peasants could do pretty much whatever they wanted with the land, including bequeathing the usufruct to their children or selling it to another peasant. Over time, tradition turned the peasants' usufruct into a virtual ownership of the land. The landlord, however, was still the lord of the land and continued to enjoy the privileges that being the lord conveyed. Ownership of the land often conferred additional obligations on the peasant and privilege to the lord. Landlords could sometimes demand a fixed amount of labor from a landholder to work on the noble's land or to make repairs around the village. They could claim a kind of death tax when property was transferred from one generation to the next. They also had rights to enforce local laws and collect the fines that were imposed.

Ownership of the land was a crucial issue because the main form of economic activity in the rural world was farming. The whole social life of the village was built around the rhythms of sowing and the harvest. In most of northern Europe, agriculture was based on a three-field crop rotation system. All of the different parcels of land owned by different villagers were divided up into three great fields which were worked with the combined labor of all the villagers. One year, a field would be planted with the principal grain crop of the region, either wheat or rye. The next year, it would be planted with a different grain that was often reserved for feeding livestock, usually oats. The third year, the soil would be exhausted, so it would be left fallow, plowed with manure, to recover its nutrients for the next year's planting.

With this system, grain yields were fairly low, usually only five times the seed sown, which placed a limit on how much extra food a village was likely to produce. The small yields were intensified by prevailing weather conditions. The seventeenth century was known as the "Little Ice Age" because temperatures were much lower than in the previous century or the century after. The vast majority of the rural population was almost completely dependent on grain for their diet. For most rural dwellers, meat was too expensive to eat regularly. Cattle were kept more for the manure they produced to fertilize the fields than for the meat or milk they produced.

Agriculture was organized by the village, as well as by the individual household. That made the village second only to the family in its impact on the lives of most Europeans. Villages were made up of anywhere from three or four households to several hundred inhabitants. Though villagers may have been subject to the laws of kings and local lords, villages were also partly self-governing bodies, with their own traditions and bases of power. Participation in the communal life of the village was usually confined to the male heads of households. Women played an informal role in maintaining internal order. Sometimes even the youths of the community would contribute to village culture by staging a *charivari*, a ritual hazing, of someone who was not conforming to communal standards. The village oversaw the distribution of work in the fields. Village elders often served in the misdemeanor courts to hear cases. Most villages had a village assembly that met to determine policy for the village as a whole. Lords relied on these assemblies to carry out their rules and regulations, because it was hard for kings to ensure that their officers were there to enforce laws in every village in the kingdom. But for that very reason, village assemblies could also serve as the focal point of resistance to lords.

Peasant uprisings were a common event in early modern Europe. France was particularly notorious for peasant rebellions, with one historian counting 450 between 1590 and 1715 in southwestern France alone. Often, the uprising consisted of just a village or two, but sometimes whole regions broke out in revolt, such as the *nu-pieds* (bare feet) rebellion in Normandy in 1639. Village officials often played a major role in encouraging regional uprisings. The causes of such uprisings varied, though they often centered on some new demand for taxes that was being put on the village.

Contemporary commentators often noted the extent to which peasants were exploited. A popular French print of the era had the title *Born to Suffer*. It showed a weather-beaten peasant at his meager farmstead and explained how he worked all the time, but had nothing. Another popular print showed a peasant giving his payments to a lord. In the corner of the print was an image of a spider and a fly, with the comment that the spider is like the lord, while the fly is like the peasant. The eighteenth-century German commentator J.M. von Loen described the peasant's plight as follows:

Allegory of lord and peasant as spider and fly. Seventeenth-century engraving by Jacques Laguiet (Snark/Art Resource, NY)

The peasant is brought up in complete ignorance like a mere animal. He is plagued continually with feudal services, running messages, beating up game, digging trenches and the like. From morning till night he must be digging the fields, whether scorched by the sun or numbed by the cold. At night he lies in the field and becomes little better than a beast of the fields, to keep the beasts from stealing his seed, and what he saves from their jaws is taken soon afterwards by a harsh official for arrears of rent and taxes. The countryman today is the most wretched of all creatures. The peasants are slaves and their men are hardly to be distinguished from the cattle they tend.[7]

Even within the world of peasants, there were social distinctions. By the early seventeenth century, a characteristic pattern had emerged in many villages, in which a small number of families held large farms that could produce more than enough to support their members, while a growing number of families had to get by with very small parcels or even no land at all. The large farming families tended to monopolize the offices of the village assembly and regulated the planting of the fields and allocation of village commons in their own interests. The land poor and landless were dependent on day labor or crafts to survive and were often on the brink of starvation. They relied on parish alms to get through the hardest times. In the village of Allfeld in Germany in 1700 there were seventy-five households able to pay the poor tax, but seventy-nine households exempt from the tax because of their poverty. This division between "haves" and "have nots" could lead to strife within the village instead of solidarity against lords and their oppression.

The Urban World

The Nuremberg cobbler-poet Hans Sachs's *Book of Orders*, published in 1568, illustrated 114 different occupations, from the pope and Holy Roman emperor down to the peddler. Just three of the occupations were performed primarily in villages. That illustrates one of the fundamental divisions in European society in the seventeenth century: the distinction between town and countryside. Towns were an entirely distinct social and political world that operated on quite different principles from the village. Though villages performed the one key task that was essential for the preservation of all society, the growing of food, almost all other production worth mentioning (at least in the early seventeenth century) was controlled by a town.

That was not because villages did not want to have carpenters, weavers, or metalsmiths, but because they were not allowed to have them. Only towns held privileges of forming guilds, closed corporations of craftsmen (artisans) who had a monopoly on producing a particular product. Towns were as committed to the system of privileges as were the nobles, because their superior position over villages was determined by those privileges. A common saying of the era was that "town air makes you free." What that meant was that a town was a self-governing community, usually with a mayor, town council, and lawcourts, and often with land of its own over which it was landlord. Self-government is the common feature that held together the vast array of places that called themselves towns. Some towns were scarcely larger than villages in terms of population. But they had town walls, a right to a market, and formal institutions of government that distinguished them immediately. At the other end of the scale, some towns were magnificent large places where the greatest sums of wealth in Europe tended to congregate. Great cities like Amsterdam, London, Paris, or Seville had products that were unimaginable in the countryside. Though not large by today's standards, they were growing rapidly. The population of Paris, for example, grew from around 130,000 in 1550 to nearly 500,000 in 1650. In all, perhaps 58 European cities had more than 20,000 inhabitants in 1600.

In most larger European towns (over 10,000 inhabitants), there were two broad social groups that contended for control: a semiaristocratic elite known as the patriciate and the productive artisans of the town organized into guilds. These two groups made up the commune of the town, with all of the privileges and responsibilities that went with that. We call those privileged members of the commune the burghers or bourgeoisie. The bourgeois was a legal status in early modern Europe, not a social class. It was acquired by conforming to the requirements of the specific town, usually by owning a house and business and paying taxes to the town collectors for a specific period of time. The patriciate of a town usually consisted of great merchants in long-distance trade, bankers, lawyers, and other learned trades. In some towns, such as Nuremberg, they dominated the town council and effectively shunted out the guilds from any role in government. In others, they were able to "rise above" the everyday politics of the town and maintain their position more by their international contacts than by their base in the town. As a rule, the larger the town, the more likely it was to be dominated by a patriciate. In the smaller towns of less than 5,000 inhabitants, the patriciate was very small, so control of the government fell into the hands of the most prosperous members of the guilds.

Many people lived in towns who were not burghers. At any given time, perhaps 10 percent of the town's population would consist of vagrants and beggars, who might occasionally find employment as day laborers, but mostly lived on formal and informal alms. Another quarter of the population may have been servants, working for the patriciate, guild masters, and foreign visitors. All of these "non-burghers" were subject to the laws of the town, but had no role in making those laws.

Almost all of the manufacturing work in towns was organized into guilds. The guilds had a local political role in the town and were also connected to fellow guildsmen in other towns. In their own town, they acted as an advocacy group for guild members, enforced their monopoly on producing or selling, and ensured that members adhered to guild regulations. Most guilds wanted to prevent an oversupply of whatever they produced in the town, so they deliberately limited the number of masters who could run a shop. They alone decided who could become a master and who could not. Naturally they were inclined to favor the children of the current guild masters to fill the rare openings. Guilds were, therefore, privileged in the same sense that towns and nobles were privileged.

In the economy as a whole, guilds ensured that the specific skills of their trade were maintained and that a labor force was available to supply those areas that needed it. If a boy (girls were rarely permitted to join guilds as apprentices: the few women who participated in guilds did so by marrying into the guild as wife of a master) wished to join a guild, he began his career at a very early age as an apprentice in the shop of a master. As an apprentice, he did the most menial tasks of the shop, sweeping up or gathering scraps, while the main work of the shop was done by others. At a certain point, he would be old enough to really learn about the craft. At that point he registered with the guild as a journeyman, and received a letter from his local guild explaining his status. He then wandered from town to town, looking for work in a master's shop. If a job was available, he worked for a while under that master's supervision. If no work was available, he got one free night's lodging at the guildhall and was sent on his way to the next town. In this manner, he was expected to learn all of the skills of the trade, so that, when he returned to his hometown, he would be eligible for entry as a master in the guild, by producing a "masterpiece."

However, not everyone who set out as a journeyman would eventually become a master, because the number of masters' positions in most towns was limited. Instead, journeymen often developed a distinct worker's culture within the guild, with their own rituals and habits. In the hatting guilds of France, for example, journeymen effectively enforced a rule that they would make no more than two hats a day.

The presence of so many journeymen meant that guildmasters had to be constantly on watch to be sure that journeymen did not set up in the countryside as competitors, making the same product as the masters in the town. That is why guilds were so adamant in defending their mo-

nopoly on production against rural interlopers. Guildmasters and journeymen had their own notions of honor that they strove to enforce. Some
workers were shunned by the "proper" guild members because the work
they did was viewed as inherently dishonoring. The town hangman or
executioner was especially to be avoided, so much so that even touching him was said to be dishonorable. One of the watchwords of the guild
member was "the guilds must be as pure, as if they had been gathered
together by doves."[8]

Nations and Composite Monarchies

For most Europeans, the frame of social reference was local. People
identified themselves with a particular town or village. Beyond that,
people identified with the region that they were from, such as Essex, or
the Nivernais, or East Frisia. It was comparatively rare for people to
identify primarily with either a nation (like France) or a large political
unit (like the Holy Roman Empire). As a result, the political structure of
Europe allowed a great deal of regional autonomy, even if the regions
officially belonged to a larger kingdom. The quickest way for a king to
buy political loyalty from a distant region was to confirm it in its privileges, even if they diverged dramatically from those in other parts of the
kingdom. There was a lot of talk about "service" to the king as the primary function of the nobility, but in practice, local nobles mostly served
themselves. Political theorists like Jean Bodin rationalized this "brake"
on royal authority by arguing that kings needed advising in order to rule
properly and nobles were the natural advisors who had the best interests
of the land at heart.

At the highest levels, politics was run on many of the same principles
as the more mundane concerns of peasant families. Monarchs, like peasants, were bound by lineage, and inheritance played a major role in their
calculations. For that reason, historians generally call the kingdoms of
the era dynastic states—meaning that the key element of politics was
the dynasty, or family name, not the country. Monarchs were lords: they
ruled kingdoms that were, literally, their estates. Though people sometimes spoke of "France," or "Spain," or even "Germany" as a political
and cultural unit, the real political units were the different chunks of
territory that kings and princes managed to cobble together. A king's
ownership of these different chunks was always mentioned in the long-
winded prefaces to all proclamations and treaties, which usually pro-

ceeded from the highest titles to the most obscure pockets of territory (and in descending order from the most prestigious title to the least prestigious). For example, the Holy Roman Emperors presented themselves as

> Emperor of Austria; King of Hungary, of Bohemia, of Dalmatia, Croatia, Slavonia, Galicia, Lodomeria, and Illyria; King of Jerusalem, etc; Archduke of Austria; Grand Duke of Tuscany and Cracow; Duke of Lothringia, of Salzburg, Styria, Carinthia, Carniola, and Bukovina; Grand Duke of Transylvania, Margrave of Moravia; Duke of Upper and Lower Silesia, of Modena, Parma, Piacenza, and Guastella, of Ausschwitz and Sator, of Teschen, Friaul, Ragusa, and Zara; Princely Count of Habsburg and Tyrol, of Kyburg, Görz, and Gradiska; Duke of Trient and Brizen; Margrave of Upper and Lower Lausitz and in Istria; Count of Hohenembs, Feldkirch, Bregenz, Sonnenberg, etc.; Lord of Trieste, of Cattaro, and above the Windisch Mark; Great Voyvod of the Voyvodina, Servia, . . ."[9]

As the reference to King of Jerusalem indicates, kings and princes made sure to include any chunk of territory that they could construct even the flimsiest title to, just to ensure that their claims to them would not lapse. Thus, throughout the early modern era, the kings and queens of England claimed to be not only King of England, but King of France, too.

Given the importance of inheritance for building up the different chunks of territory that made up a dynastic state, marriage was one of the weightiest issues of statecraft. Though it was assumed that succession to any territory took place through the firstborn male line, there were moments when there was only a female heir to extensive properties. The best known example is the succession of Mary, and later Elizabeth, to the throne of England. But often, the full impact of an inheritance through a female line became apparent only in the next generation. In the early sixteenth century, the Holy Roman Emperor Charles V concentrated in his hands not only his native Burgundy and the Netherlands, but also the lands of Spain (and, by extension, all of Spain's lands in the New World). This concentration occurred in stages. He acquired Burgundy when his father died unexpectedly in 1506. He acquired Spain from his mother's side. She was heir to Ferdinand and Isabella; but the land passed to Charles when Ferdinand died in 1516. The Habsburg family's success in building a dynastic state through marriage was acknowledged at the time with the Latin phrase *Bella gerant alii tu felix, Austria nube,* which roughly translates as "what others gain through war, you, lucky Austria, get by marriage."

The principle of dynastic states created three of the most common causes of war and rebellion in the early modern era. The first was a disputed succession. In general, it was clear who the legitimate successor to a king or prince was. Every kingdom had its clearly stated rules for who should be next in line. In fact, one of the strengths of France in the years after 1610 was that there were no disputed successions to the throne. But in cases where the claimants were, for example, cousins of the previous ruler, the rules of succession became murky. Previous marriages had forged multiple links between different ruling houses and the pool of potential marriage partners at the level of king and queen was limited. When a disputed succession emerged, each ruling family felt obligated to defend its position and honor against other ruling families.

The second cause of war in the era was the disgruntled relative, often a younger brother, fomenting unrest. This rarely led to international warfare, but often produced internal instability. The brother of the king usually had a major clientage network of nobles eager to come to his service. Sometimes they would gravitate around a disgraced minister or eager upstart who would challenge the policies of the king's current minister. The conflict usually would not be directed against the king himself, but against his minister, who would be accused of leading the king astray. At base, though, these struggles almost always were about who would get to exercise the real power, the king or his relatives.

The third cause of war in the era was the hostility of one region under a ruler's regime to the central tendency of that regime. Because states were made up of a combination of smaller regions, it was common for "foreigners" to rule any given territory. When territories where different languages were spoken and very different traditional customs were observed were grouped together under a single ruler, they created a "composite monarchy." The Habsburgs, with their marriage policy, were the models of composite monarchy and suffered the most from its inherent problems. In 1568, for example, the Dutch, ruled by a Spanish Habsburg, revolted against their overlord because of hostility to the "Spanish" practices of their king and his advisors. The Dutch feared that the Habsburgs were using tax money collected from the Low Countries to finance extravagance in Spain.

But Spain's problems with local feelings of autonomy did not extend only to the Netherlands. Even within Spain itself there was resentment of the advantages one region gained over another. Castile and Aragon had their distinctive customs and institutions of government. In the 1640s,

Catalonia rose up in revolt against the oppressive "Castilian" policies of the Crown. Throughout Europe, kings in composite monarchies found it difficult to command obedience from territories where a different language was spoken, were not geographically contiguous, and had distinct local customs.

Profile: The Return of Martin Guerre

In the summer of 1556 a man came to the village of Artigat in the south of France. He claimed to be Martin Guerre, who had left the village eight years before to participate in the wars between the kings of France and Spain. The man did indeed look rather like the Martin who had left so long ago, and he was able to recall incidents and stories from his youth, so his relatives greeted his return with enthusiasm. He went to the house of his wife, Bertrande, and his now nine-year-old son, Sanxi, and resumed his position as head of the family.

And so things stayed for the next four years until Martin became involved in a dispute with his uncle, Pierre, who had helped run the farm and keep the accounts in his absence. When Martin asked for a precise accounting of expenditures and profits and payment of his share of the account, his uncle began to doubt that he was who he claimed to be. But how could Pierre be sure? No one in those days had identity papers with pictures. He voiced his doubts, but Martin's wife Bertrande insisted that this was indeed her husband, and she ought to know. Also, Martin's sisters were convinced that this was their brother. On the other hand, Martin had forgotten all of the Basque language that he had learned as a youth. The shoemaker noted that the foot blank he had made for Martin before he left was much smaller than the "new" Martin's foot. Surely a foot could not change that much in eight years.

The village began to break into factions. Some supported Pierre and argued that the returned Martin was trying to usurp family property that was not rightfully his. Others supported Martin and argued that Pierre was just trying to hold onto money that was rightfully Martin's by means of blackmail. The argument became so heated that it developed into a court case, where it came to the attention of the chief judge of the *parlement* (law court) of Toulouse, Jean de Coras. After weeks of contradictory testimony, Coras seemed persuaded by Bertrande's insistence that she knew that this was her husband. Besides, Martin himself seemed very quick-witted for a peasant and was able to recount a number of obscure stories from his youth that only a village resident would know. Pierre could raise doubts, but he could not convince the judge that the returned Martin was an impostor. Coras was prepared to announce his verdict in favor of Martin when a one-legged man came limping into court: he claimed that *he* was the real Martin Guerre.

With the appearance of this new claimant, the first Martin's case began to unravel. First the sisters and then his wife had to acknowledge that the man who had just walked into court was the real Martin Guerre. The story of the impostor quickly came out. His real name was Arnauld du Tilh. Arnauld came from a poor peasant family and had been in awe of the comparative riches of the Guerres, who were one of the richest families in the village. He claimed that he had never met the real Martin, but had been inspired with the idea of taking his place when a village had mistaken Arnauld for Martin. Arnauld then used his own powers of observation to flesh out the stories and learn who was who.

With Arnauld du Tilh's confession, the case of Pierre against Martin was closed. Though there was no precise crime of "identity theft," Coras was convinced that it was a high crime to have attempted to usurp someone else's place, let alone his wife and property. Coras questioned Bertrande extensively, and she blamed her misidentification of her husband on her simplicity and Arnauld's cunning. Though Coras may have had his doubts— could Arnauld have been so successful an impostor without Bertrande's help?— she was finally exonerated of wrongdoing and told to live in peace with her true husband. Arnauld was not so lucky. He was forced to march through the village saying penance and then he was hanged.

The story of the impostor Martin Guerre was well-known among the intellectual elite of the late sixteenth century. Jean de Coras published a pamphlet on the case. It was also discussed by the great essay writer Michel de Montaigne in one of his essays. In this one instance, at least, the experiences of a peasant were deemed worthy of the attention of nobles and bourgeois, and an intensely local event achieved universal significance. For the story of Martin Guerre involved bloodlines, property, kinship, and the authority of law, the abiding concerns of all Europeans, whatever their estate.

Important Dates

1347–1350	Black Death in Europe
1381	Peasant uprising in England

1525	Peasant's War in Germany
1556	Case of Martin Guerre
1568	Publication of Hans Sachs's *Book of Orders*
1639	Nu-pieds revolt in Normandy

Further Reading

James Amelang, *Honored Citizens of Barcelona: Patrician Culture and Class Relations, 1490–1714* (Princeton, 1986)

Susan Amussen, *An Ordered Society: Gender and Class in Early Modern England* (Oxford, 1988)

William Beik, *Urban Protest in Seventeenth-Century France: The Culture of Retribution* (Cambridge, 1997)

Joseph Bergin, *The Making of the French Episcopate, 1589–1661* (New Haven, 1996)

François Billaçois, *The Duel: Its Rise and Fall in Early Modern France* trans. Trista Selous (New Haven, 1990)

Laura Brace, *The Idea of Property in Seventeenth Century England: Tithes and the Individual* (Manchester, 1998)

M.L. Bush, *Noble Privilege* (Manchester, 1983)

M.L. Bush, *Rich Noble, Poor Noble* (Manchester, 1984)

James Collins, *Classes, Estates and Order in Early Modern Brittany* (Cambridge, 1994)

David Cressy, *Birth, Marriage and Death: Ritual, Religion, and the Life Cycle in Tudor and Stuart England* (Oxford, 1997)

Natalie Davis, *The Return of Martin Guerre* (Cambridge, MA, 1983)

Natalie Davis, *Society and Culture in Early Modern France* (Stanford, 1975)

Jonathan Dewald, *The Formation of a Provincial Nobility* (Princeton, 1980)

Jonathan Dewald, *The European Nobility, 1400–1800* (Cambridge, 1996)

Barbara Diefendorf, *Paris City Councillors in the Sixteenth Century* (Princeton, 1983)

Mary J. Dobson, *The Contours of Death and Disease in Early Modern England* (Cambridge, 1997)

Amy Louise Erickson, *Women and Property in Early Modern England* (London, 1995)

Cissie Fairchilds, *Domestic Enemies: Servants and Their Masters in Old Regime France* (Baltimore, 1984)

James Farr, *Authority and Sexuality in Early Modern Burgundy, 1550–1730* (Ithaca, 1994)

James Farr, *Hands of Honor: Artisans and Their World in Dijon, 1550–1650* (Ithaca, 1988)

Jean-Louis Flandrin, *Families in Former Times: Kinship, Household and Sexuality* (Cambridge, 1979)

Anthony Fletcher, *Gender, Sex and Subordination in England, 1500–1800* (New Haven, 1996)

Christopher Friedrichs, *Urban Society in an Age of War: Nordlingen, 1580–1720* (Princeton, 1979)

Christopher Friedrichs, *The Early Modern City, 1450–1750* (London, 1995)

Kristin Elizabeth Gager, *Blood Ties and Fictive Ties: Adoption and Family Life in Early Modern France* (Princeton, 1996)

Pierre Goubert, *The French Peasantry in the Seventeenth Century* (Cambridge, 1986)

Laura Gowing, *Domestic Dangers: Women, Words, and Sex in Early Modern London* (Oxford, 1996)

Richard Grassby, *The Business Community of Seventeenth-Century England* (Cambridge, 1995)

Louis Haas, *The Renaissance Man and His Children: Childbirth and Early Childhood in Florence, 1300–1600* (New York, 1998)

Stephen Haliczer, *Sexuality in the Confessional: A Sacrament Profaned* (Oxford, 1996)

Joel Harrington, *Reordering Marriage and Society in Reformation Germany* (Cambridge, 1994)

Felicity Heal and Clive Holmes, *The Gentry in England and Wales, 1500–1700* (Stanford, 1994)

George Huppert, *The Bourgeois Gentilhommes* (Chicago, 1977)

George Huppert, *After the Black Death: A Social History of Early Modern Europe* (Bloomington, IN, 1986)

Arthur Imhof, *Lost Worlds: How Our Ancestors Coped with Everyday Life and Why Life Is So Hard Today* trans. Thomas Robisheaux (Charlottesville, 1996)

Martin Ingram, *Church Courts, Sex and Marriage in England, 1570–1640* (Cambridge, 1990)

Sharon Kettering, *Patrons, Brokers and Clients in Seventeenth Century France* (Oxford, 1986)

Robert Kingdon, *Adultery and Divorce in Calvin's Geneva* (Cambridge, 1994)

Peter Laslett, *The World We Have Lost: England Before the Industrial Age* (New York, 1971)

Emmanuel Le Roy Ladurie, *The French Peasantry, 1450–1660* trans. Alan Sheridan (Berkeley, 1987)

David Luebke, *His Majesty's Rebels: Communities, Factions, and Rural Revolt in the Black Forest, 1725–1745* (Ithaca, 1997)

Alan Macfarlane, *The Family Life of Ralph Josselin* (New York, 1970)

Alan Macfarlane, *The Origins of English Individualism* (Oxford, 1978)

Alan Macfarlane, *Marriage and Love in England, 1300–1840* (Oxford, 1986)

Sara Maza, *Servants and their Masters in Eighteenth Century France: The Uses of Loyalty* (Princeton, 1983)

Raymond Mentzer, Jr., *Blood and Belief: Family Survival and Confessional Identity among the Provincial Huguenot Nobility* (West Lafayette, IN, 1994)

Michael Mitterauer and Reinhard Sieder, *The European Family: From Patriarchy to Partnership from the Middle Ages to the Present* (Chicago, 1982)

Mark Motley, *Becoming a French Aristocrat: The Education of the Court Nobility, 1500–1715* (Princeton, 1990)

Roland Mousnier, *Social Hierarchies from 1450 to the Present* trans. Peter Evans (New York, 1973)

Helen Nader, *Liberty in Absolutist Spain: The Habsburg Sale of Towns, 1516–1700* (Baltimore, 1990)

Kristin Neuschel, *Word of Honor: Interpreting Noble Culture in Sixteenth Century France* (Ithaca, 1989)

Ruth Pike, *Penal Servitude in Early Modern Spain* (Madison, WI, 1983)

Linda Pollock, *Forgotten Children: Parent-Child Relations from 1500 to 1900* (Cambridge, 1983)

Thomas Robisheaux, *Rural Society and the Search for Order in Early Modern Germany* (Cambridge, 1989)

Peter Roebuck, *Yorkshire Baronets: Families, Estates and Fortunes* (Oxford, 1986)

Lyndal Roper, *The Holy Household: Women and Morals in Reformation Augsburg* (Oxford, 1989)

David Sabean, *Kinship in Neckarhausen, 1700–1870* (Cambridge, 1997)

David Sabean, *Property, Production and Family in Neckarhausen, 1700–1870* (Cambridge, 1991)

David Sabean, *Power in the Blood: Popular Culture and Village Discourse in Early Modern Germany* (Cambridge, 1984)

Thomas Max Safley, *Let No Man Put Asunder: The Control of Marriage in the German Southwest* (Kirksville, MO, 1984)

Peter Sahlins, *Boundaries: The Making of France and Spain in the Pyrenees* (Berkeley, 1989)

Ellery Schalk, *From Valor to Pedigree: Ideas of Nobility in France in the Sixteenth and Seventeenth Centuries* (Princeton, 1986)

Tom Scott, *Regional Identity and Economic Change: The Upper Rhine 1450–1600* (Oxford, 1997)

Jay M. Smith, *The Culture of Merit: Nobility, Royal Service, and the Making of Absolute Monarchy in France, 1600–1789* (Ann Arbor, 1996)

Margaret Spufford, *Contrasting Communities: English Villagers in the Sixteenth and Seventeenth Centuries* (Cambridge, 1974)

Lawrence Stone, *The Crisis of the Aristocracy 1558–1641* (Oxford, 1965)

Lawrence Stone, *The Family, Sex and Marriage in England, 1500–1800* (New York, 1977)

Lawrence Stone and Jeanne Fawtier Stone, *An Open Elite? England 1540–1880* (Oxford, 1984)

Kathy Stuart, *Defiled Trades and Social Outcasts: Honor and Ritual Pollution in Early Modern Germany* (Cambridge, 1999)

Peter K. Taylor, *Indentured to Liberty: Peasant Life and the Hessian Military State, 1688–1815* (Ithaca, 1994)

Maarten Ultee, *The Abbey of St. Germain des Pres in the Seventeenth Century* (New Haven, 1981)

David E. Vassberg, *The Village and the Outside World in Golden Age Castile: Mobility and Migration in Everyday Rural Life* (Cambridge, 1996)

Mack Walker, *German Home Towns: Community, State, and General Estate 1648–1871* (Ithaca, 1971)

Jeffrey Watt, *The Making of Modern Marriage: Matrimonial Control and the Rise of Sentiments in Neuchâtel, 1550–1800* (Ithaca, 1992)

Charlotte C. Wells, *Law and Citizenship in Early Modern France* (Baltimore, 1994)

James B. Wood, *The Nobility of the Election of Bayeux, 1463–1660* (Princeton, 1980)

Keith Wrightson and David Levine, *Poverty and Piety in an English Village: Terling, 1525–1700* (New York, 1979)

Heide Wunder, *He Is the Sun, She Is the Moon: Women in Early Modern Germany* trans. Thomas Dunlap (Cambridge, MA, 1998)

Chapter Four

The Mental Universe

What Everyone Knows

"Common sense," wrote the philosopher René Descartes in 1637, "is the most equitably divided thing in the world, for even those who are hardest to please in everything else usually do not want more of it than they have,"[1] and this chapter will start off by exploring the ordinary, common-sense ideas that ordinary people had about the world. In the early seventeenth century, people's ideas about themselves and the world were shaped by certain assumptions: that they were in the center, and at the focus, of a universe designed for humanity on God's plan, that the microcosm of their bodies was affected by the macrocosm of the universe, that women were by nature physically similar, but mentally and emotionally very different from men, that magic and witchcraft were real forces in the world (though there was some dissent on the latter issue).

The Rule of Order

God had given people two ways of understanding His design, people believed: the holy book of the Bible, and the book of nature. Both, understood correctly, should reveal the same truth. God had created man and given him dominion over all the earth: it was from that dominion, political theorists like Robert Filmer believed, that the authority of kings over subjects, and fathers over households, ultimately derived. The authority of men over women was so much taken for granted that people used the words "man" and "mankind" to mean "all of humanity." The earth on which people lived was a sphere, whose circumference, scholars and navigators like Christopher Columbus knew, had been carefully calculated by the Greeks about 200 B.C.E. Even uneducated people had learned it from the European voyages of discovery of the fifteenth and sixteenth centuries. By 1600, it was known that the circumference of the sphere was approximately 25,000 miles. Magellan's fleet had taken three years to sail around it. The early explorers had discovered new continents, still only partly explored and popularly believed to be composed chiefly of monsters, fabulous cities, gold and silver mines. Travelers' tales played into this belief, but so did the reality: the reported wealth of the East Indies, the silver mines of Peru, the apparently inexhaustible forests of North America.

However expanded this sphere of people's dominion from the time of the Greeks, most people still believed in the system of science, known as natural philosophy, they had described. Just as people were all born into their rightful order or estate, so too all parts of nature were created with a rightful place. The earth, motionless, was fixed in its rightful place as center of the universe. Its great weight ensured it could never move, for just as a ball or any other heavy body, thrown up in the sky from any part of it, comes back to the earth, so too the earth, if it ever could be moved from the center of the universe, would fall back to its rightful place again. All the substances on earth were made up of combinations of four elements: earth, water, air and fire. Heavy substances were composed primarily of earth, and so their rightful place was close to the earth. For that reason, they always fell straight down, as if trying to reunite with the earth itself. Liquids were made up primarily of the element water. They did not fall, but rather poured, and they would always seek the lowest level surface. Air neither fell nor poured, but spread out to fill every empty space. Nature abhors a vacuum, as the great Greek philosopher Aristotle had said, and all philosophers agreed, for who had ever seen a space with no substances whatever in it? Fire, the last element, again behaved differently from the other three, for instead of falling, pouring, or spreading, it always rose upward, as if trying to escape from the earthly world and ascend directly to heaven.

Around this world circled the heavenly bodies, or orbs. They were weightless, as everyone knew, for otherwise they would fall down to earth like other weighty bodies, and they were carried around the earth by equally weightless spheres. Closest to earth was the moon; next was the sun, giver of warmth and light. Then came the rest of the planets, Mercury, Venus, Mars, Jupiter, and Saturn, each of which circled the earth in orbits that varied by planet. Beyond the planets were the fixed stars, which did not move with respect to each other and which made up the constellations. Popular opinion said that each sphere was moved by angels and that God sat in majesty on the outermost sphere and moved the whole heavens once each day. Educated opinion was more circumspect, saying only that there was a sphere beyond the sphere of the fixed stars, called a First Mover, in Latin a *primum mobile*, that moved the heavens all the way around the earth once each day. All agreed that the sun moved, though, so that the side of the earth that faced it had day and the side of the earth that faced away from it had night.

This was, above all, an orderly universe, which followed the laws of nature, by which was meant, explained the English clergyman Richard Hooker, "that manner of working which God has set for each created thing to keep."[2] As Hooker's contemporary, the playwright William Shakespeare wrote,

> The heavens themselves, the planets, and this centre,
> Observe degree, priority, and place,
> Insisture, course, proportion, season, form,
> Office and custom, in all line of order[3]

All created things, from the lowest worms to higher animals, to people, and above people to the angels and God Himself, were links in a chain uniting the universe in a divine harmony. Take away order, and the links of the chain would be broken, resulting in chaos, as Shakespeare depicted:

> What plagues and what portents, what mutiny,
> What raging of the sea, shaking of earth,
> Commotion in the winds, frights, changes, horrors.

The divine order that governed the daily motion of the heavens around the earth also governed the yearly motion of the sun on its orbit through the most important set of constellations in the heavens, the zodiac. Then, as now, everyone knew that the "sun sign" was the sign of the zodiac in which the sun appeared at a particular time of the year. They knew, too, that the path of the sun caused the seasons, for it was self-evident in an agricultural society that summer brought longer working days, and winter, shorter ones. Everyone knew about the moon's orbit, too, which took approximately a month as the moon waxed and waned, and sensible folk arranged long journeys to coincide with the full moon. The motions of the rest of the planets were much harder to determine, requiring abstruse calculations: to find them, everyone knew, one went to an astrologer.

For everyone knew that the macrocosm of the heavens could affect the microcosm of the human body and of human affairs. The basic principle was simple: for any minute of any day, it was possible to draw up a chart, called a horoscope, to find out the positions of planets in the zodiac. For people, the position of each planet at the precise date and time of their birth, or nativity, was believed to give it a specific influence over their lives. Though the most important planet was the sun, the position of the moon, other planets, and particularly influential stars could all affect the horoscope. The mathematics for finding the positions of the other planets, which can be done today in minutes on any home computer, took days of elaborate calculations. Everyone knew, though, that it was well worth the effort. In medicine, astral influences, as the effects of the heavenly bodies were called, were believed to determine the course and treatment of illness. The astrologer Richard Napier painstakingly drew horoscopes for all his patients, in a process that seems to us to mirror a kind of psychotherapy, in order to show them "how to prevent many evils proceeding from the influence of the stars."[4] Astrology was also believed to reveal clues about the future, and people consulted astrologers to find out when to commence lawsuits, avoid plagues, and even fight wars.

But did the stars determine human events or merely influence them? Could they determine human nature or merely influence it? More sophisticated writers believed that the stars influenced, but did not determine, the future. Like the modern debate between nature or nurture in child-rearing, there was a seventeenth-century debate over the interaction between inborn disposition (as revealed by the horoscope), personality, and external circumstances. The Oxford professor John Aubrey, famous for his *Brief Lives*, a series of short biographies of notable men of his age, believed that "we are governed by the planets, as the wheels and weights move the hands of a clock," and that parents should use astrology to determine what occupations are best for their sons. He believed, though, that astrology needed to be more fully studied and regarded his biographies as kind of research tool to correlate astrological data with biographical information.[5]

Many believed that the stars could determine temperament. Those born with Mars as a dominant influence were warlike, martial, choleric, while those born with Jupiter were cheerful, jovial. Those born under Saturn were melancholic, under Mercury, mercurial, and under Venus, amorous. Physicians believed that each temperament was associated with certain characteristic diseases—choleric with apoplexy, for example, and melancholic with depression—and prescribed treatments to counteract unfavorable influences. These treatments included rules on eating, drinking, sleeping, and exercise as well as medication and, collectively, were called a regimen. A choleric person could counteract a predisposition to apoplexy by watching diet, drinking cooling liquids, and listening to soothing music. But we can turn to Shakespeare again for the alternative view: "This is the excellent foppery of the world, that, when we are sick in fortune—often the surfeit of our own behaviour—we make guilty of our disasters the sun, the moon, and the stars; as if we were villains by necessity; fools by heavenly compulsion; knaves, thieves, and treachers by spherical predominance; drunkards, liars, and adulterers by an enforced obedience of planetary influence; and all that we are evil in, by a divine thrusting on."[6]

Nature and Human Nature

But what was human nature itself? Men and women of the seventeenth century all looked to their religion to give an answer to that question, and all the Christian faiths agreed that people had been made in God's image and that, though the body was made from clay, the soul could achieve salvation. The soul set people apart from other living things, though they all experienced the corruption and decay of the body: "We attribute but one privilege and advantage to man's body above other moving creatures," wrote the poet and clergyman John Donne, "that he is not as others, groveling, but of an erect, of an upright form, naturally built, and disposed to the contemplation of Heaven."[7] Men and women of the seventeenth century did not define themselves by biology, or science, or citizenship, but by their relationship to God. A good man, of whatever estate, was to fear God, respect his parents, remain chaste and sober, avoid bad company, shun the deadly sins of lust, rage, pride. He was to look after his wife, financially, spiritually, and morally, for he was her lord and therefore accountable to God for her well-being and obedience. Husbands who desired to live in peace with their wives were given three rules: "Often to admonish: seldom to reprove and never to smite her."[8]

For though equally beloved by God, men and women were not equal in authority, in religious matters as elsewhere. The early Christian writings of Saint Paul had placed the blame for Adam and Eve's expulsion from the Garden of Eden squarely on women: "For Adam was formed first, then Eve; and Adam was not deceived, but Eve was deceived and became a transgressor. Yet woman will be saved through bearing children, if she continues in faith and love and holiness, with modesty."[9] All religious traditions and civil law in the seventeenth century were patriarchal, giving authority to husbands over wives, though it was supposed to be authority tempered with gentleness. "Ye husbands, dwell with your wives according to knowledge, giving honor to the wife, as unto the weaker vessel, and as being heirs together of the grace of life," went the Lutheran table of duties for husbands, while wives were told to "submit yourselves unto your husbands as unto the Lord—even as Sarah obeyed Abraham, calling him lord."[10]

The image of the dutiful, subservient wife, bowing to the will of her husband, is counteracted by other images from art and literature. A woman could act as an agent of the devil, tempting man by playing on his love for her. The most frequently cited example of this was Eve, whose own will, reason, and intellect were weakened, wrote the humanist scholar Erasmus (ca. 1466–1536), and who was able to tempt Adam "because of his immoderate love for his wife to whose desires he gave preference over obedience to God's commandments."[11] Women were believed to be more lustful than men and for that reason more easily corrupted; they were more emotional, less rational, less upright, given to idle gossip and frivolous activities. All the more reason for her to be reminded that she was made from one of man's ribs "under his arm to show that she should be under the hand and guidance of her husband." It was his job to fear God and advance his estate in an often hostile world, while it was his wife's task to maintain a moral, well-ordered household.

And yet, though the social roles, and nature, of men and women were considered to be quite distinct, biologically their roles were not as differentiated as we now consider them. Of course, the fundamental fact of women, not men, bearing children, was not usually questioned. But male and female sexual organs were regarded as very similar, with what we now call the vagina considered to be the penis turned inward. Like many other seventeenth-century ideas, this went back to Aristotle, who believed that males of any species were more perfect, and therefore better formed, than the females. Female bodies, then, represented a kind of lesser males, having all the same parts, but in less perfection: inward, rather than outward, because of lack of sufficient heat to form them perfectly.

It seemed plausible that women could, on occasion, turn into men. One famous story was that of Marie Germain, who had lived and dressed like a girl until sometime in her teens. One day, however, while jumping across a ditch, "his masculine organs came forth."[12] Marie ran back to her mother, who took her to medical men, all of whom assured her that her daughter had become her son. The local bishop rebaptized her/him as Germain, and he took on the life of a man, becoming a servant of the king of France. Women and men, then, were not two distinct biological sexes, as we now think of them, but merely less perfect and more perfect forms of the human species. This did not mean that women were entitled to act like men, however. Another young French woman dressed up as a man and worked as a weaver; she even fell in love and married another woman. But she was recognized, exposed as a woman, and executed, saying she would rather undergo being hanged than go back to being treated as a girl.

Similar to the reciprocal duties and obligations between husbands and wives were those between parents and children. "Children, obey your parents in the Lord: for this is right," went the Lutheran table of duties, and all Christian teachings agreed, going back to the Biblical commandment, " Honor thy father and thy mother." Though early childhood was recognized as a time of special indulgence, from the age of five or so children were expected to prepare themselves for their roles as Godly adults. Parents were instructed to "bring them up in the nurture and admonition of the Lord,"[13] and it was a common practice for children to kneel to receive the blessing from their parents. For children above a certain age, beating and whipping were common.

Whether people were born good or bad, naturally inclined to virtue or vice, remained subject for debate. "Natural inclinations," according to one writer, "are by institutions helped and strengthened, but they neither change nor exceed,"[14] but "infants' manners are moulded by the example of their parents, much sooner than the stars that reign at their nativities," according to another. Still, in child-rearing, too, the message from religious authorities was kindness, not coercion: the lord of the patriarchal household, like the sovereign of a state or the Lord Himself, was to be loved as well as feared.

On these points, all the Christian teachings were united, but they disagreed decisively on what men and women could do to ensure their salvation and entrance into God's kingdom. According to orthodox Catholicism, Adam had been created with uncorrupted reason and uncorrupted will, Erasmus wrote, "which remained quite free, if he wished to choose also evil. . . . In man, will was so good and so free that even without additional grace it could have remained in a state of innocence, though not without the help of grace could it attain the blessedness of eternal life, as the Lord Jesus promised his people."[15] Faith in God, and the carrying out of good works, would lead to salvation. Luther vehemently disagreed: people were created with corrupted wills, and without God's grace would continue to sin. "I believe that I cannot by my own reason or strength believe in Jesus Christ my Lord, or come to Him," repeated thousands of Lutheran children each day; only God's grace could lead them and sanctify them, "in like manner as He calls, gathers, enlightens, and sanctifies the whole Christian Church on earth."[16] Calvin's teachings went even further in stressing the helplessness of people and the power of God's grace: "For what is more consistent with faith than to acknowledge ourselves naked of all virtue, that we may be clothed by God; empty of all good, that we may be filled by him; slaves to sin, that we may be liberated by him; blind, that we may be enlightened by him."[17] Calvin went further, too, in emphasizing that some few, the elect, had already been chosen by God for salvation, and Calvinist preaching emphasized God's love for a humanity so sinful that people should be grateful he would save anyone: "Here is God's love that I am out of Hell, not roaring with the damned. . . , this is love indeed."[18]

The effect of these doctrines on their respective communities, repeated in catechisms, in sermons, in religious writings that went through many editions, led people to ongoing introspection about their relationship with God. St. Teresa of Avila, in her memoirs of her life, recounted the many times she sinned, and feared she was damned, and how only slowly she came to understand "from plentiful experience that if I resolutely persist in a purpose from the beginning, and it is done for God's sake only, His Majesty rewards me even in this life in ways which only one who has known their [these] joys can understand."[19] The Puritan— that is, English Calvinist—joiner Nehemiah Wallington devoted some 50 volumes to his constant self-examination. As a young man, his fears of damnation nearly drove him to suicide; if his life was so filled with sin, he reasoned, it would be the more godly path to end it early. Yet he, like St. Theresa, sometimes felt religious rapture, when "the Lord (like a tender Father or Mother) comes softly on me, withdraws the curtain, looks on me."[20]

Witchcraft, Magic, Folk Belief

Belief in magic and witchcraft had existed in Europe throughout the Middle Ages, but the Reformation gave it new emphasis. All faiths emphasized the role of Satan in deceiving God's faithful, and civil and religious authorities who preached so vigorously against the works of the devil on Sundays had no difficulty in believing in Satan's presence during the rest of the week. Everyone knew that the devil constantly traveled throughout the earth, looking for people whose souls he could steal, from Dr. Faustus in the play of that name by Christopher Marlowe, who sells his soul to the devil in exchange for "a world of profit and delight / Of power, of honor, of omnipotence,"[21] to the poor woman in an English village who did the same for two and sixpence, only to find that the devil refused to pay it and "complained of the hardness of the times."[22]

When confronted with unexpected misfortune, then—illness of family members, death or injury to animals, financial loss—men and women often assumed it to be caused by witchcraft and immediately looked around for the suspected witch. Indeed, "it is astonishing," wrote one learned author, "that there should still be found to-day people who do not believe that there are witches." When one man, while threshing corn, was "suddenly stricken down to the ground and taken lame, both in his right arm and left leg, and so continued until his death," and his daughter "pined away to skin and bones and so died," the family accused a local woman of causing both deaths by witchcraft. Contemporary writers did not all approve the wholesale tendency to blame witches for all misfortunes: physicians cover up their own ignorance by claiming witchcraft, wrote one; when "he cannot find the nature of the disease, he saith the party is bewitched," and "when a country wench cannot get her butter to come," observed another, "she says the witch is in her churn." But few questioned the belief that witches could exist and could cause injury, which would only cease once the witch was tried and executed: the curse, wrote one legal authority, "is prevented or cured in the execution of the witch."[23] Legal procedures were also the only ones approved by civil and religious authorities, who forbade, though they could not prevent, the two most usual responses on the part of victims: countermagic or personal assault on a suspected witch.

In the small, intolerant, and very public communities of early modern Europe, it was never hard to find someone who had reason to dislike the family or who had a bad reputation in the village. But, of course, the belief in witches and the ability to decide who the witches must be were not new in the seventeenth century. What defined witchcraft in the period between 1550 and 1650 was the dramatic increase in the number of accusations and the extent to which one set of accusations led to a chain of further accusations. The effort to root out witches gave rise to witch crazes. There were perhaps 100,000 witch trials throughout Europe in the sixteenth and seventeenth centuries, and perhaps 50,000 executions. About 80 percent of the accused were women.

That new phenomenon was shaped as much by the legal apparatus as by the belief in witches by itself. On the one hand, there was an increasingly lurid concern with wanton sexuality supposedly inspired by the devil. For legal experts, witchcraft was a threat to the community not because of evil magic, but because of the breakdown of "normal" order that went with it. It is the legal manuals, not the folk beliefs, that are filled with graphic descriptions of great orgies of women having sex with the devil and his demons. On the other hand, legal experts who tried to solve the fundamental problem of overcoming the trickiness of the devil also created the mechanism for the crazes: they endorsed the use of torture as a method of interrogation of suspected witches. Since most spells were cast without witnesses, the only guarantee of guilt was a confession, which could usually be extracted only after hard interrogation. Under torture, the accused would implicate other participants at the great orgies with the devil, who would, in turn, have to be tortured to extract further accusations. By this method, a single accusation against a marginal member of the community could become an all-encompassing accusation against almost everyone.

Like epidemics, witch crazes exploded and then receded. By the mid-seventeenth century, an increasing number of critical voices on the reality of witchcraft were heard. Yet the decline of witch crazes after about 1640 (the Salem witch trials in New England were a very late offshoot of the European phenomenon) was not caused by a decline in the belief that witches existed so much as by the inability to come up with a sure way of proving who was or was not a witch.

The Specialists

In the early seventeenth century, as today, there were specialists in one or another branch of knowledge. Though they might share the common opinions of common folk outside their specialty, within it they were experts. Like today, they disapproved of people outside their specialty meddling in their subjects or holding contrary opinions to their own.

The Universities

There were almost 200 universities in Europe in 1600, each intended to impart learning and knowledge to young men, for women were excluded. In Catholic countries, the universities were often run by religious orders, such as the Dominicans and Jesuits; in Protestant countries, the universities usually required students to repeat an oath of faith to the confession of that country. Only Anglicans, for example, could attend the English universities of Oxford and Cambridge, while students at the University of Wittenberg had to repeat the Augsberg Confession of the Lutheran faith. Generally, the universities were organized into four faculties: the arts faculty, for Latin, Greek, and the general knowledge suitable for a gentleman, medicine, law, and theology.

Student life differed from country to country and from town to town. Students might live in colleges, as was common in Oxford and Paris, or board in private lodgings, as in Leyden. In colleges, whether Catholic or Protestant, their day was strictly regulated, usually beginning and ending with religious exercises. Even in private lodgings students were usually required to attend the university chapel. Teaching itself was done by lecturing, with students taking notes—or perhaps copying their friends'—by memorization of a passage, or by disputation of a set theme, called a thesis. The social backgrounds of students were mixed, for sons of noblemen often went to universities for their general education, which included drinking and dueling as well as Latin and Greek, while poor boys could get scholarships, usually for a career in the church, for all faiths actively recruited clergymen.

Professors of the universities were equally varied. Some regarded their positions as merely steppingstones on the way to more prestigious careers, like the professor of medicine who left to become town physician, the law professor who left after a year or two to become advisor to his prince, or the theology professor who left to become a bishop. Others became distinguished scholars, teachers, and writers. Justus Lipsius, for example, was professor at Louvain whose study of the Roman army served Dutch military reformers as a model. His political writings were read, translated, and even plagiarized throughout European courts: many of the greatest monarchs of the seventeenth century learned their political theory through his work, *Politica*. Indeed, Lipsius saw himself, not as the subject of a particular prince at a particular university, but as a genuine expert, one who might converse, on his own specialty at least, as an equal with princes and lords. This attitude took hold in universities throughout the seventeenth century, reinforced by students who moved from university to university, seeking the best professors in any subject.

Professors at most universities covered standard subjects. The arts faculty, usually the first subjects studied, taught logic, ethics, mathematics, and natural philosophy. The higher faculties were law, medicine, and theology. The basic texts in all areas were the classics of the ancient world, such as Aristotle for logic and natural philosophy, the Institutes of Justinian for law, and Galen and Hippocrates for medicine, while the texts for theology varied depending on the confession of the university. By 1600, though, professors dealt with these texts differently. Some still revered them as the greatest works of learning and scholarship, but others, particularly in natural philosophy and medicine, began to sift through and critique them, challenging their authority in the world of scholarship.

Religion

The main product of most universities in the seventeenth century was trained clergymen. The theology faculty was usually the largest and most prestigious in the university. As the doctrines of Catholicism, Lutheranism, and Calvinism became more defined and rigid in the late sixteenth century (a process often referred to as confessionalization), territorial rulers developed a strong interest in ensuring a properly trained clergy to enforce confessional uniformity. So, for example, when the two branches of the house of Hesse in Germany began to diverge in religious culture, the Lutheran branch of Hesse-Darmstadt founded a new university at Giessen, so that it would not have to rely on clergy trained at the Calvinist university at Marburg. When Hesse-Darmstadt reclaimed Marburg and reinstituted Lutheran teaching there, the ruler of Hesse-Kassel opened a competing university at Kassel to train his territory's clergy.

Priests and pastors were probably the only specialists that the vast majority of the population ever encountered. The Council of Trent, which met between 1545 and 1563 to reform abuses and clarify the doctrine within the Catholic Church, sharply reduced the number of Catholic parishes without a resident priest. The general level of knowledge about basic Catholic doctrine increased. One principle of confessionalization was that the clergy was distinct from the population it served and its primary task was the reinforcement of social order. In the early seventeenth century, the clergyman was often the only person in a village who could read and write. In the course of the century, instruction in reading and writing in village schools increased, usually under the purview of the clergy in the parish house. Thus, in addition to providing an essential religious function, clergy contributed to the integration of local communities into a wider network of information.

The Law

After the clergy, probably the most numerous products of the universities were jurists, people trained in the law. In much of Europe, the legal code remained local customary law. Local nobles or town governments usually controlled the courts, but juries were often composed of ordinary villagers or townspeople whose decisions sometimes depended on the memories of the village elders, literally the oldest people in the community who could remember the farthest back about how things had been done. Specialized legal training was rarely necessary in these courts.

In contrast, the new courts of law that began to develop in the early sixteenth century were populated by jurists, experts in law who had trained at the universities. In France, for example, the number of courts increased fifty-fold between 1450 and 1550 and continued to expand into the seventeenth century. The spread of legal training coincided with the rediscovery of the Roman law codes of Justinian and their elaboration. Roman law, meaning written law with extensive layers of interpretation, called glosses, from later authors, began to compete with customary law based on local memory. Also, more and more customary laws began to be written down, acquiring their own glosses that needed legal interpretation. And finally, territorial rulers began to issue their own ordinances and laws, which sometimes substituted for local customs and sometimes addressed issues that had previously been unregulated. Jurists came to be essential for writing and enforcing those laws;

then they became essential for interpreting those laws at the local level. In the early sixteenth century, few villagers would have ever seen a lawyer. By the end of the seventeenth century, some villages had their own lawyers on retainer to plead their cases in the lords' courts.

Natural Philosophy

In 1500, all those who called themselves natural philosophers could have fit into one good-sized room, for the subject was not regarded as very interesting even among educated people. Most of the problems had been settled by the Greeks: geometry by Euclid, physics by Aristotle, astronomy and geography by Ptolemy, medicine by Hippocrates and Galen. By 1600, that had changed, as a new set of ideas in astronomy and physics arose to challenge the belief that the earth stood still and the heavens moved. The ideas arose in part because of a serious astronomical problem: the mathematical calculations necessary for establishing the date of Easter, the start of the new year, did not appear to be working very well. Easter, from time immemorial, was calculated as the first Sunday after the first new moon after the spring equinox, the date at which there are equal hours of night and day. To calculate it, it was necessary to predict, with some accuracy, the motions of the sun and moon. The popes were particularly interested in this, for it was one of the administrative tasks of the Catholic Church to set the church calendar, with its many holidays and feast days. Calendars, in 1500 as now, had to be set many years in advance. It was clearly not possible simply to wait until the spring equinox occurred, then announce that the next Sunday after the next new moon would be Easter, any more than it would be possible now to wait for Halloween to announce the date of Thanksgiving.

It was partly to solve this problem, and partly to work out his own mathematical ideas, that Nicholas Copernicus (1473–1543), a canon from Frauenberg, now in Poland, began to investigate the motions of the sun and moon. He was a true Renaissance scholar, versed in medicine, law, and classical Greek, and his goal was to renovate and reform the abstruse mathematics of the great astronomical treatise of the ancient world, the *Almagest* of Claudius Ptolemy, written in the second century A.D. Copernicus had no new astronomical observations to work with: in fact, his measurements of the positions of the stars and planets were probably worse than Ptolemy's. Nor did he discover any new data, any new information about the heavens, to make him think that the earth moved and the sun stood still. Instead, he was led by strict adherence to the mathematical principles he set himself, including the perfect circular motion of the heavenly bodies, to write his book *On the Motion of the Heavenly Spheres*. Published in 1543, it was the first astronomical treatise since the ancient world to propose that the sun was in the center of the solar system and that the earth and all other planets revolved around it.

Copernicus's ideas had circulated in manuscript before they were published, as was customary, and were rejected by most people out of hand, for who could believe, against the evidence of one's own senses, that the earth moved? If it moved, why did we feel no wind draft? Why did we observe no difference in the position of the fixed stars at different seasons of the year? But other learned astronomers discussed Copernicus's work seriously. One such astronomer, Tycho Brahe (1546–1601), was a Danish nobleman who established an observatory on the North Sea island of Hveen, where he ruled his court and built the most elaborate and expensive astronomical instruments of his day. He established the precise positions of nearly a thousand stars and accumulated hundreds of thousands of equally precise observations of the sun, moon, and planets. He never believed that Copernicus could be correct, for if the earth moved, he said, his instruments should be able to detect some change in the appearance of the stars, as people on board a ship sailing close to land can detect changes in the position of buildings on the coast. He intended his magnificent data to support his own, hybrid theory, in which the sun, moon, and other planets revolved around a stationary earth, while Mercury and Venus revolved around the sun. When the Danish king, tired of Tycho's highhanded ways, asked him to leave Hveen, Tycho became the Imperial Astronomer to the Holy Roman Emperor Rudolf II in Prague, hoping to devote the rest of his life to proving his theory.

Tycho, though a brilliant observer, was not a skilled mathematician, and he needed one, he knew, to bring order out of his observations. He hired a young, brilliant astronomer, Johannes Kepler (1571–1630), as his assistant. Kepler had learned of Copernicus's theory while a student at the University of Tübingen, one of the centers of mathematical astronomy, and he became a passionate convert to the idea of the sun-centered solar system. His first position had been as mathematics teacher in the small Austrian town of Graz, and when that ended he was happy to accept Tycho's offer to become his assistant, though Tycho continued to be highhanded and Kepler was seldom paid. The two astronomers engaged in an ongoing tug of war, each intent on using the data to support his chosen theory. This tug of war ended in 1601 with Tycho's death, when Kepler, now Imperial Astronomer, simply took the volumes of data and refused to surrender them despite the fury of Tycho's family. In 1609 he published the result of years of exhausting calculations, which showed that the orbits of the planets were ellipses, not perfect circles; in 1627, using this theoretical framework and Tycho's data, he published a set of astronomical tables with far more precise predictions of the motions of the sun, moon, and planets than anyone had ever seen.

Though not all astronomers found the new theory convincing, they seriously debated its merits, and the authority of Aristotle and Ptolemy began to decline. Discussion of these new ideas in natural philosophy had already begun to extend to the educated public as well: In 1576 the English mathematician Thomas Digges had published the first English translation and discussion of Copernicus's theory. Like Copernicus, Digges placed at the outermost edge of heaven the sphere of fixed stars, now immovable. Within that, he said, orbited the planets, which he named in order, together with the period of their orbit, like any modern astronomy textbook. But the new philosophy did nothing to destroy the old belief in astrology, for Digges's description of Copernicus's ideas was attached to his popular astrological book *Prognostication Everlasting*, which went through many editions in the next half century. Nor was Digges alone in mixing astronomy and astrology. As a young math teacher, Johannes Kepler had the task of drawing up horoscopes for his town of Graz, Austria, where he accurately predicted a cold snap and an attack of the Turks. He drew them for the weather, for his own weddings, and, when appointed Imperial Astronomer, for the prominent general Albrecht von Wallenstein. For many people, the new philosophy did not change the essential idea of a closed universe, with people as the most important part of God's plan, the moral, if not the physical center of the universe. "This is nature's nest of boxes," wrote John Donne; "The heavens contain the earth; the earth, cities; cities, man."[24]

Galileo and the Telescope

The invention of the telescope took natural philosophy out of the hands of mathematicians and placed it in the hands of anyone within reach of a lens grinder. The first spyglasses, as they were called, were invented in the Netherlands and used for identifying ships at sea. A professor of physics at the University of Padua, Galileo Galilei (1564–1642), heard of the instrument and developed his own. He was an ambitious, pugnacious man, who, like Kepler, had become convinced that the Copernican theory was correct. He was convinced, too, that the theory of a moving earth required a complete revision of the laws of physics as developed by Aristotle and taught in the universities, and the results of his carefully framed experiments on falling bodies are taught in all introductory physics classes today. Though only tangentially interested in astronomy, he was interested in new inventions that might spur his fame. He carefully ground lenses until he had an instrument with far greater magnification and resolving power than other telescopes, and pointed it at the night sky. What he saw surprised even him: the first glimpse of craters on the moon, which he thought were seas, the first sight of the phases of Venus as it revolved around the sun, and the first sight of four of the moons of Jupiter, which he called the Medicean planets in honor of the de Medici family, rulers of Florence. The telescopes which he sent to astronomers throughout Europe, and his book, *The Starry Messenger*, describing his discoveries, made him the most famous astronomer of his day.

Scholarly controversy was often very combative in the seventeenth century, and Galileo had angered a number of professors with his previous attacks on Aristotle's teachings, the staple of the university curriculum. Now, his publication on the telescope provoked new controversy, for Galileo published it in Italian as well as Latin, opening up his discoveries to anyone who could read. No previous astronomer had done so, and many, like Kepler, thought it a bad idea, for it would take astronomy away from mathematicians and expose it to religious controversy. In fact, that is what happened. In 1616, Galileo went to Rome to discuss Copernican theory with the astronomers in the Vatican, hoping to persuade the Catholic Church to make the theory its official position. But his many controversies had made him many enemies among the more conservative church officials, and the decision of the committee appointed to examine the astronomical debate went against Galileo and the Copernican theory. The idea that the sun was the immovable center of the universe was declared "foolish and absurd, philosophically false and formally heretical,"[25] and Galileo was told not to hold or defend it again.

Over the course of the next twenty years, as fighting between Catholic and Protestant forces convulsed central Europe, many Catholic astronomers discreetly adopted Tycho Brahe's theory of the solar system as a compromise position. Not Galileo, who remained convinced both of the truth that the earth moves and of his obligation to educate the church. In the 1630s he thought his time had come. The liberal Cardinal Barberini, an amateur astronomer and long-standing supporter, was elected pope as Urban VIII. Galileo sought, and received, permission to discuss the theories of the motion of the earth, as long as he did not appear to be holding the position that Copernicus was right. His book, *Dialogues on the Two World Systems*, was published in 1632, in Italian. The result was a disaster, for him and for the church. For the *Dialogues,* though it claims to merely discuss the theories of the heavens, in fact is a brilliantly written polemic, in which the supporters of the Copernican theory win every argument and have all the best lines. Galileo was ordered to come to Rome, where he faced trial by the Inquisition. He was well treated, as befit Italy's most prominent astronomer, but he was strictly questioned. As a result of the trial, the publication of the *Dialogues* was forbidden—as Galileo had expected—and Galileo was told to confess his disobedience and abjure having appeared to hold opinions which the church considered heretical—which he had not. He obeyed, as an obedient Catholic, but he thought the sentence misguided and intolerant, the result of intrigues by his enemies. He spent the rest of his life under fairly comfortable house arrest, working once again on the physics problems that had interested him as a young man, but he took his disgrace very much to heart. As for the Catholic Church, it had turned its back on the new astronomy that it had done much to inspire, and natural philosophers in Italy carefully chose their research to avoid controversy.

Ironically, the calendar reform that had first inspired Copernicus, based on tables derived by using his system, took place under the pope's auspices in all Catholic countries in 1582. Protestant countries rejected the pope's calendar with his authority, and though support of the Copernican theory became a cause célèbre in Protestant countries, calendar reform according to the Copernican system was accepted only in the eighteenth century.

Profile: William Harvey and the Witchcraft Trials

William Harvey (1578–1657), anatomist and physician to King Charles I of England, was one of the most prominent medical men of his day. Harvey studied medicine first at Cambridge, then at the University of Bologna, which had a distinguished history in anatomy. Andreas Vesalius, famous for publishing *De Fabrica* (1543), the first modern illustrated anatomy text, had taught there. He, like Copernicus, whose book on the sun-centered theory was published the same year, had wanted to produce a new, revised version of an ancient Greek text, in Vesalius's case Galen's work on human anatomy. Like Copernicus, he had ended up questioning many of the ancient ideas, and his questions had been taken up by his successors, such as Gabriele Fallopio, discover of the Fallopian tubes, and Hieronymo Fabricius, Harvey's anatomy teacher.

Harvey built on his predecessors' work in his own investigation of the heart. In 1628 he published *On the Motion of the Heart and Blood*, which showed by careful anatomical research and experiments that blood was pumped through the body in a circuit, from the arteries to the veins, then back to the heart. Harvey's theory on the circulation of the blood made him one of the most respected physicians and philosophers of his day, and contributed to the decline of the authority of the ancient Greeks in natural philosophy. As Harvey himself told John Aubrey, he was one of the few men to see his own revolutionary theories accepted in his own lifetime.

King Charles regarded Harvey as an authority on all matters of medicine and natural philosophy, and it was in that capacity that Harvey became involved in the trial of seventeen witches in Lancaster in 1634. A year earlier, Edmund Robinson, aged eleven, had claimed to have been present at a witches' meeting in a nearby house and had accused nearly thirty people from the area as having been there. Seventeen of them were found guilty, based on their having unusual marks on their bodies, for it was a common belief that the devil placed his mark on his disciples. One of the women, Margaret Johnson, actually claimed that she was a witch and that the devil had appeared before her and "offered her, if she would give him her soule, he would supply all her wants, and at her appointment would help her to kill and revenge her either of men or beast, or what she desired." King Charles heard of the case, and ordered another examination of some of the surviving women—three had already died in prison—to be carried out by midwives (female medical practitioners experienced in childbirth and in diseases involving women and children) under Harvey's instruction. The midwives found "nothing unnatural in . . . any . . . part of their bodies, nor any Sign that any such thing hath ever been"[26]; even Margaret Johnson, they said, had only natural birthmarks, no signs or marks of the devil. All the women they examined were pardoned by the king. Margaret Johnson's comments on her pardon were not recorded, so we do not know her response to the specialists' opinion that she was not a witch. The boy, Edmund Robinson, was later questioned and confessed to having made up the whole story. The curate at one of the churches where he had identified witches was David Webster, who published *The Displaying of Supposed Witchcraft* in 1677, one of the works most influential in bringing to a close the age of witchcraft trials. Belief in witches and magic, however, remained common in rural areas through the twentieth century.

Important Dates

1545–1563	Council of Trent
1543	Publication of Copernicus's *On the Motion of the Heavenly Spheres*; publication of Vesalius's *De Fabrica*
1550–1640	Height of witch hunting in Europe
1582	Introduction of revised calendar in Catholic countries
1601	Death of Tycho Brahe
1610	Publication of Galileo's *The Starry Messenger*
1627	Publication of Kepler's *Rudolfine Tables*
1628	Publication of Harvey's *On the Motion of the Heart and Blood*
1632	Publication of Galileo's *Dialogues on the Two World Systems*
1677	Publication of Webster's *The Displaying of Supposed Witchcraft*

Further Reading

Jonathan Barry, Marianne Hester, and Gareth Roberts, eds., *Witchcraft in Early Modern Europe: Studies in Culture and Belief* (Cambridge, 1998)

Wolfgang Behringer, *Witchcraft Persecutions in Bavaria: Popular Magic, Religious Zealotry and Reason of State in Early Modern Europe* (Cambridge, 1997)

Mario Biagioli, *Galileo Courtier: The Practice of Science in the Culture of Absolutism* (Chicago, 1994)

Ian Bostridge, *Witchcraft and Its Transformations, c.1650–c.1750* (Oxford, 1997)

Thomas Brennan, *Popular Drinking and Popular Culture in Eighteenth-Century Paris* (Princeton, 1988)

Robin Briggs, *Witches and Neighbours: The Social and Cultural Context of European Witchcraft* (New York, 1996)

Robin Briggs, *Communities of Belief: Cultural and Social Tension in Early Modern France* (Oxford, 1989)

Peter Burke, *Popular Culture in Early Modern Europe* (New York, 1978)

Sandra Cavallo, *Charity and Power in Early Modern Italy: Benefactors and Their Motives in Turin, 1541–1789* (Cambridge, 1995)

Louis Chatellier, *The Religion of the Poor: Rural Missions in Europe and the Formation of Modern Catholicism, c.1500–1800* (Cambridge, 1997)

Stuart Clark, *Thinking with Demons: The Idea of Witchcraft in Early Modern Europe* (Oxford, 1997)

Stillman Drake, *Galileo: Pioneer Scientist* (Toronto, 1990)

Sara Schechner Genuth, *Comets, Popular Culture, and the Birth of Modern Cosmology* (Princeton, 1997)

Carlo Ginzburg, *Ecstacies: Deciphering the Witches' Sabbath* (New York, 1991)

Carlo Ginzburg, *The Cheese and the Worms: The Cosmos of a Miller in Sixteenth Century Italy* (Baltimore, 1980)

Carlo Ginzburg, *The Night Battles: Witchcraft and Agrarian Cults in the Sixteenth and Seventeenth Centuries* (Baltimore, 1983)

R. Po-Chia Hsia, *Social Discipline in the Reformation: Central Europe 1550–1750* (London, 1989)

R. Po-Chia Hsia, *The World of Catholic Renewal, 1450–1770* (Cambridge, 1998)

Ronald Hutton, *The Rise and Fall of Merry England: The Ritual Year 1400–1700* (Oxford, 1994)

Ronald Hutton, *The Stations of the Sun: A History of the Ritual Year in Britain* (Oxford, 1996)

Susan Karant-Nunn, *The Reformation of Ritual: An Interpretation of Early Modern Germany* (London, 1997)

Joseph Klaits, *Servants of Satan: The Age of the Witch-Hunts* (Bloomington, 1985)

Alan Kors and Edward Peters, eds., *Witchcraft in Europe 1100–1700: A Documentary History* (Philadelphia, 1972)

Michael Kunze, *Highroad to the Stake: A Tale of Witchcraft* (Chicago, 1987)

Christina Larner, *Enemies of God: The Witch Hunt in Scotland* (Baltimore, 1981)

Anthony J. LaVopa, *Grace, Talent, and Merit: Poor Students, Clerical Careers, and Professional Ideology in Eighteenth-Century Germany* (Cambridge, 1988)

Brian Levack, *The Witch-Hunt in Early Modern Europe* (Bloomington, 1987)

H.C. Erik Midelfort, *Witchhunting in Southwestern Germany* (Stanford, 1972)

E. William Monter, *Witchcraft in France and Switzerland* (Ithaca, 1976)

Edward Muir, *Ritual in Early Modern Europe* (Cambridge, 1997)

Pietro Redondi, *Galileo, Heretic* trans. Raymond Rosenthal (Princeton, 1987)

Lyndal Roper, *Oedipus and the Devil: Witchcraft, Religion and Sexuality in Early Modern Europe* (Oxford, 1994)

Pieter Spierenburg, *The Broken Spell: A Cultural and Anthropological History of Preindustrial Europe* (New Brunswick, 1991)

Keith Thomas, *Man and the Natural World: Changing Attitudes in England 1500–1800* (New York, 1983)

Keith Thomas, *Religion and the Decline of Magic* (New York, 1971)

Gerhild Scholz Williams, *Defining Dominion: The Discourses of Magic and Witchcraft in Early Modern France and Germany* (Ann Arbor, 1995)

Deborah Willis, *Malevolent Nurture: Witch-Hunting and Maternal Power in Early Modern England* (Ithaca, 1996)

Chapter Five

Politics or Religion?
The Thirty Years' War

At the beginning of the seventeenth century, there was a subtle shift in the political landscape of Western Europe. The previous century had been dominated by three great issues: the tensions between Protestantism and Catholicism, the gradual emergence of regional and national consciousness as a motive for political action, and the rivalry between the ruling families of Spain and France for the preeminent position on the European stage. In the second half of the sixteenth century, those issues had produced two grand struggles that reverberated throughout Europe: the French Wars of Religion and the Dutch Revolt. While France and the Netherlands were wracked by bitter religious wars, the neighboring Holy Roman Empire, the home of the Reformation, had remained remarkably stable. Protestants and Catholics had chafed at some of the provisions of the Peace of Augsburg of 1555, which had established that German princes could choose between Lutheranism and Catholicism, but which had provided no mechanism for settling disputes between the two faiths. None of the flare-ups, though, had been severe enough to plunge Germany into turmoil.

Around 1600, as the conflicts in France and the Netherlands calmed down, the situation in the Empire became more tense. The conversion of King Henry IV of France from Calvinism back to Catholicism, combined with the Edict of Nantes, which guaranteed some freedom of worship to Calvinists, defused the most virulent fighting in France. Henry's astute internal policies and kingly bearing brought surprising stability to the country, which persisted even after he was assassinated by a Catholic zealot in 1610. In the Netherlands, financial exhaustion of the two sides produced a willingness to stop the bloodshed, at least temporarily.

In the Netherlands, Jan of Oldenbarnevelt led a peace party, while the Spanish were forced to make a deal to avert yet another default on their massive debts. In 1609, a twelve-year truce was concluded. It was clear that neither side was really satisfied with the terms of the truce, so there was widespread fear in Europe that a new conflagration would break out in 1621 when the truce expired. However, events in the Holy Roman Empire accelerated that conflagration by three years. The war that broke out was a continuation of the struggles of the late sixteenth century in some respects. But it also inaugurated a new era in warfare and diplomacy that was to shape the rest of the early modern period.

Thirty Years' War

One reason why the Holy Roman Empire had been spared the worst of religious warfare in the last decades of the sixteenth century was because the emperor, Rudolf II, was distracted by two things: an invasion of Hungary by the Ottoman Turks and his own mental instability. The former meant that he had to rely on both Protestant and Catholic princes in the Empire to supply troops, so he could ill afford a confrontation over religion within the Empire. The latter meant that the House of Habsburg was unable to work out any coordinated policy. Frustration over Rudolf's indecisiveness and "melancholy" eventually prompted his brothers and nephews to try to give formal power to his brother Matthias (1557–1619). When Rudolf refused give up his authority, they went one step further and mobilized troops to force him to recognize Matthias as the head of the Habsburgs, if not as emperor himself. Rudolf's court was in Prague in Bohemia, while Matthias was stationed in Vienna. To gain allies in his fight against Matthias, Rudolf was compelled to make extensive concessions to the Protestant nobles who dominated the Bohemian Diet (representative assembly). His "Letter of Majesty" of 1609 reinforced the belief of Bohemian nobles that they themselves controlled the terms by which the Habsburgs ruled their territory. When Rudolf II died in 1612, Matthias was compelled to renew the Letter of Majesty as a precondition for gaining Bohemian support.

It was galling for the Austrian Habsburgs to have to tolerate such a strong Protestant independent streak in their hereditary lands, particularly because the Catholic cause had begun to make a strong comeback within the Empire through the tireless efforts of Duke Maximilian of Bavaria. After all, what good was the principle of *cuius regio eius religio* if the most prominent Catholic ruler in Europe was unable to apply it in his own lands? Lutheranism was on the defensive against both Catholicism and Calvinism, both of which gained converts. The conflict between Lutherans and Calvinists meant that they could not cooperate in resisting expanding Catholic influence. For example, when Bavaria annexed the city of Donauwörth in 1609 as punishment for the attack by a Protestant mob on a Catholic religious procession, Protestant princes could not agree on a united protest. Though both Catholic and Protestant rulers within the Empire organized themselves into defensive alliances, called the Catholic League and the Protestant Union, the Protestants wrangled over the relative weight of Calvinist and Lutheran elements. The Catholics, in contrast, remained united under Maximilian's leadership.

Within the Austrian Habsburg family, the ruler who best emulated Maximilian of Bavaria's arch-Catholic strength was a cousin of Rudolf's, Ferdinand of Styria (1578–1637), whom the childless Matthias designated as both successor to the Habsburg hereditary lands and as emperor in 1617. Transfer of the imperial title would have to wait until Matthias's death, but Ferdinand was given immediate administrative authority over the hereditary lands, including Bohemia. He immediately installed an aggressively Catholic administration, which the Bohemian Protestants reviled as a violation of the Letter of Majesty. When, in early 1618, Matthias's adminstrators ordered the destruction of two Protestant churches that had been built on Catholic lands, an angry mob, instigated by Protestant nobles, confronted them in the main palace in Prague and tossed them from a high window into the dry moat below. This "defenestration" (a fancy way of saying "thrown from a window") marked an irrevocable break between the Bohemian Protestants and the Catholic Ferdinand. The leaders of the rebels announced that Ferdinand had been imposed on them in violation of the fundamental principles of the Bohemian monarchy, which required the approval of the "estates," so he was not rightfully their king. They then began the search for a new king who would recognize their rights. There was now no way to avoid war between the Bohemian Protestants and Ferdinand. The only question was, who else would become involved?

Several factors made it likely that the strife in Bohemia would spill over into the rest of Europe. First, there was the issue of the Netherlands. The primary architects of the Twelve Years' Truce between Spain and the Dutch both came to ignominious defeats, just as the events in

Bohemia unfolded. Scandals forced the duke of Lerma to renounce his position as chief minister of Spain and retire to a monastery in 1618. Jan of Oldenbarnevelt faced an even worse fate. Criticism of his peace policies combined with sharp doctrinal debates within the Dutch Calvinist church led to a mob uprising against him. He was arrested in 1618 and executed the following year. With these voices for moderation out of the way, both sides began to prepare for the lapse of the treaty in 1621. Second, the elderly Matthias died less than a year after the defenestration of Prague. If he had lived longer, the Bohemian issue might have remained an internal, Habsburg affair. With his death, though, the Holy Roman Empire as a whole became involved, because, although Matthias had designated Ferdinand as his successor, the position of emperor was elected, not conferred automatically by birth.

The problem was the composition of the electoral body. There were seven electors, almost evenly divided by confession. The archbishops of Mainz, Trier, and Cologne were Catholic, while the princes of Saxony, Brandenburg, and the Palatinate of the Rhine were Protestant. The seventh vote was held by the kingdom of Bohemia. So it mattered a great deal whether Ferdinand, who had just been "deposed" by the estates of Bohemia, was legitimately king or whether the rebels' claims would be recognized. The matter was further complicated by the dissension within the Protestant ranks. Saxony, home to Martin Luther, had traditionally been the most respected of the Protestant powers and it was strongly in favor of a conservative interpretation of imperial affairs. That meant that the Duke of Saxony was perfectly ready to recognize Ferdinand in Bohemia and in the empire, as long as Ferdinand was willing to continue the settlement worked out in the Peace of Augsberg. Brandenburg had traditionally deferred to Saxony's judgment, so it was willing to vote for Ferdinand as well. The Palatinate of the Rhine, on the other hand, was an upstart power, the most aggressive of the newly Calvinist territories in the empire. The ruler of the Palatinate, Frederick V (1596–1632), saw the Bohemian struggle as the ideal opportunity to rise to the forefront of the Protestant cause. He entered into negotiations to become king of Bohemia, while trying to stall the inevitable election of Ferdinand as emperor. Unfortunately for him, the negotiations took too long, so that by the time the offer of the kingship came from Bohemian nobles, the election of Ferdinand as emperor was already complete.

The Winter King

As Frederick accepted the invitation to become king of Bohemia, he claimed that it was "a divine calling, which I must not disobey. My only end is to serve God and His church."[1] The comment is partly self-serving, since it is obvious that he also would personally profit from the enhanced prestige of the title of king. But it shows the extent to which political calculation was intertwined with religious faith. Frederick's opponents were equally motivated by a combination of political calculation and religious faith, but they could also claim that Frederick subverted the natural political order by accepting the Bohemian rebels' claim that they had the right to depose a king. One reason why the rebels had chosen Frederick was that he was the son-in-law of James I, the king of England. They were counting on English backing for their cause. But James strongly cautioned Frederick against accepting the Bohemian crown and did little to support his son-in-law after he did.

The English were not the only Protestants who were dubious about the Bohemian situation. John George of Saxony categorically refused to support Frederick, because Frederick was a Calvinist. In fact, John George sent the Saxon army to support Ferdinand against the Bohemians. For him, the principle of legitimate monarchical authority took precedence over the principle of religious liberty. The Protestant Union also refused to attack the emperor directly. Instead it dissolved in disunion over how much support to lend to Frederick. Only a few minor radical Protestant princes offered their support to Frederick. Thus, he began his kingship with significant weaknesses.

Ferdinand, on the other hand, was able to secure a number of allies. The change in ministers in Spain meant that the Spanish were willing to lend both financial and direct military support to Ferdinand. Within the empire, Maximilian of Bavaria offered the army of the Catholic League, under the experienced general Tilly, to help suppress the rebels. The military campaign turned out to be a great mismatch. At the Battle of White Mountain near Prague in 1620, the rebel army was decimated. Frederick was forced to flee Prague less than a year after he had arrived. His short stay earned him the sarcastic nickname "the Winter King." The fate of the Bohemian rebels was sealed. Those who were caught were executed; the rest had their lands confiscated.

From Bohemian Rebellion to German War

The original question concerning the Bohemian monarchy was resolved, but the war did not end. Later writers would claim that a comet blazed across the sky for thirty days in 1618 to mark the beginning of thirty years of war. At the time, however, few suspected that the war would be so long or so costly. The Thirty Years' War lasted thirty years primarily because each solution to some issue in the war raised a new question that had to be dealt with. With the military defeat of the Bohemian rebels, the question now became what to do about Frederick. Frederick escaped unharmed from Prague and fled to the Netherlands, where he remained in exile during the war. Surely he had to be punished for his actions, but what kind of punishment was appropriate? The Spanish army had begun to invade his home territory of the Palatinate and Ferdinand wanted to take advantage of that situation to punish Frederick by confiscating his lands. But while James I and John George of Saxony had cautioned Frederick against joining the Bohemian rebels, they were not willing to see him lose his own lands. On the other hand, both Spain and Bavaria were not only willing, but eager to see Frederick lose his land. Spain wanted to remove a belligerent Calvinist from a strategic position along the Rhine, the main supply route for Spanish troops once the war in the Netherlands resumed. Bavaria wanted the Palatinate, and its privilege of electing the emperor, as compensation for its actions on behalf of the Catholic cause. Emperor Ferdinand, indebted to both, fulfilled their wishes.

When Ferdinand announced that he had banned Frederick and was turning over his lands to Maximilian of Bavaria, he dramatically increased the resistance and suspicions of the Protestant states within the empire. Saxony did not turn against the emperor, but it did refuse to acknowledge Maximilian's claims to the Palatinate. Several smaller Protestant states became active opponents of the emperor. They gained financial, and some military, support from the Dutch, who had renewed their war with Spain. Thus, the war spread. Militarily, the first years of the war were a series of great victories for the emperor's allies; but each victory only heightened the fears that the Habsburgs aspired to a "universal monarchy," in other words that they would destroy the traditional powers of the territories within the empire and rule as if all were their kingdom. That meant that there was always one Protestant state willing to take up the challenge when another one was defeated. But it also meant that new parts of the empire became caught up in the war—first Bohemia, then the Palatinate, then southwest Germany and Alsace, then central Germany, and then northern Germany. The war even spilled beyond the borders of Germany, as seemingly unrelated conflicts became caught up in the struggle between the Habsburgs and the Protestants. A fight over the succession in the Italian duchies of Mantua and Montferrat linked northern Italy into the war. Dutch expeditions in the New World against the Spanish, including the capture of Brazil in 1630, turned the German war into perhaps the first world war.

The Generals: Wallenstein

Until 1626, all of Ferdinand's accomplishments were achieved by proxy. He did not really have an army of his own, but depended on Bavaria and Spain to fight for him. When Denmark took up the Protestant cause in 1625 as part of a great coalition that included, at least nominally, England and the Netherlands, Maximilian began to fear that the Bavarian and Spanish forces would not be enough and he urged Ferdinand to create his own imperial army.

An ambitious Bohemian nobleman, Albrecht von Wallenstein (1583–1634), had already offered more than once to raise an army out of his own funds and place it at the emperor's service. This seemed the time to take up the offer. Wallenstein was born into a minor Protestant noble family in Bohemia. In his youth, he converted to Catholicism and was one of the few Bohemian nobles to remain loyal to the Habsburgs during the Bohemian rebellion. That paid off nicely for him, because he was able to buy up confiscated estates at very low prices after the Battle of White Mountain. He became a very rich and powerful man. He was, therefore, well positioned to make his offer to Ferdinand.

With Wallenstein's army in the field, the power of the emperor seemed all the more dangerous. Wallenstein developed an innovative system of recruitment and supply that actually made it easier to keep his army large than to keep it small. By 1628, he had more than 100,000 men under his command, which made his by far the largest of the Catholic forces in the field. After the Danes and their allies were defeated by a combined action of Wallenstein and Tilly in 1626, there were no major powers ready to come to the rescue of the Protestant cause. Ferdinand began to overreach himself. First, he decided to reward Wallenstein with an unprecedented elevation in rank. He deposed the Duke of

Mecklenburg, who had been an ally of the Danes, and declared that Wallenstein would become the new duke. This was viewed as even more outrageous than the decision to give the Palatinate to Maximilian of Bavaria: Maximilian was at least descended from the same noble family as Frederick, while Wallenstein was a rank upstart. Wallenstein had had no connection to Mecklenburg before his armies occupied it and, despite his newfound wealth, came from a much lower noble status than a hereditary duke. If Ferdinand had the power to raise Wallenstein to the same level as the other territorial rulers within the empire, other princes feared, maybe he really was about to institute a universal monarchy. Even the Bavarians began to warn that it would perhaps be safer if Wallenstein were removed from command of his army, so that he could not threaten the liberties of other territories.

Maximilian of Bavaria agreed wholeheartedly with Ferdinand's other move, however—the publication of the Edict of Restitution in 1629. The Edict of Restitution confirmed the Protestants' worst fears about Ferdinand, because it rolled back the territorial gains of the Protestants since 1552 and restored property that Protestant princes had confiscated from the Catholic Church. Handpicked assessors were to determine what properties had been illegally occupied by Protestants. Under the Edict, even John George of Saxony might be compelled to give back land that had been in Saxon hands for half a century. The Edict also reaffirmed that Catholicism and Lutheranism were the only religions that territorial rulers would be allowed to adopt. All Calvinists were to be treated as rebels against the empire. Tilly and Wallenstein immediately began to enforce these statutes. The Edict was issued from a position of strength, on the assumption that there was no one who could resist it. But, shortly, the situation would be dramatically changed.

The Generals: Gustavus Adolphus

One sign of Ferdinand's overconfidence in the wake of the Edict of Restitution is that he listened to Maximilian of Bavaria and finally removed Wallenstein from command of his army, placing overall command in the experienced hands of the head of the Catholic League, General Tilly. At almost the same moment, King Gustavus Adolphus of Sweden entered the fight. The Swedes had kept out of the war till then, in part because they were unwilling to be tied up in an alliance with their regional enemy, Denmark, and in part because they were busy fighting

Portrait of Gustavus Adolphus, King of Sweden (1594–1632) (Erich Lessing/Art Resource, NY)

the Poles. When France brokered a peace treaty between Sweden and Poland and offered subsidies for the Swedish army if it should get involved in the empire, Gustavus Adolphus agreed.

Gustavus Adolphus (1594–1632) became king of Sweden in 1611 at the age of seventeen. Though Sweden was not as wealthy as some of its rivals, Gustavus was an astute politician, able to extract resources from his nobility to pursue an active foreign policy. From the beginning, his reign was marked by warfare—against Denmark from 1611–1613 and against Poland from 1617–1618. Gustavus was a tireless campaigner. He also devoted himself to the study of warfare and applied the new principles of the Dutch tactician Maurice of Nassau to reforming his own army's organization. He thereby welded together an extremely effective fighting force.

Gustavus had many motives for getting into the war. He wanted to support the Protestant cause, but he also wanted to establish the superiority of Sweden in the Baltic and thought he could acquire the Duchy of Pomerania on the Baltic coast to help with that design. Perhaps equally important was a desire for glory. He wanted Sweden to be taken seriously among the major powers of Europe, instead of being treated as a second-rate power. That would only be possible if Sweden got involved in the affairs of state currently convulsing central Europe.

By the time Gustavus landed in Germany there was almost no one left to be his ally. The deposed Dukes of Mecklenburg signed on, but their lands were in Wallenstein's hands. The only territory who opposed the emperor not already occupied by Catholic troops was the Protestant-dominated archbishopric of Magdeburg, which immediately became the target of the imperial army. Gustavus was unable to prevent Tilly from capturing the city of Magdeburg after a long siege. But Tilly's victory proved almost as costly as a defeat. A fire that started during the assault burned much of the city to the ground. Meanwhile, the attacking troops lost all control in wreaking vengeance on the city. The destruction of Magdeburg was a public relations disaster for the emperor, which only pushed wavering territories closer to Gustavus.

Not long after Magdeburg, John George of Saxony finally abandoned his deference to the emperor. He forged an alliance with Gustavus, and the combined Saxon-Swedish army headed off Tilly's invading force near the city of Leipzig. At the resulting battle of Breitenfeld in 1631, Tilly's army was crushed. The tables were suddenly turned. Now the Catholics were on the defensive, as Gustavus swiftly marched first towards the Palatinate and then directly into Bavaria, which he deliberately devastated. It seemed as if Gustavus would march directly on Vienna and impose a Protestant solution to the war. The emperor quickly recalled Wallenstein, who was able to divert Gustavus back into Saxon territory. At the battle of Lützen, in 1632, Wallenstein's army suffered a loss, but the loss to the Swedes was even greater, because Gustavus himself was killed while leading his troops.

Without their leader, the Swedes seemed temporarily stunned. But Gustavus's chief minister, Axel Oxenstierna, took over direction of Swedish policy, while Wallenstein dithered about how to exploit his advantage. In fact, Wallenstein's actions became so erratic that the emperor began to fear that he intended to use his army against the emperor instead of the enemy. The emperor gave the order that Wallenstein was to be deposed, by force if necessary. On February 25, 1634, Wallenstein was assassinated by officers of his own army.

It was becoming increasingly difficult to determine what the belligerents were fighting over, except to hold on to as much of the gains, or recoup as much of the losses, as they could before the war was over. In November 1634, the emperor's army won a major victory over the Swedes at the Battle of Nördlingen. The desire for peace was strong enough that the emperor was able to win over most of Sweden's allies for a comprehensive peace settlement in 1635. He could no longer demand terms as harsh as those of the Edict of Restitution, but he could come out stronger than he had been before the war.

Richelieu and Reason of State

The war might have ended there, had it not been for the entrance of the French. Under Henry IV, France had taken an active interest in German affairs. But after his assassination by a Catholic fanatic in 1610, France had been preoccupied with internal matters. The new king, Louis XIII (1601–1643), was just eight years old, which meant a long period of regency. In 1614, a meeting of the French parliament, called the Estates General, was convened to advise the king as he approached maturity. The Estates General suggested various reforms, most notably an end to the practice of selling political offices, but its effects were limited and the occasion is most notable for being the last time that the Estates General met until 1789.

Louis XIII's early reign was dominated by court intrigues, but amidst the intrigues, he encountered the young bishop of Luçon, Armand du Plessis, Cardinal Richelieu (1584–1642). Richelieu had originally trained for a military career, but family dynamics made it more practical that he follow a clerical career, as the bishopric of Luçon had traditionally been part of the family's possessions. Richelieu had made a favorable impression on the king during the Estates General of 1614, and in 1624 he was named chief minister to Louis XIII. He held on to that position, despite vocal and powerful opposition from, among others, the king's mother Marie de Medici, primarily because he was always able to earn the king's trust.

Richelieu had not been sorry to see the Habsburgs, traditional rivals of the French, exhaust their resources in a long, destructive war. Later in his career, he expressed his goals for the monarchy: "Three things entered my mind: first, to ruin the Huguenots and render the king absolute in his state; second, to abase the House of Austria [the Habsburgs]; and third, to discharge the French people of heavy subsidies and tailles [taxes], enabling the king to repossess his domains which are capable by themselves of sustaining him handsomely."[2] For much of the 1620s, he could not deal with the second issue, because he was distracted by the first and third. Despite the Edict of Nantes, the independence of the Huguenots in the regions they dominated was an obvious limitation on Louis XIII's control of his realm. In the 1620s he began a more aggressive policy against the main strongholds. Richelieu helped him carry out that policy, which culminated in a long siege of the key Huguenot stronghold of La Rochelle in 1627. La Rochelle counted on aid from England, but all rescue attempts were unsuccessful. Louis XIII and Richelieu persisted in the siege, despite its tremendous expense, and when the garrison surrendered in 1628, the military independence of the Huguenots was broken.

All during his conflict with the Huguenots within France, Richelieu was pursuing a policy of support for the emperor's enemies in Germany. His diplomats expended much effort to detach Maximilian of Bavaria and other Catholic princes from their alliance with Ferdinand, but much of Richelieu's support had to go to Protestant powers. At the treaty of Bärwalde in 1631, Richelieu agreed to subsidize the Swedish army in Germany in exchange for a promise that the Catholic religion would be protected in Swedish-occupied regions. The Swedes did little to keep that promise, but the French still supported them.

How could a cardinal of the Catholic Church justify such blatant support for Protestants against a Catholic power? First of all, it was nothing new for the French crown to have dubious allies in its fight against the house of Habsburg. Under Francis I it had even had a diplomatic understanding with the Turks. But under Richelieu, the doctrine became more pronounced that the first responsibility of the king and his ministers was to the security and glory of their state, not their religion, a doctrine known as "reason of state." Louis XIII expressed the idea to an ambassador of the pope who was trying to negotiate a settlement of a dispute between France and Spain: "interests of state must not be mixed in any way with religious ones."[3]

In 1635, it became necessary to draw the final conclusion from that principle. If the German Protestants and Swedes could not thwart the Habsburgs on their own, then France would have to join the struggle directly. France formally declared war against Spain, but the main theater of conflict was Germany. With France now officially on the side of the Protestants and the religious passions of the first decade of the war starkly reduced by the inconclusiveness of the war, reason of state came to be the guiding principle of all of the belligerents.

The last decade of the war was, if anything, even more confusing and inconclusive than the first two decades. Despite the entry of France into the war, the Spanish concentrated as much on defeating the Dutch as the French. There were violent outbreaks against the rising taxes that were necessary to finance the war in several of the major states: in 1636 in Austria, in 1637 and 1639 in France, and in 1640 in Catalonia and Portugal against Spain. There were also a number of impressive and bloody battles, but they served mainly to build up the hopes of one side or the other that they could extract extra concessions at a final peace treaty. But despite years of fighting, no one side emerged victorious. Even the Battle of Rocroi in 1643, where the French inflicted a severe defeat on the Spanish, did not directly affect the tide of events in Germany. Even as the last provisions of a peace treaty were being hammered out in 1648, Swedish troops were launching a furious assault on the city of Prague, now defended by ardent backers of the house of Habsburg.

The Armies

The Thirty Years' War marks the end of one important era of military development and the beginning of a new one. Gunpowder weapons were already commonplace on the battlefields of Europe in the sixteenth century. By the end of the war, they were being deployed in innovative ways that increased firepower and made battles much bloodier affairs. The infantry squares called *tercios*, with which the Spanish had dominated the battlefields of Europe in the sixteenth century, were replaced with more flexible formations that relied on length rather than depth

The constant presence of war for thirty years brought about changes in the overall organization of warfare that were probably more profound than these tactical changes. Especially in the early years, the Thirty Years' War is notable for the number of independent military contractors who operated. For example, forces raised by Count Ernest of Mansfeld were hired consecutively by the Piedmontese, the Bohemians, the Palatinate, the Dutch, the English, and the Danes. To keep their mercenary armies in the field, both sides had to rely on stopgap financing methods. The countryside suffered from both unregulated plundering by undisciplined troops and official plundering in the form of "contributions," a kind of tax that invading armies were allowed to place on the areas they occupied, while the mercenary captains had to be bought off with huge reimbursements or new titles and lands. By the end of the war, the system of contributions became regularized and the princes who hired the armies gained the upper hand in administering them. Wallenstein contributed to this trend as both a positive and negative example. He was adept at using his personal estates as protected havens that produced the necessary supplies for his army. But his arrogance and independence also demonstrated to many princes the dangers of keeping powerful armies in private hands. Thus, an almost inadvertent result of the war was that the state gained more control over the army. After 1648, it was no longer possible for a minor nobleman to raise an army on his own account to challenge one of the kings of Europe.

Destruction in a Village

In 1642, the pastor of the village of Reichensachsen in central Germany wrote in his parish register, "Anno 1642, all the misery continued just as bad as in the previous year, so that the despair pressed all the harder . . . whoever has not himself seen and lived through such circumstances cannot believe what I note here."[4] Indeed, for large numbers of ordinary people the war was an unimaginable catastrophe. The novelist Grimmelshausen experienced the war as a child growing up in the Spessart near Frankfurt. His fictional account, *Simplicius Simplicissimus* ("Simple the Simplest"), first published in 1669, depicted "the horrifying and quite unheard of cruelties sometimes perpetrated in this our German war," including rape, burning alive, application of thumbscrews, garroting, and having buckets of dung poured down the throat. These horrors were presented graphically in a series of engravings by Jacques

Callot (1592–1635), entitled "The Miseries and Calamities of War," produced in 1633. Callot, like Grimmelshausen, saw the impact of the war
firsthand in his native Lorraine and believed it was his responsibility to
illustrate the horrors that war represented.

Books and works of art reflected reality. Though the number of civilians who died as a direct result of attacks by troops was comparatively
small, the coming of an army was always a terrible ordeal. Villages and
towns sent messengers in all directions to keep track of the movement
of troops, so the inhabitants would know when to flee and take their
possessions with them. Whole villages would hide out in the nearest
fortified town or in the most impenetrable parts of the woods.

The indirect effects of the war were sometimes even more devastating than the direct effects. The armies of the era were great breeding
grounds for disease, and plagues spread throughout Germany on more
than one occasion. Resistance to disease was reduced because food was
in short supply. The armies sucked the resources of the countryside dry
and left almost nothing behind. They could strip whole fields and leave
nothing for the villagers who remained. Constant flight from invaders
disrupted the ordinary routines of tending the fields, so yields were
sharply reduced. It was not unusual to find villages that had more than
fifty families before the war left with just five or six families in the
worst years of the war. The rest had either died from disease or starvation or left the village for good.

It is no wonder that preachers, poets, and propagandists made the call
for peace one of the standard pleas of the era. The satirist Philipp Michael
Moscherosch entitled one of his poems "Germany which sighs for peace,"
while the villagers of Grandenborn concluded a letter to their ruler with
the phrase: "God the almighty change things for the better and give us
his merciful grace and remove the burden of war from us and grant us
poor Hessian subjects dear peace, so help us God."[5]

Peace Treaties of Westphalia

The peace that came was a combination of tradition and innovation. For
the first time, all the combatants met at the bargaining table (or actually
two bargaining tables, because the negotiations were divided between
two cities, the Westphalian towns of Münster and Osnabrück), for a
series of negotiations that took four years to complete. Much of what
was decided merely codified the situation from before the war. The Edict

88

Europe in 1648 (Copyright: Hammond World Atlas Corporation, NJ Lic. No. 12504)

EUROPE IN 1648
AT THE PEACE OF
WESTPHALIA

of Restitution was repealed, so Protestant princes kept the former church territories. The son of Frederick of the Palatinate was reinstalled in his lands along the Rhine as Elector of the Palatinate, though Bavaria was made the eighth elector and allowed to keep the region bordering on Bavaria called the Upper Palatinate. The authority of the territorial rulers within their own territories was recognized: the emperor had to agree not to intervene in internal affairs, including religion. Calvinism was given equal legitimacy with Lutheranism and Catholicism in the imperial constitution, although the irony there was that Calvinism had lost much of its social dynamism and ceased to be a potent political force in the empire after 1648. The treaties also recognized in law things that were already de facto circumstances. Both the Netherlands and Switzerland were formally recognized as independent of the Holy Roman Empire. Furthermore, Spain recognized the independence of the Dutch Republic.

The French had urged an even more radical revision of the constitution of the Holy Roman Empire, one that would have made the emperor a mere figurehead and prevented the Habsburgs from monopolizing the office, but the plan foundered on the resistance not only of the Habsburgs, but of the great majority of the Protestant states as well. The small German states were well aware of the dangers of too much independence in a world where the major powers could be so aggressive. Instead, the Treaties of Westphalia added France and Sweden as guarantors of the security of the empire. From now on, the strength of the empire was to depend on the weakness of the powers within it.

Both Sweden and France were awarded territories within the Holy Roman Empire. France's territories were mostly taken directly from the Austrian Habsburgs, pushing the French frontier closer to the Rhine. The Swedes occupied part of the Duchy of Pomerania and the Bishopric of Bremen and also received a large sum of money to help pay off their demobilized troops. But otherwise the internal territorial map of Germany was little changed. The most dramatic political change as a result of the war was that Bohemia was now populated almost exclusively by ardent Catholics who were intensely loyal to the Habsburg dynasty.

Though the Holy Roman Empire did not disappear as a political entity, no emperor was ever again in a position to attempt to build a strong central government. In 1657, Leopold I, a Habsburg, was elected on two conditions. First, he was to give no help to his Spanish cousins: the Habsburg domination of the ruling houses of Europe had come to an end. Second, the emperor would not seek to interfere in the internal government of the German principalities. This was the beginning of the Habsburgs' concentration on their own territorial possessions of Austria and (after the failure of the Ottoman attack on Vienna in 1683) Hungary.

The war also had consequences for the practice of European warfare. Everyone was sick of the brutality of war, so it was the beginning of discipline in armies. The Thirty Years' War was the last religious war in Europe, the last of the crusades, as after 1648 Richelieu's "reason of state" became the primary objective in war. It was the single most destructive war in European history until World War I. In fact, it has much in common with World War I. Both can be considered European civil wars, emerging from the division of European polities into increasingly rigid alliances; both did little to change the map of Europe itself.

Perhaps the most far-reaching effect of the Treaties of Westphalia was to heighten awareness of the principle of "balance of powers." One of the reasons for the many twists and turns of the war was the fear that one family—the Habsburgs—was in a position to dominate too much of Europe. It would be essential in the future, many believed, for states to defend themselves by forming alliances whenever it appeared that any one principality or ruling family was becoming too large and powerful. Ironically, the power that had been most adamant in exploiting that fear, France, was soon to have the principle invoked against it. This shift in Europe from a network of royal alliances, joined by marriage, to a network of international diplomacy, elaborated by treaties, was a decisive step in the creation of the modern world order.

Profile: Coping with the War—Two Strategies

Thirty years was more than a generation for most Europeans of the era. Few of the principals at the beginning of the war survived to see its end. Yet two rulers who did were among the most important in all phases of the war: Maximilian of Bavaria (1573–1651) and John George of Saxony (1585–1656). Their experiences can tell us as much about what the war was really about as can the lives of more famous participants.

Maximilian of Bavaria was the main organizer of resurgent Catholic power in the Holy Roman Empire before the war. He was a brilliant administrator, one of the few in the era to bring his state out of debt and to create a firm financial footing for his diplomacy. He was also perhaps the only Catholic ruler within the Holy Roman Empire to ensure that no

Protestant movement emerged either in the towns or among the nobles in his territory. He deliberately fostered the cult of the Virgin Mary within his territory, turning several miraculous sites into pilgrimage destinations. He also projected the most aggressive posture among Catholics in the political maneuvers of the Empire. He was aided in this practice by strategically placed relatives. His brother, for example, was archbishop of Cologne, one of the electors. In the wake of the Donauwörth incident, Maximilian organized the Catholic League to challenge Protestant princes.

Maximilian's fierce Catholicism put him squarely on the side of the Habsburgs in their fight with the Bohemian rebels. But Maximilian was too astute a statesman to squander his full treasury simply for the sake of protecting Catholicism in someone else's territory. For all of his prominence in the Catholic camp, the fact that Bavaria was not one of the seven electors meant that it was a second-status power within the empire. Maximilian saw it as his duty to rectify that. In exchange for bringing the army of the Catholic League into the conflict with Frederick and the Bohemian rebels, he extracted a promise that he and his successors would be granted the right of electing future emperors. The only way that Ferdinand could make good on that promise was to transfer Frederick's electoral rights to Maximilian. (Although Frederick and Maximilian were on opposite sides in matters of religion, they were both members of the family of Wittelsbach. The two lines had diverged more than a century previously, when a ruler had divided his inheritance between two sons, just as the Habsburgs had done in 1555, separating their Spanish and Austrian lines.) This was accomplished in 1623. For the rest of the war, Maximilian's policies were shaped by his determination to hold on to this concession, which depended on the success of the Habsburgs in achieving peace on their terms.

Having achieved his purpose in the war in 1623, Maximilian spent the rest of the war trying to balance his enthusiasm for the Catholic cause with his own reason of state. He endorsed the Edict of Restitution because it brought glory to Catholicism. He opposed Wallenstein's techniques for supplying his troops because they undermined the power of territorial rulers like himself. He was not eager for the emperor to gain absolute power within the empire. As he explained his opposition to Wallenstein's policies: "It is not only the prosperity and liberty of the whole Empire, and of all the states of the Empire, which is at stake, but also the dignity and prerogatives of the Electors."[6] Maximilian's ambivalence about the power of the emperor prompted the French periodi-cally to try to get him to join their side, without success. But in the end, Maximilian achieved his objective. The Treaties of Westphalia explic-itly recognized Bavaria as the eighth elector and granted him possession of part of the territories he had occupied from the Palatinate during the war. When he died in 1651 (from a cold caught during a pilgrimage to one of the shrines of the Virgin Mary), he could be well satisfied that he had raised Bavaria to the top rank of the German states.

If Maximilian of Bavaria chose a course to follow at the beginning of the war and clung to it doggedly no matter what the consequences for thirty long years, John George of Saxony was buffeted into a series of compromises and hard choices by the twists and turns of events in the war. He never really had an objective except to keep things pretty much as they had been. He was genuinely scandalized by the thought that Bohemian noblemen could simply toss aside their God-given ruler and choose a new one. In fact, the rebels approached him first about becoming their king, but he refused even to consider it. He believed strongly in the principle of le-gitimate authority and minimal change. He agreed to help Ferdinand in the suppression of the Bohemian revolt in exchange for a promise that reli-gious practices in the staunchly Lutheran Silesia would not be changed. John George was not willing to assist in the suppression of the Palatinate, but he was equally unwilling to come to Frederick's aid.

Some have claimed that John George lacked diplomatic vision be-cause of a fondness for drink. His court was notorious for the amount of beer consumed. But mostly he was simply caught between conflicting values. He kept his territory out of the war until 1631, despite increasing worries about the consequences of Habsburg power. All the while, he used the regular channels of the empire, especially his position as the most se-nior secular elector, to write letters of protest against what he perceived to be violations of the empire's constitution. But when Tilly and Gustavus Adolphus confronted each other after the destruction of Magdeburg, he had no choice but to choose sides. With great reluctance, he chose for the Swedes. The enforcement of the Edict of Restitution simply threat-ened too much of what he considered to be legitimate (including several of his own territories) for him to support the emperor any longer.

From that point on, Saxony became one of the main battlefields of the war. John George disliked being dependent on Gustavus Adolphus and Oxenstierna. He did just the bare minimum to fulfill his obligations towards them, but also tried to open up the possibility of a "third party" between the Swedes and the emperor, that might be able to force the two to accommodate. After the battle of Nördlingen, he was able to detach himself from his alliance. He agreed to the Peace of Prague in 1635, even though it was highly advantageous for the emperor, primarily because he thought it provided the best opportunity for a legitimate solution to the war. He had built an alliance of the great majority of the German states to back up the peace—there were only a few holdouts, such as the landgrave of Hesse-Kassel and the Elector of the Palatinate. Unfortunately for him, the intervention of the French undermined his plans. Saxony continued to be ravaged by enemy troops and John George switched back to the emperor's side, fighting against the Swedes.

By the end of the war, Saxony was devastated and John George's state finances were ruined. By following the middle path, John George gave himself little leverage to extract concessions at the peace conference. Perhaps his greatest accomplishment was to convince both sides that 1624, not 1618 or 1627, would be the ideal compromise for territorial settlements between Protestants and Catholics. With that date, the only Protestant territory to surrender land to a Catholic territory was the Palatinate, which gave part of its territory to Bavaria. The irony is that the final peace settlement arrived at a position not unlike John George's stance at the beginning of the war. His state had suffered because of forces beyond his control; it was never again to play the same role in German affairs.

Important Dates

1598	Edict of Nantes
1609	Letter of Majesty for Bohemia issued by Rudolf II
1609	Donauwörth incident in Germany
1609	Twelve Years' Truce signed between Netherlands and Spain
1610	Assassination of Henry IV of France
1612	Death of Emperor Rudolf II
1618	Fall of the duke of Lerma in Spain
1618	Arrest and condemnation of Jan of Oldenbarnevelt of the Netherlands
1618	Defenestration of Prague begins Thirty Years' War
1619	Death of Emperor Mathias; Frederick V of the Palatinate becomes king of Bohemia; Ferdinand II confirmed as emperor

1620	Battle of White Mountain; Maximilian defeats Bohemian rebels
1624	Richelieu becomes chief minister of France
1625	Christian IV of Denmark enters war against Emperor Ferdinand
1626	Albrecht von Wallenstein raises army for emperor; defeat of Danish army
1627	Huguenot stronghold of La Rochelle surrenders
1629	Edict of Restitution
1632	Death of Gustavus Adolphus
1635	France directly enters Thirty Years' War
1634	Assassination of Wallenstein
1642	Death of Richelieu; Mazarin becomes chief minister
1648	Treaties of Westphalia

Further Reading

Ronald Asch, *The Thirty Years' War: The Holy Roman Empire and Europe, 1618–1648* (Houndsmills, England, 1997)

Frederic Baumgarten, *From Spear to Flintlock: A History of War in Europe and the Middle East to the French Revolution* (New York, 1991)

Joseph Bergin, *Cardinal Richelieu: Power and the Pursuit of Wealth* (New Haven, 1985)

Robert Bireley, *Religion and Politics in the Age of the Counterreformation* (Chapel Hill, 1981)

Richard Bonney, *Political Change in France under Richelieu and Mazarin, 1624–1661* (Oxford, 1978)

William Church, *Richelieu and Reason of State* (Princeton, 1972)

J.H. Elliott, *The Count-Duke of Olivares: The Statesman in an Age of Decline* (New Haven, 1986)

J.H. Elliott, *Richelieu and Olivares* (Cambridge, 1984)

Myron Gutmann, *War and Rural Life in the Early Modern Low Countries* (Princeton, 1980)

R.J. Knecht, *Richelieu* (London, 1991)

Paul Lockhart, *Denmark in the Thirty Years' War: King Christian IV and the Decline of the Oldenburg State* (Selinsgrove, PA, 1996)

Howard Louthan, *The Quest for Compromise: Peacemakers in Counter-Reformation Vienna* (Cambridge, 1997)

J. Russell Major, *From Renaissance Monarchy to Absolute Monarchy: French Kings, Nobles and Estates* (Baltimore, 1997)

Golo Mann, *Wallenstein, His Life Narrated* trans. Charles Kessler (New York, 1976)

A. Lloyd Moote, *Louis XIII: The Just* (Berkeley, 1989)

Geoffrey Parker, *The Military Revolution: Military Innovation and the Rise of the West, 1500–1800* (Cambridge, 1989)

Geoffrey Parker, *The Thirty Years' War* (London, 1984)

J.V. Polisensky, *The Thirty Years' War* trans. Robert Evans (Berkeley, 1971)

J.V. Polisensky, *Tragic Triangle: The Netherlands, Spain and Bohemia 1617–1621* trans. Frederick Snider (Prague, 1991)

Erik Ringmar, *Identity, Interest and Action: A Cultural Explanation of Sweden's Intervention in the Thirty Years' War* (Cambridge, 1996)

Michael Roberts, *Gustavus Adolphus: A History of Sweden* 2 vols. (Oxford, 1953, 1958)

Michael Roberts, *Gustavus Adolphus* 2nd ed. (London, 1992)

Magdalena Sanchez, *The Empress, the Queen, and the Nun: Women and Power at the Court of Philip III of Spain* (Baltimore, 1998)

R.A. Stradling, *Philip IV and the Government of Spain, 1621–1665* (Cambridge, 1988)

John Theibault, *German Villages in Crisis: Rural Life and the Thirty Years' War in Hesse-Kassel, 1580–1720* (Atlantic Highlands, NJ, 1995)

C.V. Wedgwood, *The Thirty Years' War* (London, 1938)

Chapter Six

Who Should Rule in England?

The Stuart Kings and Divine Right

During the sixteenth and early seventeenth centuries, all continental Europe had found out how explosive religious differences could be when associated with conflict over legitimate political authority. Now the three kingdoms of England, Scotland, and Ireland, united under the crown of James I and VI of England and Scotland (1566–1625), were to learn the same lesson. Up to the mid-seventeenth century, England had been spared religious wars, largely because Elizabeth I's diplomacy had kept violent religious differences in check. Still, those differences existed. The Church of England, also called the Anglican Church, was the only lawful church, but there were wide variations in how Anglicanism was practiced. In regions closest to the court, the practices adhered most closely to the reforms instituted by Henry VIII; in others, much more of the Catholic ritual had been retained; in others, English Calvinists, called Puritans, had established the austere churches, and the meetings of elders, associated with Calvinist reforms on the Continent.

This diversity of practices pleased no one. True Catholics had little power in England and lost what little support they had after the discovery in 1605 of the Gunpowder Plot, an alleged plot by Roman Catholic conspirators to blow up the King and both Houses of Parliament. The opposition was most fierce between the supporters of the bishops and ritual of the Church of England, called High Churchmen, and the strictest Puritans, who wanted to see the established church reformed along Calvinist lines with no bishops. The High Church Anglicans saw themselves as the only true, pure religion, in which civil and religious authority flowed from the king as head of the church through to the bishops, his administrators in religion just as the king's sheriffs were his administrators in justice. Their enemies were, on the one hand, the Catholics, whom they regarded as vessels of that Antichrist, the pope, who, as everyone knew, had called for the murder of Elizabeth I as a holy act, and whose agents, the Jesuits, were feared as spies and troublemakers. On the other hand there were the Puritans, viewed by the High Church bishops as bigoted fanatics, similar to the crazed Anabaptists of the preceding century who had taken over the town of Münster; their goal in attacking bishops, many believed, was to attack the King and all lawful government. Puritans had their own brand of vehement and intolerant invective: agreeing with Anglicans in regarding Catholics as enemies of the godly, they considered the High Church so close to Catholicism that its adherents must be themselves agents of the pope, retaining bishops and ritual as merely a temporary ploy to lull the people of England into a false sense of security so that they could reimpose Catholicism. And while supporters of bishops had the law on their side, the Puritans had the passionate conviction that they were God's anointed, commanded to bring true reformation to the country.

In a world where tolerance was seen as close to atheism, and few believed that those who thought differently from them could be sincere, these ideas were bound to disturb the peace of the realm. They became far more dangerous when, in the early years of the reign of King James I, they became caught up in the struggle between two opposing ideas of government in England. The first became known as the theory of the "divine right," of which James was an early adherent. Both a good scholar and a lively and topical writer, James believed that God made a king "a little God to sit on his throne, and rule over other men." "God gives not Kings the style of God in vain," he wrote in the opening lines of a set of instructions to his son on the duties of kings,

> For on his throne his scepter do they sway:
> And as their subjects ought them to obey,
> So Kings should fear and serve their God again.
> Observe the statutes of your Heavenly king,
> And from his Law, make all your laws to spring.[1]

Law was the cornerstone of political sovereignty, or authority, and, in James's view, all laws came ultimately from the king. True, a king who ascended the throne of an already-existing country, like England, with its laws, customs, and privileges, should make it a point to obey existing laws, to follow existing customs, and to protect existing privileges, for "a good king will not only delight to rule his subjects by the law, but even will conform himself in his own actions thereunto." Still, James had no doubt that the king was not bound by the law, but only followed it out of good will, "and for good example-giving to his subjects," for "the King is above the law, as both the author and giver of strength thereto." No just king would make a law without looking into the state of the country, by calling the country's representatives to a Parliament, the institution established for the framing (not initiating) of laws, "the honourablest and highest judgement in the land (as being the King's head Court) if it be well used." Unfortunately, it could be abused by factions using it to their own advantage, in which case it became "the injustest judgment-seat that may be": therefore hold no Parliaments, James counseled his son, "but for the necessity of new laws, which would be but seldom, for few laws and well put in execution, are best in a well ruled commonwealth."[2]

Parliament and the Ancient Constitution

In his views on law and the role of Parliament, James had history on his side, for many of the laws in England and Scotland had been imposed on the country by the Norman conquest in 1066, and throughout the medieval and Renaissance period the king's law had been the resort for justice and equity against the powerful local interests of the great nobles. As James VI of Scotland, he had brought order to a notoriously turbulent country by increasing royal power over the nobility and clergy. However, his argument was not intended for historians, but as a practical guide to politics against specific claims: that the law, and true political authority, came from ancient tradition embodied in the common law, law based on custom and precedent. According to this claim, it was for Parliament, the true representatives of the commonwealth, to propose new laws to the king, and any such laws should, if not unlawful, be ratified. Those who held this position felt, too, that they had history on their side, for they believed that all English law emanated from an ancient, Anglo-Saxon constitution that predated the Norman conquest and thus the present king. It was the task of Parliament to interpret this ancient constitution and apply it to modern law.

The Parliament about which these claims were made had come a long way from its original, medieval institution. The English Parliament, like the Estates General in France and the Diet in many German principalities, was originally an advisory body called by medieval kings. Medieval kings could wage war only if they were able to gather knights—their nobles—to support their cause. In theory, all nobles in the kingdom owed obedience to the king, but in practice, kings could only ask, not demand, support. The House of Lords in England began as the council called by the kings of England to ask advice, in order to get service, from the lords of England. Church lords—archbishops, bishops, and abbots—were included in the House of Lords, because they could give both financial assistance and their own knights to the king's cause, and Anglican bishops continued to be members of the House of Lords after the Reformation. In the reign of King John I, the Lords had been powerful enough to wring from the king an important concession, embodied in a document that became known as the Magna Carta, the Great Charter: the crown could not pass certain kinds of taxation without the approval of Parliament.

Over time, the practice of warfare became more and more costly, and the wealth of medieval England more and more spread to towns and counties as well as to lord's estates. Edward III, during the Hundred Years' War, was the first king to realize that the wealth of his kingdom lay in the commons as well as the lords, and he called together the first meeting of the House of Commons. It included representatives from the wealthiest towns and counties in England. Edward had no intention of giving his commons a say in the government: he called them together solely to ask them to gather funds for his enterprise and then dismissed them. But in return, the representatives then present asked for, and were granted, a privilege hitherto unknown among commoners: the privilege that, when the king called them together, they could present their grievances.

Over the succeeding 200 years, the House of Commons did not meet very frequently: Elizabeth called them as little as possible, since they inevitably used their privilege to beseech her to make war on Spain, to get married, or to reform the church, none of which she wished to do. Yet the period had also strengthened the Commons in ways that the Crown had not anticipated. During the Reformation, Henry VIII had confiscated church lands and sold them to the great nobles, thus setting up the most active land market that had ever appeared in England. Much of the land eventually passed to the younger sons and daughters, or nephews and nieces, of the nobility, enriching a group of wealthy landowners who, while not legally noble themselves, retained close ties to their aristocratic cousins. This group, called the gentry, made up the main representatives to the House of Commons. They were not representative in the modern sense, for voters had to be freeholders with property worth forty shillings per year, and those elected had to be substantial landowners, wealthy enough to leave their estates for the time Parliament was in session. Nor were they representative of religious feeling in the kingdom, for a majority of members of Commons were Puritan, though Puritans were a minority, though a vocal one, throughout the country as a whole. Still, members of Commons were literate and educated, often coming from families who had been elected to serve for several generations. They were established enough to feel themselves independent of the nobility, and they dominated local politics as sheriffs and justices of the peace. Particularly when confronted with a foreign, Scottish king, they felt themselves to be truly the representatives of the English nation.

The Expenses of Government

The struggle between Crown and Parliament began, and continued, as a struggle over the expenses of government. The tradition in England, as elsewhere, was that the king should live at his own expense, that is, support himself, his court, and the entire apparatus of government, off the revenues from his own lands. By 1600, however, the machinery of government everywhere had grown so that that was as impossible a task as expecting a modern president to support himself, his cabinet, and Congress out of his own income. Elizabeth I had been known for her parsimony, but she left her successor James I a debt of £400,000, the equivalent of a full year of royal revenue. The only solution was to ask for subsidies and raise taxes, for which the crown, by immemorial custom, had to call Parliament. Once called, members of Parliament had the privilege to express their grievances, which, over the course of the twenty years of James's reign, became a positive program. The king should purify the Anglican Church to bring it more in line with Calvinist doctrine, they argued. Far from looking for more sources of revenue, he should cease giving money to his favorites and abolish some traditional practices by which the Crown gained money, like the sale of monopolies. And, after war broke out in Germany in 1618, Parliament urged that England should take on the task of defending the Kingdom of God from the Antichrist by supporting the Protestant cause, especially of Frederick of the Palatinate, married to James's daughter Elizabeth.

James had no intention of carrying out any of these policies. The former two would have weakened his control over the church and the Crown revenues; the latter would have involved England in a disastrous foreign war and himself in complete dependence on Parliament for funds to prosecute the war. He called Parliament, in fact, as seldom as possible, treating it to long-winded speeches on its duties and the limits to its prerogatives, on occasion making concessions in exchange for Parliamentary loosening of those all-important purse strings. But he never acquired the talent that Elizabeth I had exhibited and that has become a standard technique of the executive branch of all modern representative government, of finding members of the Commons to argue for, and channel debate towards, his own policies. The result was that Crown and Parliament acted as competing, rather than cooperating, institutions of government.

Charles I

The conflict continued with the death of James I and the accession of his son, Charles I (1600–1649), to the throne in 1625. Charles was a quiet, affectionate man to his family and friends, but he had absorbed his father's views on the divine right of kings without his father's statesmanship or administrative ability. Like his father, he inherited an enormous debt. He also inherited the expenses of a foreign war, for in his last years James, urged by Charles himself, had entangled England in the war on the Continent. They were obligated to provide soldiers to the Dutch, to attack Spain from the sea; within a few years, Charles's marriage to, and quarrel with, the French princess Henrietta Maria led to war with France. The domestic quarrel was resolved and the two became a most loving couple, but the foreign conflicts could not be handled the same way. Now that England was at war, Charles had to ask Parliament for money.

The king had every reason to assume that Parliament would grant the money, for had it not insisted that he support the Protestant cause in Europe? But Parliament did nothing of the kind, giving him only £140,000, less than a quarter of what he had asked for. Charles was furious, but he was also desperately in need of funds, and he presented the House of Commons with a detailed account of all his outlays. Still Parliament would not be moved. Many members had sat in Parliament under James I, and they believed it was necessary to check the growing power of the monarchy, as they saw it. They distrusted Charles's chief minister and dearest friend, the Duke of Buckingham, disliking his bad advice, his extravagance, and his hold over the king; they distrusted, too, the influence of High Churchmen, such as William Laud, a vocal opponent of Puritans. They requested that Charles enforce the existing strict laws against Catholics and that he begin in earnest to reform the church along Puritan lines. They gave point to their requests by granting Charles the revenue from custom duties for only one year, instead of for life. Charles responded by dissolving Parliament.

This scene was to be repeated over and over again in the next few years, for Charles was repeatedly in the position of having to ask Parliament for money, only to dissolve it when its privilege of expressing grievances took the form of attacks on his ministers or demands for reform. The two sessions in 1628 and 1629 were especially stormy. In order to carry out his military campaigns, he had disregarded the customary laws and imposed his own taxes; he had then imprisoned some of those who had refused to pay them. When, after all, the military maneuvers were unsuccessful, he had to call Parliament once again to avert "the common danger," a two-front war against the most powerful countries in Europe, France and Spain. Commons refused to vote subsidies until they voiced their grievances, including the specific taxes levied by Charles, the imprisonment of those who refused to pay without just cause, the billeting of returning soldiers on his citizens, and the use of martial law to contain the protests caused by the billeting. "They do therefore humbly pray your Most Excellent Majesty," Commons concluded, that no man be forced to pay taxes that were not voted by Parliament, that no man be imprisoned without just cause, that soldiers not be billeted among civilians without their consent, that martial law not be established in peacetime, "all which they most humbly pray of your Most Excellent Majesty, as their rights and liberties according to the laws and statutes of the realm." Agreeing to this document would have barred Charles from using any form of force, legislative or military, against his subjects to make them obey.

This document, called the Petition of Right, was to have far-reaching effects in constitutional history, but for the moment it was merely another volley in the battle between king and Parliament. Charles appeared to accept it in order to gain the much-needed subsidies, but he later changed his mind, giving force to the arguments of his opponents that he could never be trusted. When Parliament met again in 1629 many members were angry, and the Commons again refused to consider granting money for the war until domestic matters were taken care of. Chief among these was religious reform, for it seemed to many Puritan members that the Anglican church was growing closer and closer to Catholicism: Oliver Cromwell, a new member, stated that one of the king's appointments to a bishopric was reported to be preaching "flat popery."[3] Angry at what he called the "undutiful and seditious" behavior of Parliamentary leaders, the king ordered an adjournment, but Commons, in defiance of all tradition, refused to adjourn until it had passed highly inflammatory motions attacking the king's policies on religion and taxation. It then voted its own adjournment, as if to underscore the point that it was not dependent on the king's pleasure. Even those in the country at large who supported its proposals felt that some "fiery spirits in the house of commons" had gone too far in their attacks on the king, and that this outburst marked the "most gloomy, sad, and dismal day for England that had happened in five hundred years." But Charles again showed his lack of political sense by arresting eleven members of the House for sedition, switching public sympathy in their favor. Ten were released, but one died in prison, instantly becoming a martyr to what became known as the "eleven years' tyranny," the decision on Charles's part to rule in the future without calling Parliament at all.

This "tyranny," as it was termed by Parliamentary supporters, might more properly be called "Charles's personal rule," for it was not a tyranny in the usual sense of the word: there were no extraordinary imprisonments or interference into the lives of most subjects. Once Charles had made peace with France and Spain, it was, in fact, a time of prosperity in England. Royal administration of existing laws was, on the whole, efficient and fair, and though Charles levied customary taxes without Parliament, he was able to show plausible legal precedent. Charles himself was a patron of the arts and sciences. He appointed the brilliant architect Inigo Jones (1573–1652) as Surveyor of the King's Works, and Jones took on the task of building and rebuilding old medieval churches, public buildings, and private mansions in the new, ornate classical style. Among the most visible of his accomplishments was the renovation of the Cathedral of St. Paul's in London, turning a piece of urban wasteland—used variously as a garbage dump, market, and children's playground—into one of the city's chief ornaments. Charles was a patron of the Flemish artists Peter Paul Rubens and Anthony Van Dyck, and put together one of the finest art collections in all of Europe.

There is no sign that anyone in the country except for the members of Parliament themselves cared whether the king levied taxes with or without Parliament. It seemed to one writer, looking back years later, that in 1639, "England enjoyed the greatest measure of felicity it had ever known."[4] Certainly there was no widespread outcry in the country about fiscal matters. When trouble came, it came not from taxes or tyranny, but from that perpetual powder keg, religion. Charles's patronage of Inigo Jones's building program was related to his religious policy: the ornate, imposing churches mirrored royal preference for High Church Anglicans who emphasized ceremony, ritual, and royal power. His chief advisor was Archbishop of Canterbury William Laud, who agreed with the king that the time was passed for toleration of diversity within the Anglican faith. Puritan insistence on simplicity in church architecture was ignored; Puritan objections to Anglican ritual were ignored; Puritan resistance to the High Church reforms was severely punished. With the success of his policy—as it seemed to him—in England and in Ireland, Laud decided the time had come to export it to Scotland as well.

In the 1630s Scotland was a small nation associated by its crown with a greater one, which had for a long time been its mortal enemy. Throughout the medieval period up through the reign of Elizabeth, Scotland and England had been natural rivals, with the ruling house of Scotland more closely allied to France than to its southern neighbor. The Reformation that had brought Calvinism—Presbyterianism—to Scotland had changed that, paving the way for James VI of Scotland to become James I of England in 1603. But though the crowns were united, the countries retained traditional differences. James I, who had grown up among the fierce religious rivalries in his native country, had refrained from imposing the Anglican church on Scotland. Charles had no such compunction, or caution. In 1637 a new prayer book, based on the Anglican prayer book, was introduced into St. Giles Cathedral in Edinburgh. This is popery, yelled Jenny Geddes, among a storm of protest from other parishioners, and she threw a stool at the officiating bishop. Riots broke out throughout Scotland, and the Scots Calvinists swore an oath, called the National Covenant, to resist all outside religious innovations. They raised an army and marched south into England. In 1639, Charles's advisors told him that he had no choice: he had to call a Parliament in England to raise troops to meet the Scots.

Road to Civil War

Charles and his advisers hoped that, faced with a war with Scotland, Parliament would rally behind the king and grant the huge sum— £840,000—needed to raise and equip an army. But the Parliament that met in 1640, with a majority of Puritans, had much sympathy for the Scots Calvinists. Moreover, they had had to be silent for eleven years and now were prepared to air their grievances. John Pym (1584–1643), a Puritan and member of Parliament for twenty years, took the lead in declaring that "a Parliament is that to the Commonwealth, which the soul is to the body."[5] Intense and serious, he, like many in the Commons, was from a long-standing Parliamentary family, in which fathers, sons, uncles, and cousins regularly represented their districts. The rights and obligations of Parliament may have seemed a part of his own soul, and since the soul governed the body, his assertion was no less than that Parliament should govern the kingdom. Before they voted supplies, the House of Commons declared, the king had to agree to limit his authority. After only three weeks the king dismissed them, but when his military campaigns against the Scots ended in disaster he was forced to call another Parliament. On November 3, 1640, the new members met in what was to become known as the Long Parliament, because it did not adjourn for the next fifteen years.

They met determined to oppose the king. To his theory that all law emanates from the king they opposed the theory that the king must be bound by the fundamental laws of the land that only Parliament could interpret. Each side believed that both God and history supported its claims. Based on its reading of those laws, Parliament attacked, and had executed, Charles's chief ministers and reversed the rulings on prisoners convicted of offenses against the crown in the preceding eleven years. From his palace in London, Charles could hear both the anti-monarch riots and the cheers of the crowd as the prisoners were released. Bands of young men with swords were everywhere, some violently attacking courtiers, bishops, and churches, and some as violently defending them. "Both factions talk very big," reported one officer, "and it is a wonder there is no more blood yet spilt, seeing how earnest both sides are." "Reformation goes on . . . as hot as toast,"[6] announced one member of Commons, but as bill after bill was passed, formally clarifying but really extending Parliamentary power, observers began to call it not reformation, but revolution. In the summer of 1641, Pym pushed through the

House of Commons the Grand Remonstrance, which was both a detailed list of all grievances and a piece of legislation. It included all the stipulations contained in the Petition of Right, together with the provision that Parliament had to meet at least every three years and could not be dissolved without its own consent. It passed by only eleven votes; already a more moderate party had begun to detach itself from Pym's supporters. Charles angered his enemies by giving orders for the arrest of five of the members, including Pym; but he angered his friends by not acting with the necessary decisiveness, so that they escaped. They were sheltered by the city of London, like most towns a walled city with its own militia. London itself was in an uproar, sure it would be attacked by the king's armies and determined to resist. To ensure that the king could not raise an army against it, Parliament passed a new bill, requiring the king to give it control of all the armed forces of the country. "By God!" Charles exclaimed "Not for an hour."[7] Forced to leave London, he sent his wife and older children, including the Crown Prince Charles, to France. Setting up court in Oxford, Charles I began raising an army. Parliament began to raise its own, declaring that all those who did not support it were delinquents and that their property was forfeit. The Civil War had begun.

Oliver Cromwell and the New Model Army

The English Civil War was a polite affair compared to the destruction on the Continent. Only about three out of every hundred men took an active part in it. Many viewed it as a kind of private quarrel between king and Parliament, and one farm laborer only heard when advised to keep out of the line of fire that "them two had fallen out."[8] Countryfolk, it was said, did not really care what government they lived under "so long as they may plough and go to market," and many regions tried to remain neutral. Yet for many of the gentry and the lords, as well as the merchants and shopkeepers who comprised the militia of the towns, choosing sides required heartbreaking searching of individual conscience. Parliament had its strongest support in London and the southeast; the king, in the north and in western England and Wales. Everywhere, though, families and communities were divided between supporters of the king, called Cavaliers, and supporters of Parliament, called Roundheads because Puritan hats did not have hatbands. "I beseech you consider," wrote one Cavalier, "that majesty is sacred; God saith 'Touch not mine anointed.'"[9] The Roundheads were rebels and traitors, whom God would not suffer to prosper. To this the supporters of Parliament had their own answer. King Charles was a man "against whom the Lord had witnessed," wrote Oliver Cromwell. Charles had taken up arms against his own subjects and had thus betrayed the most fundamental trust of government; he must be resisted, in order to preserve "the true religion, the laws, liberty, and peace of the Kingdom."[10]

Oliver Cromwell (1599–1658) came, like so many of his fellow members of Commons, from a gentry family with a long history of service in Parliament and in local politics. Raised as a Calvinist, he had undergone a religious experience that convinced him that he was one of God's elect, who had been placed on earth to devote himself to God's cause and the creation of his kingdom on earth. When the war began, he was the representative from the city of Cambridge, and he immediately returned there, recruiting soldiers, setting guards to prevent valuables from the town reaching royal troops, capturing the city castle and its ammunition, and arresting Royalists. Cromwell began his own military by raising a small troop of horsemen that was promptly driven off the field in their first engagement. He tried again, and more effectively, recruiting officers and men, not from the usual mixture of adventurers and landless laborers, but "such men," he wrote, "as had the fear of God before them and as made some conscience of what they did." They were not allowed to plunder, get drunk, fornicate, or even swear, all the usual pastimes of soldiers, and officers and men held prayer meetings together. A company of Cromwell's men, made up of "honest sober Christians" and disciplined soldiers, commanded by a "plain russet-coated captain that knows what he fights for and loves what he knows,"[11] stood in stark contrast to the traditional armies raised by young noblemen. In contrast, too, was Cromwell's policy of paying officers and men well and promoting them for competence with no regard to social rank.

Cromwell's army was largely responsible for the defeat of King Charles's best general, Prince Rupert of Nassau, at the battle of Marston Moor in 1644. His resounding victory paved allowed him to convince Parliament that the entire army should be reorganized along similar lines: it should be a truly professional, well-paid force, with freedom of conscience for all Calvinist groups. Though officially Cromwell himself was only second in command, it was clear he was its dominant force. The New Model Army, as it was called, was decisive in the defeat of Charles's troops in the Battle of Naseby in 1646. Charles fled north to

Portrait of Oliver Cromwell by Peter Lely (Alinari/Art Resource, NY)

Scotland, hoping to raise support from the Scottish nobles who had traditionally supported the Stuarts, but John Pym had concluded a treaty between Parliament and the Scots Protestants before his own death in 1643. In 1646 the Scots turned Charles over to Parliamentary custody on the payment of £400,000.

The Trial and Execution

With King Charles now a prisoner, serious divisions began to appear among his opposition. Members of Parliament were divided between the more conservative men who wanted to restore the king to the throne as long as he would agree to Parliamentary control of the army and reforming the church along strict Calvinist lines, and the more radical "Independents," who wanted toleration for different religious groups within Protestantism, distrusted the king, and had the support of the New Model Army. The mood within London was as uncertain as it had been six years earlier. Radical religious groups proliferated, each claiming to be God's elect; men and women claimed to be seers and prophets. The continental demand for news-sheets, the earliest newspapers, had been forbidden under the king, but they circulated during the Civil War, spreading news of military events, the capture of the king, and actions taken by Parliament. Rumor and gossip as well as news circulated rapidly. There was political unrest as well. Many were tired of the warfare and of the heavy taxes Parliament had had to impose to sustain it; there was growing sympathy for the King and for the "good old days" before the war began. Members of Parliament were no longer sure they could keep control either over the country or over their own members. More ominously, they were not sure they could keep control over the New Model Army, firmly in Cromwell's hands. Perhaps, after all, it would be better to treat with the king.

King Charles's confinement was not arduous, and he was always treated with the respect and dignity due a king. Yet, from the first, Parliamentary commissioners sent to negotiate a treaty were wary. Charles had entered into negotiations at various times during the preceding six years, but they always foundered over the abolition of bishops, for Charles, no less than his opponents, felt that God had called him to fight for the religion he had sworn to uphold. Moreover, Charles had made promises before and reneged on them. Letters captured after the battle of Naseby had shown that Charles was negotiating with foreign powers, even, with Henrietta Maria's help, the king of France, to raise a foreign army and invade his own kingdom. Even now, as Charles listened carefully to his captors' proposals, he had entered into a correspondence with the Scots, promising them control over the church of Scotland if he regained the throne; he wrote to supporters in Ireland, too, saying he would deny any agreement he made with the rebels once he was free. In his own mind, the ends justified the means: his subjects had rebelled against him, and he owed them no apologies for his behavior. Yet such duplicity, as it was viewed by his opponents, was fatal to his own cause. In 1647 Charles attempted to escape, and there were Royalist uprisings, quickly put down by Cromwell. He became convinced that Charles was too deceitful to be allowed to govern. In a move widely supposed to have been instigated by Cromwell, the army marched on London and expelled from Parliament any members who supported negotiation with the king. The Rump, as the remainder were derisively called, voted to try King Charles for high treason. Even with the army as a constant presence, the vote carried in Commons by only 26 to 20, and the House of Lords, attended by now by only half a dozen peers, refused to consider it. Cromwell himself was not present at the trial, though he was the dominant force: "We will cut off the King's head with the crown on it," he reportedly said.[12]

And yet Cromwell, and the Rump, were governed by the conviction that the trial had to be a real, legal trial. Kings had been murdered, or assassinated, by their own subjects before. It was vital to Cromwell and his supporters that King Charles be neither murdered nor assassinated, but legally judged by the law of his land, the law that, in their eyes, he had so seriously violated. Charles himself rose to great dignity in the trial. He refused to answer the charges, claiming that he was not brought before a court properly constituted according to the law, but merely men who were in power: "It is not my cause alone, it is the freedom and liberty of the people of England."[13] On Tuesday, January 30, 1649, he was publicly executed.

Interregnum

The king was dead. But who should rule England? Parliament, in the last hours before Charles's execution, had declared England a republic and passed a law making it illegal to proclaim anyone king. In England, Royalist supporters, Irish nobles, and even the Scots nobles who had started the rebellion against Charles I declared his eldest son king as Charles II. Cromwell, now Lord General of the army, was able to put down all rebellions and repel a Scottish invasion, but Parliament was less able to govern. The task before it seemed clear to many: it had to form a constituent assembly to create a new constitution, after which it had to dissolve itself and call for new elections. Yet in April 1653, when all foreign enemies had been repelled and Cromwell, acting as mediator between Parliament and army, demanded a new assembly, members of Parliament responded that "there was no more fitting moment to change the Lord General."[14] Angered by what he viewed as the self-interest of the Rump he himself had helped to create, Cromwell marched into the House of Commons with musketeers from his own regiment and declared Parliament disbanded. By the end of the year his supporters had drawn up a new "Instrument of Government," with Cromwell as Lord Protector of the Commonwealth.

In foreign policy, Cromwell was an excellent chief executive. In the five and a half years that he led the Commonwealth, the English army and navy gained renewed respect from foreign powers. Charles II could gain no assistance from any other monarch, and he was even asked to leave France, since the French king preferred not to offend the new English government. "According to the opinion of all the world," one writer noted, "the Crown is only wanting to this government to establish and confirm the authority upon the head of the Lord Protector." But the problem was that Cromwell had no crown—he was not a king, inheriting by immemorial custom—and no one was precisely sure what legitimate authority a Lord Protector should have. At home, Cromwell confronted the same difficulties as Charles I, for he could not get on with his Parliaments, who promptly challenged the legitimacy of his Instrument of Government, and he could not get on without them, for only Parliament could raise enough money to enable him to govern. His government put into practice the religious reforms long demanded by Puritans—the abolition of bishops and ritual, the removal of art and sculpture from churches, the prohibition against ungodly activities such as dancing and theater—but in many areas these reforms were unpopular. Cromwell faced both attempted rebellion and assassination; neither Ireland nor Scotland ever forgave him for the brutal manner in which he waged war against them; and by the time he became ill in 1658, worn out by the cares of government, he was one of the most hated men in Britain.

Radical Religious Sects

Cromwell believed all his life that God had called him to assist his country, and he believed all his life in liberty of conscience for individuals. His Instrument of Government allowed freedom of religion for all those not professing either Catholicism, reimposition of bishops, or atheism—

that is, for all those groups whose beliefs, he felt, did not undermine the civil government. Though more limited than modern freedom of religion, it allowed unprecedented freedom for Protestant religious sects to grow and flourish. Millenarian sects such as the Fifth Monarchists believed that the end of the world predicted by the Bible had come and that the kingdom of the righteous was to be established in England, by the sword if necessary.

The most successful and longest lasting of the sects was the Society of Friends, also called the Quakers, gathered by a shoemaker, George Fox, in the 1650s. By 1660 they numbered approximately 60,000 members. Unlike most other Protestant groups, in which women were excluded from all positions of scholarship and authority, Quakers believed that women, too, could be called by God to preach and prophesy. Quakers had meetings in which people sat in silent contemplation until called by an inner voice to speak, rather than the formal religious services of other faiths, so that knowledge and scholarship outside the Bible was not necessary. Elizabeth Hooten, a married woman of fifty, was Fox's first convert. She became a Quaker preacher and traveled around England, mixing religious with political messages: "You make yourself ridiculous to all people who have sense and reason," she wrote to Oliver Cromwell; "your judges judge for reward," while poor people lie in prison "worse than dogs for want of straw."[15] Margaret Fell was thirty-eight, the wife of a member of the Long Parliament, when she was moved by the Lord, she said, to preach His word. She also established a Fund for the Service of Truth to help pay the expenses of preachers and their families as they traveled or, as often happened, when put in prison for disturbing the peace. Quaker women preachers faced both opposition and personal violence. Rebekah Travers was knocked down in the street by an angry mob after telling one London parish that she set before them "all this day, life and death . . . that you may . . . love and follow that which condemns all injustice, deceit, vain, wanton and unprofitable words and actions, and leads to justice, righteousness and soberness."[16] Yet Quaker women persisted, traveling as missionaries throughout Britain and New England, preaching and organizing philanthropic societies, in what grew into a long tradition of religious conviction, social work, and political activism.

John Milton

From within the government of the Commonwealth, John Milton (1608–1674), Secretary for Foreign Tongues and finest poet of his age, spent the years of the Interregnum putting his incomparable mastery of the English language to work in the service of the Puritan cause he believed in. A Londoner born and bred, he called his native town "this vast city; a city of refuge, the mansion house of liberty,"[17] and had supported first Parliament, then Cromwell, against the king. The victory at Marston Moor in 1644 inspired him to write a pamphlet, *Areopagitica*, which became one of the classic defenses of a free press. "I deny not," he wrote, "but that it is of greatest concernment in the Church and Commonwealth, to have a vigilant eye how Books demean themselves, as well as men. . . . For Books are not absolutely dead things, but do contain a potency of life in them to be as active as that soul was whose progeny they are. . . . And yet on the other hand unless wariness be used, as good almost kill a man as kill a good book; who kills a man kills a reasonable creature, God's Image; but he who destroys a good book, kills reason itself."[18]

Milton received his position as secretary as much for his writing ability as for his religious and political commitment. Early in 1649 he wrote a pamphlet entitled *The Tenure of Kings and Magistrates; proving, that it is lawful, and hath been so through all ages, for any, who have the power, to call to account a tyrant, or wicked king, and after due conviction to depose and put him to death,* in which he stated that "the power of kings and magistrates is nothing else, but what is only derivative, transferred and committed to them in trust from the people, to the common good of them all."[19] The new Commonwealth had need for so polished and committed a propagandist, for soon after the execution of Charles I in 1649 a pamphlet appeared, *Eikon Basilike, the Royal Image,* which depicted his death as a holy martyrdom. It was enormously popular, doing much to promote the Royalist cause, and went through sixty editions in the first year alone. Milton's official duties in his position were to sit in meetings with foreign powers and assist at translations, but his real duties were to combat *Eikon Basilike* and other antigovernment writings as they appeared.

Milton is most famous, however, not for his pamphlets but for his poetry, which has influenced every generation of English language writers since his own day. His great epic poem, *Paradise Lost*, is a deeply personal religious retelling of the story of Adam and Eve and their expulsion from the Garden of Eden. Though there was a long tradition of religious poetry, no English writer had ever transformed it into epic with so much success. Milton's angels are more vividly realized, "real" angels than had ever been attempted, and the power of Milton's Satan as a fallen angel has been felt by generations of readers:

> He, above the rest
> In shape and gesture proudly eminent,
> Stood like a tower; his form had not yet lost
> All her original brightness, nor appeared
> Less, than Archangel ruined.[20]

Thomas Hobbes

After the turbulent years of the Civil War, the political philosopher Thomas Hobbes (1588–1679) passed the period of the Interregnum in comparative peace. His father was a country clergyman, and, after study at Oxford, Hobbes became tutor to William Cavendish, the future second Earl of Devonshire. Tutor to the son of a noble household was a good career for a young man with intellectual interests and no other means of support, for it provided him with contact with those in influential circles, with time and leisure to read and write, and with opportunities to travel. When Cavendish grew up, Hobbes remained in his service as secretary and friend. When Cavendish died in 1628, though, Hobbes had to look for another position. He was briefly tutor to the son of a rich landowner, then entered the service of the third Earl of Devonshire as, again, tutor, then friend and secretary.

Hobbes's peaceful life, like that of so many others, was affected by the political events of the 1630s and 1640s. The Earl of Devonshire had tried, unsuccessfully, to have Hobbes elected as member of Parliament for Derby in Charles I's first, brief Parliament in 1640. Hobbes responded more effectively to those events by writing *The Elements of Law*, a Royalist pamphlet that argued that no subject could maintain rights of private property against "the absoluteness of the sovereign." Though not published, the pamphlet circulated in manuscript and acquired notoriety in London, where the conflict between the Long Parliament and king was heating up. When, in November 1640, John Pym denounced anyone who supported the ideas of absolute monarchy, Hobbes fled to Paris. By this time he was well-known among philosophers and writers, and he was asked to be the mathematical tutor to the future Charles II when he and his brother James escaped from England in 1645.

Hobbes spent the next few years completing his great work of political theory, *Leviathan, or The Matter, Form, and Power of a Common-Wealth Ecclesiastical and Civil.* Hobbes, deeply interested in the natural philosophy of his day, was influenced by those philosophers who believed that all matter was composed of uniform atoms, perpetually in motion. He used that principle to explain human behavior and politics. He argued that all people were by nature equal; but instead of that being a good thing, it was the cause of the inevitable tendency of people to fight one another. Only when people voluntarily give up their natural equality and agree to submit themselves to the sovereign authority of someone else will the "war of every man against every man" cease. Hobbes made two additional points about the sovereign authority that created what he called a commonwealth. First, once people gave up their natural equality, the authority of the sovereign was absolute. The ideal form of government was absolute monarchy. Second, once a commonwealth with sovereignty was created it could never be revoked. "And therefore, they that are subjects to a Monarch, cannot without his leave cast off Monarchy, and return to the confusion of a disunited multitude."[21]

Hobbes may have assumed that these sentiments would please Charles II, whom he presented with a copy in manuscript in 1651. Part of the book, though, contained a vehement attack on Catholicism, and it offended both Henrietta Maria and the French clergy. Even worse, Hobbes's entire structure deliberately removed religion and morality as justifications for government. His exclusive reliance on what he considered scientific principles led critics to charge him with atheism. Once again in danger of arrest, Hobbes fled back to England, to the household of the Cavendish family. Here he resumed his reading and writing with no interference from the government, though with growing notoriety as the author of *Leviathan*.

Restoration

Cromwell's death in 1658 once again raised the issue of legitimate authority. His son Richard Cromwell attempted to rule in his place, but he had no legitimacy: a son of a king might inherit a kingdom, but seventeenth-century political theory held no such protected succession for the son of a Lord Protector, and Richard himself was a mild-mannered man with no real interest in government. Once again the army decided the future of the government, this time led by General George Monk, who marched from his position in Scotland to London, gathering followers as he went. He ordered a new, free Parliament to be elected, and a majority of those elected were Royalists who opened negotiations with Charles II to return as king. On April 4, 1660, Charles agreed to "grant liberty to tender consciences"[22]—that is, to grant a general pardon to the country at large—and to leave the punishment of those exempt from pardon, as well as the settlement of questions of property, to Parliament. On May 29, Charles arrived in London and was received with an outpouring of joy.

Charles II (1630–1685) kept his promise in awarding a general amnesty. Only those who had actually signed his father's death warrant were prosecuted: some had died, and some fled, but eleven were executed with the full rigor of the law. Government civil servants like John Milton were not disturbed, and his daughter later reported that he was even "invited to write for the Court"[23] but that he turned down the offer. Handsome and easygoing, Charles II and his court became known for gaiety and amorous intrigues, and theater in London during the Restoration was as licentious as the Puritans had been severe. Charles was generous to his old friends—he gave Hobbes a pension for some years—but he was also determined to retain his throne and the backing of the Anglican bishops who had been restored with him. When Hobbes tried to reprint *Leviathan*, with its still-controversial anticlerical opinions, in 1670, he was not granted a license.

Profile: The Putney Debates

In October 1647, with King Charles I in captivity and the government of the country in disarray, members of the army's Council of Officers met in Putney Church, London, to debate proposals for the reorganization of government proposed in a document called "The Agreement of the People." It had been drafted by a vocal minority within the army known as the Levellers, who wanted, now that the king no longer ruled, to see political as well as religious reforms put into effect. They were opposed by the more conservative officers, many from landed estates, and were distrusted by Parliament.

Among the most radical of their views at the time was that all inhabitants of England should vote in Parliamentary elections, "that the poorest he that is in England," as their most eloquent spokesperson, Colonel Thomas Rainsborough put it, "hath a life to live as the greatest he; and therefore truly, sir, I think it's clear, that every man that is to live under a government ought first by his own consent to put himself under that government" by voting for it. The conservative position was put forward by General Henry Ireton (1611–1651), Cromwell's son-in-law and an astute political strategist. "I think that no person," he said, "hath a right to an interest or share in the disposing of the affairs of the kingdom . . . that hath not a permanent fixed interest in this kingdom" in the form of landed property. The debates were tumultuous, with little hope of compromise between the positions, and Rainsborough spoke for all participants when he replied that "Truly, sir, I am of the same opinion I was, and am resolved to keep it till I know why I should not."

The Putney debates had no immediate effect on political affairs. Rainsborough was assassinated by Royalists, and Ireton managed to delay presenting the army's policy on the proposed, much more moderate reforms to Parliament until just before the king's execution, thus ensuring it would be set aside. As with many of the political issues raised by the events described in this chapter, debates over suffrage would recur again and again.

Important Dates

1603	James I becomes king of England
1605	Gunpowder Plot
1625	Death of James I; Charles I becomes king of England
1628	Petition of Right
1637	Book of Common Prayer introduced in Scotland, to great resistance
1639	Scottish uprising
1640	Short Parliament; beginning of Long Parliament
1641	Parliament under John Pym passes Grand Remonstrance
1642	English Civil War begins
1644	Oliver Cromwell defeats army of Charles I at Marston Moor; John Milton publishes *Areopagitica*
1646	New Model Army defeats Charles I at Naseby
1647	Putney Debates
Late 1640s	Elizabeth Hooton converts to Quaker doctrine
1649	Trial and execution of Charles I
1651	Thomas Hobbes writes *Leviathan*
1653	Cromwell becomes Lord Protector
1658	Death of Cromwell

1660   Restoration of Charles II
1667   Milton publishes *Paradise Lost*

Further Reading

Robert Ashton, *Counter-Revolution: The Second Civil War and Its Origins, 1646–1648* (New Haven, 1995)

G.E. Aylmer, *Rebellion or Revolution? England from Civil War to Restoration* (Oxford, 1987)

Stephen Baskerville, *Not Peace But a Sword: The Political Theology of the English Revolution* (London, 1993)

Martyn Bennett, *The Civil Wars in Britain and Ireland, 1638–1651* (Oxford, 1996)

Glenn Burgess, *Absolute Monarchy and the Stuart Constitution* (New Haven, 1996)

Charles Carlton, *Going to the Wars: The Experience of the British Civil Wars, 1638–1651* (London, 1992)

Charles Carlton, *Charles I* 2nd ed. (London, 1995)

Alan J. Cromartie, *Sir Matthew Hale, 1609–1676: Law, Religion, and Natural Philosophy* (Cambridge, 1995)

Julian Davies, *The Caroline Captivity of the Church: Charles I and the Remoulding of Anglicanism 1625–1641* (Oxford, 1992)

Alan Everitt, *The Community of Kent and the Great Rebellion* (Leicester, 1973)

Mark Charles Fissel, *The Bishops' Wars: Charles I's Campaigns against Scotland, 1638–1640* (Cambridge, 1994)

Anthony Fletcher, *A Country Community in Peace and War: Sussex, 1600–1660* (London, 1975)

Jerome Friedman, *Blasphemy, Immorality and Anarchy: The Ranters and the English Revolution* (Athens, OH, 1987)

Jerome Friedman, *The Battle of the Frogs and Fairfield's Flies: Miracles and the Pulp Press during the English Revolution* (New York, 1993)

Peter Gaunt, *Oliver Cromwell* (Oxford, 1997)

Cynthia Herrup, *The Common Peace: Participation and the Criminal Law in Seventeenth Century England* (Cambridge, 1987)

Christopher Hill, *God's Englishman: Oliver Cromwell and the English Revolution* (New York, 1970)

Derek Hirst, *Authority and Conflict, England 1603–1658* (Cambridge, MA, 1986)

Ann Hughes, *Politics, Society and Civil War in Warwickshire 1620–1660* (Cambridge, 1987)

William Hunt, *The Puritan Moment: The Coming of Revolution to an English County* (Cambridge, MA, 1974)

Mark Kishlansky, *Parliamentary Selection: Social and Political Choice in Early Modern England* (Cambridge, 1986)

Mark Kishlansky, *The Rise of the New Model Army* (Cambridge, 1979)

William MacDonald, *The Making of an English Revolutionary: The Early Parliamentary Career of John Pym* (Rutherford, NJ, 1982)

Brian Manning, *The English People and the English Revolution* (London, 1976)

Peter E. McCullough, *Sermons at Court: Politics and Religion in Elizabethan and Jacobean Preaching* (Cambridge, 1998)

Michael Mendle, *Henry Parker and the English Civil War: The Political Thought of the Public's 'Privado'* (Cambridge, 1995)

John Morrill, *The Revolt of the Provinces: Conservatism and Revolution in the English Civil War, 1630–1650* (London, 1980)

Jane Ohlmeyer, *Civil War and Restoration in the Three Stuart Kingdoms: The Career of Randall MacDonnell, Marquis of Antrim, 1609–1683* (Cambridge, 1993)

Conrad Russell, *The Causes of the English Civil War* (Oxford, 1990)

Lois G. Schwoerer, *"No Standing Armies!" The Anti-army Ideology in Seventeenth Century England* (Baltimore, 1974)

Buchanan Sharp, *In Contempt of All Authority* (Berkeley, 1980)

Kevin Sharpe, *The Personal Rule of Charles I* (New Haven, 1992)

David L. Smith, *Constitutional Royalism and the Search for Settlement, c.1640–1649* (Cambridge, 1994)

Nigel Smith, *Literature and Revolution in England, 1640–1660* (New Haven, 1994)

David Underdown, *Fire From Heaven: Life in an English Town in the Seventeenth Century* (New Haven, 1992)

David Underdown, *A Freeborn People: Politics and the Nation in Seventeenth Century England* (Oxford, 1996)

David Underdown, *Pride's Purge: Politics and the Puritan Revolution* (London, 1985)

David Underdown, *Revel, Riot, and Rebellion: Popular Politics and Culture in England, 1603–1660* (Oxford, 1985)

David Underdown, *Somerset in the Civil War and Interregnum* (Newton Abbot, 1973)

Susan Wiseman, *Drama and Politics in the English Civil War* (Cambridge, 1998)

Austin Woolrych, *Commonwealth to Protectorate* (Oxford, 1982)

Blair Worden, *The Rump Parliament* (Cambridge, 1974)

Part II

ca. 1660–1720

Chapter Seven

Louis XIV and Absolute Monarchy

In February 1649, young Louis XIV (1637–1715) of France heard of the execution of his uncle, Charles I of England, at the hands of the English Parliament. "This is a blow to make kings tremble,"[1] his mother told him. Louis may not have trembled, but the similarities between his own and his uncle's troubles with unruly subjects may have aroused all his pride and anger. For King Louis, together with his younger brother, his mother, Queen Anne, then regent, her chief minister, Cardinal Mazarin, and the rest of the court loyal to them had had to flee Paris in January because of the civil war known in France as the Fronde (1648–1653). The twelve-year-old king was not amused by the sight of the court sleeping on straw (he himself had a camp bed) and going short of food. More important, he never forgave the attack on the authority of the king.

The Fronde in France, like the Civil War in England, started over taxes. In 1648, Queen Regent Anne, together with Cardinal Jules Mazarin (1602–1661), had issued new taxes to pay for what they hoped would be the last stages in a war intended to exalt French power above that of the Austrian and Spanish Habsburgs. To them, as to most rulers, European politics was a competition between more or less ancient and powerful royal houses: as the fortunes of the Habsburgs declined, those of the Bourbon would rise. But France had been at war for forty years. There were reports of widespread poverty and famine in the villages and of widespread corruption among royal tax officials. The judges in the *Parlement* of Paris, the law-court which had the formal power to register royal edicts, refused to register the new taxes unless the queen regent looked into the question of both widespread poverty and widespread corruption. The queen refused to do so and tried to arrest the leading judges. She was prevented by the Paris militia, who barricaded the narrow streets so that none of the king's soldiers could get in. Forced to negotiate, the queen released the judges and pretended to consider Parlement's demands, all the while planning the escape from Paris which took place in early 1649. By that time, however, several of the great noble families had taken advantage of the confusion to rebel against the queen and Mazarin as well. Their aim was not to overthrow the young king, but rather to acquire greater wealth and power within the government by extorting concessions from the ruling family in return for support. For nobles were still needed as the main instruments of royal authority, especially once King Philip IV of Spain took advantage of the rebellion to attack France while recruiting some of the rebellious nobles to his own service.

Could civil war in France really lead to execution of the king, as it had in England? The similarities between the two situations seemed more obvious at the time than they do today. To monarchs and their ambassadors, all rebellions tended to look alike as assaults on the majesty of the king, but to us, the French government looks very different from that of England. France was in some respects more like the decentralized Holy Roman Empire than the centralized government of England. The greatest nobles still retained their private armies. Some, like the Duke of Lorraine, owed allegiance to the kings of France for a part of his domain, but to the Holy Roman Emperor for other parts. Many saw no reason why loyalty to the king should prevent their raising their own armies, establishing their own courts, and ignoring royal edicts when it suited them. Louis XIII and his chief minister, Cardinal Richelieu, had done their best to strengthen royal authority against that of the nobles, but throughout history the greatest danger to any French king had always come from the most powerful nobles in France—that is, from his own uncles, cousins, and even his own brothers.

There were other differences as well. Despite the similarity in name, the Parlement of Paris was very different from the English Parliament. It was, first and foremost, a law court, consisting of judges appointed by the king. Its routine function was thus much closer to the modern Supreme Court than to a legislative body, but the Paris Parlement was not in any sense "supreme," as other important cities in France had their own Parlements. Certain families had long-standing traditions as Parlement families, and, as in the English House of Commons, members developed a kind of esprit de corps, taking seriously their task of protecting the innocent and punishing wrongdoing. But they were not elected and therefore had no legal status as representatives of the nation.

They had no legislative function and did not debate or advise the king on laws. The only time they might advise the king was in connection with their formal task of registering—not debating—new laws, for they could remonstrate if the new law seemed inconsistent, in a purely legal sense, with legal precedent.

France did have a governmental institution with the same medieval origin as the English Parliament, called the Estates General. It consisted of representatives from the clergy, dominated by the church lords, abbots, and abbesses (the first estate), the nobles (the second estate), and the commons (the third estate). Like most such bodies, the Estates General was called only when the Crown needed it; when the kind called it, it had the privilege of expressing grievances. The last time the Estates General had been called was in 1614. Despite almost continual war on several fronts, Louis XIII had never needed to call it again, because he, not the Estates General, controlled the collection of taxes. That constituted the main difference between the power of the French and English kings in 1648: the great wealth of the kingdom of France and the ability of French kings to raise money from the vast, fertile land they controlled.

The Fronde, which began as an appeal for relief from the rigors of war, led to five years of increased devastation and the deaths of thousands of French subjects. Cardinal Mazarin was able to preserve the monarchy by buying off some of the noble rebels and defeating the rest in battle. The Crown's greatest weapon, though, was the young king himself, who turned thirteen in 1651 and was able to rule in his own name. Courteous, well-spoken, commanding, he was already a potent political force. During the rebellion he had made carefully planned appearances through contested territory, where more than one fortress held by a rebel noble had surrendered, protesting its loyalty, at the sight of the king. That, like the escape from Paris and the treachery of some of the greatest nobles, became part of his political education. Louis XIV was determined to make royal power absolute in practice, not just in the writings of political theorists. He had learned to trust no one, not out of anger, but out of sound policy: "in wise and able kings," he wrote later, "resentment and anger towards their subjects is only prudence and justice."[2] The political theorist Bishop Bossuet, the most influential churchman of his day, later proclaimed that Louis was God's lieutenant on earth: he "was the whole State, and the will of all the people was locked in his."[3] From the first, Louis XIV of France had decided to show the world how to reign with both divine authority and divine power.

The Sun King

Throughout the 1650s, Louis ruled with the assistance of his mother and Cardinal Mazarin. Indeed Mazarin, as chief minister, retained most of the power, for Louis deferred to his judgment in all public affairs. In 1661, however, Mazarin died. Paris was filled with powerful nobles and important men at court, all hoping to replace Mazarin as chief minister or gain wealth and rank as a royal favorite. After all, for most of the previous century, monarchical government in Europe had been defined by a king working *with* a favorite minister: Louis XIII and Richelieu in France, Phillip IV and Olivares in Spain, Charles I and Buckingham in England, Gustavus Adolphus and Oxenstierna in Sweden. It was difficult to imagine a kingdom without a favorite.

Louis had already gained a reputation for self-control—"No one has ever seen him in a rage or heard him complain or lie, even in jest," wrote the Venetian ambassador. "He affects the utmost indifference towards everybody, to such a degree that even among his familiars none can boast of any evidence of partiality or trust." He gave no hint of his intentions to any of the courtiers. The day after Mazarin's death, he announced that he intended to appoint no chief minister. "It is time for me to govern by myself," he told the Council of State, the chief advisory body to the king. "You will assist me with your advice when I ask for it." Outside the normal course of business, none of his counselors was to sign a single order, not even a passport, to make a single financial decision, to take any action without his command.[4]

This was what became known as "absolute rule," the control of all branches of government by the king. Strong-minded kings had managed to dominate their countries before this, but in practice all European monarchs had delegated entire branches of the government—the army, finances, religious policy—to ministers, who were generally richly rewarded for their service to the king. Wise kings chose their ministers for their abilities; less able rulers chose personal favorites, who might or might not carry out their delegated tasks well. In France, influential ministers to the king were often members of the church, like Cardinal Richelieu and Cardinal Mazarin, but they could also be important nobles, "princes of the blood," who were related to the king and had often grown up with him. All such ministers had opportunities to gain enormous wealth and power. Mazarin, for example, went from an obscure Italian churchman to one of the wealthiest men in France, in part by using his privileged position to engage in highly unethical financial speculation. Kings traditionally tolerated or even encouraged their ministers in these practices, regarding such enrichment as payment for good service. Ministers were, in this view, rather like stewards of an estate: their job was to carry out the tedious business of administration, so that kings could enjoy the resources and privileges of their own position.

Louis XIV had no objection to his ministers enriching themselves within reasonable limits. What he did object to was their gaining power that could come only at the expense of his own. He knew his recent history: Cardinal Richelieu's reputation had eclipsed his father's on the world diplomatic stage; most recently, Cardinal Mazarin's had eclipsed his own. "In my heart I valued above all else, more than life itself, a high reputation," he later wrote. "A governing and overriding passion for greatness and glory stifles all others."[5] He probably never really said the famous words attributed to him, "L'état, c'est moi" (I am the state), but there is no doubt that he identified himself with France. The words "my dignity, my glory, my greatness, my reputation," come up frequently in his writings, and to him the words meant the same as France's dignity, France's glory, France's greatness, France's reputation. Though short, he had a commanding and charismatic presence, habitually speaking as if he were "master of himself and of the universe"; his realm, divided in so many ways, was united in adoration of its young king. Among his earliest acts as king was to force the monarchs of Europe to acknowledge French greatness: Spain had to formally apologize for an incident in London in which servants of the Spanish ambassador attacked those of the French, and the English navy had to agree to salute French ships before being saluted in turn.

When Spain and England bowed before Louis, how could his ministers fail to do likewise? Louis deliberately did not appoint high-ranking nobles to his inner circle and kept his promise to make all but the most routine decisions himself. He devoted six or eight hours a day to administrative affairs, keeping himself "informed about everything . . . knowing at any time the numbers and quality of my troops and the state of my strongholds, unceasingly giving my instructions upon every requirement, dealing directly with ministers from abroad, receiving and reading dispatches . . . regulating the income and expenditure of my State." One minister made the mistake of giving lengthy, but false, reports to the king, believing that Louis would soon tire of financial matters and leave them all to him. But Louis loved administration, seeing each dispatch,

Louis XIV as Sun King from the facade of Hotel des Tresoriers, Paris
(Giraudon/Art Resource, NY)

each decision, as the expression of his own glory: "I do not know what other pleasure we would not give up for this one," he wrote; "I felt an enjoyment difficult to express." He could listen to the most complicated reports, then make an instant decision. He expected his ministers to do the same, and to ensure that he would suddenly go into minute detail on some subject when the minister "least expected it, so that he should realize that I might do the same in other contexts at any time." His own answer to any unforeseen question was always "I'll see."[6] His own council of state was reduced to three men, all serious, competent, and hardworking, but without noble connections or independent power. "It was not in my interest," Louis wrote, "to take subjects of a higher degree . . . it was not my intention to share my power with them. It was necessary that they should entertain no higher hopes for themselves than I might be pleased to gratify."[7] Their power, and their own glory, came solely from their efforts on behalf of the state. Over the course of Louis's long reign, the entire business of government was carried out by himself, his three chief ministers, and perhaps an additional fifty functionaries. These men were, literally, the French state.

At the end of his first year of rule, Louis chose what became the most enduring symbol for his reign, the sun. He chose the sun, he said, "because of the unique quality of the radiance that surrounds it; the light it imparts to the other stars, which compose a kind of court; the fair and equal share of that light that it gives to all the various climates of the world; the good it does in every place, ceaselessly producing joy and activity on every side; the untiring motion in which it yet seems always tranquil; and that constant, invariable course from which it never deviates or diverges—assuredly the most vivid and beautiful image of a great monarch."[8] His court and his kingdom, watching him carry out as much work as the most assiduous of his ministers, ride, hunt, manage diplomatic coups, and father children with his wife, Maria Theresa of Spain, as well as with his mistresses, agreed that the king could have no fitter emblem than the brilliant light that outshines all others in the sky.

Absolute Rule

For Louis to truly dominate his kingdom, he needed more than a brilliant emblem. Monarchs of France faced opposition to their authority from pockets of privilege everywhere, from the leaders of the Estates to towns and provinces who had, from time immemorial, the privilege to exact their own laws and collect their own tolls. Wherever possible, Louis moved to attack all privilege that opposed his authority, claiming—and believing—that only the king could decide what was best for

France, "since there is scarcely any order of the realm, church, nobility, or Third Estate that has not at some time fallen into fearful error."⁹

In the first year of his reign, Louis dealt with challenges from all three orders. The Assembly of the Clergy, which acted as an interest group for the highest-ranking church positions in France, after one meeting refused to disperse until the King signed certain edicts regarding church policy. Louis, as he later wrote, "let them understand that nothing more was to be gained by these kinds of methods," and forced them to withdraw. Only then did he sign their edicts. He acted to weaken the second estate, the nobility, by limiting its control over military forces. When the colonel in chief of the infantry, a high-ranking nobleman, died, Louis took over the position himself. Despite the fact that France was now at peace, he kept a substantial force of those troops most loyal to the king. Military commanders had previously acted like independent contractors, raising an army and offering it to the king—or, as Louis well knew, to the king's enemies. He forbade commanders to raise money for troops, "which made them too absolute and too powerful"¹⁰; in future, all armies raised would be in the king's name, and only with the king's permission. As for the third estate, Louis made clear that he would tolerate no resistance to his authority. He declared that all parlements were to register his edicts at once, with no discussion or deliberation. Once they were registered and became law, the parlements could respectfully submit any remonstrances; Louis would answer yes or no, and that would be that. He also made it clear that he would hold the parlements in their respective towns responsible for any local disturbances or revolts against royal authority. By 1679 his minister of finances, Jean-Baptiste Colbert, wrote with satisfaction that "Parlementary troubles are out of date. So much so that they are quite forgotten."¹¹

All Louis's declarations were backed up by his troops, and when sporadic protests did occur—"coming close to disobedience," as Louis put it—he had them suppressed immediately and forcefully, regarding such severity as necessary for order and the glory of France, "the greatest kindness I could do my people. "Yet he could use his power to alleviate the sufferings of his people as well. When poor harvests led to famine in some provinces, causing the majority of peasants to fall below the line separating the merely poor from the starving, Louis commandeered food from provinces unaffected by the famine. He purchased grain in Danzig at royal expense and had it distributed free to those who needed it. He forbade, and ruthlessly punished, speculators in grain who attempted to profit from the disaster by selling grain to the highest bidder, and he required shopkeepers to sell bread at a price accessible to the poor. Louis's actions stood out against both the inactivity of nobles, who had done little to relieve their tenants, and the bourgeoisie of the towns, who tried to get rich from the miseries of the countryside by speculating on grain. The image of the king as defender of the least of his subjects against the "thousands of petty tyrants" within his kingdom further enhanced his own glory: it was kings, not church or parlements, he wrote, "whom God appoints the sole guardians of the public weal."[12]

Jean-Baptiste Colbert and Financial Reform

Louis's generosity during the famine had been suggested to him by his minister of finance, Jean-Baptiste Colbert (1619–1683). Colbert came from a family whose wealth came from international trade and finance. He had been the confidential financial agent of Cardinal Mazarin, through whom he had learned all there was to know about how an individual in the king's service could enrich himself at the expense of the state. Colbert served Mazarin loyally, and Mazarin rewarded him by recommending him to Louis XIV. By that time Colbert already had decided that the finances of France needed to be completely reorganized, so that the king would be completely in command of the wealth of his kingdom. It was a decision entirely in agreement with Louis's own policies, and the two men formed a bond that lasted the rest of Colbert's life.

The finances of France to that point had been run according to practices that had arisen during the Middle Ages. The king, like other lords, raised taxes on his own estates, as well as on certain customary items, like salt. He spent his revenues until they were gone. Then he had to look for other ways to raise money. These included selling governmental offices, which were often created for the sole purpose of raising money. They also included selling government bonds, which of course then had to be paid out. And they included creating new taxes, which were then farmed out to office-holders known, appropriately, as tax farmers, who promised to raise a specified sum from a specified region. The position of tax farmers were also sold, generally at a very high price, because they were so lucrative. Tax farmers, like military commanders, acted like independent contractors. All they had pledged was to provide the king a specified sum at a specified time. Any additional money that they could collect above that was theirs to keep, and no one investigated the methods they used to collect it. Moreover, there was usually a gap between the time at which taxes were collected and the time at which they had to be paid into the royal treasury, which meant tax farmers had an enormous sum of money to invest or otherwise speculate with. Any amount they made from such speculation was theirs to keep as well.

The peasantry of France, on whom most of the tax burden fell, hated the tax farmers for their extortionate practices and their wealth. Colbert disliked them too, less for reasons of equity than of inefficiency. If there was money to be made from tax collection, he believed, it should go to the king, not private individuals. He also hated the system by which deficits in royal revenues were made up by heavy borrowing. The expenses for any governmental action—war, overseas exploration, subsidies for trade—were supposed to be borne by the king, but since the royal revenues were often exhausted, French monarchs had to contract huge loans, often at enormous interest. Individuals in a position to make such loans were often supposed governmental servants, who used their positions to become enormously wealthy, lent money to the king, and became even wealthier from interest payments. Colbert's former employer, Mazarin, had done just that, amassing a huge fortune, though he was ready at a moment's notice to lend all the money in his possession to the king.

Colbert made it his business to change this obsolete system. He worked closely with the king in imposing order and providing careful accounting for all the expenses of the state. He abolished thousands of offices created in the previous thirty years to raise money and still held by officials who collected a salary. He set up a special commission to investigate tax farmers, requiring even descendants to pay any moneys that the commission found owing to the government. Anyone suspected of defrauding the government was prosecuted, and both the investigation and new regulations acted as a deterrent to the worst evils of the system. In some cases, Colbert simply canceled whole classes of government bonds that had been sold, in the desperation of immediate need, at an interest rate he felt was too high.

From a modern point of view, Colbert and Louis's reforms did not go far enough. The basic tax structure of France was both inequitable and, from the point of view of royal revenues, inefficient. The main tax on personal wealth, called the *taille*, fell only on the peasantry, artisans, and lower ranks of the merchants, because members of both the clergy and nobility were exempt from it. For that reason, patents of nobility constituted an important kind of tax evasion and were freely sold: almost any form of local government position, and the purchase of many estates, conferred nobility, as if, in modern terms, tax-exempt status for life could be bought with every house sold at a certain price or with every election to a school board. If a family's wealth increased, there would come a point at which the patent of nobility would be worth its purchase price in the money saved from having to pay taxes. This meant that, in France, the poorer a family was, the more taxes it paid, a system both unjust and, from the government's point of view, not cost-effective. If the Devil himself had been given a free hand to plan the ruin of France, one contemporary commented, he could not have devised a tax system more suitable for his purpose.

Louis was to attack many privileges, but he never instructed Colbert to broaden the taille, for it was too entrenched a system. Colbert, in any case, had larger goals than just fiscal reform, important as that was. He believed that financial speculation on grain, on tax collection, on public offices was diverting investment from France's industry and trade, and he set up a system of governmental subsidies to encourage France's underdeveloped manufacturing. He supervised the building of roads and canals to facilitate internal trade; developed the Gobelin tapestry works; supported colonies in Canada; rebuilt decayed urban centers throughout France. He was determined that Paris, still in many respects an overcrowded medieval city, should become a modern capital like London and Amsterdam, so he carried out a host of building projects to revitalize the city, widening boulevards, developing squares and gardens, and completely renovating the Louvre, the traditional royal palace. Paris should have the same relationship to the rest of France as the city of Rome had to the Roman Empire, Colbert said, for "being the capital of the kingdom and the residence of the king, it is certain that it sets in motion the rest of the kingdom; that all internal affairs begin with it."[13] Under his administration, Paris turned into a dazzling center of French cultural life, and it began to supplant even Italy as an obligatory stop on the Grand Tour.

As a minister, Colbert was notoriously stern and unbending to all those seeking special favors. "The man of marble" was one of his nicknames, and Madame de Sévigné , whose letters to her daughter provide detailed descriptions of life at court, referred to him as "the waiting ice." She went to him to request a pension for her son-in-law, and "I will not tire myself," she wrote to her daughter afterwards, "if I quote his reply: 'Madam, I shall see to it.' And he walked me to the door, and that was it." Colbert himself became an extremely wealthy man, collecting rare books, acquiring an estate that he ruled like a nobleman, exhorting the priest to "incite . . . my inhabitants to live proper lives," and requiring his tenants to exhibit "faith and homage" when he visited. But he never used his position to enrich himself unlawfully, and he never forgot that his wealth and honor came from the king's service: "Consider well and reflect often," he wrote to his son, "upon what your birth would have made of you if God had not blessed my labors, and if these labors had not been extreme."[14]

Versailles

Louis XIV had enough confidence in Colbert that the minister could, politely, disagree with Louis's policies and projects, and Colbert expressed his strong disagreement over a new building project begun in 1661, the creation of a royal residence in the otherwise undistinguished town of Versailles, fifteen miles outside of Paris. Louis showed no interest in Colbert's elaborate building projects for the capital city. He had never liked the city and its history of rebellions: too many pockets of privilege resided in Paris, from the law courts to the Sorbonne to great princes of the realm with their fine town houses. Moreover, he felt, a king who could compare himself to the sun required a new, radiant palace. The palace at Versailles, which was to grow into a huge château complex surrounded by stables, hunting lodges, and acres of formal gardens requiring the most up-to-date irrigation techniques, was and has remained the visible expression of the Sun King's glory. One of the earliest visitors, Mademoiselle de Scudéry, made this point in print in 1668. The king goes to Versailles, she wrote, "to relax and put aside for a moment his great and illustrious but tiring duties." This allowed "his prompt return to work with the same fervor as that with which the sun begins to illumine the world when he rises from the waters where he has rested himself."[15]

Colbert continually protested the cost—Versailles took 60 percent of the royal revenues for the first twenty years of its construction—but it became a showpiece for French art, music, theater, furniture, and other luxury items, stimulating a demand for goods made in France instead of imported from Italy and the Netherlands. "This is a château that might be called an enchanted palace . . . perfect," wrote one of the first public

Panoramic View of Versailles in 1668 by Pierre Patel (Giraudon/Art Resource, NY)

accounts of Versailles. "It charms in all possible ways . . . everything is so highly finished, so well laid out, so well cared for, that nothing is the equal of it. Its symmetry, the richness of its furnishings, the beauty of its walks and the infinite number of its flowers, as well as of its orange trees, make the surroundings of this spot especially extraordinary."[16] As the building progressed, Louis commissioned ever more elaborate decorations, with the theme of himself as Apollo, the Greek god of the sun, surrounded by figures representing Justice and Force. The Hall of Mirrors, built in the 1670s, was intended to stand out for sheer magnificence in a palace where room after room was designed to display splendor. It is nearly two stories high, 246 feet long, and thirty-three feet wide. Its high, vaulted ceiling is covered with Baroque painting and its floor decorated in marble. Sunlight from seventeen tall windows on one side is reflected in tall mirrors on the opposite wall. Today it is opulent enough with its decorations of statues and candelabras; on formal occasions under Louis's reign, it was decorated with tapestries, additional statues, and small trees as well. Visitors to Versailles were dazzled, as they were intended to be.

Versailles was more than just a costly symbol; it was also an efficient strategy for taming the French nobles. Louis XIV made it clear that any noble family who wished for royal patronage for any favor, from command of an army to a favorable decision in a property case, had to come to his court. Those who refused, from independence or lack of interest, might find a royal official at their door, inquiring whether they were, after all, really of noble birth and asking to see their letters of nobility. This was a serious threat, for nobility conveyed clear legal and fiscal privileges; loss of noble status meant a quick descent into the ranks of the merely bourgeois, a failure of generations of marriage and family strategies, a deep humiliation. In Brittany, 2,500 nobles were investigated in this way. And so the nobles came, spending their days in Versailles instead of looking after their semi-independent estates and, perhaps, plotting rebellion.

The success of the strategy did not end there. For Versailles was horrendously expensive. Court custom required expensive and elaborate court dress, and all visitors had to pay for their own upkeep. Since Versailles was in the country, an army of tailors, wig-makers, furriers, goldsmiths, and victualers sprang up, each anxious to make the most money possible out of the ghetto of nobles determined to display their rank and status. Attendance on the king meant, literally, daily attendance, from the moment when he awoke to when he went to bed. It was an honor to be admitted to his room to see him dress and an even greater honor to be allowed to hand him his shirt, his breeches, or his shoes, for the rumor was that Louis was more likely to agree to a petition before breakfast. Those honored in this way had special titles, and the titles were sold for large sums; the titles were even scalped, like tickets to a modern-day rock concert, for much higher prices to noble petitioners. Attendants at Versailles had to be seen at meals, where they had to maintain strict etiquette and protocol in entering and leaving the room; they had to accompany Louis on his promenades, to his theatrical performances, to his other diversions. One of the few breaks came when the king went hunting, for Louis, an excellent hunter, preferred to concentrate on the chase, not on petitions. Finally, the favored courtiers had the privilege of watching him undress and go to bed.

It could cost as much to stay at Versailles as to maintain a private estate with hundreds of men-at-arms. That was part of the point: nobles jockeying for order of precedence in entering the ballroom were safer for Louis than nobles with the means to take their quarrels onto the battlefield. It was possible—even easy—to go bankrupt at Versailles while waiting on the king's pleasure, for the king "loved magnificently lavish abundance," one visitor said; "indeed, one way to win favor was to spend extravagantly on the table, clothes, carriages, buildings and gambling. For magnificence in such things he would speak to people."[17] And a conversation with the king, or even a smile or a nod from Louis, might be enough to save an estate from foreclosure and a once-proud family from ruin. Versailles, despite its magnificence, was extremely uncomfortable. Nearly 10,000 people crowded into the complex, and nobles with magnificent town houses in Paris and châteaux of their own had to cram themselves and their servants into one or two small rooms. It was also very boring, for no discussion of politics, religion, or any other controversial subject was allowed, another rule that ensured that nobles could not plot rebellion. However, the stakes for which this game was played were very high, for under the king's absolute authority all favors, large and small, were determined by him.

Louis's goal was to reduce his nobles to courtiers, and to help him do that, he eliminated, wherever he could, their governmental functions. They were still lords in their own territories and could exact, as rent on their estates, payments in labor—repairing bridges, building new roads— as well as payments in money or goods. Louis broke with the existing tradition of appointing as the royal administrators of a region, called intendants, men who had links to the territorial nobles from that region. Instead, he appointed new men, without ties to the local nobility, to the positions. They were usually sons of wealthy landowners, often with legal training, who saw royal administration as their career, with loyalty to the king their first concern.

Men and Women of Letters

Both Louis XIV and Colbert saw clearly that writers, like artists and architects, could be pressed into service as propagandists for the king. In 1668, when Mademoiselle Madeleine de Scudéry (ca. 1607–1701) visited Versailles, she was the most popular novelist in France. She was descended from a poor, but aristocratic family. Like many of her heroines, she was orphaned when young, and she was raised by an uncle, who gave her a more extensive education than was usual for young ladies. After he died, she lived in Paris with her brother, who had already acquired a reputation as a writer. She attended literary salons, informal meetings of all those interested in arts and literary matters (letters), which attracted some of the wittiest and most elegant people in Parisian society. Later, she established her own salon, which met every Saturday afternoon. Her first novel, *Ibrahim*, was published in 1641. It is a historical romance, like her next two, *Cyrus* and *Clélie*, the bestselling novel of the century.

Mademoiselle de Scudéry did not publish her novels under her own name—as a noblewoman, she did not want to be known as a mere author—but her authorship was an open secret in the social world of Paris and the court. Her description of Versailles came from a short novel, *The Promenade in Versailles*, as always involving a beautiful heroine and several love stories. In this case, though, Scudéry was acting as an official publicist for the king, to whom the novel is dedicated. The king in the novel is clearly Louis, who is praised for the magnificence of the palace, which illustrates his glory, and for festivals, which Scudéry described in enough detail for us to identify the play being performed. Contemporary readers would also have understood the political message of the remark made by one of the characters: "A hundred times I have considered in astonishment that men who have established so many different kinds of government have never succeeded so well as when they give up their own wisdom to rely upon that of a higher order. Never have they encountered the grandeur, tranquility, and durability of state as when they choose their ruler from one family, father to son, accepting whom God has chosen for them." Scudéry received a pension from Louis, and when she went to court to thank him, "she was received in utter perfection," Madame de Sévigné wrote to her daughter; "the king spoke to her and before she could kneel to kiss his knees he lifted her to his embrace."[18]

Madame de Lafayette (ca. 1634–1693) was another novelist whose literary efforts earned the favor of the king. Born Marie-Madeleine de la Vergne, she too came from the minor aristocracy, but became maid of honor to the Queen Regent Anne in 1650 and made friends with ladies in court who later became her patrons. She married the Count de Lafayette in 1655 and had two children, but after six years the couple lived separately, with Madame de Lafayette remaining in Paris, cultivating both court and literary circles. She was known for her intelligence—"one of the finest wits of our court," for her business sense in settling her husband's lawsuits, for her "divine reason," and for her expertise in acquiring influential connections to further her family's and friends' careers. Her novels, like Scudéry's, were published anonymously, and she pretended to be angry if asked whether she was the author, but her authorship was, again, well-known in court circles. The most famous, *The Princess of Clèves*, was circulated in manuscript in literary circles before being published in 1678. It was an immediate hit and within a year was translated into English with the somewhat redundant subtitle "The most famed Romance written in French by the greatest Wit of France."

Madame de Lafayette's literary abilities as well as her charm and social contacts came in useful to the king's ministers, who used her as a publicity agent in negotiations with one of her childhood friends, the Duchess of Savoy. Like Scudéry, Lafayette was rewarded with a personal interview with the king, including a tour of Versailles in his carriage, with a pension, and with positions in the army for her children. As Madame de Sévigné noted, "Never has a person, without leaving her place, done such good business. . . . See how Madame de Lafayette is rich in friends on every side and of every rank: she has a hundred arms, she reaches everywhere. Her children appreciate this and thank her daily for having such a winning nature."[19]

Besides these informal publicists, the king also patronized professional writers, approving pensions for a range of authors on a list drawn up by Colbert, including three famous French playwrights, Corneille, Racine, and Molière. Pierre Corneille (1606–1684) was the son of a judiciary official from Rouen. He studied law, but turned to writing in the 1620s, a time when French theater was limited to either visiting Italian companies or traveling groups of actors who performed at fairs and market days. His first play, *Mélite*, performed in 1629, ensured both his own success as an author and the success of his theatrical troupe, for playwrights in this period wrote for a particular group of actors. His tragedies involved heroic characters, larger than life, caught up by passion and politics in duels, murders, and epic events. When his best known play, *Le Cid*, was first performed in Paris in 1636, audiences gasped, shuddered, and cried. Corneille wrote comedies, too, depicting scenes from Parisian daily life, as the hero and heroine take time off from the plot to visit the most fashionable shops and discuss Scudéry's novels. Over his lifetime, Corneille's heroic style fell out of fashion, and his later plays were much less successful. Yet he was honored as the founder of modern French drama. "You know in what condition was the French stage when he began his work," proclaimed Racine on Corneille's death. "Such disorder! such irregularity! No taste, no knowledge of the real beauties of the theater. . . . In this chaos . . . Corneille, against the bad taste of the century, inspired by an extraordinary genius, . . . put reason on stage, but a reason accompanied by all the pomp and all the ornaments of which our language is capable."[20]

Jean Racine (1639–1699) was the most famous playwright of the next generation. Although he was generous in his eulogy, he and Corneille had been bitter enemies, for Racine had deliberately set out to topple "the great Corneille" from the height of fame. He, too, was known for his tragedies, but his characters are portrayed with greater psychological insight: they suffer not because they are caught up by events, but because of conflicts within themselves. Though his tragedies, like Corneille's, are often set in far-off times and places, they followed popular taste by depicting characters who seemed to come straight out of fashionable Parisian life. Corneille, wrote one commentator, depicted men as they should be, while Racine depicted them as they are. Though some critics complained of his lack of historical accuracy, Racine himself believed that the "first rule" of playwriting was "to please and to touch the heart: all the others exist only as means to achieving the first."[21] In addition to his skill as a dramatist, Racine was an excellent courtier who first came to the notice of Louis XIV when he wrote a poem on the king's marriage in 1660. He charmed everyone at court when invited four years later, at which point he received his first pension, and he was appointed Royal Historian in 1677. Troubled by religious scruples, he gave up writing plays at the age of thirty-eight, but he remained a courtier all his life, and his widow and children received a pension from the king after his death.

In the 1660s, when Racine first drew the king's attention, Louis also made another theatrical discovery. A theater company, headed by Jean Poquelin, better known by his stage name Molière (1622–1673), was performing two of his comedies at a private performance for Cardinal Mazarin and his guests. At the end of the performance, Molière was summoned and given a tip equal to five years of the initial pension awarded to Racine. "This man Molière suits me," Louis told Mazarin; "he is amusing and clearsighted," and Mazarin told Colbert (in 1660 still his personal agent), "Molière must continue to receive favors. He shows promise of a comic genius which could be very useful."[22] Molière became chief comedian to the king, acting as well as writing, giving command performances in a specially constructed theater in Versailles as well as performing to packed houses in Paris. When his satire on religious hypocrisy, *Tartuffe*, aroused indignation at court, Louis protected him, and when Louis remained silent after seeing *The Would-Be Gentleman*, a play he had specially commissioned, Molière was reported to have shut himself in his room for five days. Yet all ended happily: After another performance, Louis said to Molière, "I did not speak to you about your play after its first performance because I thought I had been deceived by the way it was acted; but indeed, Molière, you have never amused me more, and your comedy is excellent."[23]

All these writers, and many others on Colbert's list, accepted Louis's favors knowing they had made a tacit bargain "to become heralds of the King's virtues."[24] But none saw a pension from the king as interfering with their artistic integrity. Though Colbert did his best to regulate artistic creation, awarding pensions, insisting that the various academies founded or revived under Louis's reign—the Academy for Fine Arts, the Academy of Sciences—have regular meetings and take notes, he could not dictate genius. Fortunately he did not have to: the artists, sculptors, writers, and musicians of seventeenth-century France were happy to lend their talents to the glory of Louis's reign.

Ironically, one of the best publicists for Louis XIV was a woman who published nothing at all in her, or his, lifetime, Marie de Rabutin Chantal,

Marquise de Sévigné, known as Madame de Sévigné (1626–1696). Born in Paris, she married, moved to Brittany and had two children, but when her husband died she returned to Paris to become another of the brilliant, fashionable ornaments to court society, friends with everyone: "Joy is the true state of your soul,"[25] Madame de Lafayette wrote to her. When her daughter, Françoise-Marguerite, married and went to live in Provence, in the south of France, Madame de Sévigné wrote her hundreds of letters evoking, for her daughter's pleasure, the events of town and court. After her death the letters remained in the family vault. A selection of them was published in 1726, captivating first Paris, then the rest of France, then the world with the eyewitness account of life in France during the reign of the Sun King.

The Glory of War

Despite pensions and other outlays, despite the enormous expenses of Versailles, the king's net income doubled from 1661 to 1671. He was probably the only king in Europe whose surplus increased from year to year. From the first, though, he had plans for that surplus: the creation of an army and navy larger and more powerful than any other in Europe. For war, to Louis, was the ultimate theater for glory: military victory was a far more important testimonial to his magnificence than even his glittering court at Versailles. Victory had practical purposes as well, in his view: it would extend the borders and increase the revenues of France.

In 1665, Philip IV of Spain died, leaving only a sickly four-year-old as his successor. Louis laid claim to the remaining Spanish territories north of the Pyrenees, southern Flanders and the Franche Comte, on the basis of a dubious legal connection. He bribed Charles II of England to remain neutral, for Charles, trying to build up the navy and maintain his court, was happy to use French funds as an alternative to asking Parliament for money. In 1667 the French army, consisting of 70,000 men, the largest in Europe, marched into Flanders. They expected easy victory on the field, and they got it. But the Dutch, alarmed at the prospect of an aggressive France at their southern border, raised the specter of "universal monarchy" to convince other nations that France could become as dangerous as the Habsburgs had been during the Thirty Years' War. The United Provinces, Sweden, and Great Britain—for Parliament, unaware of Louis's subsidies to Charles II, had already voted funds for the war—formed a Triple Alliance. It was successful in keeping Louis from all the territories he had sought, though France retained some cities in the former Spanish Netherlands. It was the Dutch whom Louis, correctly, blamed for the defeat, and he was appalled that a nation of "cheese merchants" and "sea peddlers" should have been able to halt both his diplomatic maneuvering and his magnificent army. There was a rumor that the Dutch had a medal struck, depicting themselves as Joshua, who had made the sun stand still. Louis XIV determined on revenge, he wrote in 1668. He was merely postponing the punishment for another time. His military attempts at punishment were to lead to a series of wars that would occupy the rest of his reign.

Profile: Versailles Abroad

Louis XIV continued building at Versailles throughout his long reign. The château became a symbol of absolutism, and many monarchs explicitly copied it in developing absolutist principles in their own countries. Peter Romanov, Czar of Russia, took Versailles as the inspiration for the Peterhof when he created a new capital for Russia at St. Petersburg at the end of the seventeenth century. Frederick II Hohenzollern of Prussia likewise took it for his model in establishing his court in Potsdam in the middle of the eighteenth century. Even minor princes decided to emulate Versailles by abandoning their traditional capitals for nearby palace complexes. The Electors of the Palatinate moved their court from Heidelberg to Mannheim, and the Dukes of Baden-Durlach moved from Durlach to Karlsruhe.

In the history of art and architecture, Versailles also became a showplace for the highest quality in the art of design. The Swedish monarchy kept a full-time representative on the staff of its ambassador in Paris from 1693 to 1718 whose task was to report back to the Swedish royal architect on the progress of the arts in France. Blueprints, sketches, technical details of locks, window hooks, and curtain rods were all faithfully copied and sent back to Sweden. When, in 1694, war overseas meant there was no money in France to pay workers on any royal project, the Swedish representative wrote gleefully home that "poverty and unemployment are general and that we can really hire the very best craftsmen in the world for next to nothing. . . . If the king of Sweden would like to have furniture or tapestries made, the cost will come to about half of what it would ordinarily."[26] Even Louis's most determined opponents copied the designs of his artists and architects. His later career consisted of almost constant war with the United Provinces and Great Britain, but French architects were employed in both countries in both private houses and public buildings. Prince William of Orange, Stadtholder of the United Provinces and later William III of England, spent much of his life fighting French military expansion, but his favorite residence *Het Loo* has been called a "little Versailles" from the clear French influence. Blenheim Palace in England was built to commemorate a later English victory over Louis XIV, but its design was based on French principles. Elements of French style appeared in residences throughout Europe, as budding architects from all over came to study "the interior decoration of buildings as well as...gardening," the Swedish royal architect said, "because it is in these areas they excel in France."[27]

Important Dates

1636	Corneille's *Le Cid* first performed
1648	Fronde begins
1653	Fronde ends
1654	Publication of Mademoiselle de Scudéry's *Clélie*
1659	Treaty of Pyrenees ends war between France and Spain
1661	Death of Mazarin; Louis XIV becomes his own first minister; construction begins on Palace of Versailles
1664	Molière's *Tartuffe* first performed
1667–1668	War of the Devolution
1677	Racine becomes Royal Historian
1678	Publication of Madame de Lafayette's *Princess of Clèves*
1684	Death of Corneille

Further Reading

Nancy Barker, *Brother to the Sun King: Philippe, Duke of Orleans* (Baltimore, 1989)

William Beik, *Absolutism and Society in Seventeenth Century France* (Cambridge, 1985)

Robert W. Berger, *A Royal Passion: Louis XIV as Patron of Architecture* (Cambridge, 1994)

Peter Burke, *The Fabrication of Louis XIV* (New Haven, 1992)

William Church, *Louis XIV in Historical Thought* (New York, 1976)

James B. Collins, *The State in Early Modern France* (Cambridge, 1995)

Jonathan Dewald, *Aristocratic Experience and the Origins of Modern Culture* (Berkeley, 1993)

Richard Golden, *The Godly Rebellion: Parisian Curés and the Religious Fronde, 1652–1662* (Chapel Hill, 1981)

Pierre Goubert, *Louis XIV and Twenty Million Frenchmen* trans. Anne Carter (New York, 1972)

Joseph Klaits, *Printed Propaganda Under Louis XIV: Absolute Monarchy and Public Opinion* (Princeton, 1976)

Emmanuel Le Roy Ladurie, *The Ancien Régime: A History of France, 1610–1774* trans. Mark Greengrass (Oxford, 1996)

W.H. Lewis, *The Splendid Century: Life in the France of Louis XIV* (New York, 1978)

John A. Lynn, *Giant of the Grand Siècle: The French Army, 1610–1715* (Cambridge, 1997)

Louis Marin, *Portrait of the King* trans. Martha M. Houle (Minneapolis, 1988)

Alain Merot, *French Painting in the Seventeenth Century* (New Haven, 1995)

Roger Mettam, *Power and Faction in Louis XIV's France* (Oxford, 1988)

Chandra Mukerji, *Territorial Ambitions and the Gardens of Versailles* (Cambridge, 1997)

Inès Murat, *Colbert*, trans. Robert Francis Cook and Jeannie Van Asselt (Charlottesville, 1984)

Orest Ranum, *Artisans of Glory* (Chapel Hill, 1980)

Orest Ranum, *Paris in the Age of Absolutism* (Bloomington, IN, 1979)

Orest Ranum, *The Fronde: A French Revolution* (New York, 1993)

Lionel Rothkrug, *Opposition to Louis XIV* (Princeton, 1965)

Herbert H. Rowen, *The King's State: Proprietary Dynasticism in Early Modern France* (New Brunswick, 1980)

John Rule, ed., *Louis XIV and the Craft of Kingship* (Columbus, OH, 1970)

David J. Sturdy, *Louis XIV* (New York, 1998)

Andrew Trout, *Jean-Baptiste Colbert* (Boston, 1978)

Guy Walton, *Louis XIV's Versailles* (Chicago, 1986)

John B. Wolf, *Louis XIV* (New York, 1968)

Chapter Eight

The Arts in the Age of the Baroque

Even though Spain and the United Provinces of the Netherlands were two of the main belligerents in the Thirty Years' War (1618–1648), both countries also experienced a golden age of culture in the seventeenth century. In Spain, this culture was above all associated with the court of the Spanish monarchy, based in Madrid. Like Louis XIV of France, Philip IV (1605–1665) and his ministers recognized that art and architecture could play a major role in expressing a monarch's glory. The style of arts known as the *Baroque*, which developed at the end of the sixteenth century, was especially well-suited to represent confident nobility and a resurgent church.

It is not easy to define the Baroque, which has been applied to many styles and genres of the seventeenth century. It began in Italy, where a succession of Counter-Reformation popes commissioned major building projects to beautify Rome and celebrate the ritual and mystery of Catholicism. In contrast to Renaissance art, which emphasized harmony, balance, and classical proportions, Baroque was quite consciously emotional and grandiose. Baroque worked best on the largest scales because that is where the swirl and mass of details could be harnessed to create a single overpowering effect. One of the most characteristic monuments of the Baroque was a great colonnade and piazza designed to grace the entrance to St. Peter's Cathedral in Rome (completed in 1657)—the "home" church of the pope.

Other Roman churches, especially those of the new Jesuit order, were built or rebuilt and lavishly decorated with gold and ebony ornamentation. They were often crowned by elaborate painted ceilings deliberately designed to give the illusion of the heavens, adorned by angels, in which richly detailed religious scenes take place. *Trompe l'oeil* (optical illusion) effects are frequent. For example, in the ceiling of the church of St. Ignatius, dedicated to the founder of the Jesuits, the ceiling consisted of a view extending upwards, depicting St. Ignatius's ascent to heaven.

Giovanni Lorenzo Bernini (1598–1682), who designed the colonnade outside of St. Peter's, became the emblematic artist of the Baroque. Raw emotionalism and exuberant color and design were characteristic of Bernini and other Baroque artists. The emotionalism was apparent in Bernini's sculpture of *The Ecstasy of St. Theresa*, which showed the sixteenth-century saint swooning from receiving an arrow to her heart from Christ. The look on her face was akin to sexual excitement. His canopy for the interior of St. Peter's, called the *Baldacchino*, was even more exuberant. Twisting columns, gold, ivory, and ebony, inlaid in fine, multicolored marbles, created an overpowering ensemble effect that was widely imitated.

From Rome, the stylistic principles of Baroque architecture spread to the rest of Italy, Catholic Germany, and Spain. In those territories, the combination of powerful nobles, fervent and militant Catholicism, and lavish display and ornamentation led to the adoption of the Baroque as the distinctive artistic style. In France, England, Protestant Germany, and the Netherlands, the Baroque unfolded in a more restrained style that adhered more closely to classical ideas of harmony. In fact, when Louis XIV invited Bernini to come to Paris and redesign the Louvre palace, Bernini's plans were rejected as too exaggerated for French tastes. Yet even French and English architecture adopted the Baroque tendency for the grand gesture and elaborate control of interior space. This undercurrent was apparent in other arts besides architecture that flourished in the mid-seventeenth century.

The Golden Age of Spain

By the 1620s, shortly after the accession of the sixteen-year-old Philip IV to the throne, Spain had already entered its golden age, according to one writer: "The happiness in the government of this fortunate monarchy proceeds in glory; the reign of our seignior Philip IV the king is for Spain a golden century."[1] The writer, a publicist for the king, may well have been receiving a subsidy from the crown. As a prophet of political events, he was to be sadly mistaken. Though still, in the 1620s, the most powerful king in Europe, Philip wrestled throughout his reign with

Baldacchino at St. Peter's Basilica by Giovanni Lorenzo Bernini (Scala/ Art Resource, NY)

irresolvable problems. Long years of warfare had depleted his treasury, and the silver mines of the New World that had supported Spanish military power for 150 years were finally drying up. Spain, like many principalities, consisted of different semiautonomous provinces: even Aragon and Castile, formally united by the marriage of the Catholic Monarchs Ferdinand and Isabella in 1469, continued to have separate governments. The great noble families united only to protect their privileges, otherwise jostling with each other for rank and royal favor. War, taxes, and a harsh penal code fell most heavily on the peasantry, leading to rural unrest. The territories of Catalonia and Portugal rebelled against royal authority at the same time as Spain confronted an increasingly militaristic northern neighbor, France. By Philip IV's death in 1665, Louis XIV had ascended the French throne, and France, not Spain, was the dominant power in Europe.

Yet in the arts, the writer was correct: the seventeenth century was to be known as Spain's golden age. Under Philip III, Madrid had been made the official capital of the monarchy; under Philip IV, it became a major urban center comparable to London under Charles I. One contemporary commentator wrote that "little by little it began growing and extending itself, almost arriving at the grandeur and splendor in which we now see it; . . . the far-removed fields on its outskirts were converted into attractive streets, its cultivated fields into large buildings, its small chapels into parish churches, its hermitages into convents and its common lands into plazas, common markets and places of exchange."[2] Spanish noble families built town houses and laid out gardens, and Philip IV himself commissioned a palace designed to house and represent his glory, the Buen Retiro, "this temple, this matchless marvel,"[3] as it was called by the playwright Calderón. This conjunction of noble patronage and literary and artistic talent gave seventeenth-century Europe some of its most enduring images.

Miguel Cervantes (1547–1616)

Paradoxically, the author for which seventeenth-century Spain is best known never had any patronage at all and lived most of his life in poverty. Miguel Cervantes wrote his first poetry at the age of twenty-one, on the death of the king, Philip II. His writing career was interrupted by his taking part in a duel, however, as a result of which he had to flee Madrid. He went to Italy and became a soldier in an Italian regiment, taking part in the famous battle of Lepanto of 1571, in which the Otto-man navy was defeated. He stayed in the army for another four years, but then he was captured and taken to Algiers. He remained in captivity for the next five years, despite four attempts to escape. According to witnesses, his behavior in prison was exemplary: "None among the cap-tives was more charitable than Cervantes, nor behaved more honorably."[4] His family finally managed to pay his ransom and have him released.

Once home, Cervantes set about trying to earn a living. He wrote about thirty plays, "without," as he later wrote, "receiving the tribute of cucumbers or other missiles,"[5] but equally without earning enough money to support himself and his family. He became a government commis-sary, in charge of raising supplies for the military, but found that the Spanish government, like many others, often did not pay its officials. At one point he was even imprisoned for not being able to satisfy royal officials that his accounts were in order. And it was during the two months that he spent in the Seville jail, "where every discomfort is lodged and every dismal noise has its dwelling,"[6] that he came up with the idea for his masterpiece, *Don Quixote*.

Don Quixote began as a satire on the romance novels fashionable in the seventeenth century, filled with valiant knights, beautiful ladies, and fearsome giants. It is the story of a gentleman who, "having lost his wits completely" from reading romances, "believed that it was necessary, both for his own honor and for service of the state, that he should be-come a knight-errant, roaming through the world with his horse and armor in quest of adventures."[7] He is accompanied by his down-to-earth servant, Sancho Panza, who can be counted on to point out that the wind-mills Don Quixote thinks are giants are really windmills and that the inn his master thinks is a castle is really an inn. "Do you not hear the neigh-ing of the horses, the blaring of the trumpets, and the rattle of the drums?" asks Don Quixote in a field. "I hear nothing," answers Sancho, "but the bleating of the sheep and lambs."[8] One reader even suggested that the book's title be changed to *Don Quixote and Sancho Panza*, "for Sancho is worth as much as his master and amuses and comforts us even more."[9]

The first part of *Don Quixote* was published in 1605, and within a year the book was famous. By the time the second part appeared in 1615, Cervantes was known all over Europe. Cervantes told the story of one medical student who was overjoyed to meet him, and "seizing me by the left hand he cried out: 'Yes, yes, it is surely he. It is the hero with the maimed hand, the happy, the famous author.'"[10] The mad, yet noble and chivalrous Don Quixote has had an assured place in every literary tradition since his author first created him.

Spanish Theater: Lope de Vega and Calderón

Although Cervantes's first set of plays were performed, his later ones were not, for he could not find a company of actors to put them on. He understood why all too well: his own plays had been overshadowed by those of Lope de Vega (1560–1635), "Nature's monster,"[11] according to Cervantes, but the greatest playwright of his day. Plays in Madrid were performed to demanding audiences. Every afternoon, except during Lent, plays were performed in the two theaters in Madrid, the Corral del Príncipe and the Corral de la Cruz. The theaters were, in fact, truly "corrals," unroofed courtyards surrounded on three sides by houses. The stage took up the fourth side of the theater and consisted of merely a platform. It had no front curtain, but it did have a back curtain to create a backstage area. The entire population of Madrid seems to have attended the plays, though they did not necessarily mingle with one another. The most expensive seats were in the windows of surrounding houses, where wealthy ladies and gentlemen sat together in what were, in effect, box seats. Noble families sometimes rented their window seats for the entire season. In the rest of the theater, there was one price for admission, and another, higher price if the viewer wanted to sit down. Men, women, and the clergy each sat in separate sections. The most boisterous section was in the front and along the sides of the stage, where the audience participated by booing, heckling, or commenting on the action. In these theaters, like their Elizabethan counterparts, audience participation was very much part of the play, and the most popular actors, and playwrights, knew how to incorporate it into the drama.

Certainly Lope de Vega knew how to do so, writing and presenting 1,500 plays by his own count, though modern scholars think 800 is a more reasonable figure. Either way, it was an immense output. The style he developed and made popular was the *comedia*, a three-act play in verse. Strictly speaking the comedia need not be a comedy, in the sense of a humorous play. Lope de Vega liked to mingle comedy and tragedy, because, he said, "such variety gives great delight." Very few, though, are real soul-wrenching tragedies, like the plays for which the French playwright Racine was famous. Lope deVega himself explained why: the desire to please his audience. When he wrote a play, he said, he locked up the rules of classical drama that came from ancient authors and were much studied in the French theater. Instead, "I write in accordance with the art of those who seek popular applause," he said, "for as it is the public who pay, it's only fair to write the kind of nonsense that they like."

What kind of drama did they like? Much of it we would call melodrama, with murders, ghosts, revenge, and ladies dressed up as gentlemen, for again, Lope de Vega said, "male disguise usually gives great pleasure."[12] There are star-crossed lovers, as in the Elizabethan theater, and one of Lope de Vega's many plays is a Spanish variant of the plot of *Romeo and Juliet*. As in Shakespeare and Cervantes, there is one kind of speech for noble characters and another kind, more down-to-earth and, often, to a modern ear, more entertaining, for peasants. The peasant speech is also more evocative of Spanish life, as in this girl's declaration that she refuses to be seduced by a lord: "I would far rather put a slice of ham on the fire in the early morning and eat it with my homemade bread and a glass of wine stolen from my mother, and then at noon to smell a piece of beef boiling with cabbage and eat it ravenously, or, if I have had a trying day, marry an eggplant to some bacon; and in the evening, while cooking the supper, go and pick a handful of grapes from the vines (God save them from the hail) and afterwards dine on chopped meat with oil and pepper, and so happily to bed murmuring 'Lead us not into temptation.'"

There were three main themes in the comedias. The first was religion and the duty owed to God, which was always treated with great seriousness. The second was love and its frequent companion, jealousy. The third, and most distinctive theme, was honor, a pervasive theme throughout Spanish culture. Spanish nobles adhered to a very rigid code of honor, which demanded that the slightest affront to oneself or one's family be punished by the death of the perpetrator. This led to frequent duels, in life as well as on stage. Onstage it also provided a number of plots, for example when a nobleman came to believe his beloved wife guilty of adultery. His own code of honor demanded that he kill her and her lover, even if he had no conclusive proof (and if, as was often the case in drama, she was in fact innocent). The impact of this plot on its audience may have come from the fact that it was supported by the Spanish penal code: a husband was legally permitted to kill an unfaithful wife and her lover, as long as he discovered them in the act and killed them both.

Wives had no legal permission to murder their husbands for adultery, or any other cause, and when they defended their honor onstage, it was not for a mere insult, but for outright rape. One of Lope de Vega's most famous plays, *Fuenteovejuna*, has as its detestable villain a nobleman, the seigneur of a village, who makes a point of seducing and raping village girls. "It is unfair to try to take away our honor," protests one of the villagers, but the lord, like his real-life counterparts, denies that peasants could have any: "Honor? Do you have honor?" Only after repeated episodes does the village rebel. One of the lord's victims, Laurencia, first incites the men to avenge her; then she turns to the women: "Every man, boy, and child is rushing furiously to do his duty. Is it fair that the men alone should have the glory of a day like this, when we women have the greatest grievances . . . I propose that we all band together and perform a deed that will shake the world." "Only women know how to take revenge," says another. "We shall drink the enemy's blood." The villagers do kill their overlord and must face the king's judgment. They remain united in the conviction that they have done right, and "either you must pardon them all or kill the entire village," the king's judge informs him. Since the *comedia* audiences preferred happy endings, the village is pardoned.[13]

Popular as plays were in Madrid, they also had their opponents, who accused them of promoting immorality both among theater companies and among their audiences. Lope de Vega's own life provided enough material for scandal. His first, well-documented affair was with a married actress. He married twice, keeping a mistress in a separate household for at least part of the period of his second marriage. At the age of fifty-two he became an ordained priest, but two years later he fell in love with a young married woman, who eventually bore him a child. After the death of her husband, he arranged to live near her, together with his four children, legitimate and illegitimate. This lifestyle was not confined to either theatrical circles or priests, but it created additional notoriety for the theater. Theater was entertaining, but was it art? And was it respectable?

The playwright who did most to elevate Spanish drama to a more respectable art form was Pedro Calderón (1600–1681), who became the dominant playwright in Madrid from the 1620s. He was born into a noble family and received an excellent education; though his plays adhere to the forms of the comedia, they were intended for a more elite audience. They feature elaborate plots, intricate language, and interplay of music and dancing. It is easier to imagine them being performed to a select group of nobles than in the rough-and-ready atmosphere of the corrals, and in fact Calderón became one of the principal playwrights for Philip IV's many theatrical entertainments at Buen Retiro. The performance of his play *Andromeda and Perseus* at the Coliseo, the theater built at the Buen Retiro, featured elaborate stage settings, full of trompe-l'oeil paintings, ingenious machines for producing special effects, and *automatons* (statues which could be made to move). This elaborate spectacle was Baroque theater in all its glory. In Philip IV's Spain as in Louis XIV's France, it had been harnessed to promote the glory of the king.

Velásquez and Rubens

The image of the king was very much on the mind of the young court painter, Diego de Silva Velásquez (1599–1660), when he painted his first portrait of Philip IV in 1623. The portrait went through successive stages. In its first version, it was an accurate likeness of an ugly man, imposingly presented. The king was pleased with it, and his chief minister, the powerful Count of Olivares, declared that before Velásquez, no one had really painted Philip. Yet over the next ten years, as Velásquez continued to paint portraits of the king and his family, he gradually transformed Philip into a model of an absolute monarch of a powerful state, head back, shoulders squared, his whole body imbued with royal dignity. As a result of the first portrait, Velásquez became the official court painter, the only painter with the privilege of painting the king and his family. He was given a monthly salary as well as substantial payment for each new painting. For a young man only recently arrived from Seville, it was a triumph.

Velásquez remained the king's painter for the rest of his career, one of the coterie of artists and playwrights who accompanied the court wherever it might be. This may be one reason why there are comparatively few Velásquez paintings, for he was given other honorary duties as a mark of the king's favor. His best-known paintings are his portraits, brilliantly lit figures usually placed against a plain background. Like many seventeenth-century artists, he was fascinated with the interplay of light on different surfaces and textures, so that many of his paintings are notable for realistic, almost photographic representation of glass, pottery, and shiny objects. His most famous paintings combine these interests in group portraits. *The Surrender of Breda* (1634–1635) commemorates the victory of the Spanish troops over the town of Breda in the Netherlands after a long siege in 1624. The armies stand on one side

Diego de Silva Velásquez's painting *Las Meninas* (*The Maids of Honor*)
1665 (Erich Lessing/Art Resource, NY)

of the painting, talking and jostling, while the Dutch commander sur-
renders to the Spanish general. Nearly all the figures in the painting are
absorbed in their own world, as Velásquez recreates the scene, but here
and there a few faces look directly out from the painting, as if to say to
the viewer, "Do you see what is going on?"

Velásquez's most famous painting is *Las Meninas* (1656), a group
portrait of the young *infanta* (princess) Margarita and her small court,

including ladies-in-waiting, dwarves, and dog. It is both an extremely accurate group portrait—all but one of the people in it can be precisely identified—and a deliberate play on light and reflection. The infanta, and all her ladies, appear to be looking intently out of the painting at the viewer. With careful attention, we can find out why: a reflection of Philip IV and his wife appear in the mirror behind the infanta, which means that they must have been standing right in front of the people portrayed in the painting—in fact, right where the viewer now stands. What appears to be a portrait of little girls is really a portrait of a painting session in progress, caught at the moment when the king and queen appear in the room. Velásquez painted himself in *Las Meninas* too, caught with paintbrush in hand.

Of all the honors Velásquez received from the king, the one he wanted the most was a knighthood. In order to obtain one, he had to prove he was descended from noble ancestry, with no hint of Jewish or Moorish background; he also had to prove he was a gentleman who never worked for a living. He could show that he was not descended from Jews or Moors, but since it was impossible to prove he was of noble birth—in truth, he wasn't—that requirement was waived. It was also completely untrue that he had never worked for a living, but that was no problem: he was able to get 140 people to sign a statement that he had never had a painting "business," that he had never sold any of his pictures, that he had merely painted for his own pleasure and for that of his king. The strategy worked, and at the age of sixty, Velásquez was made a knight of the Order of Santiago. The emblem of the order, a chain worn around the neck, was added to his self-portrait in *Las Meninas*.

In his capacity as court painter, Velásquez had the opportunity to meet many great men, but his most significant meeting for the history of art came in 1628, when the great Flemish artist and diplomat Peter Paul Rubens (1577–1640) came to Spain. He had been brought up in the city of Antwerp, once the greatest commercial center in Europe. But the destructive wars of the Dutch revolt, culminating in the sack of Antwerp in 1576, had brought a long period of economic decline to Flanders and Brabant, the largest provinces remaining in the Spanish Netherlands after the war was over. The young Rubens was intended by his family to become a courtier to one of the local noble families, a good career for an intelligent, well-educated young man. But his artistic talent was so impressive that Rubens went, at the age of twenty-three, to Italy, the center of the art world, to study and to seek his fortune. He quickly met his first patron, the Duke of Mantua, and entered his service as painter. As the duke soon found, Rubens could be put to other uses, for he was clever, ambitious, and charming, all excellent qualities in a budding diplomat. Thus began the career that was to last Rubens's whole life: his art won him noble patrons, who were then happy to employ his considerable diplomatic skills in international affairs.

After eight years in Italy, Rubens returned to Antwerp and entered the service of the regents Isabella (1566–1633) and Albert (1559–1621), who governed the Spanish Netherlands for the Spanish crown. Isabella believed that the key to restoring the prosperity of her territories was to maintain peace, but this required delicate political maneuvering among the territorial ambitions of France to the south, the United Provinces to the North, and Spain itself. Rubens became a key player in these maneuvers and one of Isabella's most trusted negotiators, since he could be sent as a diplomat to any court with the pretext that he was just a painter carrying out a commission. Not that many were deceived: "Rubens has gone to Spain, where he *says* he is summoned to paint the king," wrote one observer of the trip in which Rubens met Velásquez, and he was known in diplomatic circles as "a person capable of things much greater than the composition of a design colored by the brush."[14]

Useful as he was as a diplomat, Rubens's great achievement was as an artist. He realized early on in his career that he preferred to work with very large canvases, suited to the great palaces and large public displays of seventeenth-century monarchs. To carry out these works, he had a whole studio of assistants and students, and he also worked with other, well-known artists. Rubens would design the work and complete the most important parts; the rest would be sketched in chalk and left for other artists, or his assistants, to fill in. Rubens would provide the finishing touches. When working out the commission with his patrons, he would clearly specify whether the work was to be "an original by my hand," or an "original by my hand except a most beautiful landscape, done by the hand of a master skilful in that department," or copies done by students and then "so well retouched by my hand that they are hardly to be distinguished from originals."[15] The price of the finished work would vary accordingly. The artists employed in the studio also had the job of making engravings and woodcuts based on Rubens's paintings, which were then sold to a more general public: Rubens's works were so popular that he had to patent them to prevent other engravers from stealing them. In between running the studio as a thriving business, taking part in delicate negotiations, and doing his own art-collecting of seventeenth-century masters, it is a wonder Rubens found time to paint. But he did, and his artworks were among the greatest treasures of seventeenth-century palaces.

Dutch in the Seventeenth Century

When the seventeen provinces of the Low Countries began fighting against their Spanish rulers in 1572, the most populated and prosperous part of the territory was in the south, in Flanders and the Brabant. By 1609, when a truce was declared, the seven United Provinces in the north had succeeded in gaining effective independence from Spanish rule. They had also gained economically. Calvinists from the southern provinces had fled north, bringing their families, their movable property, and their traditions of skilled craftmanship. The major commercial cities of Bruges, Ghent, and Antwerp had suffered from attacks and blockade, and the northern commercial centers of Amsterdam, Utrecht, and Leyden had seized the opportunity to take over their trade. The war against Spain had coincided with a great effort to reclaim land from beneath sea level, and the success of both efforts led to a period of economic and cultural expansion known as the Dutch golden age.

In all the provinces, public affairs were dominated by the interests of wealthy city merchants, and the Dutch Republic, as the United Provinces were often called, became the trading center to the world. For centuries, merchants from the Netherlands had been the middlemen between northern Europe and the Mediterranean; in the seventeenth century, Dutch merchants expanded the position to cover North America and India as well. In 1602, the States General chartered the Dutch East India Company, a state-sponsored trading company with a monopoly on the territory from Europe to the Indian Ocean. In 1621, they established the Dutch West India Company for trade with Africa and the Americas. By the end of the Thirty Years' War in 1648, when Spain formally recognized the United Provinces, Amsterdam was the shopping center of a far-flung trading empire. There were over 230 shop signs in the main street, one observer remarked. Visitors could buy rice, indigo, spices, and porcelain from Japan and China, mahogany and sugar from Brazil and the Caribbean, and beaver and otter from North America.

The Dutch themselves believed that their great prosperity was a sign of God's special favor. The majority religion was Calvinist, and every household had its Bible. The story of the Dutch Revolt, especially, was taught to schoolchildren as the victory of the Righteous—the Good Guys, as we might say—against the Wicked. Though Catholics, like members of other religions, were officially allowed freedom of worship, their churches were increasingly turned over to Calvinists, and many Catholic families migrated south to the Spanish Netherlands. Other countries were not convinced that the hand of God was all that was responsible for Dutch trading supremacy, particularly as the East and West India Companies backed up their enterprises with warships. But no one could help being impressed with the sheer wealth of the cities. "All the buildings stand tall," one traveler wrote of the most fashionable street in Amsterdam, "some of them two, others three and four stores high; sometimes their great cellars filled with merchandise. Within, the houses are full of priceless ornaments so that they seem more like royal palaces than the houses of merchants, many of them with splendid marble and alabaster columns, floors inlaid with gold, and the rooms hung with valuable tapestries or gold- or silver-stamped leather. . . . You will also find in these houses valuable household furnishings like paintings and oriental ornaments and decorations so that the value of all these things is truly inestimable."[16]

As the Dutch became known for conspicuous consumption, the most impressive area of that consumption was art: paintings, emblems, woodcuts, and engravings. Even butchers, bakers, blacksmiths, and cobblers bought paintings, wrote one visitor in amazement. In fact, any household with disposable wealth was likely to purchase art to hang in its public rooms, and even doctors and lawyers could become substantial collectors. The result was a thriving bourgeois (urban, or middle class) art market in Holland, which fostered art as memorable as that sponsored by the court patronage of Spain or France.

Rembrandt (1606–1669)

There were thousands of Dutch artists in the seventeenth century, but the man whose art dominated them all was Rembrandt Harmenszoon van Rijn (1606–1669). He was born in the university town of Leyden and, after studying art in Amsterdam, returned to Leyden to set up shop as an artist. Like Velásquez and Rubens, his talent was recognized early by an important and helpful patron, in Rembrandt's case the statesman, scientist, and art collector Constantin Huygens. Through Huygens,

Rembrandt received commissions in Amsterdam, where he spent most of the rest of his life. He was very prolific, and over 2,300 works of art by Rembrandt have survived. Still, there were artists who produced even more: according to one account, the Delft artist Michiel van Miereveld produced more than 10,000 portraits in his sixty-year career.

Rembrandt's contemporaries were especially impressed by his technical innovations. He treated paint as a physical object in its own right and experimented with different textures, sometimes scraping it almost smooth and sometimes piling it on so thick, wrote one observer, that paintings of jewels looked as though they had been chiseled into the canvas. He also made excellent use of the new technique of etching, in which the artist first applied resin to a copper plate, then scratched away the design with a needle. The plate was then placed in acid, which bit away the metal wherever the resin had been removed. The plate was then used to print the design, which could be easily changed or added to. Rembrandt's etchings were in demand from the beginning of his career, with collectors eager to gain each new version of the print as he reworked the design.

Rembrandt's group portraits first established his reputation. Group portraits are difficult to carry off: each individual member of a group has to be portrayed accurately, but if individuals are merely painted side by side, the painting can be very dull. (Class pictures may be good souvenirs for graduating seniors, but they are not great art.) The key Rembrandt found was to position each individual so that he or she seemed to be engaged in a common enterprise. In *The Anatomy Lesson of Doctor Nicholas Tulp* (1632), seven men cluster around a dead body, intently watching the arm being dissected by Dr. Tulp. Each individual is a precise portrait. As in Velásquez's paintings, two of the men look out at the viewer as if to say "Do you see what is happening here?" And the effect, as in Velásquez's *Las Meninas*, is almost that of a candid snapshot of a group caught at the moment of activity. Rembrandt used the same effect in his painting *The Company of Captain Frans Banning Cocq and Lieutenant Willem van Ruytenburch* (1642), better known as *The Night Watch.* He was commissioned to paint a group portrait of the eighteen members of the regiment, but instead of lining them up to paint, he presented them in the act of marching out behind their captain on a crowded city street. The viewer becomes a spectator of the military parade, as, once again, one of the men looks straight out of the painting to make sure the viewer is paying attention to the scene.

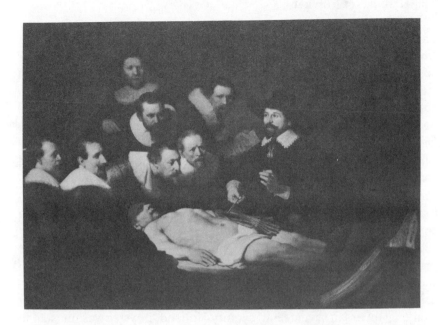

Rembrandt's painting *The Anatomy Lesson of Doctor Nicholas Tulp,* **1632** (Giraudon/Art Resource, NY)

After *The Night Watch*, Rembrandt's reputation declined. A deeply religious man, he was especially attracted to Biblical subjects, which he depicted with great feeling and care. He was unusual in drawing people from the Jewish community in Amsterdam to use as models for scenes from the Old Testament. His interests were not shared by the Dutch public, however, and they began to turn to other artists. Though he earned a great deal of money as an artist, he spent even more of it, especially on art. Eventually he had to declare bankruptcy. His financial affairs affected his personal life. His beloved wife, Saskia, who had been a model for some of his early pictures, had died at the age of thirty. Her will had been a conventional one, but by its terms their son, Titus, would suffer financial loss if Rembrandt remarried. A few years after Saskia's death, Rembrandt's servant, Hendrickje Stoffels, became his lover (as well as his model), but Rembrandt never felt financially secure enough to marry her. In Calvinist Amsterdam, cohabitation without marriage was a serious matter, and Hendrickje was banned for a time from attending church. Despite this, the two lived together as a loving couple until Hendrickje's death in 1663.

The Urban Art Market

The Dutch art market was so competitive that most painters lived and worked in a single city. Franz Hals (1580?–1666) was the most popular portrait painter in the city of Haarlem. His parents were Protestants from Flanders, who immigrated north after the Spanish sack of Antwerp in 1585. Like Rembrandt, Hals was often commissioned to paint group portraits, in which each individual person had to be painted accurately. One group portrait, of an Amsterdam guard company, was never finished, because Hals refused go to Amsterdam to finish it, and the guard company refused to come to Haarlem. Even paintings which do not appear to have been commissioned portraits, such as *The Laughing Cavalier* (1624), were painted with such attention to detail that they appear to be as good a likeness as a photograph.

Judith Leyster (1609–1659) was another Haarlem artist who made her living with portrait-painting. Her own self-portrait, painted when she was only about nineteen, could have been used as a kind of advertisement of her skill to attract commissions. Although there were other women painters in seventeenth century Holland, Leyster was unusual in that her father was not an artist. Instead of joining a family business, she chose to set up her own studio, which she operated independently. In addition to portraits, she, like many other Dutch artists, produced genre paintings, paintings of set scenes that were much in demand. These scenes included children playing, young men gambling or drinking, and musicians playing their instruments. Thousands of scenes of this type were painted by Dutch artists and sold in studios or at fairs.

Leyster married the artist Jan Miense Molenaer in 1636. The couple had five children, and Leyster seems to have been actively involved in running Molenaer's studio. She may have also assisted with his commissions, but the only painting of hers that can be documented after her marriage was a tulip (1643). Tulips can be bred into beautiful and unpredictable variations, and tulip breeding and collecting became a craze in the early seventeenth century. Rich collectors spent huge sums of money for rare bulbs, while ordinary people bought hardier, more common varieties. In the 1630s, speculators moved into the tulip market. Tulip bulbs were dug up in June and planted in the autumn, and it was impossible to predict, until they bloomed, what the flowers would look like. Investors began to buy up bulbs at high prices, hoping to sell them at even higher prices; some speculators mortgaged their houses or spent their life savings to buy up bulbs they thought would make their fortunes. In 1637, the tulip market crashed, and all speculation came to an end. Tulips continued to be bought, sold, and painted, as Leyster's example shows.

In contrast to the incredible productivity of Rembrandt and other Dutch artists stands the art of Johannes Vermeer (1632–1675), who lived and worked in the city of Delft. He was not famous in his own time, and only forty of his paintings are known today. Today they are prized for their exquisite attention to detail, for Vermeer's paintings look more like photographs than any other art of his day. In fact, he used in his painting an early version of a camera, a *camera obscura*, a box with a set of lenses in which images were projected onto a screen. Vermeer was also fascinated with the play of light on textures, and most of his paintings take place in one of two rooms, each lit by beautiful windows. Although he painted genre scenes, he appears to have done so with little attention to popular taste, and we do not know if he sold any of his paintings in his own lifetime.

Despite the high quality of Dutch art, few artists grew rich. When Vermeer died, he owed money to his baker; since his heirs could not pay it, the baker agreed to accept two paintings. It is likely that the baker did so reluctantly, for paintings were commonplace in Delft. Those two paintings have never been identified, but Vermeer's works are now so rare, and so highly prized, that they could have made the baker's descendants millionaires many times over.

Profile: The Story of Don Juan

In addition to Don Quixote and Sancho Panza, Spanish authors contributed another enduring character to European literature, the nobleman Don Juan, the relentless philanderer who makes a conquest of every woman he meets. He makes his first appearance in a play by Tirso de Molina (1580?–1648), entitled *The Trickster of Seville and the Guest of Stone*. Don Juan in this version is an unscrupulous seducer, but he is not a rapist like the nobleman in *Fuenteovejuna*. Instead, he is indeed a trickster, who takes advantage of the fact that marriages in noble Spanish households were arranged for family advantage, not love. "But when you mutually adore," a servant asks his master,

> And neither in your faith miscarry,
> What difficulty is there more—
> What is preventing that you marry?

His master's answer is

> Such weddings are for lackeys, slaves,
> And laundry wenches. . . .

This custom of arranged marriages gives Don Juan his opportunity. He looks for pairs of young lovers who have no chance to marry under this system; then, disguising himself as her sweetheart, he seduces the young lady. He considers himself safe, for the lady would be ruined if the secret came out; or if it does, she can name only her lover, not him. In Molina's play, Don Juan is eventually punished, and all lovers wed to their respective sweethearts.

The story of Don Juan was retold in a play by Molière and in an opera by Wolfgang Amadeus Mozart (1756–1791), to name only two subsequent versions. His character was often depicted with greater subtlety and psychological insight than in *The Trickster of Seville*. But in the following lines, Tirso de Molina succinctly captured the essence of the unscrupulous seducer. Don Juan, on the run, has been saved by a fishing girl, Thisbe. He discusses her seduction—in effect, her ruin—with his servant, Catalinón.

> Catalinón: But surely, Sir, you won't abuse her,
> Who saved your life?
> Don Juan: As a seducer
> You've always known me. Why, then ask me,
> And with my own true nature task me?. . .
> Catalinón: Too well I know you are the scourge
> Of womankind.
> Don Juan: I'm on the the the verge
> Of dying for her. She's so good.
> Catalinón: How generously you repay
> Your entertainment.
> Don Juan: Understood.[17]

Important Dates

1605	Publication of Cervantes's *Don Quixote*
1616	Death of Cervantes
1623	Velásquez becomes court painter to Philip IV
1634	Completion of Buen Retiro; Velásquez paints *Surrender of Breda*

1635	Death of Lope de Vega
1638	Rubens paints *The Horrors of War*
1640	Death of Rubens
1642	Rembrandt paints *The Night Watch*
1656	Velásquez paints *Las Meninas*
1657	Bernini completes colonnade at St. Peter's
1659	Death of Leyster
1660	Death of Velásquez
1665	Death of Philip IV of Spain
1666	Death of Hals
1669	Death of Rembrandt
1675	Death of Vermeer
1681	Death of Calderon
1682	Death of Bernini

Further Reading

Svetlana Alpers, *The Art of Describing: Dutch Art in the Seventeenth Century* (Chicago, 1983)

Svetlana Alpers, *The Making of Rubens* (New Haven, 1995)

Svetlana Alpers, *Rembrandt's Enterprise: The Studio and the Market* (Chicago, 1988)

Jonathan Brown, *Kings and Connoisseurs: Collecting Art in Seventeenth-Century Europe* (Princeton, 1995)

Jonathan Brown, *Velazquez: Painter and Courtier* (New Haven, 1986)

Jonathan Brown and J.H. Elliott, *A Palace for a King: The Buen Retiro and the Court of Philip IV* (New Haven, 1980)

Wayne Franits, *Paragons of Virtue: Women and Domesticity in Seventeenth-Century Dutch Art* (Cambridge, 1995)

Frederick Hammond, *Music and Spectacle in Baroque Rome: Barberini Patronage under Urban VIII* (New Haven, 1994)

Francis Haskell, *Patrons and Painters: Art and Society in Baroque Italy* (New Haven, 1980)

Elizabeth Alice Honig, *Painting and the Market in Early Modern Antwerp* (New Haven, 1998)

Pamela N. Jones, *Federico Borromeo and the Ambrosiana: Art Patronage and Reform in Seventeenth-Century Milan* (Cambridge, 1993)

R.O. Jones, *A Literary History of Spain: The Golden Age; Prose and Poetry, The Sixteenth and Seventeenth Centuries* (London, 1971)

Madlyn Millner Kahr, *Dutch Painting in the Seventeenth Century* (New York, 1978)

Jose Antonio Maravall, *The Culture of the Baroque: Analysis of a Historical Structure* trans. Terry Cochran (Minneapolis, 1986)

Melveena McKendrick, *Theater in Spain, 1490–1700* (Cambridge, 1992)

John Michael Montias, *Vermeer and His Milieu: A Web of Social History* (Princeton, 1989)

Jeffrey M. Muller, *Rubens: The Artist as Collector* (Princeton, 1989)

Christian Norberg-Schulz, *Baroque Architecture* (New York, 1971)

Michael North, *Art and Commerce in the Dutch Golden Age* (New Haven, 1997)

Steven N. Orso, *Velazquez, Los Borrachos, and Painting at the Court of Philip IV* (Cambridge, 1994)

Simon Schama, *The Embarassment of Riches: An Interpretation of Dutch Culture in the Golden Age* (Berkeley, 1988)

Simon Schama, *Rembrandt's Eyes* (New York, 1999)

Peter N. Skrine, *The Baroque: Literature and Culture in Seventeenth Century Europe* (London, 1978)

Seymour Slive, ed., *Frans Hals* (Munich, 1989)

Margaret A. Sullivan, *Bruegel's Peasants: Art and Audience in the Northern Renaissance* (Cambridge, 1994)

Paul Taylor, *Dutch Flower Painting, 1600–1720* (New Haven, 1995)

Susan Verdi Webster, *Art and Ritual in Golden-Age Spain: Sevillian Confraternities and the Processional Sculpture of Holy Week* (Princeton, 1998)

James Welu and Pieter Biesboer, *Judith Leyster: A Dutch Master and Her World* (New Haven, 1993)

Arthur Wheelock, Jr., *Vermeer and the Art of Painting* (New Haven, 1995)

Christopher White, *Rubens and His World* (New York, 1968)

Chapter Nine

Trade, War, and Monarchy in the Seventeenth Century

The Mercantile World

By 1672, Louis XIV was ready for his great enterprise, designed to teach the United Provinces the lesson that no nation could defy the Sun King. He had been preparing ever since his defeat in 1668. He had an even greater army than before, armed with a brand-new weapon, the bayonet, so that his well-trained infantry (foot soldiers) could first fire on command, then charge while their enemy struggled to reload. He had bribed Charles II of Great Britain, who was always in need of money, to avoid an alliance between the British and Dutch, and in fact English warships joined French ones sailing against the Dutch. His ministers had bribed the German and Austrian princes to stay out of the conflict.

Formally, the United Provinces and the French were allies, but to Louis that only meant the Dutch should be punished for their "ingratitude and intolerable vanity" in not submitting to his authority. When the States General of the United Provinces asked the purpose of the military buildup on their border, Louis's only reply was that "he would make such use of his troops as was required by his dignity, for which he owed account to no one." In April, French troops marched north towards the Low Countries, and by June the States General were ready to sue for peace. The peace terms proposed by the French would have required the Dutch to pay heavy fines and turned their country, in effect, into a northern province of France. Each year, they would have had to send a medal to Louis, "on which the engraving would read that they [the Dutch] received their liberty from His Most Christian Majesty."[1]

Revenge for his former humiliation was, all too obviously, on Louis's mind. But there were other considerations for his war with the Dutch, considerations that affected international diplomacy throughout the century. These considerations were based on a cluster of economic ideas now known as mercantilism, though at the time they would have been thought of as part of "reason of state." According to mercantilist ideas, the wealth of a country was based on its resources, such as population, agricultural produce, or gold and silver mines. The more resources the country had, the wealthier its monarch, just as in private life, where the more gold and silver an individual had, the wealthier he was. In this model, the discovery of the silver mines of Peru had added more resources to the crown of Spain, and the Spanish kings had become richer. Colbert's improvements to French manufacturing had added directly to the wealth of the king of France. And according to this model, monarchs should be actively involved in economic activity, licensing trading companies, promoting overseas colonies, and establishing laws protecting their own economic activity at the expense of that of other nations, because all those practices would increase the wealth of their own countries.

Trade, a country's imports and exports, was, according to this model, part of the resources of that country, just like its forests, agricultural produce, or gold and silver mines. Trade was, in fact, thought of as a kind of war, for seventeenth-century economists believed that, just as there was only so much gold and silver in the world, there could be only so much trade. If Spain had Peruvian silver mines, and France did not, then Spain would be richer in silver than France. If France went to war with Spain and conquered Peru, France would own the Spanish silver and thus be wealthier than Spain. But the United Provinces had, over the preceding century, acquired Spanish silver without fighting, simply by trading their manufactured goods: they had thus acquired additional resources, and wealth, without having to go to war for them. Countries like the United Provinces were considered to be "rich" in trade, just as other countries were rich in silver or timber or grain.

The Dutch themselves had made ample use of this idea to promote their own interests: they zealously protected their own commercial routes and trading ports, by force wherever necessary, while calling for "free trade" whenever they wanted to establish trading relations with a port controlled by another country. Conflict with the British over colonies and trading rights led to a series of Anglo-Dutch wars throughout the seventeenth and early eighteenth centuries. In general, seventeenth-century observers believed the Dutch to come off the clear winners in the first phase of these commercial conflicts: "I think the Devil shits Dutch-men," snarled one English observer.[2] This anti-Dutch sentiment was in part responsible for the English warships joining the French off the Dutch coast in 1672. And mercantilist ideas were expressed clearly in the advice given by Colbert to Louis XIV about the advantages of his own Dutch wars: "If the King were to subjugate all the United Provinces to his authority, their commerce would become the commerce of the subjects of His Majesty, and there would be nothing more to ask."[3] Just as Louis believed he could take over Dutch territory and turn it into a French province by marching in his armies, so too he believed he could take over Dutch trade in the same way. The piece of pie owned by the Dutch, so to speak, would then become French pie instead.

Yet world trade is not, in fact, a pie to be carved up, and the Dutch, driven to desperation by Louis's proposed peace terms, continued to fight. The Dutch navy drove off the French and British fleet, as it had done before, and the Dutch opened the dikes and flooded their country-side, their farms, their fine houses filled with artwork and curiosities from around the globe, and the fine French infantry. Internal struggles had brought William III (1650–1702), Prince of Orange, to power as stadtholder, and he took command of the army. He also took command of creating an alliance of European powers against France and Louis, raising fears that Louis was trying to dominate all of Europe. Sweden joined the alliance; so did the Habsburg Emperor Leopold I; so did the king of Spain. Louis tried to keep Charles II and his ministers neutral by increasing their bribes, but Parliament feared French aggression and Catholicism more than Dutch naval supremacy. When William III married Mary (1662–1694), the niece of Charles II and daughter of his brother James, the heir apparent to the British throne, it was considered through-out Europe as a diplomatic coup for the United Provinces. By 1678 peace was concluded on favorable terms to the United Provinces.

Louis XIV was proclaimed "the Great" by his own subjects, but his territorial ambitions had alarmed his neighbors, who continued to watch closely for any further military buildup. In 1685 he took another step that alarmed his Protestant neighbors even more: he revoked the Edict of Nantes, which had protected Calvinist worship within France. Hu-guenots had to convert to Catholicism or leave France. Many chose to leave, and their primary destination was the United Provinces. In mer-cantilist terms, this policy was a mistake, for the human population of a country was also part of its resources, and the Huguenots were particularly active in commerce and manufacturing. France lost, and other countries gained, skilled craftsmen, the wealth of large numbers of families: "enemy nations swelled by the addition of eight or nine thousand seamen," according to one French commentator, "their armies by five or six hundred officers and ten to twelve thousand soldiers far more seasoned than their own."[4] In one stroke, then, Louis had deprived himself of, and provided his neighboring countries with, valuable resources.

Glorious Revolution

In 1685, the year of the Revocation of the Edict of Nantes, Charles II of England died. He left no legitimate sons to inherit the throne, and his brother James inherited as James II (1633–1701). His reign was controversial even before it began, for James was a Catholic, as was his second wife. England had not had a Catholic monarch since the Reformation, when Mary I, a Catholic, had tried to reconvert all of England to Catholicism. Charles II's alliances with Louis XIV had raised fears in many members of Parliament that he was too sympathetic to the Catholic cause, and those fears had grown when Charles had proposed establishing religious tolerance in his realm. Nowadays religious tolerance is considered a virtue in politics, but this was not true in the seventeenth century. French Catholics had cheered when Calvinists were harassed or forced into exile through the revocation of the Edict of Nantes, and British Anglicans were outraged at the suggestion that Catholics and Dissenters (Protestants of other denominations) should enjoy the same privileges as they did. Parliament had responded by refusing to grant money unless the king backed down. In addition, it passed a new law, the Test Act (1673), which stated that anyone holding public office had to belong to the Church of England. This act effectively barred Catholics and Dissenters from any public office until the nineteenth century.

Throughout the 1680s, fear of Catholic influence grew in Parliament, leading to the formation of the first political parties (coalitions formed around opposing political viewpoints). The issue over which political opinion split was James's expected succession. By the law of inheritance that governed succession in Britain, James was next in line to the throne. But by the Reformation policy that stated that the king of England was the head of the Church of England, the king could not be Catholic. Those who supported James as the next king came to be known as the Tories; those who wanted the next king to be Protestant came to be known as Whigs. In 1679, the Whigs introduced a bill to require that the throne pass to the next *Protestant* heir, thus excluding James. Charles II, to protect his brother, dissolved Parliament to ensure that the bill could not pass, but the religious and political tension remained. Rumors spread through London that there was a "popish plot" to massacre Protestants, and several prominent—and innocent—Catholics were arrested and executed. The Whig leaders began to champion Charles's oldest illegitimate son, the duke of Monmouth, as the heir to the throne in James's place. But for the rest of the country, this came very close to treason, and even those who had believed Catholic conspiracy theories were not prepared to support what they viewed as Whig rebellion against the king. Most Englishmen believed that a monarch given by God "is not in our power to change."[5] Monmouth was arrested, convicted, and executed, and his Whig supporters went into hiding.

James II came to the throne, then, in an atmosphere of religious distrust, which he exacerbated by his policies. He called for repeal of the Test Act, thus allowing all religions equal rights, and he followed it up by appointing Catholics to any position he could, in defiance of Parliament's law. As long as his Protestant daughters from his first marriage were next in line to the throne, his opponents might have waited to see what happened. But on June 10, 1688, James's wife gave birth to a son, who thus became the next heir to the throne. Whig leaders opened negotiations with William III, husband of Mary, James's oldest daughter. William had been watching English affairs for some years, anxious to protect his wife's inheritance. He was also anxious that a Catholic monarch in Britain would renew Charles' pro-French policy, a policy that had given Louis considerable advantages for the preceding twenty years. In November, William landed in England, set up camp, and waited to see what would happen. James, too, waited, only to find his support eroding daily. Throughout England, William was welcomed: he "comes only to maintain the Protestant religion," people said; "he will do England no harm." Scotland supported its Stuart kings, but it was not enough to save James's throne for him. He, his wife, and his son fled to France. Parliament, dominated by Whigs, declared his flight an "abdication" and formally invited William and Mary to rule Great Britain together.

This, then, was the Glorious Revolution, "glorious" because it was bloodless, at least in England. It was revolutionary because, for the first time in Britain, ruling monarchs received their legitimacy from Parliament, not from their own hereditary succession. The power of Parliament was emphasized by the law passed in 1689, the Declaration of Rights. It stated that only Parliament had the right to make or unmake laws. All moneys could be raised only by Parliament. Armies could be raised only by Parliament. Parliamentary elections and debates must be free of influence of the crown. Later bills established that a new Parliament must meet every three years and that two independent witnesses were needed for trials of treason. The result was a true "constitutional monarchy," with the king bound by the laws of the nation. It was not a democracy, for the laws were still interpreted by the great nobles in the House of Lords and the wealthy landowners who were elected to the Commons. Monarchs continued to have substantial influence on Parliament debates and elections through the nineteenth century.

William continued to govern his own lands on the European continent, and he took the precaution of making sure that Parliament could not meet when he was out of the country. He was, in fact, often out of the country, for he had acquired the British throne as part of his lifelong fight against Louis XIV. Louis at first refused to accept William and Mary as legitimate rulers and supported an attempted invasion by James II. From 1688 to 1697, France was at war with a Grand Alliance of the Dutch, British, and Holy Roman Empire. One result of the inconclusive peace that followed was that Louis agreed to accept William and Mary as rulers in Britain. Another, far more important, was that it confirmed the superiority of British sea power, for the British navy had been a crucial advantage to the anti-French allies. From this point on, Britannia began to rule the waves.

John Locke (1632–1704)

In February, 1689, as William and Mary announced their acceptance of the throne, the political writer, former government servant, and Whig propagandist John Locke returned to London from Holland. Educated as a physician, he had become the friend, associate, and political advisor of the first earl of Shaftesbury, a Whig leader. Shaftesbury was one of the most influential politicians in Britain, and Locke's position was much like that of a congressional staff member. Locke's job was to keep abreast of political matters, to investigate and write up current issues of interest to the earl, to find arguments and compose treatises to support Whig positions, and to help Shaftesbury influence "public opinion," that is, Parliamentary opinion. Fiercely suspicious of "popery," he and his associates had accused prominent Catholics of conspiracy in the "popish plot" and had seen them executed, on little evidence. In 1683, the Tories had their revenge, as many Whigs were indicted and executed for their role in the duke of Monmouth's rebellion. Shaftesbury and Locke fled to Holland, where Shaftesbury died and Locke remained, watching developments in England, in particular the negotiations with William III. With the success of the Glorious Revolution, Locke was one of a group of Whig exiles who returned home to reap the political rewards of victorious political party members.

One of Locke's first acts on his return was to arrange the publication of *Two Treatises on Government* (1689), originally composed in the 1680s. These treatises have given international significance to what would otherwise be just another dynastic struggle. They were formulated in response to Tory political philosopher Robert Filmer. Filmer had claimed that the king took authority over subjects from the dominion God had given Adam over all the earth. On this basis, all members of a family were subservient to the father and owed him full obedience, or else they were disobeying God's original settlement. That is the legal justification for the father's authority over his wife and children. For the same reason, all subjects should be obedient to the king. Kings allowed subjects to live peacefully and acquire property, but subjects still owed life, and liberty, and property, to kings, as children owed it to fathers.

This was a convincing argument because it supported all kinds of existing authority: kings, magistrates, and fathers. To counter it, John Locke responded by ridiculing the idea that kings actually were descended from Adam. How was the lineage of this inheritance to be traced? he asked. "I go on to ask whether in the inheriting of his paternal power, this supreme fatherhood, the grandson by a daughter hath a right before a nephew by a brother? Whether the grandson by the eldest son, being an infant, before the younger son, a man and able? Whether the daughter before the uncle? . . .Whether the elder son by a concubine, before a younger son by a wife?"[6]

Even more important, Locke presented an alternative starting point to political systems, the state of nature. Imagine, he said, a world in the state of nature, with no governments, though there are people. That would be "a state of perfect freedom to order their actions and dispose of their possessions and persons as they think fit." In that state, there would also be perfect equality, for each individual would have the same perfect freedom. Together with the state of nature, though, would be a "law of nature," "and reason, which is that law, teaches all mankind who will but consult it that, being all equal and independent, no one ought to harm another in his life, health, liberty, or possessions."[7] In this state of nature, two people might come together and decide to make a compact, an agreement, to join forces for defense, or to get food, or to punish wrongdoers. When each individual member of the group agrees to the compact, when each agrees to give up his individual privilege of protecting his life, liberty, and property to the rule of the law, when each agrees to accept the arbitration of the community, then the group forms a true civil society. "And thus . . . the community comes to be umpire by settled standing rules . . . the same to all parties."[8] That, said Locke, is the true origin of governments.

Who, in modern societies, acted as that "umpire"? The law-making branch of government, was Locke's decisive answer, for "it is in their legislative that the members of a commonwealth are united and combined together into one coherent living body. This is the soul that gives form, life, and unity to the commonwealth." By the "legislative," Locke clearly means a body like the House of Commons, and when any other person "shall take upon them to make laws, whom the people have not appointed so to do, they make laws without authority, which the people are not therefore bound to obey."[9] In the inflammatory political climate of the 1680s, the "any other person" clearly included the King. What if a king, or any other person without legitimate authority, should go ahead and attempt to pass laws without the consent of the people? In that case, the authority which he held from the community "is forfeited," and legitimate authority "reverts to the society, and the people have a right to act as supreme and continue the legislative in themselves, or erect a new form, or under the old form place it in new hands, as they think good."[10]

When they were written, the *Two Treatises* were intended as justification for Monmouth's rebellion, for what many people viewed as treason. Locke was therefore prudent to leave for Holland when he did. His treatises circulated in manuscript, though. When they were published in 1689, they had the express permission of William III, since they provided an excellent political argument for his taking over the throne from James II. Locke was a prudent man, though, and recognized that the *Two Treatises* could be considered as justification for treason. They were published anonymously, and Locke refused ever to admit that he had written them. The Glorious Revolution, however, represented, for many, the triumph of Locke's views. Locke became an elder statesman, influential in political life and much sought-after by the younger generation.

Imperial Sweden

When Gustavus Adolphus, king of Sweden, launched his country into the Thirty Years' War in 1631, he knew that he confronted a problem of succession. He had a daughter, Christina, then age seven, and his wife seemed unlikely to bear another child. That made Christina the heir to the throne, but could a woman really rule the great power Sweden had become? Gustavus entrusted the education of his daughter to his chief minister, Axel Oxenstierna (1583–1654). Christina's later praise of him shows the qualities she admired most in a statesman: "He was remarkably efficient and possessed a thorough knowledge of international politics. He was aware of the strengths and weaknesses of all European countries."[11] When Gustavus Adolphus died unexpectedly in battle, just two years after he launched his German campaign, Oxenstierna became regent and de facto ruler of Sweden until Christina reached maturity. He kept Swedish policy firmly focused on achieving imperialist expansion throughout the ups and downs of the Thirty Years' War. Christina did eventually ascend the throne in 1644, but the government of imperial Sweden proved a more troublesome issue than even Gustavus Adolphus and Oxenstierna had supposed.

In many respects Queen Christina (1625–1689) seemed the perfect type of ruler for an age of absolutist monarchs. She was highhanded and arrogant, convinced that God had created her for greatness. She was also a consummate politician. At the time she inherited the throne, Sweden controlled the Baltic, ruling Finland and Estonia on the eastern coast of the sea, Livonia, western Pomerania, Bremen-Verden, and Wismar on the southern coast, and two Norwegian provinces. Christina devoted much of her reign to giving her court the kind of splendor she felt suitable for such an empire, encouraging philosophers, such as Descartes, and commissioning the works of artists and musicians.

With her empire, however, Christina inherited serious problems. Sweden had always been sparsely populated, and the victories of the Thirty Years' War had drained the country of peasant manpower. Some villages lost as many as 80 percent of their inhabitants. Throughout the Swedish countryside, village women found themselves doing the work of men; while this increased their power and authority, at least temporarily, it also was a drain on scarce resources. Like many rulers, Christina was unconcerned about changes in village life and the hardships they entailed for her subjects. But her treasury, too, had been depleted of

Portrait of Queen Christina on horseback by Sebastian Bourdon (Scala/ Art Resource, NY)

scarce resources, and so she decided to sell large tracts of land tradition-ally held by the crown to great nobles in order to raise money. The move benefited the royal treasury; moreover, awarding land to nobles was a time-honored way of rewarding their faithful military service and sup-port. But many of the nobles had been influenced by the social organi-zation of land ownership they had seen in Sweden's eastern possessions, with serfs instead of free peasants. The Swedish peasants living on those lands therefore found themselves with new masters, and new taxes, duties, and restrictions, so that their tenure looked less and less like freehold and more and more like serfdom.

The non-noble estates represented in the Swedish Diet, the traditional representative body, pleaded with the queen to take action to curb the power of the nobles. Christina pretended to consider, but for her own ends. Despite her conviction that God had created her for great things, she no longer wished to rule Sweden. She believed herself incapable of marrying and bearing children to ensure a successor, the political obligation of every queen. Moreover, she was disgusted with the strict Lutheran faith in which she had been raised and began to be attracted by the scientifically minded Catholicism current in the mid-seventeenth century, in which any question of science and religion could be discussed, as long as it was not expressly forbidden. The religious conversion of a Protestant queen—especially the daughter of Gustavus Adolphus—was an international affair, and Christina had to keep her interests a secret from her own subjects. Secretly, she sought the support of the kings of France and Spain; secretly, she received the Jesuit emissaries of the pope. No doubt the Catholic powers hoped that, through her, they might convert all of Sweden. Christina's own goal was different: abdication of the throne for life in a freer, more congenial environment.

In this she succeeded. By playing off the non-noble estates against the nobles, she gained the support of the Diet, first, for naming her cousin, Karl Jasper, as her heir presumptive if she died without children. In that way she ensured the succession. It took more time to convince her ministers of the need for her to abdicate, but in 1654, she succeeded in that as well. Her cousin took over as King Karl X Gustav (1621–1660). Christina left Sweden to spend much of the rest of her life in luxurious exile in Rome, converting to Catholicism en route and becoming an international cause célèbre.

Christina's departure from Sweden did nothing to resolve the plight of the peasants, and though King Karl X Gustav was an able statesman and general, he continued the policy of selling royal lands to raise money for the crown and reward nobles for military victory. It was his son, King Karl XI (1655–1697), who finally ended the process. The incessant warfare necessary to maintain the Swedish empire had drained the treasury so much that in 1680 the young king called the Diet to find some way to increase revenue. The non-noble Estates once again looked to the Crown for assistance, calling for an absolute monarchy to repossess the state lands and restore freedom to the peasantry. This time the monarch listened, spending the rest of his reign taking back the territories and promising peasants protection against serfdom as long as they paid taxes and served faithfully in his wars. By the end of the century, Sweden's population grew, its trade expanded, and its army was rebuilt. These results were seen as the triumph of absolutist rule. The Swedish royal architect took careful notes on the architectural innovations at Versailles as he designed the new, splendid Royal Palace in Stockholm. The Diet, for its part, declared its gratitude to Karl XI, "an absolute sovereign king, whose commands are binding on all, and who is responsible to no one on earth for his actions."[12]

Leopold I of Austria (1640–1705)

As other monarchs jockeyed for position in the north and west of Europe, Leopold I, Holy Roman Emperor since 1657, consolidated the position of the Habsburgs in central Europe. The Thirty Years' War had produced disease and depopulation, and heavy taxation had led to economic depression, but after the Treaties of Westphalia in 1648, the area made a rapid comeback. The traditional Habsburg territories of Austria and Bohemia were rich agriculturally; there were important iron and silver mines; Silesia was a major center for linen manufacture. Counter-Reformation political and religious policy had driven out Protestants, but the Catholic noble families who had benefited from this policy were prepared to support Habsburg rule. Leopold I himself was a mild-mannered, courteous ruler whose great passion was music. He did not make any great innovations in government. His own lands, including many different peoples and governmental systems, were too diverse for him to attempt to create strong central authority like Louis XIV in France or Karl XI in Sweden. Instead, he performed the traditional balancing act of Habsburg rulers, holding together extensive territories that had little in common with each other except being ruled by Habsburgs.

By default, Leopold had to assume the role of senior partner in the Habsburg dynasty. Spain was also ruled by a Habsburg, but in the late seventeenth century the glory years of Spain had passed and it entered a period of decline. The decline was most notable at the top. In 1665, at the age of five, Charles II became king of Spain. Charles was both physically and mentally handicapped. He was constantly ill, so the courts of

Europe spent much effort speculating on when he would finally die. His physical handicaps made it impossible for him to produce any heirs, so the question of when he would die went hand in hand with the question of who would be his successor. As it happened, Charles defied the odds and lived until the age of forty, without ever clarifying his commitment to his Austrian cousin.

Leopold's enemies, too, were the traditional ones of Habsburg rulers: the Ottoman sultan in Constantinople and the king of France. The kingdom of Hungary was claimed by both Habsburg and the sultan, and the fiercely independent Magyar nobles who governed their estates there had learned to play the two against each other to their own advantage. The major cattle drives from the Danube to Vienna made Hungary an important resource, just as cattle drives were to be much later in the American West. After two decades of skirmishes between Habsburg and Turkish armies, the Turks invaded Austria and besieged Vienna in 1683. They were narrowly defeated, and Leopold's armies followed up their victory with the rapid occupation of all of Hungary. The defeat of the Turks, however, did not mean that all the Hungarian nobles were won over to Leopold's government. Many of them were Protestant, and though Leopold did not prohibit their religion, he did favor Catholics at every opportunity. The result was that Hungary remained a center of "unrest and revolution"[13] against Habsburg authority for the next century.

Leopold's victory over the Turks was celebrated throughout Europe as a victory of Christians over infidels, but he himself considered his most dangerous enemy to be His Most Christian Majesty, Louis XIV. Throughout most of their long lives, he and Louis fought over their expected inheritance of Spanish Habsburg territory. Leopold was forced to give up the territories of Alsace and Lorraine, on the Rhine, to French control in 1673, and from then on Leopold joined forces with William III of Orange in his efforts to contain France. When, in 1700, the king of Spain died, Louis XIV claimed the throne for his grandson, Philip V, while Leopold claimed it for the Habsburgs. All of Europe rallied against the specter of France ruling both sides of the Pyrenees, commanding the seacoast from the southern Netherlands to Coruña. William III once again marshaled the United Provinces and Great Britain, while Leopold called on the Holy Roman Empire. The resulting war, known as the War of the Spanish Succession, was not fully settled until 1714. According to the peace treaty, the Peace of Utrecht, Philip V was accepted as the king of Spain, but he was barred from inheriting the throne of France. France and Spain would remain separate kingdoms. Great Britain was the big winner in the negotiations, primarily because of its colonial acquisitions. The Austrian Habsburgs received Spanish territories in the Netherlands and Italy. Future Habsburgs would once again face the balancing act of uniting diverse cultures under their authority.

Brandenburg-Prussia

Northern and northeastern Europe had always been a war-prone region. When Sweden entered the Thirty Years' War, the bellicose tendencies of the whole region became more central to the diplomatic affairs of western and southern Europe as well. But the warlike tendency persisted. One previously obscure territory was forged by the continuing wars into the main point of connection between the northeast and the rest of Europe: Brandenburg-Prussia.

The state of Brandenburg-Prussia rose out of the ashes of the Peace of Westphalia. Elector Frederick William (1620–1688) came to power in 1640, but most of his scattered lands were devastated by war. He decided to use the resources remaining to him to build up his army, both to enhance his authority at home and to act as an ally for the big powers. The strength of his army came to be of paramount importance to Frederick William and his successors. In 1653, the Diet of Brandenburg, a representative body much like the English House of Commons, met and demanded a greater role in government. It was the last time, for Frederick William, unlike Charles II, had the independent military force necessary to sustain his resolve. He extracted a concession from the Diet: the right to collect taxes under his own authority. When war broke out between Sweden and Poland again in 1655, he used that concession to build an especially strong army. When the war ended in 1660, instead of demobilizing the army, as was traditional in earlier decades, he insisted on keeping it at near full strength. Prussia now had a "standing army," ready for use whenever Frederick William wanted it and with a steady source of revenue to keep in going.

Frederick William was able to achieve centralized power by making an alliance with his nobles. The highest positions in government and army were reserved for the most important nobles, thus buying their support. Nobles were also given the privilege to govern their estates however they wished, and neither non-noble landowners, professionals, or merchants had political power. More restrictive labor practices called a "second serfdom" were imposed on the peasants. In Prussia, especially, the nobles, called *Junkers*, used the reimposition of serfdom and their dominant political position to consolidate their holdings into vast estates. In Brandenburg-Prussia, the saying went, "Rulers ruled; aristocrats gave orders, burghers worked, peasants toiled." Frederick William was so successful in reviving central authority that he was given the nickname "the Great Elector."

This cluster of policies was continued by Frederick William's son, Frederick I (1657–1713). He aided Emperor Leopold I in his fight against France in the War of the Spanish Succession and was rewarded with the title of "King" instead of "Elector" in 1701. He was one of the major beneficiaries of the decline of Swedish power in the Baltic. Like many other seventeenth-century monarchs, he chose one city, Berlin, to build up as a cultural center to reflect the glory of his court, even founding an Academy of Sciences. He also took advantage of the Revocation of the Edict of Nantes, providing refuge for the exiled Huguenots and the skills they brought with them.

Still, the foundation of the Prussian state was the army. When King Frederick William I (1688–1740) inherited the throne, the still obscure state of Brandenburg-Prussia had one of the most powerful armies in the world. He pursued the goal of building the army up still more with a passion that bordered on fanaticism. The greatest present another prince could give him was a new recruit for his special regiment of soldiers more than six feet tall. He so loved drill and discipline that he earned the nickname the "Soldier King." The army grew from 40,000 to 83,000 during his reign. Other places, the saying went, were countries with an army; Brandenburg-Prussia was an army with a country. In fact, Frederick William loved his army so much that he refused to endanger it with combat during the entire span of his reign.

Peter the Great of Russia (1672–1725)

Russia, lying on the outskirts of Europe, was ruled by the Romanov family and had a long history of palace intrigue and turmoil. It was characterized by a powerful nobility, with a powerful church as well, Eastern Orthodox, whose patriarch had the status of a lord in his own right and was thus largely independent of the czar. Traditionally isolated from the rest of Europe, it was also isolationist, suspicious of "German"—as the Russians called all other Europeans—innovations.

Peter I Romanov, known as "the Great," changed all that, bringing Russia into the greater European orbit. He inherited a kingdom that was unstable at best, prone to palace intrigue. His early interests were in military affairs, and he personally trained a regiment of crack troops. They proved valuable allies in the faction-ridden palace. Peter himself began as a "junior" czar in a joint czardom between his older brother, Ivan, and his sister, Sophia, but he was ultimately able to wrest power for himself, and to keep it. Traditionally, Russian rulers had looked east, and Peter's reign began with an alliance with Leopold I against the Turks. But Peter himself was fascinated by western ways, which he was convinced were the way to increase Russia's power. He went on a tour of Europe in 1697, ostensibly in disguise but with a large retinue which betrayed his presence. It was impossible to hide the fact that the Russian czar was visiting, wrote one observer: "the rumor is so widespread that people run after every Muscovite thinking that it's His Majesty."[14] He asked questions everywhere and studied all that he saw, especially army and navy administration. Peter was, in fact, "too interested in foreign countries for anyone to mention the possibility of his returning home," but in 1698 he did have to return to Russia to put down an uprising. He did so in brutal fashion. At that point, he took control of the country himself, determined, like his idol Louis XIV, to rule without a chief minister or even an advisor.

Peter's attempt to drag Russia into the modern, European world began symbolically, by his personally shaving off the beards of Russian nobles to make them conform to the fashion current in the west. More concretely, he completely reorganized the machinery of government. Russia, like many countries, had nobles who still ruled their family territories like feudal estates, dispensing justice and maintaining private armies. Peter, copying Swedish models, set up an elaborate, unified hierarchy of authority. Each province had a governor, who reported to one of eleven administrators, who in turn reported to the czar and his ministers in the capital. Any nobleman who wished to retain his status had to have a position within the czar's government or risk his displeasure.

Naturally, many nobles resisted, but Peter joined this reform with another, the subjection of his peasantry to new, harsher controls. Like many countries, seventeenth-century Russia had variations among the peasantry, from prosperous landowners to landless laborers. Peter passed new legislation which reduced all peasants to the same level. They were subject to a new tax, to military conscription, and to forced public work, and forbidden to leave the estates on which they were born. Effectively, Peter reversed the historical trends of the preceding 400 years by making free peasants into serfs, subordinate to their lord's authority. Thus Peter compensated his nobles for their loss of autonomy—their capitulation to his absolute rule—by giving them almost absolute power over their tenants, the peasantry.

Peter also emulated the military aspirations of his hero. His ambition was to make Russia a Great Power by replacing Sweden as the military power in the northeast. He saw his chance in 1697, when Karl XI of Sweden died, leaving a fifteen-year-old son, Karl XII (1682–1718), to inherit the throne. A young ruler was often an easy target for hostile neighbors, and the kings of Poland and Denmark, as well as Karl XII's own nobility, felt the time had come to make inroads on the power of the Swedish crown. But Karl showed himself a brilliant military leader. Peter launched the Great Northern War against Sweden in 1700, but his army of 40,000 was soundly defeated by Karl's 8000 men. For the moment, a Swedish ruler was still the "Terror of the North."

Peter's defeat led him to pour money and discipline into his army, rebuilding it from the bottom up on new, modern lines. His foreign and domestic policy overlapped in the founding of St. Petersburg in 1703, on the gulf of Finland. Technically on Swedish territory, it was a mark of his self-confidence that he began building. It was also a mark of his ambition, for St. Petersburg was located on a swamp, its harbor frozen in seven months of the year. Thousands of peasants, working by conscription, perished in building it. But Peter was determined that it should be another Versailles, in both its brilliance and its strategy, for he compelled his nobles to build their own houses and live there, rather than on their own estates. Russian Academies of Sciences and of the Arts were additional French imitations.

In 1707 Karl XII reacted to Peter's challenge by sending another army. He had been fighting for one after another of Sweden's possessions for seven years, and he and his troops were exhausted. He met the Russians in Poltava in 1709, and this time his army was defeated. Though the Great Northern War between Russia and Sweden officially continued until 1721, the Swedes never again had the upper hand in the conflict. Karl XII died while fighting in Norway. When Sweden finally agreed to a peace treaty, it lost most of the rest of its possessions in the eastern Baltic. Though the loss brought a decline in international prestige, the ensuing peace led to a period of internal economic growth and domestic

Europe in 1713–1714 (Copyright: Hammond World Atlas Corporation, NJ, Lic. No. 12504)

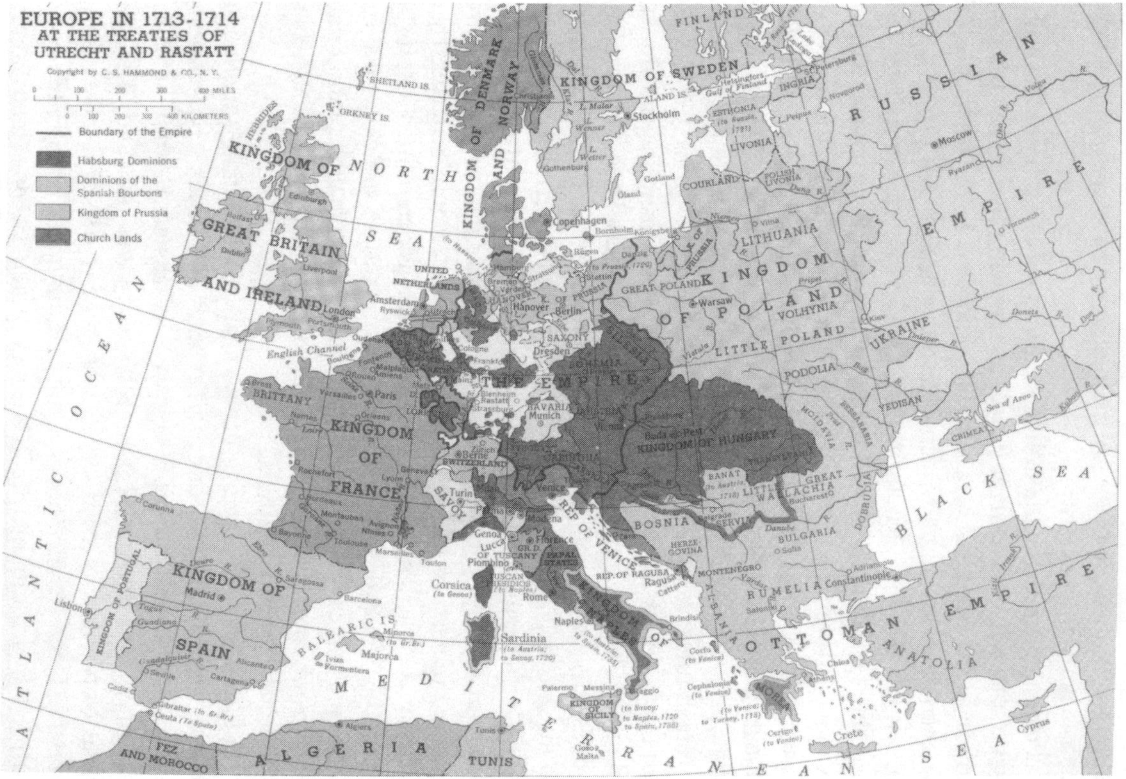

EUROPE IN 1713-1714
AT THE TREATIES OF
UTRECHT AND RASTATT
Copyright by C. S. HAMMOND & CO., N. Y.
Boundary of the Empire
Habsburg Dominions
Dominions of the Spanish Bourbons
Kingdom of Prussia
Church Lands
KINGDOM OF GREAT BRITAIN AND IRELAND
NORTH SEA
KINGDOM OF DENMARK AND NORWAY
KINGDOM OF SWEDEN
FINLAND
RUSSIAN EMPIRE
KINGDOM OF POLAND
LITHUANIA
UNITED NETHERLANDS
THE EMPIRE
KINGDOM OF FRANCE
KINGDOM OF HUNGARY
KINGDOM OF SPAIN
KINGDOM OF PORTUGAL
OTTOMAN EMPIRE
BLACK SEA
MEDITERRANEAN SEA
ATLANTIC OCEAN
ALGERIA
TUNIS
FEZ AND MOROCCO

tranquility. In the eighteenth century, Sweden was more influential for her men of science, like the botanist Carl Linnaeus (1707–1778) and the astronomer Anders Celsius (1701–1744), than for her kings.

By 1721, then, Peter had succeeded in his goal. He had wrested the Gulf of Finland from Sweden together with most of its Baltic possessions. By doing so, he had successfully challenged its supremacy in northern Europe. Russia had replaced Sweden as the great northern power to be reckoned with and courted. On Peter's death, many of his internal reforms were undone, but the position of Russia as a Great Power was assured.

Profile: The Siege of Vienna

In 1683, as Leopold I was enmeshed in warfare against Hungary in the east and France in the west, the Turkish army under the grand vizier Kara Mustafa left Adrianople and camped around Belgrade. The core of the force was 4000 *janissaries*, crack troops, but troops from allies and dependents brought the number up to 100,000. They quickly made their way down the Danube to the frontiers of Habsburg possessions in Hungary. Austrian observers looked on in dismay: there was little, they knew, that could slow the Turks in the rapid movement towards Vienna. Much, indeed, had already been done to speed their way. Louis XIV's ministers had done all that was diplomatically possible to further the Turkish cause against the Holy Roman Empire. France had been paying subsidies to support a rebellion in Hungary and additional subsidies to keep the king of Poland, John III Sobieski and his French wife, neutral. Assurances had been given to the sultan that France would keep Leopold I busy in the west if the Turks wished to attack in the east. Now it was up to Kara Mustafa to invade, and for Leopold and his allies to defend, Austria—if they could.

As the Turks grew closer, panic spread in Vienna. Leopold and his court left the city. Although he was criticized for this, it was the only way to retain his freedom of action. Great nobles and foreign ambassadors hastily packed their households and fled as well. Other residents tried to leave the city at the same time, while peasants from the surrounding countryside scrambled to enter, for the protection of the city walls. Over the next week, as Vienna awaited the onslaught, the military government took control and restored order. The imperial army withdrew north of the Danube to assemble the relief force. The Turks would come, everyone knew, and they would besiege Vienna. Everything depended on their being held off until reinforcements could arrive.

On July 16, 1683, the Turks surrounded the city. The ensuing siege was savage, with atrocities on both sides. Kara Mustafa used captives taken on the march through Hungary to dig trenches and construct defenses; then he deliberately ordered them massacred in full view of the Viennese defenders. The imperial soldiers responded by impaling the heads of captured Turks and flaying them alive. Dysentery spread through both armies as sanitation worsened, and the summer heat added to the stench of decomposing bodies. By the beginning of September, the numbers of casualties on the Turkish side had grown alarmingly, but so had the casualties in Vienna, where only a third of the imperial army was in a position to fight. The commander sent off distress rockets from the roof of St. Stephen's Cathedral in Vienna. On the night of September 7, the distress signals were answered from the surrounding hills.

Leopold, too, had marshaled his diplomats. Several of the German states sent troops, so that the imperial army could marshal nearly 50,000 men; and John Sobieski of Poland, despite the French subsidy, personally led another 20,000. Kara Mustafa had done little to protect his rear, and he was completely overwhelmed by the confronting forces. The final battle for Vienna began early in the morning of September 12, and was over by sunset, with a resounding victory against the Turks. Kara Mustafa fled and was later ceremonially strangled by representatives of the sultan for his failure. Vienna was in shambles, and Leopold wept at the sight of his capital city in ruins, filled with rubble and unburied corpses. But he and his successors rebuilt it as a glorious testimony to the great victory that marked the end of the Ottoman threat to central Europe.

Important Dates

1640	Frederick William, the Great Elector, becomes ruler of Brandenburg-Prussia
1644	Christina becomes queen of Sweden
1654	Death of Oxenstierna; abdication of Christina of Sweden
1657	Leopold I becomes Holy Roman Emperor
1665	Charles II becomes king of Spain
1672–1678	Dutch War
1673	Test Act in England

1679	"Popish plot" in England
1682	Peter the Great becomes czar of Russia
1683	Turkish seige of Vienna
1685	Revocation of Edict of Nantes; death of Charles II of England
1688	Glorious Revolution in England; death of Frederick William, the Great Elector of Brandenburg-Prussia; Frederick I becomes ruler of Brandenburg-Prussia
1688–1697	War of the League of Augsburg
1689	Publication of Locke's *Two Treatises on Government*
1697	Karl XII becomes king of Sweden; Peter the Great tours Europe
1700	Death of Charles II of Spain
1700–1714	War of the Spanish Succession
1701	Prussia elevated to kingdom
1703	Founding of St. Petersburg
1709	Battle of Poltava; Russians rout Swedes under Karl XII
1713	Death of Frederick I of Prussia; Frederick William I becomes king of Prussia
1715	Death of Louis XIV
1718	Death of Karl XII of Sweden

Further Reading

Richard Ashcraft, *Revolutionary Politics and Locke's Two Treatises of Government* (Princeton, 1986)

Stephen B. Baxter, *William III and the Defense of European Liberty, 1650–1702* (New York, 1966)

Jeremy Black, *The Rise of the European Powers, 1679–1793* (London, 1990)

J.C.D. Clark, *English Society, 1688–1832: Ideology, Social Structure, and Political Practice during the Ancien Régime* (Cambridge, 1982)

Tony Claydon, *William III and the Godly Revolution* (Cambridge, 1995)

Maurice Cranston, *John Locke: A Biography* (London, 1968)

R.J.W. Evans, *The Making of the Habsburg Monarchy, 1550–1700* (Oxford, 1979)

Robert I. Frost, *After the Deluge: Poland-Lithuania and the Second Northern War 1655–1660* (Cambridge, 1993)

Paul Halliday, *Dismembering the Body Politic: Partisan Politics in England's Towns 1650–1730* (Cambridge, 1998)

Ian Harris, *The Mind of John Locke: A Study of Political Theory in Its Intellectual Setting* (Cambridge, 1998)

Geoffrey Holmes, *Politics, Religion, and Society in England, 1689–1742* (Roncevert, WV, 1987)

Henry Horwitz, *Parliament, Policy, and Politics in the Reign of William III* (Manchester, 1977)

Lindsey Hughes, *Russia in the Age of Peter the Great* (New Haven, 1998)

Charles Ingrao, *The Habsburg Monarchy 1618–1815* (Cambridge, 1994)

J.R. Jones, *Country and Court: England 1658–1714* (London, 1978)

Vasili Klyuchevsky, *Peter the Great*, trans. Liliana Archibald (New York, 1961)

Mark Knights, *Politics and Opinion in Crisis, 1678–1681* (Cambridge, 1994)

John Marshall, *John Locke: Resistance, Religion and Responsibility* (Cambridge, 1994)

Derek McKay, *Prince Eugene of Savoy* (London, 1977)

Derek McKay and H.M. Scott, *The Rise of the Great Powers, 1648–1815* (London, 1983)

Paul Kleber Monod, *Jacobitism and the English People, 1688–1788* (Cambridge, 1989)

Steven C.A. Pincus, *Protestantism and Patriotism: Ideologies and the Making of English Foreign Policy, 1650–1668* (Cambridge, 1996)

J.L. Price, *The Dutch Republic in the Seventeenth Century* (New York, 1999)

Herbert H. Rowen, *John De Witt, Grand Pensionary of Holland: 1625–1672* (Princeton, 1978)

Herbert H. Rowen, *The Princes of Orange: The Stadholders in the Dutch Republic* (Cambridge, 1988)

Paul Seaward, *The Cavalier Parliament and the Reconstruction of the Old Regime, 1661–1667* (Cambridge, 1989)

Paul Sonnino, *Louis XIV and the Origins of the Dutch War* (Cambridge, 1988)

W.A. Speck, *Reluctant Revolutionaries: Englishmen and the Revolution of 1688* (Oxford, 1988)

John P. Spielman, *Leopold I of Austria* (New Brunswick, NJ, 1977)

Sven Stolpe, *Christina of Sweden* (New York, 1966)

Geoffrey Symcox, *Victor Amadeus II: Absolutism in the Savoyard State, 1675–1730* (Berkeley, 1983)

A.F. Upton, *Charles XI and Swedish Absolutism* (Cambridge, 1998)

Peter H. Wilson, *War, State and Society in Wurttemberg, 1677–1793* (Cambridge, 1995)

Melinda S. Zook, *Radical Whigs and Conspiratorial Politics in Late Stuart England* (State College, PA, 1999)

Chapter Ten

Europe Overseas

The wars of Louis XIV certainly merit the title "world wars." They were fought not only across the expanse of Europe, but in the European kingdoms' colonies located in the Americas and Asia as well. Beginning around 1600, the relationship between Europe and its overseas colonies underwent a fundamental change. Before that date, Europeans were primarily engaged in "discovery" and exploration. European navigators for the first time set foot on the shores of North and South America, the East Coast of Africa, the Philippines, and Indonesia during the sixteenth century. The only two countries to establish significant settlements overseas were Spain and Portugal, who, according to the Treaty of Tordesillas of 1494, were to divide world trade between them, with Spain getting the Americas and Portugal getting Africa, the Indian Ocean, and a small sliver of South America in Brazil.

By the end of the sixteenth century, small groups of Spaniards, led by *conquistadores*, managed to overthrow the two most powerful empires on the American continents and establish nominal control over most of the Caribbean, Central, and South America. New, partly Spanish, partly indigenous cultures began to emerge in the Spanish colonies. So, before 1600, "European colonization" could, more properly, be called Spanish colonization. The vast sums that poured in from the discovery of gold and silver in Mexico and Bolivia all technically belonged to Spain, though intrepid smugglers from other countries managed to skim small quantities off the top.

By the early seventeenth century, the easy money from gold and silver was ending. At the same time, European rulers tried to find ways to circumvent the Spanish and Portuguese monopolies on New World goods. A new wave of self-conscious settlement overseas began.

The intensity and variety of colonial rivalry accelerated because of the idea of mercantilism.

The Columbian Exchange

The first hundred years of European "discovery" of the Americas unleashed an unprecedented (at least for historic times) ecological transformation. European species were brought to the Americas—sometimes deliberately in order to recreate European lifestyles overseas, sometimes accidentally because of stowaways on board European ships. At the same time, curious Europeans gathered American products and brought them back to Europe to try out on their own soil. This two-way ecological transfer is known as the "Columbian exchange."

The most dramatic and controversial aspect of the Columbian exchange is the "exchange" of diseases. The native populations of the Americas were the clear losers in this exchange. Indians (we use the term Europeans gave to native Americans because the natives had no such generic term themselves and began to need such a term only when they confronted Europeans and Africans) had no immunity to several endemic European diseases, such as measles, influenza, and smallpox. When the diseases struck, they had a devastating impact. The full magnitude of the tragedy remains disputed—it depends on how one estimates the size of precontact populations, how one counts the offspring of Europeans and Indians (usually referred to as *mestizos*), and whether one views the spread of disease as primarily accidental or part of a conscious strategy by Europeans to drive the Indian population away. But one cannot dispute that the practical effect was a dramatic "ethnic cleansing." The first peoples to contact Europeans, the Tainos and Arawaks, were effectively extinct by 1540. The population of Mexico dropped from an estimated 25 million in 1519 to under 2 million by 1580. Thus, vast stretches of the mainland that had been moderately populated before contact were now deserted. Europeans were well aware that it was primarily disease that caused this depopulation. One English observer of a smallpox epidemic among the Algonquin in the 1630s noted, "Whole towns of them were swept away, in some not so much as one soul escaping Destruction."[1]

For the first century of contact, the biological balance of the Columbian exchange was almost entirely in the direction from Europe to the Americas. Wherever Europeans went, they wanted the comforts of home—beef, lamb, pork, wheat, rye, and oats. The extent of the exchange can be seen in a simple comparison of populations of people and livestock in Mexico in the first two centuries of contact. As the number of people was declining from 25 million to 1 million in the century after contact, the number of cattle, sheep, and goats rose from zero to more than 8 million. Native people were simply replaced by European livestock. The diffusion of European livestock, many of which escaped to the wild, began to alter the ecological balance of the Americas.

Europeans were slower to adapt to the new produce of the Americas. Corn (maize) and potatoes, two staples of the American diet, did not become important crops in Europe until the eighteenth century. Maize, along with another American staple, cassava, was actually adapted more readily into the African diet than the European. Undoubtedly the first American product besides gold and silver to have a noticeable impact on the lives of Europeans was tobacco. Already in 1604, King James I of England was so alarmed by the spread of the tobacco habit that he wrote a pamphlet, *A Counterblaste to Tobacco*, to discourage it. By the mid-seventeenth century the Dutch had begun growing tobacco in their own lands and even exporting up to 5 million pounds a year to the rest of Europe. Smoking had become a widespread habit among the Dutch, prompting one contemporary to observe, "a Hollander without a pipe is a national impossibility, akin to a town without a house. . . . If a Hollander should be bereft of his pipe of tobacco he could not blissfully enter heaven."[2]

The biological exchange brought about by Portuguese contacts in the Indian Ocean was more modest. Asia and Europe shared a common infectious disease pool, so there was almost no depopulation when Europeans arrived. In fact, Europeans were more susceptible to the tropical diseases that abounded in the region and so found it difficult to establish lasting settlements. Most of the products Europeans sought in the Indian Ocean, such as spices and tea, were not suited to European growing conditions and vice versa. Nevertheless, precisely because there was little biological exchange, the value of the trade coming out of the Indian Ocean in the sixteenth century was far greater than that coming out of the Atlantic, if we exclude the vast quantities of gold and silver taken from the Americas.

The Economic Organization of Colonization

The change in European colonization after 1600 had both political and economic causes. Spain was the leading colonial power, but the Dutch were the leading mercantilist country in Europe. With their specially designed cargo boats called *fluyts* they controlled a significant proportion of the trade along the Atlantic coast of Europe. They also held the key position in the trade of the Baltic Sea, where they transported grain from Prussia and Poland, and timber from Sweden. They were economic rivals of the Spanish at the same time that they were political rivals, fighting their long-running war for independence. They actively supported both smuggling, to get around the Spanish monopoly on trade with the Caribbean, and privateering and piracy. Privateering was the capture of commercial ships with the official permission of one's ruler. Piracy was the same act done without official permission. For merchant vessels, the distinction was a small one. The English and French also permitted their captains to undertake joint privateering and smuggling raids against the Spanish. For most of the sixteenth century, privateering and piracy were the main form of warfare, and one of the main forms of trade, in the Caribbean and Atlantic.

One reason for the thin line between legal and illegal raiding of trade was that most of the merchant ventures of the Dutch and English were undertaken by chartered companies or joint stock companies, not by the government. Chartered companies received permission from the king (or in the Dutch case from the States General) to exploit some trade opportunity, but they were run strictly for the profit of the stockholders. The most famous joint stock companies had thousands of investors, but most were dominated by a few key investors, many of whom were noblemen. This made them something between a business and a sovereign war-making institution. The eighteenth-century observer Edmund Burke commented, "The East India Company did not seem to be merely a Company formed for the extension of British commerce, but in reality a delegation of the whole power and sovereignty of this kingdom sent to the East."[3] Even the Bank of England, the prototype of the modern commercial bank, founded in 1694 to help finance the war against France, was at first just a group of private citizens prepared to lend to the government for eight percent interest. But at the same time, joint stock companies were highly speculative ventures, many of which failed. For example, the Virginia Company, chartered in 1606, succeeded in planting the first English settlement on North American soil at Jamestown, but went bankrupt in 1624, with all of its property being forfeited to the crown.

The most prominent joint stock companies were the Dutch East India Company (usually abbreviated from its Dutch name as VOC), founded in 1602; the Dutch West India Company, founded in 1621; the English Hudson's Bay Company, founded in 1670; and the English East India Company, first chartered in 1600, with a competing branch founded in 1694, and eventually merged in 1702. The Dutch took the lead in using their joint stock companies to wreak havoc on the older Spanish model of government monopoly. Their most noticeable advances were in the Indian Ocean with the VOC. There, they began to supplant the Portuguese as the main trading partner with the Spice Islands. Throughout the 1640s the VOC fought a long campaign against sultanates in what is now Indonesia. The Dutch secured a near monopoly in the spice trade and became the only European country allowed to trade with Japan, through its port city of Nagasaki. As the seventeenth century wore on, the Dutch supplemented their income from spices with imports of silk and tea. At the beginning of the eighteenth century they introduced coffee, originally from East Africa and Arabia, to the island of Java, thereby becoming Europe's main coffee brokers. To supply their growing presence in the Indian Ocean, the Dutch established a small colony at the Cape of Good Hope in 1652, which was one of the few European settlements on the African continent.

The Atlantic World

Colonial competition in the Atlantic turned out quite different from that in the Indian Ocean. The Dutch played a crucial, but short-lived role in transforming the Atlantic world. The flow of silver and gold into Spain in the sixteenth century may have impressed contemporaries, but it was two exceedingly mundane products that proved to be the driving economic forces behind the dramatic change in European colonization in the Atlantic after 1600: salt and sugar. The Dutch needed large quantities of salt for their herring industry. When their usual sources from Portugal were shut down during the Dutch Revolt, Dutch smugglers and privateers began to visit the massive salt deposits at Araya in Venezuela. As many as one hundred ships a year came to this remote spot at the beginning of the seventeenth century, equaling the volume of the official Spanish fleet to Mexico. The size of the trade made the Dutch a constant presence in the Caribbean, despite the supposed Spanish trade monopoly. It emboldened the English and French to pursue their own interests in the Americas as well. In 1604, James I of England managed to extract an important, though technical, concession about the Spanish monopoly of trade to the Americas. The Spanish accepted the idea that "prescription without possession availeth nothing"[4]—in other words, that the Spanish monopoly only applied to those areas already occupied by Spain; all "unoccupied" (by Europeans, that is) areas were free to be exploited by whoever could possess them. This provision reduced the danger of Spanish interference with new English colonies in Virginia and Massachusetts.

The goal of the Dutch West India Company was to make the Dutch the masters of the Caribbean trade by fighting the main Spanish fleets there. Its most dramatic success was when Piet Heyn captured the entire Spanish treasure fleet in 1628, which not only made the Company 15 million guilders richer, but ruined Spanish finances and forced the Spanish crown to declare bankruptcy. In the next two decades the Dutch captured or established settlements at Curacao, Saba, St. Martin and St. Eustatius in the Caribbean, New Amsterdam in North America, Elmira and the Cape of Good Hope in Africa, and Recife in Brazil. These Dutch actions so preoccupied the Spanish that other powers, such as England, France, and even Denmark, were able to find their own niches in a string of colonies along the Caribbean and Eastern North America.

At first, bases in the Caribbean were valuable primarily as havens for smugglers and privateers circumventing the Spanish monopoly, but the Dutch actions in Brazil pointed to another potential source of wealth that transformed the whole economy of the Caribbean. Brazil was the first American outpost to begin cultivating sugar. Sugar was native to the Mediterranean, but had spread with the Portuguese discoveries of the fifteenth century to the islands of Madeira and the Azores. By the 1580s Brazil had become Europe's major supplier. At the instigation of Dutch merchant shippers, the plantation techniques developed in Brazil began to spread to Caribbean islands in the 1630s and 1640s. The spread of the sugar plantation system dramatically altered the Atlantic world, because, unlike traditional European farming that relied on a free peasantry, sugar plantations were most cost-efficient when operated as great factories relying on slave labor. In the course of the seventeenth century, a "triangle trade" developed, in which Europe shipped finished products to Africa, exchanged them for slaves, which were then shipped to the Caribbean and exchanged for sugar, which was then shipped to Europe. Europe's sweet tooth thus changed the African slave trade from a peripheral phenomenon into a defining element of European society.

The Slave Trade

Slavery had been a small, but visible, element in much of Europe, the Middle East, and Africa for centuries. As the Portuguese began their explorations of the African coast in the fifteenth century, they established trading posts in which African captives sold as slaves were one of the commodities (though gold and hot pepper were the main products sought). In the course of the century, several hundred Africans came to Europe and to the European Atlantic islands as slaves, gradually supplanting the small number of European and Middle Eastern slaves in Western Europe. By the Treaty of Tordesillas, the Portuguese had exclusive rights to the African coast trade, so they became the primary slavers (as merchants who dealt in slaves were called).

When the Spanish and Portuguese first established their colonies in the Americas, they tried to employ Indians as the main laborers. Many Indians were simply enslaved; others were turned into dependent laborers under a system called *encomienda*, in which Europeans were given the responsibility to "civilize" and Christianize some number of villagers, in exchange for which they would be entitled to some specified amount of labor—a system reminiscent of the European serfdom. In the farming and ranching areas of Spanish America, such as Mexico, this system worked to perpetuate the native population and increase production, but in the mines and plantations disease and overwork quickly decimated the native work force. Europeans and Africans were brought in to replace the Indians. At first, more people came as indentured servants, who were obligated to work for a fixed period of time and then were free to settle on whatever land they wanted, rather than slaves. But soon large plantation and mine owners began to prefer slaves. Portuguese slavers began to profit more from their monopoly of the African coast and so they began to intensify their search for slaves, while merchants from other countries tried to break into the trade. Indeed, for the smugglers plying the Caribbean trade, slaves were one of the most valuable cargoes.

The premier example of the change in the Caribbean trade was the island of Barbados. In 1624, when the English began to settle it, it was uninhabited; by 1660 it was being called "the brightest jewel in His Majesty's crown."[5] What made it such a bright jewel? The triangle trade. By the 1640s, Barbados had become Brazil's principal rival as a producer of sugar. Almost the entire island was turned over to sugar cultivation and large processing plants that were akin to a modern factory. The demographic profile of the island changed in response. In the initial stages of the sugar plantation system in Brazil, Europeans and Africans worked in about equal numbers. On Barbados in 1645, there were still more Europeans than Africans, about 40,000 to 6,000. The influx of the slave trade and the change in working conditions led to a reversal of that proportion. By 1685, the European population was down to 20,000 while the African population rose to 46,000.

The effects of the slave trade on its victims were devastating. Europeans were not able to set up their own colonies on the African coast, but instead relied on African middlemen who captured neighboring peoples and brought them to trading forts. Some number of captives died in transit to the slaving ports, while many more died on the so-called "middle passage" to the Americas. Slave traders (and especially slave smugglers) wanted to get as big a profit as possible from their cargoes, so they shackled as many Africans as they could to planks below decks, sometimes not even leaving enough room for individuals to lie all the way down. Records of one company from the 1680s show that 23 percent of the Africans transported died en route. By the early eighteenth century, mortality rates improved to only about 10 percent. Slavers considered this an acceptable attrition rate that would probably not have dropped much if more humane conditions prevailed on board.

Conditions scarcely improved for the slaves if they survived the passage. Sugar plantation work was exceptionally physically demanding. Rations were very low and injury and death commonplace. The death rate exceeded the birth rate by a wide margin (about six to one in one plantation that has been studied in depth). The harsh conditions meant that slaves tried to escape as often as they could. Escaped slaves (called maroons) managed to set up their own colonies on the South American mainland. That was one reason why Europeans preferred small islands like Barbados for their plantations: it was harder to escape. For most of the seventeenth and eighteenth centuries it was still cheaper to import more Africans than it was to sustain the population of slaves already in place. And, in fact, the demand for slave labor in the sugar colonies seemed to be insatiable. The price of a slave increased more than threefold by the early eighteenth century. As a result, the number of imports accelerated: from about 900,000 during the entire sixteenth century, to 2.7 million during the seventeenth, to 6 million during the eighteenth. One indication of the relative importance of the sugar trade of the Caribbean in comparison to the tobacco (and later cotton) trade in North America is that, of the average of 25,000 slaves imported per year to British colonies in the early eighteenth century, 5,000 went to Virginia and the Carolinas, which specialized in tobacco, while 4,000 went to Barbados and 15,000 to Jamaica, which specialized in sugar.

Few commentators thought to object to the nature or volume of the slave trade. Some religious figures complained about how slaves were treated, but they did not object to the principle of slavery in itself, which was, after all, sanctioned by the Bible. Even political theories oriented toward widening the sphere of political participation made no effort to challenge the legitimacy of slavery. Drawing on ancient Greek concepts, most European writers insisted that Africans were "natural slaves" because they did not adhere to European political or social norms. It was not until the late eighteenth century that a significant number of agitators began to challenge the slave trade. One of the earlier voices against the practice of slavery was the French jurist and writer Montesquieu, who wrote in his 1748 book *The Spirit of the Laws,* "The state of slavery is in its own nature bad. It is neither useful to the master nor to the slave; not to the slave because he can do nothing through a motive of virtue; nor to the master because by having an unlimited authority over his slaves he insensibly accustoms himself to the want of all moral virtues, and thence becomes . . . cruel."[6]

Abolitionists in England and New England became more vocal after 1750, but were slow to develop a following. Among the most eloquent spokesmen were a former slave, Olaudah Equiano, whose biography, published in 1789, exposed the horrors of the middle passage, and another African, Ottobah Cugoano, who published *Thoughts and Sentiments on the Evil and Wicked Traffic of the Slavery and Commerce of the Human Species* in 1787. Most abolitionists focused their attention on the evils of the slave trade as opposed to slavery itself. But, of course, by that time the institution of slavery was so entrenched that ending the slave trade would do little to change the practices of slavery within the colonies themselves. The first former sugar plantation colony to abolish slavery was St. Domingue, now known as Haiti, which did so because of an armed uprising of slaves that overthrew the existing government. Despite increasingly strong agitation, the British did not abolish the officially sanctioned slave trade until 1806–1807. Smugglers continued to supply British colonies even after that date, and the practice of slavery in British colonies was not formally abolished until 1833.

European Competition on the World Scene

The moment of Dutch predominance in the Atlantic triangle trade was comparatively brief. The constant warfare against the English and the French (sometimes one or the other, sometimes both at the same time) sapped Dutch reserves. The Dutch West India Company eventually collapsed into bankruptcy in 1674, though it was quickly reestablished. As a result, it was primarily the English who came to benefit from the breakdown of the Spanish monopoly of the Caribbean. The Portuguese were able to reclaim Brazil in the 1650s, while the English seized the Spanish island of Jamaica in 1655, turning it into another major sugar producing site. Even as the Dutch lost control of the sugar trade, they tried to maintain their prominence in the triangle trade by dominating the slave trade. By 1702, the Dutch West India Company was already claiming that "the slave trade has always been considered, and always should be, one of the biggest and chief concerns of the company."[7] But even in that sector, the English were able to snatch away the Dutch advantage. The Royal African Company was founded in 1672 to make the English the leaders in the slave trade. It was symbolic of the changing dynamics of sea power that, when William III brought the English and Dutch fleets together to face the navy of Louis XIV, the Dutch fleet was subordinated to the English.

England's primary rival for predominance in the Caribbean was neither the Dutch nor the Spanish, but the French. The French also got into the sugar production business, establishing major plantations in St. Domingue, what we now call Haiti. The wars of Louis XIV on the European continent had their counterpoint in raids by English and French squadrons against the principal outposts of their adversaries in 1666–1667, 1689–1697, and 1702–1713. The English generally came out ahead in these raids, but not so much so that they were able to permanently drive the French out of the colonial scene. The Peace of Utrecht in 1713 gave the English two great prizes. The French were forced to relinquish their claims to Newfoundland, Nova Scotia, and the territories of the Hudson's Bay Company, giving the English privileged access to both the fur trade and the fishing banks of the Atlantic. But more important, even though the Spanish crown was given over to a grandson of Louis XIV, it was the English who were granted exclusive rights to trade slaves in the Spanish colonies in the Americas. The Royal African Company now effectively controlled the slave trade at precisely the moment when it was becoming even more lucrative. As many slaves were transported in the eighteenth century as in the sixteenth and seventeenth centuries combined, mostly by English traders.

While Anglo-French competition was fiercest in the Caribbean, a new area of conflict between the two countries also emerged: North America. Within a few years of the news of Columbus's first voyage, the English Captain John Cabot had rediscovered the North Atlantic route to Newfoundland and Nova Scotia. Subsequent voyages by both the French and English produced a wealth of new geographical knowledge. The Frenchman Jacques Cartier sailed up the Saint Lawrence river as far as modern-day Montreal; the Englishman Henry Hudson, sailing for the Dutch, found a passage to the north of Labrador giving access to Hudson Bay and a lucrative fur trade. But efforts to establish settlements, by the French in 1541 and the English in 1587, failed.

At the beginning of the seventeenth century, European settlements in North America began to stick. The English settled Virginia in 1607, New England in 1620, and Maryland in 1634. The Dutch established trading settlements along the Hudson River by 1624 and in Delaware by 1631. Danes established the first settlement further up the Delaware river in 1639, while a Swedish-Finnish expedition in 1643 established the first settlement in what was to become Pennsylvania. As a result of the Anglo-Dutch War of 1665–1667, the Dutch were forced to cede their North American colonies to the English, including the port of New Amsterdam. It was promptly renamed New York, in honor of its titular governor, the Duke of York. The English were more generous than most in allowing other Europeans to join in the settling of their lands. Germans (beginning in 1681), Swedes, and Danes were all integrated into the English colonies beginning in the seventeenth century. Though the numbers of settlers are not impressive in comparison to the scale of the slave trade, by the mid-eighteenth century, perhaps 1.5 million settlers of European descent were in North America.

The number of French settlers in North America was much smaller, but the French established a major position on the continent by means of exploration and formal trade contacts with Indian groups. The French explorer Samuel de Champlain finally established permanent settlements in Canada, in Nova Scotia in 1605 and at Quebec in 1608. By the end of the seventeenth century, French "lands" virtually encircled the English, as the French laid claim to Canada, the Great Lakes, and the Mississippi valley. There were French forts (really just trading posts) as far in the interior as Chicago by 1680. The French had become the main media-tors between different Indian groups in the Upper Great Lakes region. The two main propagators of French control were Jesuit missionaries and fur traders. Some French women also came to convert the natives. For example, Marie Guyart, the daughter of a baker and wife of a silkmaker, joined the Ursuline order after her widowhood in 1618 and traveled to Quebec in 1639. For the next thirty-two years she ministered to the local Huron and Algonquin population, eventually translating the catechism into Algonquin. Despite the condescending attitude that some missionaries adopted towards their charges, the Indian populations were generally less hostile to the French than they were to the farming and land-clearing English settlers.

In the eighteenth century, English settlers began crossing the Allegh-eny and Appalachian mountains toward the Ohio Valley, creating a new frontier rivalry between the English and French. There were frequent skirmishes, sometimes between the French and English directly, but more often between different Indian groups supported by one side or the other. This arrangement would shape competition between France and En-gland during the great European wars of the mid-eighteenth century: the War of the Austrian Succession and the Seven Years' War (known in North America as The War of Jenkins' Ear, King George's War, and the French and Indian War).

The Colonial "Bubbles"

Anglo-French rivalry emerged in another form as well. The French looked enviously at the success of the English and Dutch in generating great profits through joint stock companies. When a Scottish financier and speculator named John Law arrived in Paris with an innovative scheme for generating profits from a far-flung colonial network, he quickly de-veloped a following among the progressive noblemen he encountered.

John Law was born in Edinburgh in 1671, the son of a goldsmith. After a rambunctious youth, he was forced to flee from London in 1694 because of a duel fought over a woman. He made his way to Paris, where he prepared a tract called *Money and Trade Considered* (1700) that laid out his principles for generating wealth for the Crown. He argued that paper money did not have to be backed up by owning an equivalent amount of gold and silver, as it traditionally was. Instead, the currency could be backed by land, the whole domain of the kingdom. While frequenting the fashionable gambling rooms of Paris, he made the acquaintance of the Duke of Orleans, who gave him access to the Crown's treasury officials. In 1716, he founded the General Bank of Law and Company, designed to implement his system. But his system entailed more than just the domains of France to support the stocks he offered. He decided to back his bank with the lands held by the Mississippi Company, founded in 1717, which covered the entire Mississippi Valley of North America. To give some semblance of economic activity in that vast region, the Mississippi Company encouraged new settlements. But the results were desultory and New Orleans remained a small tumbled-down center.

In the meantime, the Mississippi Company and Law's bank experienced an investment frenzy. The value of the notes issued far exceeded any reasonable return that one could have expected from New Orleans. Prices increased fivefold during the summer of 1719. In May 1720, Law acknowledged the obvious and announced that share values would have to be reduced. A wave of panic selling set in, quickly evaporating the entire assets of the company. By November, the company dissolved. Law kept one step ahead of the creditors and fled to Venice, where he died in 1729.

France was not alone in experiencing the frenzy of a colonial get-rich scheme. At almost exactly the same time as the "Mississippi Bubble," the English experienced the "South Sea Bubble." The South Sea Company had been founded in 1710 to support English interests in the Caribbean. In 1720, investors suddenly started reaping great rewards, as the value of shares rose from 160 in February to 1,050 in June. But as with the Mississippi Bubble, the fact that these values were not backed with any discernible profits led to a rapid deflation. The Bubble popped in September and the South Sea Company went bankrupt.

Despite the Bubbles, the countries of Europe continued to clamor to participate in the colonial trade. Even the Austrian Habsburgs decided to get in on it, with the foundation of yet another company, known as the Ostende Company, in their newly acquired territories in the Low Countries in 1723. The Dutch responded with particular hostility to this trade initiative, which seemed to be a direct competitor. They seized ships of the company and did everything within their power to undercut their presence in the Indies. In the end, Charles VI of Austria decided to sacrifice the Ostende Company for political purposes, agreeing to disband it in exchange for Dutch and English promises to support his daughter as heir to the Austrian Habsburg lands.

Colonial Competition in the Mid-Eighteenth Century

By the mid-eighteenth century, the competition between France and England in overseas colonies was one of the key factors in European politics. French sugar production from St. Domingue, Guadaloupe, and Martinique equaled that of the British Caribbean; the Ohio Valley and Canada were both being hotly contested; and a new venue was opening up for colonial competition: India. These issues were also becoming more integral to the economies of the home countries. The colonial trade of England increased fivefold between 1698 and 1774. It is one of the ironies of colonialism that the British Empire was just beginning to move towards its peak at the moment when one small part of it, the thirteen North American colonies, were breaking away.

In the peaceful interim between the War of the Austrian Succession and the Seven Years' War, the grounds for future conflicts in both North America and India were established. To defend the Ohio Valley from encroaching British settlers, the French established a new series of forts, culminating at the easternmost point with Fort Duquesne, established in 1754 at the site of modern Pittsburgh. Meanwhile, in India, the governor of the French East India Company, Joseph Dupleix, changed the dynamics of colonial control there. Since the sixteenth century, Europeans in India had relied entirely on trade and special contracts with local princes to gain access to the wealth of India. That policy became more difficult when the Mughal Empire began to disintegrate, creating competing princedoms. Dupleix decided to gain more control over these small princedoms by supplying them with the military power to defeat rival claimants. In 1749, he backed India rulers in the Carnatic and Deccan, thereby winning privileged access to their products. The English, fretting over this development, decided to back their own claimants to the princedoms. A British force under Robert Clive drove the French from the Carnatic and established their own puppet princes in place of the French protégés. Dupleix was forced to return to France. But a pattern of European intervention in India affairs was established.

The seething conflicts became open warfare in 1756 with the outbreak of the Seven Years' War. At first, the colonial war seemed to go in favor of the French. A first British expedition against the fort system in the Ohio Valley failed; the French general Montcalm captured the town of Oswego in New York; the main British outpost in India, Calcutta, fell to a local Bengali prince. But under the resourceful leadership of the

British prime minister William Pitt, the British were able to quickly reverse the situation. A three-pronged attack against the French positions in North America led to a dramatic climactic battle on the outskirts of Quebec on September 13, 1759, in which both commanding generals, Montcalm and Wolfe, died. On September 8, 1760, the French governor of Canada, Vaudreuil, surrendered and Canada was lost.

Meanwhile, the British took advantage of their superior naval strength to strangle the French position in India. The decisive moment came at the Battle of Plassey on June 23, 1757. A small British force under Robert Clive defeated the army of the *nawab* of Bengal, who was an ally of the French. Clive rapidly exploited the victory to occupy most of Bengal, which would be the center of the British Empire in India in the nineteenth century. The French, now isolated, were forced to abandon their position in India when the fortress of Pondicherry surrendered on January 16, 1761. France would never recover its position in either North America or India. Resentment of the British was to contribute to French support for the American colonists during the American Revolution.

Profile: The Golden Age of Pirates and the "Lady Pirates" Anne Bonny and Mary Read

There have been pirates for as long as there has been seaborne trade. Pirates were so numerous and successful from roughly 1690 to 1730 that the period has come to be known as a golden age of piracy. Most of the famous legends of pirate ships that have captured the modern imagination date from that era: Captain Kidd; Edward Teach, known as Blackbeard; Stede Bonnet; Charles Vane; Thomas Tew. Some of these captains, such as Captain Kidd, were more privateers gone wrong than outright pirates, but the fine line between legitimate privateering and piracy was one of the distinguishing features of the age, where local officials often created safe havens for and cut deals with pirates in order to profit from the cargoes they brought in. Many of the stories, including that of the "Lady Pirates," Anne Bonny and Mary Read, are known primarily from a book called *A General History of the Pirates*, published by a certain Captain Charles Johnson in 1724, but often attributed to Daniel Defoe, author of *Robinson Crusoe*.

There were obvious attractions for the common seaman in the pirate life. The seaman's life was in any case hard. The English writer Samuel Johnson quipped that "no man will be a sailor who has contrivance enough to get himself into jail, for being in a ship is being in a jail with the chance of being drowned. . . . A man in jail has more room, better food, and commonly better company."[8] But unlike on merchantmen, and especially naval ships, there was a kind of democracy to the way a pirate ship was run. It was customary for the captain of a pirate ship to be elected by the crew, not self-appointed. Ordinary seamen contributed to decisions about what to attack and how to divide the rewards.

This egalitarianism may have contributed to the careers of Anne Bonny and Mary Read. Anne Bonny was the illegitimate daughter of a prominent Irish attorney, who was forced to emigrate to South Carolina because of the scandal. Her father went on to be a prosperous merchant and planter in Charleston. She, however, had no interest in the quiet life of Charleston and married, against her father's wishes, a young sailor named James Bonny. She accompanied him to Nassau in the Bahamas, a notorious congregating place for pirates. There she met "Calico Jack" Rackam, a compatriot of Charles Vane and Blackbeard, who had just obtained one of the pardons that the Crown periodically extended to pirates in order to reduce their numbers. The two quickly fell in love; but there was this awkward problem of her husband, who refused to release her from her marriage and petitioned the governor of the Bahamas to arrest Jack if he continued to see her.

Jack and Anne decided to take matters into their own hands. Jack recruited his old pirate crew, stole a merchant vessel, and he and Anne used it to prey on merchant shipping in the Caribbean. At first, Anne disguised herself as a man on board, perhaps to avoid excessive interest from the crew members. One day she developed a very strong attraction to a new sailor who had been impressed (the naval equivalent of kidnapping) from a captured merchant ship. She decided to reveal her secret to him and win his affection. But then she discovered to her surprise that the object of her affection was a woman: Mary Read.

Mary came from more humble origins than did Anne. She was born more than a year after her mother's husband had gone to sea. In order to disguise the circumstances of the conception, Mary's mother hid the pregnancy and dressed Mary in the clothing of her recently deceased brother. Mary was thus brought up as a boy. At the age of twelve she entered the navy and went on to be a cavalry soldier, where she fell in love with another soldier and abandoned her disguise. She and her new husband opened a tavern in Holland, but her husband soon died. Mary returned to the work she knew, disguising herself as a boy and joining a Dutch merchantman as a sailor. That was the ship captured by Jack Rackam from which she was impressed.

Anne and Mary became fast friends. Eventually Anne revealed Mary's secret to Jack. Soon thereafter, Mary became attracted to another sailor. When her identity was exposed, she and Anne abandoned their disguises and dressed as women, except when boarding prizes, where they continued to wear the traditional pirate outfits of jackets, trousers, and handkerchiefs tied around the head. They remained active pirates: "none were more resolute or ready to Board or undertake any Thing that was hazardous as Mary Read and Anne Bonny."[9]

Both Anne Bonny and Mary Read were still with the crew of Calico Jack when the war against the pirates took a more aggressive turn in 1720. The pickings became slimmer, while the territorial governors became more energetic in pursuing pirates. A sloop under the command of Captain Barnet waylaid the ship near Dry Harbor Bay, Jamaica. The pirate crew was captured and Calico Jack, Anne, and Mary were put on trial for piracy. All three were sentenced to be hanged. The sentence was carried out for Jack in December 1720. Mary and Anne both received a reprieve: they were both pregnant. Mary died of a fever while still waiting in prison. Anne, however, escaped execution when Jamaican planters who knew her father interceded on her behalf. Her ultimate fate is not known, though she is said to have returned to her father's house in Charleston.

The capture of Calico Jack Rackam, Anne Bonny, and Mary Read is emblematic of a change in the war against the pirates. By the 1720s provincial governors were no longer cooperating with pirate captains for their own profit. They were using all of the resources at their disposal to destroy the bases from which pirates worked.

So what of buried pirate treasure and treasure maps? For the most part, those are just fables used to embellish the pirate legend. Most pirates were oriented to the short term, not the long. As soon as a prize was captured, it was divided up. The ship then proceeded to one of the traditional ports of call, where some crewmembers might be tempted to settle down with their cash, while most spent their rewards profusely on drink and gambling. The egalitarian nature of the pirate community worked against the idea of burying any treasure, since everyone would have to be in on the secret and then it would hardly be a secret any more.

Important Dates

1492	Columbus's first voyage to America
1494	Treaty of Tordesillas
1498	Vasco da Gama circumnavigates Africa to Indian Ocean
1521	Cortes overthrows Aztec Empire
1533	Pizarro overthrows Inca Empire
1600	English East India Company formed
1602	Dutch East India Company formed
1605	French settlement of Canada begins
1606	Virginia Company formed
1607	English settlement of Virginia begins
1621	Dutch West India Company formed
1624	English settlement of Barbados begins
1628	Dutch capture Spanish treasure fleet
1641	Dutch capture Malacca in Indonesia
1652	Dutch settlement of Cape of Good Hope begins
1655	English seize Jamaica from Spanish
1665–1667	Anglo-Dutch War
1672	Royal African Company founded
1694	Bank of England founded
1720	Mississippi and South Sea Bubbles
1723	Ostende Company formed
1724	Publication of *A General History of the Pirates*
1756–1763	Seven Years' War
1757	Battle of Plassy gives British upper hand in India
1759	Battle of Quebec gives British upper hand in Canada
1789	Publication of Equiano's *Biography*
1807	End of British slave trade
1833	Abolition of slavery in British colonies

Further Reading

Kenneth R. Andrews, *Trade, Plunder and Settlement: Maritime Enterprise and the Genesis of the British Empire, 1480–1630* (Cambridge, 1984)

Philip P. Boucher, *Cannibal Encounters: Europeans and Island Caribs, 1492–1763* (Baltimore, 1992)

Charles R. Boxer, *The Dutch Seaborn Empire, 1600–1800* (New York, 1965)

Charles R. Boxer, *The Portuguese Seaborn Empire, 1415–1825* (New York, 1969)

Sushil Chaudhury and Michel Morineau, eds., *Merchants, Companies and Trade: Europe and Asia in the Early Modern Era* (Cambridge, 1999)

Noble David Cook, *Born to Die: Disease and New World Conquest (1492–1650)* (Cambridge, 1998)

Alfred W. Crosby, *The Columbian Exchange: Biological Consequences of 1492* (Westport, CT, 1972)

Alfred W. Crosby, *Ecological Imperialism and the Biological Expansion of Europe* (Cambridge, 1986)

K.G. Davies, *The North Atlantic World in the Seventeenth Century* (Minneapolis, 1974)

Ralph Davis, *The Rise of the Atlantic Economies* (London, 1973)

Richard S. Dunn, *Sugar and Slaves* (Chapel Hill, 1972)

J.H. Elliott, *The Old World and the New, 1492–1650* (Cambridge, 1970)

Richard Grove, *Green Imperialism: Colonial Expansion, Tropical Island Edens and the Origins of Environmentalism, 1600–1860* (Cambridge, 1995)

Roger Hainsworth and Christine Churches, *The Anglo-Dutch Naval Wars, 1652–1674* (Stroud, England 1998)

David Hancock, *Citizens of the World: London Merchants and the Integration of the British Atlantic Community, 1735–1785* (Cambridge, 1995)

Eric Hinderaker, *Elusive Empires: Constructing Colonialism in the Ohio Valley, 1673–1800* (Cambridge, 1997)

Jonathan Israel, *Dutch Primacy in World Trade, 1585–1740* (Oxford, 1989)

Jonathan Israel, *Empires and Entrepots: The Dutch, the Spanish Monarchy, and the Jews, 1585–1713* (Oxford, 1989)

Herbert S. Klein, *The Atlantic Slave Trade* (Cambridge, 1999)

Kris Lane, *Pillaging the Empire: Piracy in the Americas, 1500–1750* (Armonk, NY, 1998)

Sidney Mintz, *Sweetness and Power* (Baltimore, 1979)

Antoine E. Murphy, *John Law: Economic Theorist and Policy Maker* (Oxford, 1997)

Anthony Pagden, *The Fall of Natural Man: The American Indian and the Origins of Anthropology* (Cambridge, 1982)

Anthony Pagden, *European Encounters with the New World: From Renaissance to Romanticism* (New Haven, 1992)

Anthony Pagden, *Lords of All the World: Ideologies of Empire in Spain, Britain, and France, 1492–1830* (New Haven, 1995)

J.H. Parry, *The Age of Reconnaissance: Discovery, Exploration and Settlement 1450 to 1650* (Berkeley, 1981)

J.H. Parry, *The Establishment of the European Hegemony: 1415–1715* 3rd ed. (New York, 1966)

Sue Peabody, *"There are no Slaves in France": The Political Culture of Race and Slavery in the Ancien Regime* (Oxford, 1996)

Adam Potkay and Sandra Burr, eds., *Black Atlantic Writers of the Eighteenth Century* (New York, 1995)

Theodore K. Rabb, *Jacobean Gentleman: Sir Edwin Sandys, 1561–1629* (Princeton, 1998)

Robert C. Ritchie, *Captain Kidd and the War against the Pirates* (Cambridge, MA, 1986)

Irving Rouse, *The Tainos: Rise and Decline of the People Who Greeted Columbus* (New Haven, 1992)

A.J.R. Russell-Wood, *The Portuguese Empire, 1415–1808* (Baltimore, 1998)

David Harris Sacks, *The Widening Gate: Bristol and the Atlantic Economy, 1450–1700* (Berkeley, 1991)

Patricia Seed, *Ceremonies of Possession in Europe's Conquest of the New World, 1492–1640* (Cambridge, 1995)

John Thornton, *Africa and Africans in the Making of the Atlantic World, 1400–1800* 2nd ed. (Cambridge, 1998)

James D. Tracy, ed., *The Rise of Merchant Empires: Long Distance Trade in the Early Modern World, 1350–1750* (Cambridge, 1990)

Immanuel Wallerstein, *The Modern World System II: Mercantilism and the Consolidation of the European World Economy, 1600–1750* (New York, 1980)

Richard White, *The Middle Ground: Indians, Empires and Republics in the Great Lakes Region, 1650–1815* (Cambridge, 1991)

Glyndwr Williams, *The Great South Sea: English Voyages and Encounters, 1570–1750* (New Haven, 1997)

Chapter Eleven

The Pursuit of Truth

"The inquiry of truth," wrote Sir Francis Bacon, "which is the love-making or wooing of it, the knowledge of truth, which is the presence of it, and the belief of truth, which is the enjoying of it, is the sovereign good of human nature."[1] During the Renaissance, most scholars in Europe had thought that all truth about the natural world was to be found in the works of ancient Greece and Rome. By the early seventeenth century, though, natural philosophers were beginning to argue that the ancients, though great men, had not discovered all there was to know: the compass, gunpowder, and the printing press, all unknown to the Greeks and Romans, had transformed the world. Voyages of discovery had shown the existence of whole continents, peoples, plants, and animals not described in ancient books of geography; the telescope had revealed heavenly bodies, like the moons of Jupiter and rings of Saturn, that no ancient authority had discussed. Another new instrument, the microscope, showed "tiny animals" found in no ancient book on zoology. These discoveries had thrown into doubt all ancient knowledge and with it ancient assumptions about truth and certainty. The pursuit of new truth, then, became the highest priority for philosophers interested in the natural world, especially for Francis Bacon and René Descartes.

Francis Bacon (1561–1626)

Francis Bacon set out to leave his mark not on philosophy, but on law. His father, Sir Nicholas Bacon, was Lord Keeper of the Great Seal, the senior legal officer to Queen Elizabeth I of England, and his uncle was Lord Burleigh, the queen's chief minister. With that family background, young Francis was intended for a career at court and high political office. He studied at the University of Cambridge, then at the Inns of Court in London, the standard training for a young lawyer and rising politician. At the age of sixteen he went to Paris as a member of the English ambassador's staff, and he may have developed an interest in natural philosophy there. When he was nineteen his father died and he had to return home. In 1584, he was elected to the House of Commons, with the assistance of his uncle, for all parliamentary elections in the early seventeenth century required political influence. Unlike many members of Parliament, who did very little after their election, Bacon tried, and succeeded, to obtain high political office. In 1603 King James I knighted him, and his appointments mark an upward spiral of prestige: from King's Counsel, to Solicitor-General, through Attorney General, and finally, Lord Chancellor, the highest legal position in the land. But there were many others who were interested in high position at court, and the court of James I, like all others, was filled with political intrigues. Bacon's chief rival for the position of Lord Chancellor, Sir Edward Coke, accused him of bribery, and Bacon was removed from office in 1621. He spent the rest of his life working on the philosophical writings that were to ensure his fame far more than his legal career.

Bacon was not himself a scientist, but he was one of the first influential writers to recognize that the new natural philosophy of his age was a complete departure from the ideas of the ancients. The problem, he thought, was that all philosophers were going about the business of investigating the natural world piecemeal, bit by bit, while still relying on the works of Aristotle and other ancient writers. In his book *The New Organon*—intended to replace Aristotle's *Organon*, which dealt with the methods of natural philosophy—Bacon set out the stages for a new, modern intellectual structure that would completely replace the old natural philosophy. As with any new structure, it was necessary to begin by clearing away the rubble of the old one. Bacon called the obstacles to proper reasoning about natural philosophy "idols" and gave them the labels "Idols of the Tribe," "Idols of the Cave," "Idols of the Marketplace" and "Idols of the Theater." Though the labels are hard to keep straight, the concepts behind them are clear. First, our senses are imperfect. We can be deceived by what we see, and our experience of the natural world is only indirect. Second, everyone sees the world in his or her own way and believes that his or her point of view must be the true and most important one. Third, words are imprecise and do not always mean the same thing, so it is hard to be sure that knowledge has been communicated properly. And finally, there are competing philosophical systems that give order to our sensory experiences. These philosophical systems, which channel how people interpret the world, hinder communication. They are, in Bacon's view, like so many stage plays, largely fiction.

Bacon's four idols are a perceptive critique of the problems of scientific inquiry, and he is considered to be the first sociologist of scientific communities. His solutions to the problems he identified were most influential in his own time. The first solution, he said, was for scientists to come together in communities to discuss common problems. The problems of the imperfection of people's senses, of individual perceptions, of imprecision of language, of competing systems could all be worked out if natural philosophers carried out their investigations jointly, instead of each in a private study or laboratory. The second solution was to concentrate on carrying out experiments, instead of reading ancient texts or modern books of philosophy, to understand the workings of nature. Bacon felt that the ancients were wise, but that their philosophy was inadequate precisely because it lacked any understanding of experiment; instead, he praised the "mechanical arts," that is, manual trades like smelting, weaving, engraving, and agriculture, "which are founded on nature and the light of experience" and were "continually thriving and growing" as men sought to improve them. "It is well to observe the force and virtue and consequences of discoveries," he wrote, "and these are to be seen nowhere more conspicuously than in those three which were unknown to the ancients . . . namely printing, gunpowder, and the magnet. For these three have changed the whole face and state of things throughout the world; the first in literature, the second in warfare, the third in navigation."[2] Let philosophers cease wrangling over words and start investigating the natural world, torturing nature by experiment, in Bacon's phrase, to make her tell her secrets. That was the way to properly investigate the truth.

René Descartes (1596–1650)

In France, René Descartes, another wealthy amateur with legal training, turned his attention to the problem of method for the new philosophy. He was from Brittany, son of the counsellor of the parlement of Bretagne, and received an excellent education. Like Bacon, he became interested in philosophy at an early age. He had been brought up on books as a young man, he wrote in his *Discourse on Method* (1637), because he "was persuaded that through them we can acquire a clear and certain knowledge of all that is useful in life." But he found so many conflicting opinions that he became "encumbered with doubts and errors," and even the guidance of his teachers did not help, so that it seemed he had discovered no certain truth "except that I had discovered progressively how ignorant I was."

Descartes's intellectual journey took him through study of classical and modern writers. In his youth, he traveled extensively, the usual education of a young gentleman, and served for a time in the armies of the Thirty Years' War, before settling down in the Netherlands, the favorite haven for critical thinkers. His journey also took him within himself. He tried to use the principle of radical doubt, using his reason to eliminate everything that was uncertain, as an intellectual scalpel to find certainty in what was left. He could doubt all philosophy, he found, and reject it as uncertain, because he, like Bacon, found there were so many competing philosophical systems. He could doubt religion, because there were so many religions, each perfectly convinced it was the only true one (though Descartes did not doubt the existence of God). He could doubt the evidence of his senses, for he, again like Bacon, knew that our sense perceptions could deceive. But when all was said and done, he could not doubt his own existence, for he could not use his own reason to prove that there was no human being doing the reasoning. "I noticed," he wrote, "that although I wanted thus to think that everything was false, it was necessary that I, who was thinking this, be something. And noting that this truth, *I think, therefore I am*, was so firm and well assured. . . . I judged that I could accept it without scruple as the first principle of the philosophy for which I was searching."

Descartes, like Bacon, wanted to create a new intellectual structure to replace what he called the uncertain natural philosophy of his own day. Unlike Bacon, though, he did not feel a new philosophy could be based on the work of many men, for, he wrote, "we see that the buildings designed and completed by a single architect are usually more beautiful and better planned than those which many have tried to redesign, making do with old walls which had been built for other purposes." He had no doubt that he was the architect to rebuild natural philosophy, and he had no doubt of the proper method, not Bacon's experiment, but the science of mathematics, "for at bottom the method which shows us how to follow the direct order, and to enumerate exactly all the circumstances of that which we are investigating, contains everything which gives certainty to the rules of arithmetic."[3]

Descartes in fact made his name in intellectual circles with an elegant piece of mathematical reasoning, the mathematical formulae for reflection and refraction of light. His other mathematical accomplishments include the one that bears his name, Cartesian coordinates, the unification of geometry and algebra into analytical geometry. But his influence went beyond mathematical circles, for he developed a mechanical theory of natural philosophy that was widely adopted. All of nature, he said, had two primary, fundamental qualities, matter and motion. These operated according to mechanical principles, just like a man-made machine. Nature also had a host of secondary, additional qualities, such as color, light, texture, which operated, one of Descartes's followers later explained, rather like the special-effects department of a theatrical performance. It was the task of natural philosophers to look for the mechanical laws underlying natural phenomena, to try to puzzle out the way in which the special effects were carried out: "whoever sees nature as it really is simply sees the backstage area of the theater."[4] Above all, the study of nature had to be built on what Descartes called "clear and distinct ideas," simple and straightforward concepts that were clearly amenable to human reason.

Concerned about the response of the French government to his ideas, Descartes moved to the Netherlands in 1628, even for a time serving as a kind of personal philosopher to Queen Christina of Sweden. He became the most famous living philosopher, and a visit to him, even more than to the Dutch picture-galleries, was obligatory for any traveler.

Academies of Science

Bacon and Descartes were, each in his own way, the inspiration for a new type of philosophical institution, the Academy of Science. In the early seventeenth century, communities of people interested in the new natural philosophy began to come together, often in the home of a noble patron, as communities of artists and scholars had in the Renaissance. In England, mathematicians and chemists gathered together with Sir Walter Raleigh, though they were reputed to discuss magical and atheistic ideas as well as philosophy. In Italy, the Accademia dei Lincei began in 1603 under the patronage of Duke Federigo Cesi, who was interested in natural history. It was one of the first groups to which Galileo demon-

strated his spyglass, and it was members of the Accademia who chris-
tened it a "telescope." In France, a philosophically minded monk, Marin
Mersenne (1588–1648), invited anyone interested in the new philosophy to visit him in his cell and began an extensive correspondence with
the leading philosophers of his day that became, in effect, a kind of
scientific newsletter.

In England, informal meetings of those interested in, or curious about,
the new philosophy began in Oxford in the 1640s. After the Restoration,
some of those involved moved to London and petitioned the king for a
royal charter. Although Charles II was said to have laughed mightily
when he heard that some of the philosophers were trying to weigh air,
he granted the charter, dated July 15, 1662, to the Royal Society of London. It included men with all sorts of diverse interests, such as Samuel
Pepys (1633–1703), a naval administrator best known for his detailed
diaries, the political philosopher John Locke, surveyor and expert mi-
croscopist Robert Hooke (1635–1702), who first identified the cell, and
the chemist and Earl of Cork, Robert Boyle (1627–1691), who developed Boyle's law of gases. Eventually it grew to have corresponding
members and to publish papers presented to the society in its annual
publication, *The Philosophical Transactions*. The Dutch lens-grinder
Anton van Leeuwenhoek (1632–1723) published an account of what he
called his "little animals," the first description of microorganisms, in
the *Transactions*.

The program of the early Royal Society was deliberately modeled on
Bacon's call for experiment, instead of relying on texts or creating philosophical systems. Thomas Spratt, who wrote a history of the society,
claimed that no other preface was necessary than Bacon's writings.

The writings of Descartes just as explicitly inspired the work of the
other prominent scientific academy, the Académie Royale des Sciences
in Paris, founded in 1666, with its own journal, the *Journal des Scavans*.
(The word "scientist" was still not used: those interested in the subject
were called either natural philosophers, or savants, or virtuosi). Bernard
de Fontenelle, who wrote a history of the Paris academy, claimed that
the geometrical (mathematical) method proposed by Descartes had given
"a keynote to the whole of his century." Not just natural philosophy had
been affected by it, but all other branches of knowledge: "the order, the
clarity, the precision and the accuracy which have distinguished the
worthier kind of books for some time past now,"[5] he wrote, are all due to
the triumph of the mathematical method advocated by Descartes.

The Royal Society, though owing its formal existence to the royal charter, received no other funding or patronage from the king. The Académie des Sciences, in contrast, was one of the many cultural innovations designed to enhance the glory of Louis XIV, and members received a stipend. Distinguished foreign scientists were enticed by the promise of royal salaries to come to France and join the academy, for the Sun King wanted his personal retinue of philosophers to outshine any other. It, too, published scientific papers that circulated throughout Europe. Over time, members of both academies found that there could be disadvantages as well as advantages to scientific communities, as members quarreled over interpretations of experiments or over who should get credit for a theory or experiment discussed within the society. Still, all extolled the value of cooperative effort within the new academies, "where all the facts brought forth are verified by a great many eyes, all clear-seeing, where arguments are discussed by a great many minds, all enlightened. . . . It is on such works that one can, as on solid foundations, build the edifice of science without fear."[6]

Newton and Newton's Laws

Not long after the founding of the Royal Society, in 1672, it elected as a new Fellow the professor of mathematics at Cambridge University, Isaac Newton (1642–1727), who had invented a new form of telescope. Newton came from one of the wealthiest gentry families in Lincolnshire, but he had been a sickly baby and grew up an unsociable, rather bad-tempered child, with few friends and no interest in assuming the considerable responsibilities of a proprietor of a large estate. Neither his gift for mathematics—he seemed to have been born knowing geometry, since he had been able to read through and understand Euclid without being taught—nor his fascination with devising new mechanical devices seemed admirable to his mother, who despaired of his ever amounting to much. Why not send him to study at Cambridge, suggested her brother, who was kindly disposed to his difficult nephew, and Cambridge proved to be Newton's haven, where he was eventually appointed professor of mathematics. His official duties were to give a series of public lectures each year on his mathematical researches in physics, astronomy, and calculus. It was said that he gave those lectures to the four walls, for they were well beyond the understanding of all but a few. The rest of the time he was left alone, in the quiet of his own comfortable rooms, to carry out his own investigations.

Portrait of Isaac Newton by anonymous artist (Scala/Art Resource, NY)

Newton might have been personally unsociable, but he wanted his work to be generally known, and soon after his election to the Royal Society he sent an account of some experiments he had done with a prism. Everyone knew that white light, shining through a prism, emerged as colored light, and there was a debate then current in philosophical circles about whether the colors were contained in the white light or whether the prism somehow added them to the light. Newton thought the former, and he pursued this idea by directing the colored light through a second prism, and obtaining white light again. It seemed to him clear that the prism could not be adding anything to the light, or else the second prism would add something else, and the colors would emerge from it with new colors, not as white light. Newton also calculated the angle of refraction—bending—of each of the colors. It seemed to him a very pretty piece of experiment that clearly proved his hypothesis (theory) that white light contained all the colors of the rainbow, and he sent it to the society with the expectation that it would be welcomed and acclaimed.

Yet with scientific societies and publications came something that we now call peer review, the process by which all proposed theories and discoveries were "discussed by a great many minds." Newton was neither the first nor the last scientist to find out that theories that seemed so obviously proven to him were still subject to question by other people. Skilled experimenters in the society said that the prism experiments might support, but could not prove Newton's theory: it might be an ingenious hypothesis, but that did not make it the only possible hypothesis. Nor did everyone agree that the mathematical formula for the refraction of light really explained the nature of color. Newton, offended at the reception of his ideas, refused to answer any objections, and he ceased corresponding with the Royal Society altogether.

When he resumed correspondence, it was at the society's request. By 1684, the work of Copernicus, Kepler, Galileo, and other astronomers had gained great attention. Most natural philosophers accepted the theory that planets orbited around the sun, but were still wrestling with the great question of what kept the planets going. Was there a force of some kind? If so, how did it work? And what kind of peculiar force could keep the planets in orbits shaped like ellipses, as Kepler had said they must be? How could one imagine, let alone measure, such a force? It was clearly a task for a mathematician, and as clearly beyond even the most mathematically minded of the members who regularly attended the society. Why not ask Professor Newton? suggested one member. He was a difficult man, true, but a brilliant mathematician. Perhaps he could help work out the answer.

As their emissary, the Royal Society sent Edmund Halley (1656?–1743), a charming and diplomatic philosopher best known in the history of science for predicting the return of the comet that bears his name. Yes, Newton said, he knew how to describe and measure the force holding planets in their orbits; in fact, he had already calculated it, during an eighteen-month period when Cambridge had been closed for fear of the plague. He had been sitting in the garden under some apple trees, he told a friend many years later, and had observed an apple fall. "Why should that apple always descend perpendicularly to the ground, thought he to himself? Why should it not go sideways or upwards, but constantly to the earth's center?. . . There must be a drawing power in matter," and it must be in all matter, not just the earth, proportional to its "quantity," or what we now call its mass. "Therefore the apple draws the earth, as well as the earth draw the apple," and therefore this "drawing power," or attraction, must extend high up into the sky. How high, Newton wondered. To the clouds? To the moon? Perhaps "there is a power, like that we here call gravity, which extends itself throughout the universe," and he set out to calculate that power.[7]

Urged on by Halley, Newton published his research as *The Mathematical Principles of Natural Philosophy* (commonly known by the first word of its Latin title, *Principia*). It was a strikingly difficult book, but those savants who could work their way through it proclaimed it a masterpiece. It established principles of physics that were considered laws of nature, true everywhere in the universe, until modified in the twentieth century; it used those laws to develop the mathematical formula for gravity on earth; and it showed how that formula explained the orbits of the planets around the sun. It also explained the action of the moon and sun on tides, included a discussion of lightning rods, and proposed a theory of atoms that was the starting point for chemists for the next hundred years. Newton became the most famous philosopher of his day. He was knighted by the king and given a government position as Secretary of the Mint. There could be only one Newton, wrote a contemporary, because there was only one world to discover. "Nature and Nature's Laws lay hid in night," wrote the poet Alexander Pope; "God said, Let Newton Be, and all was light." When Newton died in 1727, he was buried in Westminster Abbey, in the space reserved for the greatest men of England.

The New Critical Spirit

The achievements of Newton and Descartes produced cultural competition in what was beginning to be called the "republic of letters"—in other words, a country of savants devoted to the pursuit of truth. Relations were not always cordial in the republic. Newton and the German philosopher Gottfried Leibniz (1646–1716) feuded over who deserved primary credit for the development of calculus, for example. But the emergence of the new critical spirit enabled talented outsiders to participate as well. The Jewish philosopher Baruch Spinoza (1632–1677) was widely respected for the power of his philosophical works, even though his philosophical critics charged that he was actually an atheist.

The pursuit of truth was not limited to scientists and philosophers. Bernard de Fontenelle, who as Secretary of the Académie des Sciences had the task of writing obituaries for all members who died, thought the restless, critical investigation of what had passed as common knowledge was the distinctive characteristic of all "modern philosophers, who, being independent of control by any authority, are seekers now and for ever." Fontenelle was an elegant writer, whose intended audience was the *beau monde,* the "beautiful people" in town and court. His *Conversations on the Plurality of Worlds* features a narrator who lightheartedly explains the new astronomical theories to a clever and lovely marquise; his *History of Oracles* converted scholarly, difficult texts attacking belief in oracles, omens, and portents into amusing table talk. He and other popularizers spread the critical spirit beyond universities and academies, into books and, by the end of the seventeenth century, literary journals for the growing literate public.

Blaise Pascal

Blaise Pascal (1623–1662) started out as a mathematical savant, but became a bestselling author. Like Newton, he showed precocious ability in mathematics. Though recognizing his son's genius, Pascal's father locked up all mathematical texts for fear Blaise would ignore Latin and other studies. Pascal developed his own mathematical games, which so impressed his father that he allowed his son to turn to the serious study of mathematics.

The first of Pascal's serious mathematical efforts came from his father's occupation as tax collector, which involved many thousands of fiscal calculations. To help his father, Pascal tried to find a quicker and easier method. The result was his arithmetic machine, which he completed in 1645 with the help of artisans who produced over fifty models. This machine would have been enough to secure his reputation among natural philosophers, but it was followed by a series of experimental researches. Pascal built on the experiments carried out by the Italian scientist Torricelli to develop the first barometer, using handblown glass tubes up to forty-six feet in length. He carried out experiments on the vacuum, as well, and investigated the mathematical properties of the triangle that bears his name.

In 1651, Pascal's father died, and in 1652, his beloved sister Jacqueline entered the monastery of Port-Royale, which had become a haven for followers of the writer Cornelius Jansen. Like Jean Calvin, the Jansenists, as they were called, had been greatly influenced by St. Augustine. And, though they repudiated any connection to Calvinists, their insistence on Augustine's assertion that "grace is not given to all men" seemed to Jesuit scholars uncomfortably close to Calvin's doctrine of the elect. When the professor of theology at the Sorbonne argued in favor of Jansen's ideas, he was accused of heresy. Sometime in 1654, Pascal himself underwent a religious conversion to Jansenism. Probably few cared enough about fine points of theology to follow the debate, had not Pascal published a series of *Provincial Letters* pitting the virtue, simplicity, and faith of the Jansenists against the worldliness and casuistry (self-serving arguments) of their opponents.

The narrator of the *Provincial Letters* begins by running back and forth among the Sorbonne opponents of the Jansenists to find out in what ways Jansen's doctrines differ from orthodoxy, but he cannot get a straight story. He continues on, for the remaining eighteen letters, ridiculing passages from opponents to Jansenists that imply that any action is permitted as long as it serves their ends. Murder for murder's sake is of course against church law, but since murder in self-defense might be justifiable, that excuse can be applied to fighting a duel to protect one's honor, assassination to protect one's property, even—as Pascal takes the argument to its absurd conclusion—murder to prevent the theft of an apple, if the theft would impugn the honor of the murderer.

The *Provincial Letters* were banned by censors and had to be published anonymously during Pascal's own lifetime. Yet they circulated in thousands of copies, making an obscure church controversy the hottest topic in France. They have remained in print ever since, as have Pascal's *Pensées* (Thoughts), published after his death. He had intended the *Pensées* as part of a book to be entitled *Evidences for Religion*, and they remain a testament to the power of faith, even in the new, critical world. He applied the principles of mathematical probability theory, which he had pioneered, in order to show that it made sense to "bet" that God does exist. "We must begin by showing that religion is not contrary to reason," Pascal wrote, "that it is venerable, to inspire respect for it; then we must make it lovable, to make good men hope it is true; finally, we must prove it is true."[8]

Pierre Bayle

To Pierre Bayle (1647–1706), born twenty years after Pascal, no such compromise between religion and reason seemed possible. "That is the conclusion we are bound to come to . . . , that any particular dogma [religious idea] . . . whatever it may be . . . is to be regarded as false if it clashes with the clear and definite conclusions of the natural understanding."[9] The difference may be political as well as generational. For Pascal, while denying he was a Calvinist, still lived when French Calvinists were protected by the Edict of Nantes. Bayle, whose father was a poor Calvinist minister in a town in the Pyrenees, had fled from France to Rotterdam in the United Provinces during the period of Calvinist persecution leading up to the Revocation of the Edict of Nantes in 1685. Surrounded by like-minded exiles, he became one of the foremost champions first of the Protestants, then of freedom of conscience.

Bayle had become addicted to books at an early age, studying for six or seven hours at a time, and chafed at his father's poverty, which prevented his going away to school until his older brother had finished. His first publications applied modern, critical tools to the study of comets, which traditionally were considered as portents of misfortune. This belief, Bayle said, had no logical basis, since the connection of comets with later events cannot be proven. There is no clear evidence that disasters are more prevalent in years in which comets appear, let alone that the comets have anything to do with disasters that may occur. It is as if, "because a woman cannot look out of a window" in a busy street "without seeing a lot of carriages go by, she has a right to assume that she is the cause of the phenomenon; or at any rate that her appearance at the window ought to warn her neighbours that carriages would soon be going by."[10] Carriages are carriages; human affairs are human affairs; comets are comets. The supernatural—in which category Bayle, to the scandal of many of his readers, later included God's miracles—has nothing to do with any of them.

Bayle's major work was his *Historical and Critical Dictionary*, first published in 1696. It was primarily a biographical dictionary, including figures from history, writers, and philosophers. It was the first modern reference book, and that was part of its appeal, for it put a great deal of scholarship into a concise form for a literate audience. In the footnotes, often much longer than the text, Bayle put his own ideas and opinions, carrying out his ongoing war against religious intolerance. He also included ongoing battles with other writers, for Bayle, like other seventeenth-century writers, was involved in endless controversies. The *Dictionary* was a huge task, and Bayle had to write furiously to stay one step ahead of the typesetter: only in the winter, when the printer's ink froze, could he write at a more leisurely pace. The first edition quickly sold out, and Bayle prepared a second, which spread widely in northern Europe. Smuggled copies found their way into France, like other banned books, which "despite all the precautions and vigilance of the authorities . . . manage to worm their way in." Paradoxically, the French policy of censorship meant that the books were all the more sought after, "because they are not easy to come by, because they are a rarity, because they excite curiosity, in a word, because they are forbidden."[11]

The *Dictionary* made Bayle famous, and as an old man he, like Descartes, became a stopping point for anyone on a philosophical Grand Tour. Within twenty-five years after his death in 1706, the *Dictionary* had been reprinted in a general collection of Bayle's writings, and it became one of the standard books in eighteenth-century French libraries.

The Quarrel About Women

If the old ideas of natural philosophy and religious orthodoxy could be critically examined, why not the old ideas on the nature of women? "Men persuade themselves of many things, for which they can give no reason," wrote the French curate Poullain de la Barre (1647–1723) in 1673. Among these prejudices were the belief that the sun goes around the earth, that a man's own religion is the true one, and that his own countrymen are more apt to be right than foreigners. And "amongst these odd opinions," de la Barre went on, "we may reckon the common judgement which men make of the difference of the two sexes," which holds that "women are inferior to men in capacity and worth, and that they ought to be placed in that dependance wherein we see them."[12] This belief in women's inferiority, he said, originated in men's taking advantage of their greater strength in the earliest period of human history and was perpetuated because it was in men's interest to magnify the importance of their own sex. Customary ideas of women's inability to reason, their unfitness for public office, their lack of courage, were merely the result of prejudice, perpetuated by supposedly learned men who had no better reason for believing it than what they themselves had been taught.

Poullain's writings became part of what became known as the quarrel about women, over their abilities, their virtue, and their supposed inferiority to men. In the late seventeenth and early eighteenth centuries, a number of writers, many of them women, spoke out against the misogynist view of women found in ancient authors and perpetuated by men in their own day. In France, Marie de Romieu published a poetic *Brief Discourse, showing that the excellence of women surpasses that of men* in 1591; in Italy, Lucrezia Marinella published a treatise entitled *The Nobility and Excellence of Women* in 1621. In the United Provinces, Anna Maria van Schurman wrote in *The Learned Maid, or Whether a Maid May Be a Scholar* (1659) that "God hath created woman also . . . whatsoever perfects and adorns the intellect of man . . . is fit and decent for Christian woman."[13] Poullain de la Barre joined this tradition to the new genre of writings critical of ancient authority. He had studied at the Theological Faculty at the Sorbonne and may have intended an academic career. Around 1667 he began to read Descartes, which made him as disillusioned as Pascal with orthodox theology. He may also have become convinced at that point that women were as capable as men of forming "clear and distinct notions" on many subjects. True, he admitted, women were often less learned than men, but that did not mean they were any less intelligent: on the contrary, they were often far more rational, and far better able to express themselves clearly, than the so-called learned men who had written so much to their disadvantage. Women seem born to practice medicine, Poullain wrote; they plead their own cases better than many lawyers; they are excellent managers of estates; and "A little experience is sufficient to inform us, that the women here are more fit and useful than we; for, young maids are capable to order a house, at that age when men stand still in need of a master."[14] Why should they not be doctors, and lawyers, and philosophers, and even statesmen and generals?

Poullain's writings were picked up and opposed by more conservative writers, such as the influential Bishop Bossuet, but they also found support. In Italy, the philosopher Paolo Mattia Doria wrote "in pretty well everything that matters most, women are not a whit inferior to men."[15] Poullain's writings were translated into English in 1677, and they were read and cited by feminist authors during the eighteenth century. Poullain himself later resigned his position as curate and moved to Geneva, converted to Calvinism, and eventually became a teacher at the College de Geneva. He married and had two children, but we know nothing about his family life. It is pleasant to think, though, that the man who had "taken delight to entertain my self with women, of all the different conditions that I could meet with . . . and I have found . . . more sound judgement . . ." might have remained faithful to his ideas on the equality of the sexes in his own household.[16]

Profile: Maria Sybilla Merian

Adherents of the new natural philosophy did not really believe that the mind had no sex. When Margaret Cavendish, Duchess of Newcastle (1623–1673), wanted to attend one of the Royal Society's sessions, her request provoked heated debate among members. Cavendish had been a member of an informal group of natural philosophers, including several who became members of the Royal Society, since the 1640s; she was also a generous patron of learning. She was as competent in, and far more interested in, the new natural philosophy than many of the aristocratic patrons the Royal Society did court, and she was much impressed by her visit, which included a demonstration by Robert Boyle. Yet Cavendish and all other women were excluded from formal membership in the new scientific societies, as they were from the old universities.

As Bacon had observed, though, the manual arts could be fruitful places for innovation in science, and certain manual trades, like painting and engraving, were open to women. The artist and naturalist Maria Sybilla Merian (1647–1717) was born in Frankfort. Her father, Matthias Merian, was a well-known artist, specializing in precise architectural views of cities. Though he died when Maria was three, her own interest in engraving was encouraged by her mother, Johanna Sibylla Heim, and stepfather, Jacob Marrel, another painter. She married Johann Andreas Graff in 1665 and had two children, but strong religious feeling led her to leave him and join a Protestant religious community in 1685. She continued both her engraving and her interest in natural history. She was particularly interested in the process of metamorphosis, at that time little understood, and raised silkworms and other caterpillars in her own garden.

Merian's first volume of annotated engravings, *The Wonderful Transformation and Peculiar Plant Nourishment of Caterpillars*, was published in 1679, her second in 1683, and her third in 1717. In the 1690s she settled in Amsterdam, where her older daughter married, and established herself as an artist and teacher, training other young women in watercolors, engraving, and natural history illustration. She became particularly fascinated by the insect specimens brought back by Dutch merchants from their colonies in Surinam in South America. Yet the specimens were just isolated individuals, for no one had yet documented the life cycles of the New World species. "So I was moved," Merian said, "to take a long and costly journey to Surinam," and in 1699, she and her younger daughter set sail for the Dutch colony, remaining there for two years. Merian returned to publish a pioneering study, *Metamorphosis of the Insects of Suriname*. The sixty copperplates, some of which were hand-colored by Merian herself, are also magnificent works of art, firmly establishing Merian's artistic and scientific reputation. Her work has been cited by naturalists, and admired by artists, from her own to the present day.

Important Dates

1603	Accademia dei Lincei founded
1620	Publication of Bacon's *New Organon*
1626	Death of Bacon
1637	Publication of Descartes's *Discourse on Method*
1642	Death of Galileo
1657	Publication of Pascal's *Provincial Letters*
1662	Royal Society of London founded
1666	Académie Royale des Sciences in Paris founded
1673	Publication of Poullain de la Barre's *The Woman as Good as the Man. Or, The Equality of Both Sexes*
1687	Publication of Newton's *Principia*
1696	Publication of Bayle's *Historical and Critical Dictionary*
1699	Merian's voyage to Suriname

Further Reading

Roger Ariew, *Descartes and the Last Scholastics* (Ithaca, 1999)
Ann Blair, *The Theater of Nature. Jean Bodin and Renaissance Science* (Princeton, 1997)

Peter Dear, *Discipline and Experience: The Mathematical Way in the Scientific Revolution* (Chicago, 1995)

Peter Dear, *Mersenne and the Learning of the Schools* (Ithaca, 1988)

Betty Jo Teeter Dobbs, *The Janus Face of Genius: The Role of Alchemy in Newton's Thought* (Cambridge, 1991)

William Eamon, *Science and the Secrets of Nature: Books of Secrets in Medieval and Early Modern Culture* (Princeton, 1996)

Marain Fourier, *The Fabric of Life: Microscopy in the Seventeenth Century* (Baltimore, 1996)

Roger Hahn, *The Anatomy of a Scientific Institution: The Paris Academy of Sciences, 1666–1803* (Berkeley, 1971)

A. Rupert Hall, *From Galileo to Newton* (New York, 1981)

A. Rupert Hall, *Philosophers at War: The Quarrel between Newton and Leibniz* (Cambridge, 1980)

Michael Hunter, *Science and Society in Restoration England* (Cambridge, 1981)

James R. Jacob, *Robert Boyle and the English Revolution* (New York, 1977)

James R. Jacob, *Scientific Revolution: Aspirations and Achievements, 1500–1700* (Atlantic Highlands, NJ, 1998)

Margaret Jacob, *The Newtonians and the English Revolution* (Ithaca, 1976)

Lisa Jardine and Alan Stewart, *Hostage to Fortune: The Troubled Life of Francis Bacon* (New York, 1995)

A.J. Krailsheimer, *Pascal* (Oxford, 1980)

Frank Manuel, *The Religion of Isaac Newton* (Oxford, 1974)

Lawrence M. Principe, *The Aspiring Adept: Robert Boyle and His Alchemical Quest* (Princeton, 1998)

Eileen Reeves, *Painting the Heavens: Art and Science in the Age of Galileo* (Princeton, 1997)

E.G. Ruestow, *The Microscope in the Dutch Republic: The Shaping of Discovery* (Cambridge, 1996)

Londa Schiebinger, *The Mind Has No Sex? Women in the Origins of Modern Science* (Cambridge, MA, 1989)

Steven Shapin, *Scientific Revolution* (Chicago, 1996)

Steven Shapin, *A Social History of Truth: Civility and Science in Seventeenth Century England* (Chicago, 1994)

Steven Shapin and Simon Shaffer, *Leviathan and the Air Pump: Hobbes, Boyle, and the Experimental Life* (Princeton, 1985)

Pamela Smith, *The Business of Alchemy: Science and Culture in the Holy Roman Empire* (Princeton, 1994)

Dava Sobel, *Galileo's Daughter* (New York, 1999)

Charles Webster, *The Great Instauration: Science, Medicine, and Reform, 1620–1660* (London, 1975)

Richard S. Westfall, *The Life of Isaac Newton* (Cambridge, 1994)

Catherine Wilson, *The Invisible World: Early Modern Philosophy and the Invention of the Microscope* (Princeton, 1995)

Catherine Wilson, *Liebniz's Metaphysics* (Princeton, 1989)

Perez Zagorin, *Francis Bacon* (Princeton, 1998)

Part III

ca. 1730–1790

Chapter Twelve

Public Sphere and Private Lives

Public Opinion

Throughout European history until the early modern period, what we would now call "public affairs"—government, politics, international diplomacy—was really considered to be the private business of kings, nobles, and their ministers. They made what we now call "public policy," such as laws, treaties, trade agreements, and diplomatic alliances, without any reference to what the rest of the public might think of the matter. Indeed, most ruling monarchs would have thought it absurd to ask the opinion of their subjects, except for the most powerful nobles and the richest church institutions. For what could the "ordinary people" of a country, those who spent their lives pursuing their own businesses and looking after their own families, have to tell kings and lords about the business of governing? If they were kept informed at all, it was only as a strategy to help kings raise more money in taxes.

The printing press was the first agent of change. During the Reformation, for the first time, Protestants and Catholics were able to use the printed word in pamphlets and broadsides to address their lords and their communities. Their object was to persuade, to mold public opinion, and, in many cases, to influence public policy. Martin Luther's *Address to the German Princes*, advising them how to renounce the authority of the Pope, and why, is an example. In France, during the Fronde rebellion, and in England, during the Civil War, writers composed pamphlet after pamphlet justifying their beliefs and their course of action. Governments, too, made use of the printing press. They hired their own pamphleteers to explain and justify their policies. By the beginning of the seventeenth century, many governments issued their own gazettes, or newspapers, to present official reports. Frankfurt, home of the book trade, had a newspaper published in German and Latin in 1587. By 1604, a publisher in Antwerp received official approval to publish news for the government of the Spanish Netherlands. By 1617, there were several news-sheets published in Holland. The first English newspaper appeared in 1618, and the numbers swelled throughout the late seventeenth and eighteenth centuries. By 1790 London alone had fourteen morning papers, and within the next ten years evening and Sunday papers appeared. Important provincial towns like Bristol and Norwich got into the act, and by the mid-eighteenth century there were thirty-five local newspapers throughout Britain. "Knowledge is diffused among our people by the newspapers,"[1] noted one English writer, and, he might have added, by magazines as well. At least 250 periodicals were published in Britain over the course of the eighteenth century, providing discussion of literary subjects, political analysis, "ladies' affairs," illustrations, and obituaries.

In all countries, government censors kept a close watch over what newspapers published, and there was little freedom of the press. Most governmental business was kept secret, and criticism of government policy could be prosecuted as treason. In Britain, for example, Parliamentary debates were closed to the public, and public attacks on state policies were punished severely. In France, nothing was supposed to be published without an official seal of approval from the government. Any book, print, or pamphlet that criticized government policy or attacked the social order could earn its publisher a trip to the Bastille, a prison in Paris. The virulence of some "pamphlet wars" demonstrates that strict censorship did not always succeed in suppressing oppositional voices. Controversial works were usually published anonymously, with the actual publisher disguised as well. The public only became all the more eager for news, and newspaper reporters, then as now, cultivated government sources to try to get the best and most up-to-date information.

Who was this "public" whose "opinion" writers wanted to influence? Initially, the "public" included only those who had the power to make policy. In countries in which the monarch had absolute power, political writers addressed their pamphlets and treatises primarily to them. In countries in which representative institutions had substantial power, though, members often found themselves divided into political parties, and each party used print media to support its own policies. Party leaders employed writers and artists to promote their own policies and vilify those of their opponents, often with even less regard for truth and accuracy than modern political campaigns. At first, their intended audience was fellow members of their representative body, but as political debate grew more heated, writers increasingly addressed the "general public" of voters as well. Voters had to be men of substantial property, but, political writers found, they were not the only influential groups in society, and so their intended audience expanded again. All kinds of people might be affected by public policy and be willing to exert their influence to support or oppose it. At very least they wanted to be informed. Anyone engaged in commercial activity, such as overseas trade, wanted to keep up with government policy, whether or not he could vote; anyone whose son or brother was a military officer wanted to keep up with the progress of war or peace treaties; anyone involved in a profession like law or medicine or the church wanted to be able to converse intelligently on current affairs. Anyone, in fact, who could read about current events could have an opinion on the course they ought to take, and so one of the most important discoveries of the eighteenth century was that the "public" in "public opinion" extended as far as the "literate public."

Since literacy was much higher in cities than in the countryside, "public opinion" addressed in eighteenth-century writings disproportionately reflected the views and interests of the urban, rather than the rural population, of the rich rather than the poor, and of men rather than women. Peasants, it was widely assumed, had no opinions on public policy at all, or else only the most stupid and self-interested opinions. Even powerful women with substantial influence at court, it was assumed, took their political opinions from their husbands. Moreover, the influence of "public opinion" varied greatly throughout Europe, depending on how much power representative institutions had and how much governments required their support. Still, never before had so many books, pamphlets, prints, and newspapers been available. Never before had so much information on government, on international diplomacy, on commercial policy been so widely disseminated. Never before, in other words, had public policy become so accessible to private citizens.

In Great Britain after the Glorious Revolution, the arena of public opinion was the widest within Europe. When William and Mary died, the throne went to Mary's sister Anne (1665–1714), and when she died without living children, Parliament offered the throne to George I (1660–1727), Duke of the German state of Hanover. George I was succeeded by his son, George II (1683–1760), and grandson, George III (1738–1820), but throughout the eighteenth century the monarch had to work closely with Parliamentary leaders. The issue of succession after Queen Anne kept political parties alive and well, and so did the law, established under William and Mary, that Parliament must meet at least every three years. The early years of the eighteenth century saw many hotly contested elections in Britain, with the full arsenal of political cartoons, smear campaigns, bribes, and street fights called on to marshal votes for favored candidates. Powerful lords routinely decided who should win elections in their districts and told the electors, their tenants, whom to vote for. Such districts were called "pocket boroughs" because "My-Lord-So-and-So" was said to have them "in his pocket" and to deliver them to the political party of his choice. Groups of electors, more independent, might band together and contact a local political leader, promising him their support in return for favors for themselves or their families. British parties kept the names "Whig" and "Tory" from the political battles preceding the Glorious Revolution, but their policies developed to reflect the changing political issues of the new century. The leader of the most powerful party in the House of Commons became known as the prime minister. As long as he stayed in power, he was the most important man in the British government. And in order to stay in power, he had to ensure that influential public opinion stayed on his side.

Daniel Defoe (1660–1730)

In 1706, as the former businessman and current spy and political writer Daniel Defoe left London for the Scottish capital Edinburgh, he prepared to marshal public opinion to the Crown's cause. Scotland had been formally united under the Crown of England in 1603 but had retained its own Parliament and trappings of government. Now Queen Anne and her ministers wanted the two governments united. Though called the "Union" of parliaments, the process meant that the Scottish parliament would be abolished and the traditional Scottish system of representation would stop. A small number of representatives would represent Scotland in the English parliament. From the English point of view, it made perfect sense. As an independent kingdom, Scotland was hard to govern. Its closest diplomatic ties had always been with France, and in 1706, France was at war with England. There was always a danger that French troops would be able to use Scotland as a base for an invasion of England, perhaps to put the former King James II, or his son, Charles, on the throne. (James and then Charles did in fact make two such attempts, during the "Jacobite" rebellions in 1715 and 1745.)

Even some Scots were in favor of Union. The most powerful men, who would have the privilege of sitting in Parliament, would have an entirely new avenue of political influence open to them. Men of the "middling sort," as they were called, including gentry, businessmen, and professional men, saw Union as a way of boosting the faltering Scottish economy and sharing in English prosperity. Yet many more opposed the destruction of the liberties of the kingdom of Scotland and what they feared would be the annihilation of their national identity. The Scottish parliament itself had to vote on Union, which meant that the members of parliament would be voting on a policy that would destroy their sole political function.

Here, thought Defoe, was a job for a political writer in the Crown's cause. Defoe had been born in London, the son of a prosperous businessman and long-standing participant in city government. Defoe himself had begun his adult life the same way, but overexpansion, speculation, and shady business dealings led him into bankruptcy at the age of thirty-three. As one way of recovering his solvency, Defoe turned to writing, for London booksellers had discovered that the growth of literacy led to a lucrative market for pamphlets, short stories, and poems on current events and personalities. Defoe wrote pamphlets on all sorts of topics: on the dangers of foreign invasions, on the evils of standing armies (permanent armies paid for by the monarch and garrisoned on the civilian population), on schemes for providing for the poor, on corruption in elections. When he wrote an impassioned pamphlet which had the effect of questioning government policy against Dissenters (Defoe was himself a Dissenter), though, the government accused him of "publishing a scandalous book" that contained "false and scandalous reflections upon this Parliament" and tended to "promote sedition."[2] Defoe fled, but was tracked down, placed in the pillory and sentenced to spend six months in Newgate prison.

Yet Defoe had made friends in high places, and some of them suggested to government ministers that so talented a writer could come in useful. "Some discreet writer of the Government side," wrote one, would be useful "if it were only to state facts right, for the generality err for want of knowledge & being imposed upon by the stories raised by ill-designing men."[3] Defoe did more than merely state facts. He traveled, collecting opinions and reporting them; he watched the press; he watched for people who might write or act against government policy—all in his new employers' interest. But he also watched out for his own interests, looking for areas where his talent might be especially useful. Among his contacts were influential Scotsmen, in favor of the Union. He collected information from them and researched the issue on his own. In part owing to his own initiative, he received the job of going to Edinburgh to do all that a "discreet writer of the Government side" could do to ensure that the Act of Union passed.

Defoe had his work cut out for him, because anti-Union feeling ran high in Edinburgh. Any pro-Union member of the Scottish Parliament was likely to be pelted with garbage and stones as he emerged from the day's deliberations; officials faced death threats and at least one full-scale riot. Skillful political management by pro-Union forces could ensure that the Act of Union passed, but they knew that there might be severe civil disturbance if public opinion could not be swayed in its favor. Defoe began his work by making friends with pro-Union Scots, who gave him information on each day's deliberations. He read the anti-Union pamphlets by patriotic Scots and took care to answer their arguments. And he wrote a series of pamphlets stressing the economic benefits that would come to Scotland through the Act of Union, purporting to address his arguments to *Englishmen* who feared that the Scots would benefit too much from the integration of the two countries. The Act of Union was ratified in January 1707, and Defoe was rewarded for his work on the government's behalf.

Defoe's life continued to have its ups and downs, but his commitment to writing never wavered. Over the course of a busy life he published over 200 books and pamphlets. He is best remembered for his novels, so detailed that readers in his own day often assumed that they were reading fact, not fiction. He completed his most famous book, *The Life and Strange Surprising Adventures of Robinson Crusoe*, at the age of fifty-nine.

Public and Private Spaces

In the late twentieth century, movie-viewing shifted from something that people do outside the home, in public spaces, to something that people do in the privacy of their own home. Though public movie-viewing still exists, many new markets have sprung up to accommodate the demand for private video-viewing, and even movies released in theaters are affected by it. The eighteenth century saw a similar shift in reading, from an activity done primarily outside the house, in coffeehouses or reading rooms, to something more and more people did in the privacy of their own homes. Truly individual reading, done by one person, alone, remained rare except for religious works. The most common form of "consumption" of print culture in the later eighteenth century was for fathers, mothers, or children to read to the family, for "conversation & observation," as one mother noted, as well as for entertainment.[4]

Coffeehouses, which usually served food and drink as well as coffee, subscribed to newspapers and periodicals. They often developed a regular clientele, who used the coffeehouse as a place to receive messages, debate current events, and make useful contacts. There were political coffeehouses, literary coffeehouses, and philosophical coffeehouses. In Britain, where there was a comparatively high literacy rate among all classes, even urban tradesmen and artisans visited coffeehouses. "All English are great newsmongers," noted one Swiss traveler in 1727. "Workmen habitually begin the day by going to coffee rooms in order to read the daily news. Nothing is more entertaining than hearing men of this class discussing politics and topics of interest concerning royalty."[5]

One group was excluded from coffeehouses, except as proprietors or servants: women. Women could own or manage coffeehouses, as they could own taverns and inns, and female servants were an indispensable part of any household. But no respectable woman, let alone a young lady, would visit a coffeehouse, either to drink coffee, read newspapers, or participate in the political or literary discussions. They could, however, read, and an entirely respectable place for women to go to read the morning papers was the local book club and lending library. Many booksellers also operated private libraries (just as modern video stores will sell as well as rent videos), and the more elaborate stores provided armchairs, coffee, and tea for their patrons. "There are some thousands of ladies who frequent my shop," wrote one London bookseller, "and that know as well what books to choose, and are as well acquainted with works of taste and genius as any gentleman in the kingdom."[6]

Women could also extend their traditional role as hostess, especially in countries with an established court culture, by opening a salon, a kind of regularly scheduled, private meeting that was a cross between a dinner party, a literary club, and a power lunch. A salon was a mixture of a private and public space. The hostess (in French, the *salonière*) controlled admission to her house, and the gatherings could become venues for private sexual intrigue. But they could also become forums for debate and discussion among the *beau monde* (beautiful people) who congregated there. In Paris, under Louis XIV, Madame de Scudéry had presided over a well-known salon, where the best-known and most influential people, and people who wanted to meet them, came. The tradition of salons continued throughout the eighteenth century. In Paris, there were so many that serious salonières chose their weekly gatherings so as not to conflict with other well-established salons, and carefully planned the mixture of rank, talent, and fortune they wished to attract. Just like coffeehouses, certain salons specialized in certain clientele. There were political salons, literary salons, scientific salons, even—by the end of the century—radical salons. The ambition of a salonière, commented one French male observer, was to help promote the careers of men of talent, "to be useful in bringing them together with men of power and position."[7]

The ambitions of many salonières, though, extended beyond being a good society hostess to demonstrating their own power, influence, and political or philosophical interests. One of the most famous salons of the early eighteenth century was run by Madame de Tencin, a younger daughter of a noble household. Her family had intended her to enter a convent, since it was less expensive than providing her with a dowry. Instead, she established a salon in Paris, attracting writers, noblemen, and philosophers, acquiring several lovers, and earning a fortune or two in overseas investments. She also used her contacts to advance the political fortunes of her brother and other favorites. Her illegitimate son, Jean D'Alembert, became famous as a writer and mathematician; his mistress, too, kept a salon. The prestige of France as a center of culture led to the spread of salon culture to other capital cities dominated by courts, like Berlin.

Essay and Novel

The increasing numbers of pamphlets, books, and newspapers in circulation meant that literary "conversations" could go on even among authors who never met each other face to face. Defoe's *Robinson Crusoe* showed many early eighteenth-century writers the power of mixing contemporary events with imaginative literature, and it may have been the inspiration for the combination of fiction and satire found in *Gulliver's Travels* (1726), by the Irish churchman Jonathan Swift (1667–1745). Its full title was *Travels into Several Remote Nations of the World*, and its title page listed one Lemuel Gulliver as the author. Though Gulliver's travels in the tiny world of Lilliput and the giant world of Brobdingnag are now read as a children's story, early eighteenth-century readers recognized them as sharp political satire. Even more pointed was the satire in Swift's essay *A Modest Proposal for Preventing the Children of Poor People from being a Burden to their Parents and for Making them Beneficial to the Public* (1729). Swift was appalled at the treatment of the rural Irish population. Their English and Scottish landlords had been given tracts of land in Ireland during Cromwell's reign as a means to prevent rebellion. They were most often absentee landlords whose sole use for their estates was to extract as much revenue as possible. Swift had proposed many serious remedies for the situation, such as taxing absentee landlords, promoting Irish industry, and "teaching landlords to have at least one degree of mercy toward their tenants." This time, he wrote, he had an even better idea: sell the babies of poor families for food when they were one year old. That would kill two birds with one stone: the babies would not grow up to be additional mouths to feed, at the same time that they would provide scarce food for other people. "I grant," Swift wrote, "this food will be somewhat dear [expensive], and therefore very proper for the landlords, who, as they have already devoured most of the parents, seem to have best title to the children."[8]

Besides Lemuel Gulliver, Jonathan Swift introduced to the London literary scene the astrologer Isaac Bickerstaff, another fictional character represented as author. Swift's friend Richard Steele, editor of the government-sponsored newspaper, the *London Gazette*, borrowed Bickerstaff and made him the supposed editor of a new periodical magazine specializing in moral and philosophical essays, *The Tatler* (1709–1711). Steele's collaborator was an old friend, Joseph Addison, who then held a government position as undersecretary of state. In the ups and downs of the London political scene, Addison lost his post; in the meantime, *The Tatler* had become infused with party politics. Addison and Steele decided to start a new periodical, *The Spectator* (1710–1712). Its author was supposedly a country gentleman settled in London, well-educated, who spent much of his time observing men, women, and current society. This Spectator, readers learned, belonged to a supper club who met regularly. They soon became acquainted with the members' names and characters, intended to represent the spectrum of polite (well-off and well-educated) society. The *Spectator* essays, contributed by both Addison and Steele, were a combination of sharp, witty observation and reflections on social and moral issues, designed to "bring philosophy out of closets and libraries, schools and colleges, to dwell in clubs, and assemblies, at tea-tables, and in coffee-houses."[9] Though the *Spectator* lasted for only two years, it was frequently reprinted through the eighteenth and nineteenth centuries, and frequently imitated. When Eliza Haywood (1693–1756) published her essay periodical, the *Female Spectator*, from 1744 to 1746, she adopted both the essay form and the fiction of issues contributed by members of a society with regular meetings. In this case, the spectrum of literate women in polite society included the wife of a country gentleman, a "widow of quality," and the daughter of a merchant.

The moral tone of the *Female Spectator* was in marked contrast to Haywood's bestselling novels of the 1720s, in which love and passion were gratified with an enthusiasm that made respectable mothers shudder. In *Fantomina: or, Love in a Maze*, the heroine is a young lady "of distinguished birth, beauty, wit, and spirit," who decides to dress up like a prostitute to see what young gentlemen say on such occasions. She meets one man so charming that she carries on the deception until, alas, her own virtue is lost. Still, the connection is so pleasurable that she continues it, taking on new identities as her lover tires of each of her personas. As was inevitable in the eighteenth century, she is eventually betrayed by her own pregnancy and repents, but the reader is still left more intrigued than appalled by the possibilities implied by her behavior.

By the 1740s there was a backlash against books that made amorous intrigues sound like so much fun. The novel, which from the seventeenth century had meant any prose fiction, began to develop a more restricted definition. It should be a narrative that told a definite, interesting story. Though fiction, the plot and characters had to be "true to life," that is, realistic enough to be believable. "A knowledge of the world, and of mankind, are essential requisites in the writer," noted one critic; "the characters should be always natural; the personages should talk, think, and act, as becomes their respective ages, situations, and characters; the sentiments should be moral, chaste, and delicate; the language should be easy, correct, and elegant."[10] Imaginative fiction such as the *Arabian Nights Entertainment*, that took place in far-off places with unlikely characters, became classified as romances. Both genres were very popular, whether published as books, excerpted in magazines, or described in detail in essay-reviews. Women novelists in particular took seriously the idea that novels should teach moral lessons for their own sex. "Good" characters were to be "moral, chaste, and delicate," and they were generally rewarded by their authors with marriage and an estate at the end of the book; "bad" characters received their comeuppance; and any young lady heroine foolish or susceptible enough to lose her chastity would be found dead at the end of the tale. In most cases, the demands of good morals overcame the demand that the novel be true to life. In real life, the novelist Elizabeth Griffiths broke the moral code for young gentlewomen with a clandestine correspondence with a man, then a still more clandestine marriage almost certainly provoked by her pregnancy. No such physical intimacy was ever depicted in her novels, and certainly no hint that, as in her own life, it could lead to a happy marriage.

Many women novelists were acknowledged by critics to be accomplished writers, but the two novelists who critics felt had done most to put the genre on a firm literary footing were Samuel Richardson (1689–1761) and Henry Fielding (1707–1754). Richardson's *Clarissa Harlowe* (1747) became the model of what was called the epistolary novel, a novel composed entirely of letters from one character to the other. It tells the story of a young gentlewoman, Clarissa, who first falls in love with, and then is raped by, the attractive but deceitful Lovelace. Though he eventually offers her marriage, she refuses; she dies, and he is killed in a duel with her cousin. For a novel of the earlier period, this is a very limited plot, but what fascinated readers was Richardson's skill at evoking Clarissa's world so believably. Readers believed themselves transported into the story: "When I read *Clarissa*, I am of the family of Harlowes. I am interested for one, I hate another, I am indifferent for a third. By turns, I could embrace and fight with Lovelace. . . . I interrupt the unhappy Clarissa, in order to mix my tears with hers: I accost her, as if she was present with me."[11]

Clarissa inspired a host of imitators, and those who did not imitate Richardson's epistolary style imitated the continuous and sometimes rollicking narrative of Henry Fielding's *Tom Jones* (1749). Young Tom is brought up in a country gentleman's household and falls in love with a young lady from a neighboring family. The story centers on their tribulations leading to an eventual happy ending, and again, the reader becomes engrossed in their world. "The reader's attention is always kept awake by some new surprising incident," wrote one reviewer, "and his curiosity upon the stretch . . . . so that after one has begun to read, it is difficult to leave off before having read the whole."[12] The detailed portrayal of eighteenth-century English life reached its climax in the novels of Jane Austen (1775–1817), showing how the genre had changed since the works of de Scudéry in the previous century. "I have been reading *Emma*, which is excellent," wrote the novelist Susan Ferrier (1782–1854) in 1816. "There is no story whatever, and the heroine is no better than other people; but the characters are all so true to life, and the style so piquant, that it does not require the . . . aids of mystery and adventure."[13]

The very ability of novelists to evoke a private, imaginary world, however, troubled some moralists. Novel-reading was almost always done in private spaces, whether by parents reading to children or people reading to themselves. Readers seemed oblivious to the outside world, reading on, one boy later remembered, "till it was dark, without any supper or bed. When I could see no longer, I put my little book in my pocket," and the next morning, he began reading again as soon as he awoke.[14] Like modern observers who worry about the impact of television on young people, eighteenth-century commentators worried that novelists would corrupt youth, leading them to act immorally or ignore reality. The old novels might have had immoral characters, but no one would be tempted to imitate them; charming—and successful—rakes like Tom Jones, in contrast, had an obvious appeal for thoughtless young men. For that reason, wrote one disgruntled reader, "I scarcely know a more corrupt work."[15] How deceitful are the imaginary pictures of perfect happiness depicted at the end of novels, wrote another critic, "and, we may add, how mischievous too! The young and the ignorant lose their taste of present enjoyment by opposing to it those delusive daubings of consummate bliss they meet with in novels."[16] And in Charlotte Lennox's *The Female Quixote: Or, the Adventures of Arabella* (1752), the heroine, a young heiress, lives in such a fantasy world inspired by her love of novels that she cannot recognize true love and her own happiness—until the novel's end.

Private and Public Art and Music

Reading began as an activity for a public venue and moved during the century to private spaces. In the same period, art moved the other way, from private to public spaces. Throughout European history, of course, art had been hung in public spaces, like churches or public buildings.

But it had generally been privately commissioned, and it was presented to the public to be admired, not discussed. By the end of the seventeenth century, the art market had shifted toward private collections, with works of art being seen increasingly as home decorating for the wealthy. In France after the death of Louis XIV in 1715, great noble families increasingly took up residence in Paris, building elaborate town houses and decorating them according to the latest fashion. The art they preferred is known as *rococo*, beautifully painted and highly decorative scenes abounding in gardens, cherubs, and nearly naked women. Few of the subjects were religious; instead, they showed scenes from mythology or contemporary aristocratic pastimes such as picnics in the country. What mattered was that all textures of skin, satin, fur, and water be so realistically painted that they create the illusion that the viewer could reach out and touch them, and that the painting itself be so pleasing to the eye that he would want to. It was, deliberately, art to be enjoyed, not to instruct; the more fanciful, the more elaborate, the more erotic, the better.

Yet while rococo art was being installed in these private spaces, a new, public space for art was coming into existence: the *Salon* (from *salon carré*, or square room) of the Louvre, a public exhibition of art put on by the French Academy of Painting and Sculpture every year from 1737. The academy had had some public exhibitions in the late seventeenth century, but they had been discontinued. In 1737, a new director, imbued with a sense of responsibility for what was, after all, a state agency, decided that "the Academy does well to render a sort of accounting to the public of its work and to make known the progress achieved in the arts it nurtures by bringing to light the work of its most distinguished members."[17] There was an immediate outcry on the part of the best-established artists over who this "public" was and why any accounting should be rendered at all. Successful artists, like François Boucher, had become very wealthy precisely because they understood "their" public, the nobles and wealthy financiers who commissioned their paintings. But the academy Salons, which were held annually, admitted anyone, just as theaters did, and artists were fearful that "the ignorant mob" might boo and hiss new paintings just as they did new plays. There was no such thing as a single "public," complained one opponent to the Salons; "the public changes twenty times a day . . . [there is] a simple public at certain times, a prejudiced public, a flighty public, an envious public, a public slavish to fashion, which in order to judge want to see everything and examine nothing . . . the Salon can always be filled with these same kinds of people, but believe me, after having heard them all, you will have heard not a true public, but only the mob." The academy itself, while holding the exhibitions, used its government position to prevent any negative criticism from being published. "I hold the principle," wrote one member, "that a painting, a statue, do not belong to the public in the same way a book does."[18]

And yet "the public" flocked to the exhibitions just as "the public" read new books. "The Salon opens and the crowd presses through the entrance," wrote one clearly hostile observer:

> How its diversity and turbulence disturbs the spectator! This person here, moved by vanity, wants only to be the first to give his opinion; that one there, moved by boredom, searches only for a new spectacle. Here is one who treats pictures as simple items of commerce and concerns himself only to estimate the prices they will fetch; another hopes only that they will provide material for his idle chat. . . . The inferior class of people, accustomed to adjusting its tastes to those of its master, waits to hear a titled person before rendering its opinion. And wherever one looks, countless young clerks, merchants, and shop assistants in whom unchanging, tedious daily labor has inevitably extinguished all feeling for beauty. . . .[19]

Even the beau monde, people of rank and fashion, and some of taste, came to the exhibitions. The tension between the aspirations of the artist and the public who cannot understand him continued to surface at the Salons throughout the eighteenth century. By the end of the century, though, artists had found a way to resolve that tension, by presenting art exhibitions as opportunities to educate "the public" about art. Both the tension, and its resolution, have remained a part of the art world to the present day.

Music, like art, shifted from the private to the public sphere. The composer Johann Sebastian Bach (1685–1750) spent most of his life as a salaried musician, going from one good, but unexciting position to the next. Music was in a way a family business. His father and two of his brothers were musicians, and so were four of his sons (Wilhelm Friedemann Bach, Carl Philipp Emanuel Bach, Johann Christoph Friedrich Bach, and Johann Christian Bach). J.S. Bach was, in fact, very businesslike about his music. He began as town musician, first in the small town of Arnstadt, then in the larger city of Mühlhausen. He then moved to the courts of the small German principalities of Weimar, then

Cöthen. The last twenty-seven years of his life were spent as cantor of the St. Thomas School and director of music for churches in Leipzig.

Bach was noted in his own time for his remarkable skill on the clavier (an early version of the piano) and the organ. "One is amazed at his ability," wrote one musician, "and one can hardly conceive how it is possible for him to achieve such agility, with his fingers and with his feet, in the crossings, extensions, and extreme jumps that he manages, without mixing in a single wrong tone, or displacing his body by any violent movement." He was also known as a brilliant teacher, who, in Leipzig, especially, attracted a large number of students. One wrote home that he had never heard anything like Bach's playing: "I will, if God pleases and keeps me healthy, be uncommonly industrious, for I am eager to learn his style." In his polyphonic (many-voiced) compositions, Bach was noted for maintaining the purity of each voice, telling students that the parts must behave like "persons who conversed together as if in select company."[20] Yet despite his renown among other keyboard players, he was not a public figure. Aside from trips to hear new organs and organists whenever they were within what he considered walking distance—up to 200 miles—he never traveled far from home. Although his music was performed before other people—princely courts, the students in St. Thomas School, the bereaved family when he played the organ at a funeral service—it was not usual for his musical performances to attract "the public." Nor were his performances anything that were considered "newsworthy" by the emerging periodical press.

Attracting the public was precisely what Leopold Mozart, violinist to the archbishop of Salzburg, had in mind when he set off on a concert tour with the musical phenomena of the century, his six-year-old son Wolfgang Amadeus Mozart (1756–1791) and his eleven-year old daughter Maria Anna Mozart. The two children had been performing to rave reviews, for by the 1760s periodical papers had discovered music. The Mozart children appeared before the Habsburg court in Vienna, and "Just imagine," went one newspaper account,

> a girl 11 years of age who can perform on the harpsichord or the fortepiano the most difficult sonatas and concertos by the greatest masters, most accurately, readily and with an almost incredible ease, in the very best of taste. This alone cannot fail to fill many with astonishment. But we fall into utter amazement on seeing a boy aged 6 at the clavier and hear him . . . play in a manly way, and improvise . . . for hours on end . . . and even accompany at sight symphonies, arias and

Watercolor (ca. 1763–1764) of young Mozart, his father, and his sister performing (Giraudon/Art Resource, NY)

recitatives at the great concerts. . . . What is more, I saw them cover the keyboard with a handkerchief; and he plays just as well on this cloth as though he could see the keys. . . .

The reviewer's astonishment was repeated time and time again, as the Mozarts traveled through Germany, France, the Dutch Republic, and England. Wherever possible, they tried to arrange to play at court, for such performances were welcome publicity. But they also gave public performances in the modern sense, renting concert halls and giving "the Public in general an Opportunity of hearing these young Prodigies perform." The trip was widely reported to have cost Leopold a huge amount of money. "I can well believe it" wrote one German observer, "but how much money must he not have collected?"[21]

When he grew up, Wolfgang Mozart hoped to be able to build on his early success to obtain a position as musician in one of the German courts. He was a still a musical prodigy, able to compose the most complicated scores without mistakes or cross-outs. By the 1780s, when he moved to Vienna to support himself by teaching, composing, and performing, the Austrian as well as foreign periodicals regularly reviewed new performances. Mozart's opera *The Escape from the Seraglio*, wrote one review, "is full of beauties . . . and the author's taste and new ideas, which were entrancing, received the loudest and most general applause." His sonatas, wrote another reviewer, "are unique in their kind. Rich in new ideas and traces of their author's musical genius." At one of Mozart's own concerts, the review noted, he received not only "unanimous applause" from the distinguished audience, but also substantial box office receipts.[22] Yet he, like other musicians, found it hard to make a living by relying on public performances. He hoped for a court appointment, but a combination of court intrigue, economies in the government budget, and his own sometimes obnoxious personality kept a salaried appointment tantalizingly out of reach. He was finally appointed to a position at St. Stephen's Cathedral in 1791, shortly before his own death. Many of the nearly 600 works he composed in his short life are still performed in public concerts.

Profile: Wilkes and Liberty

British Parliamentary politics in the eighteenth century was anything but a model for responsible representative government. The government most resembled an oligarchy, or rule by the rich, in which factions of great lords tried everything in their power to influence elections in their favor and for their own interest. Even those calling themselves the Opposition, who opposed the king and his ministers, were not the poor and downtrodden, but great lords in their own right. Their goal was not to overthrow the government, but to replace the existing faction as the in-group. Yet even this closed, elite world of insiders and outsiders could be influenced by public opinion.

This was the situation when, in 1762, John Wilkes (1727–1797), an MP (Member of Parliament, that is, of the House of Commons), began publishing a newspaper, the *North Briton*. "The Liberty of the Press," it proclaimed, "is the birthright of a Briton and is justly esteemed the firmest bulwark of the liberties of this country."[23] This was the first time Wilkes had ever shown an interest in liberties other than his own. His father was a prosperous tradesman, successful enough to give his son the education and some of the vices of gentlemen, and young John had spent his early years as a typical eighteenth-century wastrel, drinking, gambling, and chasing after women. He had the gift of charm and wit, though, and decided to go into politics, not out of any sense of public service, but for his own advancement. Once elected, he immediately wrote petitions to King George III's ministers asking for a position as an ambassador or governor of colonial territory in exchange for his support of govern-ment policies. He was turned down and from that point cast his fortunes with the Opposition. He turned the *North Briton* into a series of unre-lenting attacks on government policy, all published anonymously. Such attacks were common in the newspapers, as were their rebuttals by news-papers on the government side. Wilkes's attacks, though, were unusu-ally pointed and unusually witty. "Wilkes, you will die of a pox [syphilis] or on the gallows," snarled one of his political opponents. "That de-pends, My Lord," Wilkes replied, "on whether I embrace your prin-ciples or your mistress."[24]

In 1763, the *North Briton*, issue number 45, published an exception-ally vicious attack on government policy, and the government decided to act. The secretary of state issued a warrant for all those associated with the *North Briton*. The events of the next few days carried a partisan political battle into the arena of public opinion. The warrant was a "gen-eral" one, in which individuals were not named, and Wilkes refused to treat the warrant as legal for his arrest, since his name was not on it. In the meantime the government compounded the illegality by ransacking his house without a warrant and arresting dozens of men who had noth-ing to do with the *North Briton* at all. By the time Wilkes had his day in court, all London awaited the outcome. The issue, Wilkes argued, was crucial for all Britain, since it involved "the liberty of all peers and gentlemen, and (what touches me more sensibly) that of all the middling and inferior sort of people who stand most in need of protection."[25] Wilkes had never shown any interest in the "middling and inferior sort" before, but his speech was an immediate crowd-pleaser. The judge dismissed the charges, and Wilkes was escorted to his home by cheering crowds, shouting "Wilkes and Liberty!" Over the next year, legal opinion upheld his assertion that a general warrant was illegal—the warrant had to be sworn in the name of a specific person and used only against that person—and Wilkes led a successful fight for damages for false arrest on behalf of all the people arrested on that day.

Wilkes thus became a popular hero, and the next few years of persecution by King George and his ministers only enhanced his reputation. Forced to flee to the Continent, where he lived the expensive and licentious life of a gentleman, he announced his intention to run for Parliament in 1768. He was the perfect political campaigner, sharp-witted, energetic, and well-organized: "Wilkes and Liberty" was his campaign slogan, and No. 45 (for the issue number of the *North Briton*) was painted on every "Wilkite" (Wilkes supporter's) house. He won easily, and a riot of popular support broke out all over Britain. The battle to take his seat, though, took the next seven years. He had been accused and convicted of libel, and his first act after election was to peaceably agree to serve his prison sentence. During his prison term, the king made it clear that he wanted Wilkes out of Parliament. The House of Commons obediently expelled him and called for a new election in his district. Elections were held in February, and Wilkes was again elected; the same thing happened in March and again in April. After the April election, the House of Commons even tried to appoint the candidate Wilkes had defeated. This completely unconstitutional act aroused public outcry once again in Wilkes's behalf. During his prison sentence, Wilkes was elected one of the officials for the City of London; after his release, he was elected Lord Mayor of London. By 1775 the government bowed to public opinion, and Wilkes was finally allowed to take his seat in Parliament.

Important Dates

1587	First newspaper in Frankfurt
1707	Act of Union between Scotland and England
1710–1712	Addison and Steele's *The Spectator*
1714	George I becomes king of England

1719	Publication of Defoe's *Robinson Crusoe*
1726	Publication of Swift's *Gulliver's Travels*
1729	Publication of Swift's *Modest Proposal*
1737	Beginnings of annual *Salons* of French Academy of Painting and Sculpture
1744–1746	Publication of Haywood's *Female Spectator*
1747	Publication of Richardson's *Clarissa Harlowe*
1749	Publication of Fielding's *Tom Jones*
1750	Death of Bach
1752	Publication of Lennox's *The Female Quixote*
1762	Wilkes begins publishing the *North Briton*
1768	"Wilkes and Liberty" parliamentary campaign
1791	Death of Wolfgang Amadeus Mozart

Further Reading

Richard Altick, *The English Common Reader: A Social History of the Mass Reading Public 1800–1900* (Chicago, 1957)

Paula Backscheider, *Daniel Defoe: His Life* (Baltimore, 1989)

Paula Backscheider and John J. Richetti, eds., *Popular Fiction by Women 1660–1730* (Oxford, 1996)

Frederic T. Blanchard, *Fielding the Novelist: A Study in Historical Criticism* (New York, 1966)

J.C.D. Clark, *Samuel Johnson: Literature, Religion and English Cultural Politics from the Restoration to Romanticism* (Cambridge, 1995)

Thomas E. Crow, *Painters and Public Life in Eighteenth-Century Paris* (New Haven, 1985)

Hans T. David and Arthur Mendel, eds., *The New Bach Reader: A Life of Johann Sebastian Bach in Letters and Documents*, revised by Christoph Wolff (New York, 1998)

Otto Erich Deutsch, *Mozart: A Documentary Biography*, trans. Eric Blom, Peter Branscombe, and Jeremy Noble (Stanford, CA, 1966)

Peter Earle, *The Making of the English Middle Class: Business, Society and Family Life in London, 1660–1730* (Berkeley, 1989)

Ruth Halliwell, *The Mozart Family: Four Lives in a Social Context* (New York, 1997)

Catherine Ingrassia, *Authorship, Commerce, and Gender in Early Eighteenth-Century England: A Culture of Paper Credit* (Cambridge, 1998)

Michael Levey, *Rococo to Revolution* (London, 1986)

Joseph M. Levine, *The Battle of the Books: History and Literature in the Augustan Age* (Ithaca, 1991)

Carolyn Lougee, *Le Paradis des Femmes: Women, Salons, and Social Stratification in Seventeenth Century France* (Princeton, 1976)

Henri-Jean Martin, *The French Book, Religion, Absolutism and Readership, 1585–1715* trans. Paul and Nadine Saenger (Baltimore, 1996)

John Middleton Murry, *Jonathan Swift: A Critical Biography* (New York, 1967)

J.H. Plumb, *England in the Eighteenth Century* (Middlesex, England, 1972)

Roy Porter, *English Society in the Eighteenth Century* (Middlesex, England, 1983)

Peter Quennell, *The Profane Virtues: Four Studies of the Eighteenth Century* (New York, 1945)

Jeffrey Ravel, *The Contested Parterre: Public Theater and French Political Culture, 1680–1791* (Ithaca, 1999)

Joad Raymond, *The Invention of the Newspaper: English Newsbooks, 1641–1649* (Oxford, 1996)

C. John Sommerville, *The News Revolution in England: Cultural Dynamics of Daily Information* (Oxford, 1996)

Margaret Spufford, *Small Books and Pleasant Histories: Popular Fiction and Its Readers in Seventeenth-Century England* (Athens, GA, 1981)

Janet Todd, *The Sign of Angelica: Women, Writing, and Fiction 1660–1800* (New York, 1989)

J.M.S. Tompkins, *The Popular Novel in England 1770–1800* (Lincoln, NE, 1961)

Cheryl Turner, *Living by the Pen: Women Writers in the Eighteenth Century* (London, 1992)

Ian Watt, *The Rise of the Novel: Studies in Defoe, Richardson and Fielding* (Berkeley, 1971)

William Weber, *The Rise of Musical Classics in Eighteenth-Century England: A Study in Canon, Ritual, and Ideology* (Oxford, 1992)

Ioan Williams, ed., *Novel and Romance 1700–1800: A Documentary Record* (New York, 1970)

Chapter Thirteen

Enlightenment: Reason, Nature, and Progress

What Is Enlightenment?

What is enlightenment? asked Immanual Kant, the Prussian philosopher. His response came to define the age: "Enlightenment is man's emergence from his self-imposed inability" to use his own understanding without guidance from church, prince, or emperor. "Dare to know!" he wrote. "'Have the courage to use your own understanding,' is therefore the motto of the enlightenment."[1] His cry was taken up by writers throughout Europe, who came to be known collectively as *philosophes*. Though the word means "philosopher," the philosophes did not consider themselves to be ivory-tower philosophers, thinking deep thoughts irrelevant to the rest of humanity. Instead, they were activists, concerned with spreading enlightenment and the power of reason throughout humanity. The philosophe is the "preceptor of mankind," wrote Denis Diderot, author, editor, and art critic: "The magistrate deals out justice: the philosopher teaches the magistrate what is just and unjust. The soldier defends his country; the philosopher teaches the soldier what a fatherland is. The priest recommends to his people the love and respect of gods; the philosopher teaches the priest what the gods are. The sovereign commands all; the philosopher teaches the sovereign the origins and limits of his authority. Every man has duties to his family and his society; the philosopher teaches everyone what those duties are."[2] The "philosopher," then, would take over from religious and secular rulers of the previous generation in explaining nature and human nature, obligations to sovereigns and rights of citizens, not by dogmatically laying down the law for all to follow, but by enlarging the scope of man's (and woman's) understanding and allowing the clear light of reason to shine on the most complex questions.

"Reason" and "nature" were two of the watchwords of the philosophes, and Sir Isaac Newton and John Locke, two of their heroes. Newton was revered as the man who had demonstrated the power of human reason to unlock the wondrous secrets of nature. Newton had used his own genius to enlighten himself and mankind, wrote Voltaire, one of the most famous philosophes. That made him "the greatest man who has ever lived, the very greatest, the giants of antiquity are beside him children playing with marbles."[3] In order to make this triumph of human reason accessible to all, Voltaire enlisted the aid of his lover, Marquise Emilie du Châtelet-Lamont (1706–1749), herself a philosophe with a long-standing interest in physics, in writing a popular account of Newton's theories, which was widely read.

The writings of John Locke were even more widely read. He was admired in part for his political writings on government, on poor reform, and on religious toleration. His most influential works during the eighteenth century, however, were on psychology, published in his *Essay Concerning Human Understanding*. He believed that children were born without innate ideas, their minds similar to a blank slate (in Latin, a *tabula rasa*). They acquired ideas through experience, gradually associating simple ideas gained by concrete experiences into more complex, abstract ones. With this theory, based in part on Locke's actual observance of children, Voltaire believed Locke had "displayed the human soul in the same manner as an excellent anatomist explains the springs of the human body." Like Newton, Locke had spoken from observation and reason: "He takes an infant at the instant of his Birth; he traces, step by step, the progress of his understanding; examines what things he has in common with beasts, and what he possesses above them."[4] Locke, too, therefore, had used the light of reason to elucidate the workings of nature, in this case the most important part of nature: people.

If the philosophes had heroes, they also had villains, in the form of superstition, fanaticism, prejudice, and bigotry. All viewed the religious wars of the previous century as barbarous acts, unfit for civilized society. "What can we say to a man," asked Voltaire with sarcasm, "who tells you that he would rather obey God than men, and that therefore he is sure to go to heaven for butchering you"; "the most detestable act of fanaticism" he knew "was that of the burghers of Paris who on St. Bartholomew's Night went about assassinating and butchering all their fellow citizens who did not go to mass, throwing them out of windows, cutting them to pieces." Orthodox religious leaders, whether Catholic or Protestant, each of whom claimed to have the only true knowledge of God, seemed to Enlightenment writers to be perpetuating the intolerance of the previous century. The philosophes themselves differed in their religious beliefs. There were Catholic, Calvinist, Lutheran, and Jewish philosophes. Some were devout, believing in revealed religion; some were deists, believing God had created the world according to natural laws and then had withdrawn from direct intervention; some became notorious as atheists who did not believe in God at all. What they all had in common was opposition to religious zealotry. "Fanaticism is to superstition what delirium is to fever and rage to anger," wrote Voltaire. ." . . The only remedy for this epidemic malady is the philosophical spirit which, spread gradually, at last tames men's habits and prevents the disease from starting."[5]

The great weapon the philosophes used in the war against superstition was their writings, ranging from poetry and plays to newspaper articles and formal treatises. Their enemy was the censorship that was still law in most countries: Kant's book *Religion Within the Bounds of Reason Alone* was suppressed by the Prussian government, and Voltaire's *Philosophical Letters* was publicly burned by the hangman in front of the Palais de Justice in Paris. But their allies were the growing literate public, consumers of printed matter of all sorts, who showed all the more interest in books that were for some reason illicit. The people who read Defoe's *Robinson Crusoe* might also read Voltaire's novel *Candide*; consumers of Richardson's epistolary novel *Clarissa* might also read Montesqueiu's *Persian Letters* or Mary Wollstonecraft's *Letters from Sweden*. The definition of "enlightenment" with which this chapter opens was first published by Kant in a monthly journal, the *Berlinische Monatschrift*, intended for general readers.

The idea that the human race could become more virtuous and happier, that there could be progress in the human condition, was an article of faith for many philosophes. The end of fierce religious warfare, the reform of armies, the increase in wealth, the growing civility in "manners" all seemed to them to indicate that they were living in an "improved" age. Some writers sounded cautionary notes that, to the modern reader, make the philosophes seem as bigoted as their opponents: they argued that the "ignorance" of the "African" or "American" savages, or the "superstition" of the European peasants, might forever prevent their enlightenment. Others argued that just as all previous ages, like the Roman Empire, had a rise and fall, so too might their own. But one writer, the Marquis de Condorcet (1743–1794), posed the question of the limitless progress of humanity: "Is the human race to better itself, either by discoveries in the sciences and the arts, and so in the means to individual welfare and general prosperity; or by progress in the principles of conduct or practical morality; or by a true perfection of the intellectual, moral, or physical faculties of man . . .?"[6] If not, other philosophes might have replied, it would not be for want of their writing.

Voltaire (1694–1778)

The first home of Enlightenment ideas was the salons of Paris, where the "greatest wits" of the age, male and female, met to discuss literature, philosophy, sex, and court intrigues. This was the milieu of the young François-Marie Arouet, born in Paris in 1694, son of a prosperous lawyer to the aristocracy. Handsome, charming, witty, he made a name for himself by publishing satires, plays, and poetry, collecting invitations to one aristocratic château after another, and acquiring mistresses like trophies. He took the pen name Voltaire in 1717, after a brief period of not uncomfortable imprisonment in the Bastille for offending the court, and spent the next ten years as one of the stars of Parisian society, sometimes in favor with King Louis XV, sometimes out of favor, but always on everybody's guest list as a person to see and be seen with.

Then, in 1726, while attending a play at the the Comédie-Française with his mistress, Voltaire traded insults with the Chevalier de Rohan-Chabot, a nobleman sure of his privilege. Several nights later, the chevalier had his servant lure Voltaire out from dinner at the house of his friend, the Duc de Sully, and watched from a carriage as his servants beat Voltaire nearly senseless. Voltaire staggered back into the house, only to find the Duc de Sully and his other aristocratic friends closing social ranks against him, claiming that he had no business insulting a nobleman. Voltaire tried to challenge the chevalier to a duel, only to be placed in the Bastille again, this time, he was assured, for his own protection. Angry and humiliated, he fled to England, where he was welcomed by London writers such as Alexander Pope. He promptly became infatuated with English civil liberties, with the legal code which made no distinctions, at least in law, between aristocrats and mere sons of lawyers. He also became enamored of other aspects of English life, such as the stock exchange and Newton's philosophy. His *Letters Concerning the English Nation*, published in 1733, was clearly designed to both express his affection for England and to provoke established opinion in France, as in his letter on the London stock exchange. "Go into the London Exchange," he wrote, "a place more dignified than many a royal court. There you will find representatives of every nation quietly assembled to promote human welfare. There the Jew, the Mahometan, and the Christian deal with each other as though they were all of the same religion. . . . If there were only one religion in England, there would be a risk of despotism; if there were only two, they would cut each other's throats; as it is, there are at least thirty, and they live happily and at peace."[7]

The *Letters* was published when Voltaire returned to France. A warrant was issued for his arrest. It was an uncomfortable homecoming in any case, for new stars had risen in Paris and Voltaire was no longer sought after by high society. But he found a new friend and protector, the Marquise du Châtelet, with whom he lived for the next sixteen years. From an early age, Gabrielle Émilie Le Tonnelier de Breuteuil du Châtelet had been interested in geometry, physics, and astronomy, interests supported by her father and, later, her husband. She, too, circulated in Parisian salons, but her interests were always scientific, rather than purely literary. From the moment she and Voltaire discussed Newton, it was love at first sight. When Voltaire's arrest seemed imminent, the couple retreated to Madame du Châtelet's château at Cirey, near the French border. They set up a philosophic household, reading and writing physics, history, and theology, entertaining numerous guests including, occasionally, the Marquis. Yet Voltaire was not long content with philosophic retreat, and he grew restless. He began to court the great rulers of Europe, believing that they were best suited to bring enlightenment to the world. He visited the Prussian court of Frederick II; he was elected to the Académie Française and became Royal Historiographer to Louis XV. Madame du Châtelet, feeling Voltaire had abandoned her, fell in love with another man and, at 43, became pregnant. Afraid that she might not survive the pregnancy, she worked long days to finish her translation and exposition of Newton's *Principia*. She died in childbirth in 1749. Her book was finally published posthumously in 1759 and remained the standard French translation of Newton.

Voltaire was heartbroken, but resilient. He set up his own household in the town of Ferney, and it was there that he wrote the works that

Statue of Voltaire by Jean Antoine Houdon (Art Resource, NY)

brought the Enlightenment beyond the salons and royal courts to the reading public. Foremost among these was his "philosophic tale" *Candide*, which was published in 1759 and immediately became an international bestseller. The hero Candide, whose name reflects his candid, innocent nature, is exposed by his author to all the horrors the world can provide, in the service of philosophical, yet activist satire. That activist approach is also reflected in Voltaire's *Treatise on Toleration*, published in 1762. It was prompted by a notorious law case: Jean Calas, an exemplary citizen, was a Calvinist in a largely Catholic area. His son was found hanged, and Calas was accused of murdering him, on no basis other than religious prejudice. He was tortured and finally executed. Voltaire took up the case, contacting government ministers, writing letters to prominent writers, publicizing the affair in English newspapers. Because of his advocacy, the judgment against Jean Calas was annulled; though too late for Calas himself, it saved the rest of his family from further persecution. Voltaire took up numerous causes for the rest of his life, fighting above all against bigotry, superstition, and the abuse of the judicial system that becomes injustice itself: "There are many dreadful ways of being unjust. An innocent man may be racked on equivocal evidence. A man may be condemned to execution when he deserves no more than three months' imprisonment. Such injustice is meted out by tyrants, and particularly by fanatics, who always become tyrants when they are given power to do mischief."[8] His most famous French slogan was "*Écrasons l'infâme*": "Make war on the fanatics."[9]

In 1778, Voltaire returned to Paris one last time, to attend a performance of one of his plays. He was given a hero's welcome, for he had become the most famous writer in France, or in the world. But he was exhausted by the long trip and died on May 30, 1778.

Montesquieu (1689–1755)

The salon society of Paris and an extended stay in England were decisive experiences for Voltaire; they were no less decisive for Charles-Louis de Secondat, best known as Baron de Montesquieu. He was born in the family château of La Brède, near Bordeaux, and studied law first at the University of Bordeaux and later in Paris. On the death of his father, he returned to Bordeaux, where he became a judge in the local *parlement* (court of justice); on the death of his uncle the Baron de Montesquieu, Charles-Louis acquired his title, his position in the parlement, and much of his estate. He was elected a member of the Academy of Sciences of Bordeaux, a suitable interest for an enlightened nobleman, particularly one associated with the nobility of the robe, noblemen who owed their title originally to the purchase of legal or financial office but who, by the early eighteenth century, often dominated courts, landholdings, and commercial enterprise in the major cities of France. He also married a suitable young lady of good family, Jeanne de Lartigue, who was, rather less conventionally, an ardent Protestant. Even less conventionally, in 1721 Montesquieue published a witty, entertaining, and philosophical novel, *The Persian Letters*, which quickly became the toast of Parisian salon society. So did Montesquieu himself, when he went to Paris, in part to look after legal affairs of the Bordeaux academy and parlement, but mostly to fulfill the dream of all provincial writers, literary fame among Parisian high society. As a wealthy nobleman and a wit, he was welcomed at the châteaux of the regent to the king of France, at the literary salons in the capital and at gatherings of more philosophically minded writers. For though Montesquieu seems to have had in mind primarily an intent to amuse—"I venture to say that *The Persian Letters* was laughing and gay, and for that reason, was popular,"[10] he later wrote—the novel, written in the form of letters from Persian travelers commenting on their trip to Paris, expressed the Enlightenment conviction that European ways were not the measure of all things, that French customs, for example, would appear as peculiar and exotic to foreign travelers as Persian customs did to the French.

Between 1728 and 1731 Montesquieu himself became a traveler, visiting Germany and Holland as well as England, where he found himself enchanted, as Voltaire was at about the same time, by English society and civil liberties. He had a professional as well as philosophical interest in comparative legal systems, an interest developed once he returned to his estate in La Brède in his most famous book, *The Spirit of the Laws*, published in 1748 in Geneva, to avoid the French censors. It began by arguing that though all people were subject to laws established by nature, such as God, social life, and desire for peace, they were also subject to human laws which could, and should, vary according to type of government, custom, history, and even climate and population. The laws appropriate to an ancient city-state, like Sparta, might not be appropriate to a modern, civilized country like France. The laws appropriate to a democracy must inculcate the special virtues of citizens in a democracy, such as equality and patriotism; the laws appropriate to a monarchy should inculcate the virtues appropriate to a monarchy, such as desire for glory, wealth, and hereditary titles. No one set of laws, therefore, should apply throughout the world. But Montesquieu did not believe that all laws, or systems of laws, were equally good. The best were those that allowed for a separation of powers between different groups within government, so each acted as an independent check on the other. His model for this was his idealized picture of the English government, in which the House of Commons spoke for the will of the people, the House of Lords spoke for the will of the hereditary aristocracy, and the King spoke for the monarchy. Since each group was independent of the other—at least in Montesquieu's view—each could protect the country against tyranny by the other two. The result would be the "spirit of moderation," in Montesquieu's view the most important goal of all legislators.

The Spirit of the Laws was criticized by the Catholic church and put on the Index of forbidden books in 1751. Philosophes criticized the book in turn: for its wit, for its style, for displaying "much imagination on a subject that would appear to require only judgement." Despite his criticisms, Voltaire wrote, "I respect Montesquieu even when he falters, because he rises again to ascend to the very sky,"[11] and he defended Montesquieu against attacks from the Church. Though hurt by the criticisms, Montesquieu defended his work with his usual mixture of wit and philosophy, and to the end of his life projected the contented image of the most privileged, and least restless, of all the philosophes. "I don't know if it's something I owe to my physical or moral being," he wrote, "but my soul seizes upon everything. I was happy on my estate where I saw nothing but trees, and I was happy in Paris amidst that mass of men equal to the grains of sand in the sea: I ask nothing more from the earth except that she continue to turn on her axis."[12] *The Spirit of the Laws* went through twenty-two editions within two years and became one of the most widely read books on political philosophy in the second half of the eighteenth century.

The *Encyclopédie* and Encyclopedists

Far removed from Madame de Châtelet's château at Cirey, or Montesquieu's at La Brède, were the alleys and garrets frequented by the young, poor, yet hopeful intellectuals in Paris. But in the late 1740s their inhabitants were united by the most famous publishing venture associated with the Enlightenment, the *Encyclopédie, ou dictionnaire raisonné des sciences, des arts et des métiers* (Encyclopedia, or analytical dictionary of the sciences, arts, and trades). It was, first and foremost, a reference encyclopedia, intended to be a French version of the successful British publishing venture *The Cyclopedia, or Universal Dictionary of the Arts and Sciences*, first published in 1728. The editor in chief, Denis Diderot (1713–84), transformed this seemingly innocuous format into a vehicle for Enlightenment ideas. He and his collaborator, the mathematician Jean Le Rond d'Alembert (1717–83), invited their philosophe friends to write key articles, published with beautiful copperplate illustrations showing the clear light of day, a symbol for reason, shining in on the arts, the sciences, the crafts, the manufactures—all the activities accessible to human understanding. Even religion was included, for theology, philosophes believed, should also be accessible to reason. Some of the articles became notorious for their irreverance and sharp wit. Under "Anthropophagy" (cannibalism), the reader would find "see Eucharist, Communion, Altar, etc," a clear attack on the Catholic theology of Christ's real presence in the Mass. As a result, the *Encyclopédie* was prohibited by official censors from being published in France. It was published instead in Switzerland in many editions, with prices designed to meet the requirements of a range of book-buyers, and smuggled into France with great profit. Diderot himself viewed the *Encyclopédie* as part of the philosophe cause: he wrote in the article "Encyclopedia" that its aim "is to collect all the knowledge scattered over the face of the earth, to present its general outlines and structure to the men with whom we live, and to transmit this to those who will come after us, so that the work of past centuries may be useful to the following centuries, that our children, by becoming more educated, may at the same time become more virtuous and happier, and that we may not die without having deserved well of the human race."[13]

At the time he began work on the *Encyclopédie*, Diderot was leading the life of a struggling writer in Paris, where much of his income came from literary hack-work, writing reviews and translations for one or another journal. He had been born in Champagne, where his family had made cutlery—knives, scissors, surgical lancets—for two hundred years. Prosperous and industrious, family members had bought land, entered the church, and enjoyed a good local reputation. Young Denis had been given a good education and had originally come to Paris with an allowance from his father to study law. But he preferred to read languages and *belles-lettres*, as philosophy, the arts, and sciences were called, to argue with like-minded friends in coffeehouses, to attend the theater, and to think of becoming an actor. What do you want to be? asked his father, concerned that his son choose a career, but "Nothing, nothing at all," answered Diderot. "I like study; I am very well off, very happy; I don't ask anything else."[14] His father, though, disapproved of his son's life as a perpetual student in happy idleness in Paris; he disapproved even more of the woman Diderot chose to marry; and Diderot the elder cut off his son's allowance. When Diderot the younger was named editor of the *Encyclopédie*, it was his first prospect of a steady income in some years.

Diderot's writings that expressed his own ideas became notorious as soon as they were published, for he was always happiest in considering the most unorthodox, the most radical new ideas. One of his early works, *Pensées Philosophiques* (Philosophical Thoughts) was condemned by the censors to be publicly torn up and burned in 1746, for it consisted of a series of elegant, quotable aphorisms that, among other issues, questioned the teachings of the Catholic church. His *Letters on the Blind*, published in 1749, combined serious scientific discussion of the phenomena of blindness and perception with a persistent questioning of God's existence: "If you want me to believe in God, you must make me touch him!"[15] As always, both the official measures against the books and the orthodox works written to attack them only increased their readership and their sales. Diderot, like Voltaire, was imprisoned for his writings; like Voltaire, he emerged a more famous, more committed philosophe. Sociable, amorous, and incorrigibly argumentative, Diderot became the personal link among philosophes in Paris.

Another of Diderot's friends from his garret days to contribute to the *Encyclopédie* was a young artisan who had also conceived a passion for letters, Jean Jacques Rousseau (1712–1778). This passion had developed from nights spent reading with his father, a watchmaker in Geneva, and it eventually propelled him away from his relatively humble social origins into the highflying world of Parisian literary and philosophical circles. The transition from engraver's apprentice to philosophe never made Rousseau happy: uncomfortable in society, hypersensitive to any perceived insult, he developed intense friendships with fellow philosophes and patrons, only to break them off in a fit of paranoia or anger. Throughout his life he flouted convention, viewing himself as a marginal creature, set apart from other men. "I am made unlike any one I have ever met," he wrote in his autobiography, *Confessions*, in a statement that has found its echo in autobiographical writing ever since; "I will even venture to say that I am like no one in the whole world. I may be no better, but at least I am different. Whether Nature did well or ill in breaking the mould in which she found me, is a question which can only be resolved after the reading of this book."[16]

Rousseau's reference to nature was typical of Enlightenment thought, but even more than other philosophes, he made the concept the cornerstone of his work. He first came to public attention in 1750 when a treatise he wrote in a competition for the thoroughly enlightened Academy of Dijon won first prize. The topic of the competition was "Has the restoration of the sciences and arts tended to purify morals?" Rousseau's answer was a resounding No, it has not. Too much science and learning, he wrote, draws people further from the simplicity of nature and from their own true moral nature.

People's true natures also figured prominently in one of his most controversial works, the one for which he is best remembered, *The Social Contract* (1762). It is a treatise on political philosophy. Like Hobbes and Locke, Rousseau started by supposing man in a state of nature: "Man is born free, and yet we see him everywhere in chains." Hobbes had argued that people's inherent lawlessness led them to place themselves under the authority of a powerful sovereign; Locke, that people entered into a contract with a sovereign that presupposed their retaining certain inalienable rights. But where previous writers saw polities as collections of individuals, Rousseau saw them as something more, the establishment of a general will which protected "with the whole common force the person and property of each associate," while allowing each individual associate to "obey only himself and remain as free as before." This general will is created by a social contract, in which "each of us places in common his person and all his power under the supreme direction of the general will; and as one body we all receive each member as an indivisible part of the whole. From that moment, instead of as many separate persons as there are contracting parties, this act of association produces a moral and collective body, composed of as many members as there are votes in the assembly." This body, or, as Rousseau called it, this "public person . . . took formerly the name of 'city' and now takes that of 'republic' or 'body politic.'" The members of the body "take collectively the name of 'people,' and separately, that of 'citizens,' as participating in the sovereign authority, and of 'subjects,' because they are subjected to the laws of the state."[17] Rousseau's general will, then, could be seen as greater than the sum of the individual wills in the body politic, and the *Social Contract* left ambiguous whether, and in what cases, the individual associate could dissent from the general will.

The *Social Contract*, and the view of government it presents, had a profound influence on revolutionary social and political movements from the late eighteenth century to the present.

And yet the *Social Contract* was little read in Rousseau's own time: his bestselling book was a novel, *Julie or the New Heloise* (1761). The noble heroine of *Julie* is beloved by her tutor, Saint-Prieux, and she returns his love. She obeys her father's commands, however, and marries the man he has chosen for her. She forswears her earlier love, devoting herself to her husband and her two sons, yet the flame of her affection for Saint-Prieux, and his for her, never quite dies. At the end of the book, Julie dies, having exhibited the most exemplary fidelity to her father, her husband, her sons, and her former lover. No one could read the novel without weeping, and Rousseau became a cult figure, the literary champion of emotion in the age of reason. With *Émile*, a kind of novelized treatise, he became the champion of the simplicity of nature against the artificiality of fashionable life. *Émile* told the story of a boy's upbringing in order to illustrate Rousseau's ideas of education: children should be taught through their senses, through the dispositions natural to childhood, not by treating them as miniature adults. Both nature itself and a child's own natural instincts are the surest guides to education. In earlier writings, Rousseau had argued that the progress of the arts and sciences so beloved by other philosophes had weakened and corrupted human society, not improved it. People were better off in simpler, more virtuous societies. Now, in *Émile*, Rousseau was even more forceful, his talent for good first lines once more coming into play: "God makes all things good; man meddles with them and they become evil."[18]

Chemistry: The Enlightened Science

The emphasis placed by philosophes on reason and on the scientific achievements of the preceding century gave the study of natural science greater prestige and attracted more people to scientific inquiry. Even women, who had been largely excluded from scientific circles in the seventeenth century, participated more in both public discussions of science and in scientific research. The increased interest in science was particularly marked in chemistry, which up through the eighteenth century was more a collection of procedures than a theoretical discipline. It was taught in medical schools because it gave practical directions for compounding medications, and collections of recipes and techniques for crafts such as dyeing, tanning, and metallurgy were published for use in households or industry. Since the main feature uniting all these different procedures was an emphasis on practical experience—or experiment—chemistry was sometimes known as "experimental physics." And since Francis Bacon, one of the heroes of the Enlightenment, had valued experiment so highly, chairs in chemistry began to appear in the Academies of Science that spread across Europe and America in the eighteenth century.

A German chemist, Georg Stahl (1660–1734), first proposed the theory that looked, for a time, as if it would be the powerful unifying theory that the field of chemistry needed. He was interested in the many chemical operations that required the use of heat, especially the action of heat and charcoal in the operation of smelting that transformed mottled, brittle iron ore into shiny, malleable iron. He proposed that a substance, *phlogiston*, was transferred from the charcoal to the iron in the course of smelting and was responsible for the change in properties from ore to metal. This theory provided a good working explanation of the process of smelting, and phlogiston came to be regarded as a standard chemical substance.

Yet additional research in chemical techniques brought up new ideas. Air—the common air that people felt and breathed—had long been considered an element, incapable of being broken down. Yet a number of chemists from the 1750s on found that there appeared to be different kinds of "air," with different properties from common air. A candle, left burning in one of these new "airs," would burn for twice its usual length. Another candle, placed in an inverted jar filled with another type of "air," would go out at once, as though water had been poured on it. And a third, placed in yet another jar filled with yet another "air," would emit a loud noise. All these airs were apparently affected by combustion of the candle, but no one could quite explain how. Was one of these airs the mysterious phlogiston? Or were they something else altogether?

Something else altogether, thought the ambitious French chemist and wealthy government financier Antoine Laurent Lavoisier (1743–1794). He was an expert experimenter who followed the scientific literature on chemistry closely, deliberately repeating all significant experiments together with a coterie of like-minded, enthusiastic scientists. His research showed that in all cases in which it was believed that phlogiston was gained in an experiment, one specific gas, which he named oxygen, was really lost; in all cases in which it was believed that phlogiston was lost, oxygen was really gained. In other words, in every case in which existing chemical theory used phlogiston as an explanation, he and his colleagues could substitute oxygen and describe its chemical properties, and since, he proclaimed in an article read to the Paris Academy of Sciences, it is contrary to good philosophy to multiply entities needlessly, it was also contrary to good philosophy to accept the existence of phlogiston any longer. Instead, he made the newly discovered gases the basis of what he called the "New Chemistry," giving them the names by which they are known today: oxygen, hydrogen, and nitrogen.

The New Chemistry was characteristic of Enlightenment ideals in its emphasis on experiment; it was also characteristic in its concern for language. Bacon had complained that one of the factors retarding the progress of science was an absence of a common vocabulary to describe scientific phenomena, and that problem occurred again and again for one of Lavoisier's close collaborators, Louis Bernard Guyton de Morveau (1737–1816), as he tried to compile a dictionary of chemistry in the 1780s. Names of chemical substances had remained the same for hundreds of years: sulfuric acid was called "oil of vitriol," mercuric oxide "red calx of mercury," iron oxide "astringent Mars saffron." This terminology made it almost impossible to keep track of what went on in a chemical operation: two or more substances with outlandish names went in, and two or more with quite different names came out. The relationship among all those substances was impossible to specify. Working together with other members of their coterie, Guyton de Morveau and Lavoisier came up with a complete reform of the chemical nomenclature, the basis of modern chemical language. Simple substances, such as oxygen, now had simple names; compound substances, such as carbon dioxide, now had names reflecting the elements they comprised; the language used in chemical operations now reflected the way elements separated or combined, so that carbon burned in the presence of oxygen gave carbon dioxide. This chemical nomenclature, Lavoisier wrote, was intended to unite three things: "the series of facts that make up science; the ideas that recall the facts; and the words that express them. . . . The perfection of the nomenclature of chemistry . . . consists of rendering ideas and facts in their exact truth . . . it must be nothing more than a faithful mirror."[19] Reform of language as a reflection of truth, uncovered by human reason, working, as Locke had said, from simple to complex ideas: with these ideals chemistry took its place among the enlightened arts and sciences.

Profile: Enlightened Couples

Looking back on the eighteenth century, we might expect to find many women philosophes, for wealthy women, at least, had the opportunity to become well educated in the arts and sciences. Émilie du Châtelet, with her mathematical interests, her translation of Newton, and her devotion to the great intellectual questions of the age, certainly deserves the title philosophe. In her own day, however, her reputation in intellectual circles came in large part from her being the mistress of Voltaire. This was typical of the period. Women usually gained access to intellectual life through the men with whom they were associated, often as mistresses or wives.

In Paris, especially, male philosophes adopted the social mores of fashionable society. Many of them were married, but in addition had mistresses who shared their intellectual pursuits. Diderot, when a young unknown, had married a pretty, respectable, but poor woman of no particular social standing, Anne-Toinette Champion. They married for love, but Diderot was, at best, a negligent husband and seems to have quickly come to think of his wife primarily as caretaker of his household and their children. The woman he regarded as the true love of his life was Sophie Volland. He was, by the time he met her, already well established as a philosophe and editor of the *Encyclopedia*. In contrast to Anne-Toinette, Sophie was of good family and well educated. She became Diderot's confidante as well as his lover. He wanted to share with her "everything which takes place in the space that I fill and outside that space; in the spot where I am and the one where others are moving," he wrote, and "I live in the faith that nothing can separate our two souls."[20]

Women did not have to be mistresses to be associated with philosophes. They could be married to them as well. Lavoisier and his wife provide another example of the way in which women could share an intellectual life they would not have been able to enter on their own. Marie Anne Pierrette was only fourteen when she married Lavoisier. He was at that point a rising star in science and her father's junior colleague in the corporation charged with collecting taxes in France. Despite her age, she was already an accomplished hostess, and she quickly made the Lavoisier household into a kind of scientific salon for members of the Academy of Sciences as well as foreign visitors. She took lessons in chemistry, the better to assist her husband's work; she learned English so as to be able to translate chemical works; and she studied engraving to provide illustrations for her husband's textbook. Lavoisier spent six hours with colleagues and students in the laboratory daily—three in the morning before attending to financial affairs, and three at night—and six hours on Saturday, and Marie Anne sat there with him, taking notes on experiments and tabulating results. She was also an able member of the coterie surrounding Lavoisier who argued for the New Chemistry, corresponding with prominent chemists in her own right to argue for the value of her husband's theories. Like many philosophes, she liked to discuss literature, art, and politics. Once again, though, the eighteenth-century picture that has come down to us is that of a devoted assistant, not an independent philosophe. "M. Lavoisier is a pleasing looking young man, a very clever and painstaking chemist," wrote one observer. "He has a beautiful wife who is fond of literature and presides over the Academicians when they go to his house for a cup of tea after the Academy meetings."[21]

The best French example of what might be called dual-career philosophes is the Marquis de Condorcet (1743–1794), who at the age of 43 married the brilliant and beautiful Sophie de Grouchy, then aged 23. The Marquis and Marquise were at the center of progressive political circles in Paris, welcoming foreign visitors like Thomas Jefferson and Thomas Paine. Sophie de Condorcet provided the standard translation of some of the writings of the English-language philosophe Adam Smith, and she collaborated with her husband on his treatises. Though we do not know exactly what ideas or phrases Sophie de Gouchy may have contributed, we may hear an echo of their conversations in many of Condorcet's writings on women. "Women have the same rights as men," the Marquis wrote in his *Memorandum on Public Instruction* (1792). For that reason they should be given the same education as men, not only among the wealthy, as previous authors had said or implied, but among all groups. This was important for personal as well as public virtue. If education was limited to men, it would introduce "a clear inequality, not only between husband and wife, but between brother and sister, and even between mother and son. Nothing would be more detrimental to the purity and happiness of domestic life." And perhaps the Marquis and Marquise could attest to an additional benefit of equal education for women: that men who received a good education "will retain its advantages much more easily if they find that their wives have had a more or less equal instruction; if they can share with their wives in the reading necessary to keep up their knowledge; if the instruction prepared for them during the interval which separates their childhood from their establishment in their own homes is also offered to members of the other sex to whom they are naturally attracted."[22]

Important Dates

1690	Publication of Locke's *Essay Concerning Human Understanding*
1721	Publication of Montesquieu's *Persian Letters*
1726	Voltaire's incident with the Chevalier de Rohan
1733	Publication of Voltaire's *Letters Concerning the English Nation*
1748	Publication of Montesquieu's *Spirit of the Laws*
1751	First installment of Diderot and D'Alembert's *Encyclopedie*
1755	Death of Montesquieu
1759	Publication of Madame du Châtelet's translation of Newton's *Principia*
1761	Publication of Rousseau's *New Heloise*
1762	Publication of Voltaire's *Treatise on Toleration*; publication of Rousseau's *Social Contract*
1778	Death of Voltaire; death of Rousseau
1794	Death of Lavoisier

Further Reading

Keith Michael Baker, *Condorcet: From Natural Philosophy to Social Mathematics* (Chicago, 1975)

Lorraine Daston, *Classical Probability in the Enlightenment* (Princeton, 1988)

Alistair Duncan, *Laws and Order in Eighteenth-Century Chemistry* (Oxford, 1996)

Elizabeth Fox-Genovese, *The Origins of Physiocracy: Economic Revolution and Social Order in Eighteenth Century France* (New York, 1976)

P.N. Furbank, *Diderot: A Critical Biography* (New York, 1992)

Peter Gay, *The Party of Humanity: Essays in the French Enlightenment* (New York, 1964)

Anne Goldgar, *Impolite Learning: Conduct and Community in the Republic of Letters, 1680–1750* (New Haven, 1995)

Dena Goodman, *Criticism in Action: Enlightenment Experiments in Political Writing* (Ithaca, 1989)

Dena Goodman, *The Republic of Letters: A Cultural History of the French Enlightenment* (Ithaca, 1994)

Norman Hampson, *The Enlightenment* (New York, 1986)

Thomas L. Hankins, *Science and the Enlightenment* (Cambridge, 1985)

Frederic Lawrence Holmes, *Antoine Lavoisier: The Next Crucial Year, Or, The Sources of His Quantitative Method in Chemistry* (Princeton, 1998)

Ulrich Im Hof, *The Enlightenment* trans. William E. Yuill (Oxford, 1994)

Alan Charles Kors, *Atheism in France, 1650–1729: The Orthodox Sources of Disbelief* (Princeton, 1990)

Alan Charles Kors, *D'Holbach's Coterie: An Enlightenment in Paris* (Chicago, 1976)

John McManners, *Death in the Enlightenment* (Oxford, 1981)

Dorinda Outram, *The Enlightenment* (Cambridge, 1995)

Jean-Pierre Poirier, *Lavoisier: Chemist, Biologist, Economist*, trans. Rebecca Balinski (Philadelphia, 1996)

Daniel Roche, *France in the Enlightenment* trans. Arthur Goldhammer (Cambridge, MA, 1999)

Remy G. Saisselin, *The Enlightenment against the Baroque: Economics and Aesthetics in the Eighteenth Century* (Berkeley, 1992)

Judith N. Shklar, *Montesquieu* (Oxford, 1987)

Geoffrey V. Sutton, *Science for a Polite Society: Gender, Culture, and the Demonstration of Enlightenment* (Boulder, CO, 1995)

Ira O. Wade, *The Intellectual Origins of the French Enlightenment* (Princeton, 1971)

Arthur M. Wilson, *Diderot* (New York, 1972)

Chapter Fourteen

Enlightenment in
National Context

Universities and Learned Societies

In France, the Enlightenment flourished in Parisian salons and town houses, but elsewhere in Europe, men and, occasionally, women of letters (a broad term covering intellectuals and writers of all sorts) could be found in universities and learned societies. Eighteenth-century universities had changed greatly since the previous century. Though the faculties of arts, medicine, law, and theology still formed the basic structure of the universities, the curriculum had been thoroughly modernized. Many universities began to teach in the vernacular instead of Latin. Medical students no longer read Galen, but rather modern authors who prided themselves on their up-to-date knowledge of anatomy and physiology; the students attended anatomical dissections and chemical laboratories. Civil law rivaled canon law in the law faculty. Students forsook theology lectures and attended those in moral philosophy instead. And throughout Europe, universities that had once produced teachers and ministers began to attract ambitious students seeking to advance their careers in government administration. One result was that university communities became natural magnets for writers engaged in the reading and dissemination of Enlightenment ideals.

Many of these writers shared many of the values of the French philosophes, whose work they read, translated, and argued for and against. Throughout Europe, including its overseas colonies, men and women spoke and wrote about the virtues of reason, nature, progress, tolerance; they called for an end to bigotry and superstition; and they published, predominantly, for the educated elites, fearful that too much enlightenment might be bad for the peasantry, for urban artisans, or for their own servants. Where European enlightenment differed most from the French was in rejecting the antireligious message of writers like Voltaire and Diderot: for most eighteenth-century thinkers outside of France, true religion, too, could be rational, natural, progressive, and tolerant. And as philosophes in each country pondered the social and moral questions facing their own societies, the Enlightenment took on distinct national flavors.

Scotland: Society and History

In Scotland, men of letters clustered around university communities, especially in the most important cities of Edinburgh and Glasgow. Though influenced by the philosophes of France, Scottish thinkers had a specific problem to ponder: how a country, like Scotland, that had lost its independent government could maintain its identity. Scotland had lost its medieval identity when its Crown was united with England in 1603 under James VI (of Scotland) and I (of England). Its Parliament was formally joined with England's in 1707, with the result that Scotland lost its own medieval tradition of representation. From then on it was governed as part of Great Britain. Though there were important economic advantages for Scotland in the arrangement, many Scots writers deplored the humiliation of being considered a mere province, where once they had had a fierce and independent kingdom. How, they asked, could Scotland cease being a polity, that is, an independent political state, and yet still continue to be a country? What held a country together, if not its government?

In the course of the debate, Scots writers transformed the language of political theory. Where earlier political theorists had used the categories "monarchy," "aristocracy," and "republic" to discuss European states, Scottish writers used the terms "nation," "country," "people." And where other writers had focused on the structures and forms of government as providing the glue that held a polity together, Scots writers began to look to other aspects of human society in order to find the "invisible hand," as Adam Smith put it, that tied nations, and the world, together.

Adam Smith (1723–1790)

These were the questions that most interested young Adam Smith when he first went to the University of Glasgow at the age of fourteen. He was most intrigued by lectures he attended on the question of human morality. Were people moral because they had been taught by religion to behave morally, or was there a kind of "natural morality" imbued in all people, no matter what their religion? These questions continued to intrigue Smith as he went on to study at Oxford University, and his answers became the basis of his own teaching when he became professor of moral philosophy at the University of Glasgow in 1752. It was not enough, Smith said, to study morality as a matter of individual conscience and individual behavior. Instead, it was necessary to study how people behave in society—for example, the fact that each person wants to be esteemed by others—because to Smith, people were first and foremost social animals.

Smith published his ideas in the *Theory of Moral Sentiments* (1759). The book made him famous well beyond Glasgow, and it was translated into many languages. Partly as a result, Smith received an offer to become the tutor to a young nobleman. He hesitated, because he liked his professorship, but professorial positions at Scottish universities did not have set salaries. Instead, professors were paid by student fees. Smith approved of this plan, which left students in the role of rational consumers, because he believed that it made professors work hard to attract students. Salaries would just make them lazy and remove any incentive for them to keep up with their fields. Still, the system made his own professorship a chancy form of income, with no pension in sight. Becoming a tutor to a nobleman would give him a salary, a pension, and a chance to travel. He accepted the position.

While tutor he wrote *An Inquiry into the Nature and Causes of the Wealth of Nations* (1776), which became the Scottish Enlightenment's most famous answer to the question of what features of human society hold it together. The wealth of any nation, Smith said, comes from the productivity of its labor force, and from this basic principle he went into a detailed examination of economic behavior, from the production of each item, to its trade and distribution, to public trading of stocks, to the impact of government on the generation of wealth. In any complex society, even the simplest item in anyone's possession is the product of hundreds or even thousands of separate human endeavors: "The woollen coat, for example, which covers the day-laborer . . . is the produce of the joint labor of a great multitude of workmen. The shepherd, the sorter of the wool, the wool-comber or carder, the dyer, the scribbler, the spinner, the weaver. . . ." Not to mention the "merchants and carriers," who transport the materials, and the great many workmen—"ship-builders, sailors, sail-makers, rope-makers"—who are involved in producing the ships or carts in which the materials are carried. "If we examine . . . all these things, and consider what a variety of labor is employed about each of them, we shall be sensible that, without the assistance and co-operation of many thousands," even the poorest person could not be clothed, fed, or sheltered.[1] Wealth, then, was not about an individual acquiring more goods, not even if that individual were a king, as the mercantilist writers like Colbert believed. It was, instead, social behavior, involving not just the production and acquisition, but also the exchange of goods and services. Economics, like human morality, Smith believed, could be understood only if people were studied as social animals.

David Hume (1711–1776)

Adam Smith was a quiet, scholarly professor, but he was also a sociable man with a gift for friendship, and one of his best friends was the Edinburgh philosopher and historian David Hume. Like Smith, Hume was expected to go to a university, and since he quickly showed his talent for academic study, his family suggested he consider law as a career. But "the Law . . . ," he later wrote, "appeared nauseous to me, and I could think of no other way of pushing my Fortune in the World but that of a Scholar and Philosopher."[2]

Hume's first public performance as a philosopher came with the publication of A Treatise of Human Nature (1740). In writing it, he had considered himself the Newton of moral philosophy, the scholar who had effected an entire revolution in the science of understanding the human intellect. Later philosophers have agreed with him, for the Treatise contains an incisive critique of human belief in fundamental principles of science and philosophy, such as cause and effect, and the uniformity of natural laws. Hume did not seek to question a law of nature, such as gravity; what he wanted to do was examine the reasons why people believed those laws to be true and immutable. In doing so, he believed, he was establishing the "science of man, " which was "the only solid foundation for the other sciences."[3] But at the time, alas, the book's brilliance was not appreciated. It had few favorable reviews and even fewer sales, and Hume, who had hoped for a bestseller, later wrote that it "fell dead-born from the press."[4]

Hume, like other philosophers, found it was a hard way to earn a living, and he began to look around for alternatives. A position as tutor to a nobleman did not work out, and he failed in his attempt to get a position as professor at either Edinburgh or Glasgow University. Eventually, though, he found his own literary voice, in the publication of sets of essays on philosophical, historical, and political subjects. The reading public that had rejected his first, dense work of philosophy were charmed with his ideas when presented in the essay style they loved, and Hume became known as a sort of philosophically minded Addison and Steele. His literary reputation increased with the publication of the *History of England* (1754–1762), which remained the standard history for the next hundred years. "These symptoms of a rising reputation," he wrote, "gave me encouragement,"[5] and they also gave him enough of an independent income to ensure that he could continue to be a scholar and philosopher all his life.

Hume was notorious in his native Scotland as a skeptic who did not believe in God. In his *Dialogues Concerning Natural Religion* (1779), he critiqued the common argument that we can infer there must be a God from studying His works, just as when we see a house, we infer there must have been an architect who built it. Someone who follows this hypothesis, Hume wrote, "is able, perhaps, to assert, or conjecture, that the universe, sometime, arose from something like design." But he cannot go beyond that assertion to say anything about the being who designed it. This world, perhaps, "is very faulty and imperfect, compared to a superior standard," and is the work "of some infant Deity, who afterwards abandoned it, ashamed of his lame performance"; perhaps "it is the work of some dependent, inferior Deity"; or perhaps "it is the production of old age and dotage" in an elderly Deity.[6] This book, published after his death, shocked many religious people. But during his own lifetime Hume had a wide circle of friends, many of them clergymen, and many others who considered themselves devout. According to one story, the elderly mother of one of his friends, "a very respectable woman," once told her son, "I shall be glad to see any of your companions to dinner, but I hope you will never bring the Atheist here to disturb my peace." Her son had the idea of inviting Hume to dinner, but introducing him under another name. His mother was charmed with Hume, and so her son told her, "This was the very Atheist, mother, that you was so much afraid of." "Well," says she, "you may bring him here as much as you please, for he's the most innocent, agreeable, facetious man I ever met with."[7] Thus Hume became a living example of his friend Adam

Smith's theory: that natural morality is imbedded in social behavior, not religion.

Societies for Useful Knowledge

Enlightenment, like other European products, was transported to the American colonies on the same ships that regularly transported books, textiles, and furnishings across the Atlantic. In 1743, Benjamin Franklin (1706–1790), the civic-minded printer from Philadelphia, proposed the establishment of an American Philosophical Society. Though influenced by the European scientific societies, such as the Royal Society of London, Franklin's emphasis for the American society was on useful, practical knowledge. In Philadelphia, Franklin and his friends had already founded a public library, a hospital, a volunteer fire department. Now he proposed the Philosophical Society as another useful project, a way of spreading information to "improve the common stock of knowledge." The emphasis in the original proposal is all on reporting "improvements": "all new-discovered plants . . . ; improvements of vegetable juices, as ciders, wines, etc.; new methods of curing or preventing diseases; all new-discovered fossils . . . new and useful improvements in any branch of mathematics; new discoveries in chemistry; . . . new mechanical inventions for saving labor." In short, the new society was to spread word about "all new arts, trades, and manufactures that may be proposed or thought of . . . and all philosophical experiments that let light into the nature of things, tend to increase the power of man over matter, and multiply the conveniences or pleasures of life."[8] The society became a natural forum for correspondence among all philosophically minded people from the British colonies, reporting on everything from new species to the Gulf stream.

Franklin took the founding of the new society as an opportunity to publish an account of one of his own useful inventions, the Franklin stove, an improvement on the stoves then in use for heating. About the same time he became famous throughout the learned world for his experiments on electricity. Electricity was one of the great discoveries of the eighteenth century, and many scientists experimented with producing an electric charge. Franklin was fascinated by his own experiments, which included generating an electric shock large enough to kill the turkey for Christmas dinner. He decided to investigate whether lightning was a form of electricity. He began by placing an iron rod on a tall building, with a wire attached to it to conduct the electricity, but then realized that a kite, made of silk to conduct electricity, could go much higher. He went to an open field in a thunderstorm and flew the kite. At first, nothing seemed to happen, but "at length," we are told, "just as he was beginning to despair . . . he observed some loosed threads of the hempen string to stand erect, and to avoid one another, just as if they had been suspended on a common conductor." He had placed a metal key on the string, and, on touching the key with his knuckles, "the discovery was complete. He perceived a very evident electric spark."[9] This proved that lightning was nothing other than electricity. At once Franklin thought of a way to make his discovery useful, and he designed what he called a "lightning rod," an iron rod placed on the roof of a building, with a wire attached from it to the ground. Such a rod, he was convinced, would protect the building itself from destruction by lightning. Once again, he was proved right.

When the physician William Small traveled from Philadelphia to the English industrial town of Birmingham in 1765, he carried with him a letter of introduction from Franklin to the Lunar Society, a circle of men, like Franklin and his associates, interested in new discoveries and improvements. They had originally come together to finance and oversee the production of a canal system for northern England, a great improvement to the transportation network of the region. They continued to meet because of a common interest in scientific and useful projects. Members of the Lunar Society included James Watt (1736–1819), who invented and produced the first steam engine, and Josiah Wedgwood (1730–1795), who developed the process for producing and mass-marketing the porcelain tableware that bears his name.

Though it was not formally a society, the circle of writers who gathered around the London publisher Joseph Johnson had many of the same interests in useful, improving knowledge, coupled with a devotion to social reform. Johnson's commercial success came primarily from poetry, the bestselling genre of the eighteenth century: he was the first publisher of William Blake (1757–1827), William Wordsworth (1770–1850), and Samuel Coleridge (1772–1834). This success allowed him to publish political pamphlets championing a broad spectrum of social causes, such as the education of women and the abolition of slavery. He became the publisher of choice to the reform-minded writers of his generation: all those, as one observer put it, who concerned themselves with "the general melioration (improvement) of the state of man."[10]

Italy: Enlightened Patronage

In Italy, divided under different rulers, the extent to which Enlighten-ment ideas could be discussed or written about depended on the sympa-thies of the ruler. In the Papal States, Pope Benedict XIV encouraged discussion of social and economic issues, and he was particularly inter-ested in supporting scientific inquiry. He and his advisors introduced reforms into the University of Bologna and the Academy of Science. With Pope Benedict's support, a few exceptional women were admitted to both institutions. Laura Bassi (1711–1778) received a doctorate in philosophy at the University of Bologna and was appointed professor of physics there. She was admitted to the Academy of Science and, like other members, contributed papers annually, on physics and mechanics. Her husband, Guiseppi Verati, was a doctor with an interest in physics, and he, too, became a member of the Academy. Pope Benedict also tried to convince the mathematician Maria Agnesi (1718–1799), of Milan, to come to Bologna to teach. Agnesi had written a well-regarded book on differential and integral calculus, and, the Pope wrote, "from ancient times, Bologna has extended public positions to persons of your sex. It would seem appropriate to continue this honorable tradition."[11] Agnesi, devoutly religious, preferred to lead a private life at home.

From Milan, firmly under the authority of the Austrian Habsburgs, came one of the most influential works of reform the Enlightenment produced: *On Crimes and Punishments* by Cesare Beccaria (1738–1794). It argued against secret denunciations, torture, and the death penalty, part of the legal code of every country in the eighteenth century. Beccaria came from an aristocratic family and, in his mid-twenties, became part of a circle of reform-minded fellow-aristocrats, imbued with Enlighten-ment ideals and ready to change the world, or at least Milan. Like many such groups throughout Europe, they met to discuss the works of Montesquieu, Diderot, and Hume, and to debate particular topics or projects for reform. One such topic was reform of the criminal justice system. Beccaria "began to write down some of his ideas on loose pieces of paper"; his friends "urged him on with enthusiasm. . . . After dinner we would take a walk, discuss the errors of criminal jurisprudence, ar-gue, raise questions, and in the evening he would write." The work was completed and published in 1764.

Beccaria and his friends had been afraid that he might be prosecuted for having written a book attacking existing legal practices, and it was first published anonymously. But in fact Milanese political authorities were delighted with the book, as was the rest of educated Europe: "perhaps no book, on any subject," wrote one commentator, "was ever received with more avidity, more generally read, or more universally applauded."[12] In French Enlightenment circles, the book was an instant hit, and Beccaria was invited to come to Paris to enjoy his fame. Unfortunately, Beccaria was a very introverted man, who did not fit in well with salon society. Embarassed by what he felt was his own lack of wit and charm, he returned to Milan. He spent the rest of his life there, but he did not write any more books. In his own lifetime, people outside of Milan believed that the government had forced him to remain silent and that the man who had written on the horrors of torture was threatened with torture himself if he tried to write any more. This was untrue, as his Milanese associates knew: Beccaria lived well and received a succession of government appointments. If he did not write another book, it was because (unlike other philosophes) he had run out of things to say.

Germany: Reason and Intellect

"The French philosophize with wit, the English with sentiment, and the Germans alone are sufficiently sober to philosophize with the intellect."[13] In this way, the German philosopher and silk merchant Moses Mendelssohn (1729–1786) summarized national styles of writing. His opinions were shared by other German writers, who believed that enlightenment required continual and rigorous examination of the deepest truths, not the kind of popular writing associated with Parisian salons and British supper-clubs. For that reason, the German Enlightenment was more closely associated with the universities.

The first home of the early Enlightenment in Germany was the University of Halle, founded in 1694. Halle was the first German university to specialize in "Cameralism"—the eighteenth-century equivalent of public policy—so it exercised a wide influence on the politically active bureaucracy. It was also a hotbed of a more spiritual form of Lutheranism called Pietism. One individual held these strands together: Christian Thomasius (1655–1728). Thomasius spent thirty-five years as a professor at Halle, helping it to become the cutting-edge university of the era. Among his innovations was publishing his books and teaching his courses in German, instead of the traditional Latin. His writings and teaching emphasized reason as the basis for law and human society. He was a tireless advocate for religious toleration, speaking out against witch trials and heresy cases and opposing the use of torture in judicial investigations.

Thomasius also attracted another philosopher to teach at Halle, Christian Wolff (1679–1754). Wolff, even more than Thomasius, came to embody the principles of the Enlightenment for its German advocates. His most influential publication announced its commitment to reason in its very title: *Reasonable Thoughts on the Social Life of People and in particular the Common Weal. Presented for the Promotion of the Happiness of the Human Race by a Lover of Truth* (1721). Wolff tried to reconcile the requirements of religious faith with reason, but leaned far enough in the direction of reason that King Frederick William I fired him from his position at Halle in 1723 because his books supposedly supported atheism. Wolff returned to Halle in triumph in 1740, when Frederick II became King of Prussia. From then until his death, Wolff was the most widely acclaimed philosopher in Germany.

Moses Mendelssohn was an important interpreter of Wolff's system for the nonuniversity public. Though many of Mendelssohn's own works required substantial knowledge of ancient and modern philosophy, he could also write for a more general audience, in a "pleasant, sharp-witted, and entertaining" style.[14] He brought contemporary philosophy before the public with his many translations of French and English works, with his reviews in literary journals, and most of all with his personal contacts in both scholarly and aristocratic circles. He spent most of his life in Berlin, but he had an international reputation. To many, he seemed the embodiment of self-reflective enlightenment, the "Socrates of Berlin."

And yet this shining example of the German Enlightenment (*Aufklärung*) is a paradox, for he was a Jew and thus not a free citizen. Frederick II of Prussia, like his predecessor, allowed Jews to settle in his realm for economic reasons, but only under severe restrictions. "Protected" Jews—so called because they were legally protected from attacks by non-Jews—were allowed to settle only in certain areas which had been specifically designated as Jewish communities. Only a very small group, called the first class, were allowed to move freely among those communities, buy houses, acquire the same privileges as Christian merchants, and bequeath these privileges to their descendants. A handful of Jews in this group had naturalization papers that made them citizens. The second class of Jews were allowed to settle in a given area, but not to move around; they could pass on their privilege to only one

Portrait of German philosopher Moses Mendelssohn by Anton Graff
(Erich Lessing/Art Resource, NY)

son or daughter without an additional fee and to a second and third son for a set fee. The third and fourth classes practiced different kinds of professions within the Jewish community; their protected status was only for themselves and could not be transferred to their children. The fifth class consisted of "unprotected" Jews who might be resident in a community, such as the children of a protected Jew who could not inherit his status. And the sixth consisted of servants or employees of protected Jews; they were allowed to remain only as long as they were employed by a "protected" Jew.

Despite his international renown and many supporters, Mendelssohn accurately depicted his own status as "a member of an oppressed people that had to implore the ruling nation for patronage and protection, which it did not receive everywhere, and which was nowhere without restrictions."[15] He himself was the beneficiary of aristocratic patronage. He was visited by many members of the Prussian nobility, including Frederick's sister Luise Ulrike, and once was even invited to the Royal Palace to converse with one of Frederick's guests. But Frederick himself was not present, and when the Berlin Academy of Sciences elected Mendelssohn a member, the king exercised his pocket veto, refusing to ratify the election. Even as a protected Jew, Mendelssohn was still liable to harassment on the streets of Berlin, and even his limited protected status was not transferable to his children. There was never any possibility that he could become a university professor like Thomasius and Wolff.

The paradox of Jews being at the center of enlightened culture even though they were not free citizens was repeated in the many Jewish salons that developed in Berlin. The best known was kept by Rahel Varnhagen, open to all precisely because of her marginal status as a Jew. In her circle, wrote one of her visitors, "everyone, royal princes, foreign ambassadors, artists, scholars or business men of every rank, countesses and actresses . . . strove for admission with equal eagerness; and in which each person was worth neither more or less than he himself was able to validate by his cultivated personality."[16]

The position of Jews in German society was also debated among non-Jews. One of the most powerful works of drama in the era was Gotthold Ephraim Lessing's (1729–1781) *Nathan the Wise* (1779), whose title character was directly modeled on Moses Mendelssohn. Lessing had already established himself as the leading playwright of his day and a major freethinker, who, like Diderot in France, made his living primarily from his writings. Shortly after *Nathan the Wise* there was an even more dramatic enlightened debate on the status of Jews, surrounding the publication of Christian Wilhelm Dohm's *On the Civic Improvement of the Jews* (1781). Dohm argued in favor of the social and economic assimilation of Jews, without requiring religious conversion. The negative reaction to Dohm's book made it clear that such toleration would not be put into practice any time soon.

Immanuel Kant (1724–1804)

In 1763, Moses Mendelssohn wrote a review of an essay called "The Only Possible Basis of Proof for a Demonstration of God's Existence," praising the author as an "independent thinker."[17] This was the first public notice taken of the author, Immanuel Kant, now considered one of the greatest modern philosophers. Kant lived nearly all his life in the obscure university town of Königsberg, in eastern Prussia, far removed from the glittering court culture and salon life of Berlin. He came from a very poor family, and after finishing his own studies, he took a position as private tutor to a nobleman's family. He had better luck than Hume with his employers, for he was treated very well and continued to pursue his studies in philosophy. He became strongly attracted to the philosophical system of Christian Wolff, but was also able to recognize some of its shortcomings, which he planned to fix. After receiving the degree of Doctor of Philosophy in 1755, Kant decided to try to establish himself as a private lecturer, with the idea of building up enough of a reputation to get a position as university professor.

In his philosophical writings, Kant argued against the Enlightenment idea that scientific or ethical knowledge was somehow "out there," for us to discover. Instead, he said, we have inborn ideas about nature and morality that we impose on what we experience. Kant's books, *Critique of Pure Reason* (1781), *Critique of Practical Reason* (1788), and *Critique of Judgement* (1790), are deliberately technical, written for philosophers, not the general public. Unlike most philosophes, he did not want to "beguile" readers into agreeing with him for "wit and literary charm."[18] In lectures for his students, though, he "was far more genial than in his books," according to one friend, and "threw off ingenious ideas by the thousands."[19]

Eventually, in 1770, Kant was appointed professor at the University of Königsberg. By that time he was Germany's most famous philosopher, and other universities tried to entice him away from Königsberg. "I wish that persons with your knowledge and gifts were not so rare in your profession," wrote one official trying to hire him; "I would not trouble you so." But Kant was happy where he was, he responded. "A peaceful situation, nicely fitted to my needs . . . is all that I have wished for and had. Any change makes me apprehensive," and he remained in Königsberg.[20]

Swiss and Dutch Republics and the Republic of Letters

In Swiss cantons and the Dutch republic, intellectuals read and wrote about the ideas of the Enlightenment. Both regions had the reputation throughout Europe of being shining defenders of republican liberties, of civic virtue, and of tolerance for new ideas. Though in fact their governments could be repressive, particularly in times of social or political unrest, they remained the destinations of choice for philosophes seeking freedom of thought and expression. The Dutch were "industrious, honest, peaceful," yet courageous, according to one French writer, constantly persevering in the "glorious fight for the spirit of liberty."[21] Moreover, the United Provinces were a major center for book publishing, and many French philosophes, like Voltaire, turned to Dutch publishers to produce and distribute their works, censored in France. The Swiss, too, were regarded by writers like Rousseau, and by themselves, as preservers of civic liberties, resisting the corruption associated with French luxury by a purer, more moral form of life. The canton of Geneva, especially, became the publisher to the Enlightenment, producing and translating works from all over Europe.

The relationship between a philosophe and his Swiss or Dutch publisher was not always an amicable one. Voltaire, like authors to the present day, complained bitterly about the commercial aspects of publishing, in which book dealers treated the products of his pen like any other commodity, to be bought cheap and sold for a profit. Pirated editions, brought out without the permission of the author, were common. Nor did publishing a book necessarily mean that the publisher or printer agreed with its contents: "We publish you," one of Rousseau's printers is supposed to have said, "but we don't read you."[22] In particular, neither the Dutch nor the Swiss were receptive to the antireligious message of the French Enlightenment; they, like the Scots, preferred a critical spirit that could be applied to a rational Christianity.

Both Dutch and Swiss scientists made lasting contributions to natural philosophy. At the University of Leyden, Dutch physicists like Pieter van Musschenbroek (1692–1761) and Willem Jakob's Gravesande (1688–1742) pioneered the study of electricity, while in Switzerland Charles Bonnet (1720–1793) of Geneva and Henri de Saussure (1740–1799) investigated biology and geology respectively. These men, like other philosophes, used extensive private correspondence, journals, and published works to communicate with other scholars and thus become an integral part of the republic of letters.

In these republics, as elsewhere, intellectual women took to the printed page to argue for Enlightenment virtues of reason and tolerance. The novel-writing team of Elizabeth Wolff-Bekker (1738–1804) and Agatha Deken (1741–1804) also wrote essays on morality and society. Wolff-Bekker, like Sophie de Condorcet, translated foreign philosophes into her native language. And in Holland, as elsewhere, the spirit of Enlightenment could occasionally show itself in acknowedgment of the exceptional woman. As the Dutch poet Juliana Cornelia de Lannoy (1738–1782) put it in her tongue-in-cheek poem "To the Gentleman of the Board of the Poetry Society in The Hague On the Occasion of My Having Been Granted Honorary Membership,"

> Never dared I to aspire to thus become highly esteemed.
> Never has my Sex in Holland been so honorably deemed.
> You may thank me, Ladies for you can all anticipate
> That this start will lead us to a new victorious fate . . .[23]

Profile: Robert Burns, the "Heaven-Taught Ploughman"

Nearly all Enlightenment intellectuals came from what were called the "educated classes," for readers of Voltaire or Smith or Kant had to have time and education to ponder enlightened ideals. Anyone wishing to become a *philosophe* or writer had an even greater need for time, as well as for some way to make a living. Some poor boys, like Kant, could attend a university and earn a living by teaching, but even Kant had to undergo years of poverty, forced to sell his book collection to make ends meet. Most educated people in the eighteenth century took it for granted that "Enlightenment" was only for them, not for the "lower orders," such as servants, shopkeepers, artisans, or peasants. In many parts of Europe, such people could not read at all; if they could read, they could not write. How, then, could they ever read literature or philosophy? True, a farmer might sing a folk song or recite a hymn. But the educated elite did not believe that he could ever have the sensitivity to appreciate, let alone compose, his own works in any field.

For that reason, the Scottish author and literary critic Henry Mackenzie was astonished when he reviewed a collection of poems written by the young farmboy and poet, Robert Burns (1759–1796). Burns's poetry combined the lyricism and music of traditional Scottish songs with the formal conventions of eighteenth-century English poetry. "Whoever will read his lighter and more humorous poems . . . ," Mackenzie wrote, "will perceive with what uncommon penetration and sagacity this Heaven-taught ploughman, from his humble and unlettered station, has looked upon men and manners."[24] It seemed almost a miracle to him that a poor farmer's son, who had spent much of his life in hard, back-breaking labor, could produce such elegant poetry. Of course, it was not really a miracle. Scotland had a strong tradition of literacy, even in the countryside, stemming from the Reformation. Even farmers went to school, and Burns, a gifted boy, had had an enthusiastic teacher, who taught him to read and write using the Bible and Shakespeare's plays. Young Robert even learned French. As a young man on his own, he had been part of a small society of local boys who wrote essays on literary or philosophical topics, just like university students or improvement-minded city folk. He had always loved to read, borrowing books when he couldn't afford to buy them. His achievement in poetry was impressive, but it was not a miracle.

Burns took no real offense at the implication that someone from his humble station was not capable of writing poetry. He was shrewd enough to realize that the image of the poetic genius, with heaven-sent verses coming to him while at his plow, was useful publicity. Still, it was sometimes hard to be caught between the two worlds of Enlightenment culture and his own poor rural background. His poem "For a' That" attacks the social stratification he experienced, celebrating the self-esteem of a poor but independent man:

> A prince can make a belted knight,
> A marquis, duke, and a' that; . . .
> The pith o' sense, and pride o' worth,
> Are higher rank than a' that.

Social stratification could have more important effects than noble titles, though. Careful observers like Adam Smith noted that children of the poor were likely to have more diseases and die at an earlier age than children of the rich. Anyone in the eighteenth century could die young from a sudden infection, but when Robert Burns died at the age of thirty-seven, it was probably from heart disease brought on by the hard physical work and periodic food shortages of his early life as a plowboy.

Important Dates

1694	Foundation of University of Halle
1721	Publication of Wolff's *Reasonable Thoughts on the Social Life of People*

1728	Death of Thomasius
1743	Foundation of American Philosophical Society
1744	Death of Wolff; publication of Hume's *Treatise of Human Nature*
1759	Publication of Smith's *Theory of Moral Sentiments*
1764	Publication of Beccaria's *On Crimes and Punishments*
1776	Publication of Smith's *Wealth of Nations*
1778	Death of Laura Bassi
1779	Publication of Hume's *Dialogues Concerning Natural Religion*; publication of Lessing's *Nathan the Wise*
1781	Publication of Dohm's *On the Civic Improvement of the Jews*; publication of Kant's *Critique of Pure Reason*
1786	Death of Mendelssohn
1796	Death of Burns

Further Reading

Alexander Altmann, *Moses Mendelssohn: A Biographical Study* (University, AL, 1973)

Hannah Arendt, *Rahel Varnhagen: The Life of a Jewess*, ed. Liliane Weissberg (Baltimore, 1997)

Isaiah Berlin, *Vico and Herder: Two Studies in the History of Ideas* (Oxford, 1976)

Ernst Cassirer, *Kant's Life and Thought*, trans. James Haden (New Haven, 1981)

David Daiches, *Robert Burns* (New York, 1966)

Hanns Gross, *Rome in the Age of Enlightenment* (Chicago, 1990)

Deborah S. Hertz, *Jewish High Society in Old Regime Berlin* (Minneapolis, 1988)

Arthur Hertzberg, *The French Enlightenment and the Jews: The Origins of Anti-Semitism* (New York, 1990)

R.A. Houston, *Social Change in the Age of Enlightenment: Edinburgh, 1660–1760* (Oxford, 1995)

Isabel V. Hull, *Sexuality, State, and Civil Society in Germany, 1700–1815* (Ithaca, 1996)

Kenneth Maxwell, *Pombal, Paradox of the Enlightenment* (Cambridge, 1995)

E.C. Mossner, *The Life of David Hume* (Oxford, 1970)

Roy Porter and Mikuláš Teich, eds., *The Enlightenment in National Context* (Cambridge, 1981)

Peter H. Reill, *The German Enlightenment and the Rise of Historicism* (Princeton, 1975)

Robert Schofield, *The Lunar Society of Birmingham* (Oxford, 1963)

H.M. Scott, ed., *Enlightened Absolutism: Reform and Reformers in Later Eighteenth-Century Europe* (Ann Arbor, 1990)

Richard B. Sher, *Church and University in the Scottish Enlightenment: The Modern Literati of Edinburgh* (Princeton, 1985)

David Sorkin, *Moses Mendelssohn and the Religious Enlightenment* (Berkeley, 1996)

David Spadafora, *The Idea of Progress in Eighteenth-Century Britain* (Ithaca, 1990)
Richard F. Teichgraeber III, *"Free Trade" and Moral Philosophy: Rethinking the Sources of Adam Smith's "Wealth of Nations"* (Durham, NC, 1986)
Franco Venturi, *Italy and the Enlightenment* (New York, 1972)
Donald Phillip Verene, *Vico's Science of the Imagination* (Ithaca, 1981)
B.W. Young, *Religion and Enlightenment in Eighteenth-Century England: Theological Debate from Locke to Burke* (Oxford, 1998)

Chapter Fifteen

Enlightened Absolutism

In the modern world, most people would assume that an "enlightened" government would of course be a democratic one, with a system of checks and balances. In the eighteenth century, however, "democracy" still brought up ideas of "mob rule," in which the ignorant masses would be manipulated by unscrupulous politicians. To most *philosophes*, the ideal form of government was a wise king, enlightened enough to know what was right and powerful enough to put his ideals into effect. Such a king could bestow great benefits on mankind, Voltaire wrote: he would "overthrow superstition and fanaticism" and "prevent those in authority persecuting others who think differently."[1] He could ensure toleration, promote the arts and sciences, and place his subjects' welfare above all else. Voltaire for a time pinned his hopes on the Prussian king, Frederick II; Diderot corresponded with the Russian empress, Catherine II; the physician Gerard Van Swieten worked closely with the Habsburg ruler Joseph II to promote religious toleration for Protestants. These three rulers were the most important examples of what is sometimes called the political enlightenment, the application of Enlightenment ideals in government.

The same three rulers, however, also show the contradictions in the idea of political enlightenment, for they are also the most important examples of what is called enlightened absolutists, or enlightened despots, powerful absolute monarchs who were monarchs first and philosophes second. Although their interest in Enlightenment principles may have been sincere, they supported only those principles that enhanced their own authority. Overthrowing superstition and fanaticism could be beneficial to a king's subjects, and it could also weaken the ability of church institutions to challenge the king's authority. Ensuring religious toleration could encourage the settlement of skilled workers in all trades, thus increasing the taxable population of the region. Promoting the arts and sciences could likewise increase taxable revenues. Reforming the legal code, reapportioning the tax burden, building bridges, and draining marshlands would all enhance the welfare of the populace while increasing the moneys available to the monarch. And the need for more money was apparent in the course of the eighteenth century to every monarch, enlightened or not, as states continued to jockey for position among the Great Powers.

Frederick II of Prussia (1712–1786)

The childhood and adolescence of Frederick II provided the European world with its most striking example of generational conflict. His father, Frederick William I, was fanatically devoted to his army and suspicious of the wider European world. He decreed that young Frederick was to be taught army discipline and nothing else. The boy was, in fact, genuinely interested in army affairs, and he had learned all fifty-four movements of Prussian military drill by the age of five. But he was more interested in the French and Latin that he was secretly taught by his favorite tutor, despite thrashings from his father. Secure in his position as heir to the throne, Frederick persisted in his interest in music, philosophy, and culture; his father persisted in his anger. Though Frederick William's attacks on his son seemed extreme even in an age of dictatorial fathers, he had some grounds for them, for intrigue and political factions had often developed around conflict between kings and disobedient sons.

By the time Frederick was sixteen, the rift between the two seemed irreconcilable. "I . . . beg my dear Papa to be gracious to me," Frederick wrote, "and after long reflection I am able to assert that my conscience has not accused me of the smallest thing for which I should reproach myself. But if I should, without wishing it or intending it, have done anything to annoy my dear Papa, I herewith beg most humbly for forgiveness." Frederick William's response was anger against his son, "that self-willed, evil disposition, which does not love its father . . . an effeminate chap who has no manly leanings, who, to his shame, can neither ride nor shoot, and at the same time is personally unclean, wears his hair long and curled like a fool."[2] Frederick hoped for escape through marriage to the daughter of King George II of England, but his father refused. Even worse, Frederick William beat his son at a formal reception given by a neighboring king, in full view of the other guests. "Had I been treated in this way by my father," Frederick William told him, "I would have put a bullet through my head, but you have not in you even to do that."[3]

Frederick did have it in him to plan to escape to France, with his best friend, Lieutenant von Katte. The two young men were discovered, and Frederick William exploded in anger. He insisted that they be treated as army deserters and court-martialed. When the court-martial's sentence was not severe enough, Frederick William himself sentenced von Katte to death. Frederick was told only at the last minute, with just enough time to beg his friend's forgiveness, and he was forced to watch the execution. Frederick fainted and then became delirious; when he came to himself he was told that his father intended he remain a prisoner unless he mended his ways once and for all. The lesson was harsh, and certainly unjust to von Katte, but it was highly effective in showing Frederick the power of an absolute monarch. He did in fact mend his ways, and he was eventually rewarded with his own household. There he cultivated the arts and sciences, writing to Voltaire and other philosophes. He stayed on good terms with his father and seems to have felt genuine sorrow when Frederick William died in June 1740.

Frederick II inherited a full treasury, prosperous subjects, and a large and well-equipped army. Immediately he looked for a way to put those advantages to use. The state of Brandenburg-Prussia was cobbled together from several smaller territories. Immediately next to the largest piece, Brandenburg, was the rich early industrial district of Silesia, which belonged to the Austrian Habsburgs. In October 1740, the Habsburg Emperor, Charles VI (1686–1740) died, leaving his twenty-three-year-old daughter, Maria Theresa, on the throne. Charles had been worried about leaving so young a woman as ruler of so large and tumultuous a territory, for never before had a woman succeeded to all the vast Habsburg possessions. He had tried to secure her succession by persuading all the rulers in Europe to acknowledge it, an agreement known as the "pragmatic sanction." But agreements had been broken before in European history and would be again. As soon as he heard of Charles's death, Frederick II wrote a brief sketch of the political situation with respect to Silesia, concluding "that we must put ourselves in possession of Silesia before the winter, and negotiate during the winter; then we shall always find cards to play, and we shall negotiate successfully when we are in possession."[4] In December 1740, Frederick II unexpectedly led his armies into Silesia, proclaiming it part of the Prussian state. With this stroke he doubled his territory, led his country into twenty-three years of armed conflict, and earned the undying enmity of Maria Theresa.

Maria Theresa of Austria (1717–1780)

There was no conflict in Maria Theresa's childhood to compare with Frederick's. In fact, we know little about her childhood because, as a girl, she was regarded as unimportant. The Austrian Habsburg family had never failed to produce a male heir, and Maria's father, Charles VI, went on hoping for one as long as possible. The problem went beyond a simple preference for a boy. By the constitution of the Holy Roman Empire, a woman could not be emperor, nor could she rule Bohemia or Hungary. Many diplomatic observers, watching the situation closely, assumed that Maria Theresa would inherit the territories of Austria only, with the rest of the Holy Roman Empire up for grabs.

The Empire's territories included parts of Italy, German principalities, the Austrian Netherlands, Hungary, and parts of Poland. Since so many European ruling houses were related, there was no shortage of royal claimants waiting to take their share of the spoils. Frederick II had even noted that he had to move fast to take Silesia before another German prince invaded it. There was almost no border skirmish that could take place anywhere in continental Europe that did not involve some part of the Empire. Such extensive domains, in the mid-eighteenth century, required an extensive military presence, with garrisons in each region to support a standing army. But the imperial troops still depended on an antiquated system whereby each region was expected to raise its own army in case of attack. Imperial finances were even more antiquated, with the monarchy badly in debt.

Maria Theresa had the typical upbringing of a Habsburg princess, learning music and dancing, not diplomacy, finance, or military strategy. When her father died, she later wrote, she was not only grief-stricken, but also worried about her own inadequacies: "devoid of the experience and knowledge needful to rule dominions so extensive and so various because my father had never been pleased to initiate or inform me in the conduct of either internal or foreign affairs, I found myself suddenly without either money, troops, or counsel."[5] She loved her husband, Duke Francis Stephen, dearly, but he had always been excluded from govern-

Family portrait of Empress Maria Theresa grieving at the death of her husband, Emperor Franz Stephen (Erich Lessing/Art Resource, NY)

ment. Her ministers were elderly men who urged her to accept Prussia's conquest of Silesia. In this crisis, Maria Theresa quickly showed her diplomatic ability. She refused to back down, determined to defend Habsburg possessions wherever they were threatened. She appealed to the chivalry of her Hungarian nobles, appearing before them in a grand ceremony, her four-month-old son in her arms, and asking their help. "The very existence of the kingdom of Hungary, of our own person, of our children, and our crown, are now at stake," she told them. "We will die for our king, Maria Theresa!" they responded.[6] It was her first diplomatic effort, and it required hard bargaining on her part, for she could get them to support her only in exchange for confirming their traditional privileges. When reform came to the Habsburg lands, to the fury of other nobles, Hungary remained exempt.

Maria Theresa marshaled international support as well. Other rulers were not unhappy to see Prussia challenge Habsburg power in central Europe, but they were also not unhappy to see Prussia contained. Maria Theresa concluded alliances with the English and the Dutch, familiar allies since the wars of Louis XIV; Frederick, in turn, made an alliance with the French, the traditional enemies of the Habsburgs. The resulting "War of the Austrian Succession" lasted on and off from 1740 to 1748. The uneasy truce that concluded it allowed Frederick to keep his Silesia territory, but astute observers did not expect the truce to last.

The war taught Maria Theresa that her government was badly in need of reform, for much as she "detested" Frederick II's "false character," she could see that Silesia had been open to attack. Under Habsburg rule, the garrisons had been neglected, and the territory overtaxed to compensate for inefficient revenue-collection elsewhere. Frederick's first acts of government in his newly taken lands, in contrast, were to build and equip garrisons and reduce tariffs to encourage industry. The contrast was also obvious between the well-disciplined Prussian troops and the haphazard imperial forces, and between Frederick's military ability and the incompetence of Maria Theresa's generals. Maria Theresa used the Prussian threat to completely revise the tax structure of her territories. Where local representative bodies did not agree to her reforms, she simply overruled them. Within her territories, as elsewhere in Europe, the clergy and nobility had traditionally been exempt from paying taxes, thus removing substantial revenues from her reach. With a combination of insistence and diplomatic skill, she was able to remove those exemptions, putting her finances in an order never before seen in Habsburg lands. She poured the money she received into the army, tightening recruiting, imposing Prussian drill, and founding a school of artillery, a new, but increasingly important part of eighteenth-century warfare. She founded a military academy in Vienna as an answer to Frederick's in Berlin, designed to turn young nobles into an elite officer corps. Her activities were noted in Prussia. "Even in the distant future," wrote one Prussian official, "posterity will acknowledge that Maria Theresa was one of the great woman rulers of history. Surely the House of Habsburg has never had her like."[7] Frederick II agreed: she was "a woman executing plans worthy of a great man."[8]

In the early 1750s, both rulers concentrated on domestic affairs. Frederick II's reforms earned him praise as an enlightened ruler. He abolished torture and censorship of the press and eliminated some of the crueler practices of army discipline (though not flogging, considered essential in all armies through the nineteenth century). He did everything he could to promote industry and agriculture, personally touring his lands and speaking to his varied subjects. He also built up the Berlin

Academies of Arts and of Sciences first founded by his grandfather. Many of his policies were also politically expedient, such as religious toleration for the predominantly Catholic population of Silesia. Some Enlightenment ideals were not politically expedient, and so Frederick did not attempt them. In theory, he knew, serfs should be freed, but to do so would alienate his nobles. Such vacillation alienated some of his philosophe friends, like Voltaire. But Frederick himself seems to have been convinced of his own enlightened rule. A king must work hard for his subjects, he wrote. "A sovereign has not been raised to his high rank, the supreme power has not been conferred on him, to live softly, to grow fat on the substance of the people, to be happy while all others suffer. The sovereign is the first servant of the state."[9] Frederick II might be the first servant of the state, but he had no human master. He alone would decide how much Enlightenment, and in what form, he would bring to Prussia.

Maria Theresa detested Enlightenment writers as much as she detested Frederick, but her reforms sometimes achieved the same goals. She took educational institutions like the University of Vienna away from the Catholic Church, placing them firmly under governmental control. Serfs were freed on lands directly held by the Crown, though she, like Frederick, shied away from dealing with serfs under noble control. She, too, believed that a sovereign must serve her state, though she placed that obligation in a religious context. Since God had chosen "to lay on me the great burden of government," she wrote, "I resolved that so long as there was any help to be found, or any resources available, I would apply them, and that it was my duty to do so."[10]

The Seven Years' War (1757–1763)

Among the resources Maria Theresa found to apply to the service of her state were new administrators who helped carry out her financial and military reforms. One of these administrators, Anton von Kaunitz (1711–1794), became her chief advisor in international affairs and the architect of a new foreign policy for the Habsburgs. By long tradition, the arch-enemy of the Austrian Habsburgs had been the kings of France: this was so much a part of the diplomatic history of Europe that no one thought to question it. But von Kaunitz did more than question it: he asserted that the old diplomatic battle lines, based on hundreds of years of rivalry among ruling families, had to be discarded in the new international realities of competing states. It was now the king of Prussia who "belongs in the category of natural enemies," he told Maria Theresa; "he has to be considered the worst and most dangerous neighbor."[11] All foreign policy should be directed toward isolating and containing Frederick. The British had shown that they would be at best lukewarm in their support of Austria; the Dutch were busy with their own concerns; the Russians could not be counted on. France had been Prussia's ally, but Frederick had broken his side of the agreement with them three times in the course of the last war. Make an alliance with France, he urged Maria Theresa. That Habsburg had battled Valois in 1524 meant nothing in the eighteenth century. An Austrian alliance with France would mean that Prussia, when war came, would find itself at a disadvantage, fighting a two-front war on the south and west; if Prussia moved first to secure the French alliance, Austria would be the one at the disadvantage.

Such a sweeping disregard for traditional alliances was called the "diplomatic revolution," as astonishing in its day as the end of the Cold War in the late twentieth century. Despite the reservations of her older ministers, Maria Theresa agreed to von Kaunitz's plan, and he left for the Austrian embassy in Paris. Additional diplomatic maneuvers secured Austrian possessions in Italy and Belgium from attack. An agreement with Czarina Elizabeth of Russia, daughter of Peter the Great, completed the circle of alliances.

Frederick II had kept a careful eye on the international situation, and his concern led him to a major diplomatic error. Convinced that the French would never make an alliance with the Habsburgs, he concluded a treaty with the British. The French, alarmed, concluded a defensive alliance with Austria. Frederick II suddenly and unexpectedly found himself surrounded by allies of the Austrians. He had achieved his military victories—for which he was known in his own country as "the Great"— by seizing the initiative, and as he watched the international tensions build, he decided to do so once again. In 1756, he invaded Saxony, hoping to have a quick end of the war. He had no legitimate pretext for the invasion, but as he once wrote, "If there is anything to be gained by honesty, then we shall be honest; if we must dupe, then let us be scoundrels."[12] Austria and France mobilized their armies, and the war was on.

Like the wars of Louis XIV, the Seven Years' War was a world war. Even without the diplomatic revolution, Britain and France would have found themselves on opposing sides, as the two states vied for possession of colonial territories around the world. Britain sent troops and subsidies to help Prussia keep France busy on the European continent.

In North America, the Seven Years' War became known as the French and Indian War, as the British colonists, allied with the Iroquois, fought against the French, allied with the Hurons.

By 1760 it looked as though Frederick might be beaten, for the impressive army he had inherited from his father had suffered terribly, as had his country. Fortunately for him, Czarina Elizabeth died and her nephew, Peter III, became czar of Russia. Peter idolized Frederick II, and he at once made peace with Prussia. The war ended in a peace of exhaustion on all sides, but with slight gains to Prussia and Britain. Prussia kept Silesia, much to Maria Theresa's dismay, but gave up Saxony. More ominously for future conflicts, Frederick II had expended a substantial portion of the military resources his father and grandfather had so carefully built. Britain was the major colonial winner, taking over territories in North America and India from France. The alliance between France and Austria remained intact for the moment, with Maria Theresa's daughter, Marie Antonia (Antoinette), marrying the young Prince Louis, heir to the French throne.

The Treaty of Paris (1763) that ended the war was an acknowledgment of the changes in government and diplomacy that had taken place in the preceding one hundred years. It left European rulers free to concentrate on their own countries. For the most part, they did so with clear intent: to apply those aspects of enlightened thought that would support their own authority while building their country's power. Gone were the old days of dynastic succession as the ruling force in government: the idea of the personal ruler was replaced by the idea of the impersonal state, as represented by government bureaucracy, armies, laws, courts, and citizens. The principle of balance of powers, first developed out of the Treaties of Westphalia that ended the Thirty Years' War in 1648, received further support. The idea of considering Europe as composed of distinct and separate parts, noted one British writer, and "of keeping them independent, though unequal in power, and of preventing any one, by any means, from becoming too powerful for the rest," was the most important political invention of the century. In his view, it was owing to this system of "balance of power. . . that this small part of the western world has acquired so astonishing a superiority over the rest of the globe."[13]

Catherine II of Russia (1729–1796)

By the time the Treaty of Paris was signed in 1763, Czar Peter III, whose accession had been so beneficial to Frederick II, was dead under the

Portrait of Catherine the Great wearing a robe of silver silk and an ermine coat, by an unidentified artist (Erich Lessing/Art Resource, NY)

most suspicious circumstances. He had been born Duke Peter Karl Ulrich of Holstein, a small German state. He had been brought to Russia at the age of fourteen as Grand Duke Peter, heir to the childless Czarina Elizabeth. His wife had been born Princess Sophia Augusta Fredericka of Anhalt-Zerbst, an even smaller German state, and invited to Russia as Grand Duchess Catherine specifically for the purpose of providing Peter with a male heir. For Russia had a long history of political instability and palace intrigue. A young, beautiful, and impoverished German princess, like Catherine, could be expected to learn Russian, convert to the Russian Orthodox church, and have children without acquiring political influence on her own.

The best-laid plans even of czarinas can go astray. Catherine did, indeed, do all she was asked, but she was also a clever, forceful girl who spent her years as Grand Duchess observing the political arena and gaining supporters. Peter, in contrast, was foolish and infantile, with little interest in his new country and no talent for governance. His abrupt reversal of Russian policy in favor of Frederick II came after six long years of war, angering the country. Many, including his wife, thought him, quite simply, incapable of ruling, even insane. An attempt at usurpation was inevitable. For some time Catherine had been quietly building up support for herself and her son among the military and the powerful nobles. When word came back to her that Peter was planning to have her killed and their son disinherited, she decided to act. In June 1762, her supporters carried out a *coup d'état* (takeover of the state) on her behalf, proclaiming her Czarina Catherine II. It was so well planned that Peter III hardly knew what had happened to him. He signed a formal letter of abdication and was imprisoned. An official account of his death from disease was circulated six days later, but it was widely assumed— and historians have confirmed—that he was murdered by Catherine's supporters. No one was surprised: royal murders were not infrequent in Russian history.

Catherine's official statements depicted her takeover as necessary for public welfare. "By this action," she later proclaimed, "thanks be to God, We accepted the Sovereign throne of Our beloved fatherland upon Ourselves without any bloodshed, but God alone and Our beloved fatherland helped Us through those they selected."[14] Her ability to maintain the throne rested, in the early years, on her ability to inspire confidence. She had a talent for befriending powerful supporters in the nobility and the army, whom she rewarded lavishly: out of a total annual state revenue of roughly 16 million rubles, she spent about 1 million rubles rewarding those who had put her on the throne. She was also, like Frederick II, hardworking, determined to keep up with the details of the governmental bureaucracy. "Her application to business is incredible," wrote a British observer; "the welfare and prosperity of her subjects, the glory of her empire, are always present to her; and to all appearance her care will raise the reputation and power of Russia to a point which, at present, they have never reached."[15]

Catherine II was an absolute monarch out of political necessity as well as personal taste, and like other absolute monarchs she enacted policies to weaken the power of great nobles, cut down on the power of the established church, and strengthen the financial and legal position of the Crown. As a grand duchess, she had read many of the works of the philosophes, and one of her first acts as czarina was to call a special commission to debate a project on legal reform. The reforms, called the Great Instruction, which had taken her several years to write, were largely based on Montesquieu's *Spirit of the Laws*. They were intended to impress western European statesmen and westernized Russians, and succeeded in both areas. Voltaire called the Instruction "the finest monument of the age," and Frederick II noted that "we have never heard of any Female being a Lawgiver. This Glory was reserved for the Empress of Russia."[16] These instructions, and their contrast with Russia's murky past, were the basis for Catherine's growing European reputation as an enlightened ruler. But Catherine was a pragmatic ruler, and proud as she was of her Great Instruction she would not risk her throne by putting its principles into practice. Nor would she risk angering her noble supporters, or cutting down on her ability to distribute largesse, by abolishing serfdom or other feudal privileges. The Great Instruction remained on paper, where, indeed, it had great success, frequently reissued in Russian and translated into all the major European languages.

In the aftermath of the Treaty of Paris, Catherine looked to military power to enhance Russia's international position. Two wars with Turkey, between 1768 and 1774 and 1787 and 1792, gave Russia the Crimea to gain access to the Black Sea, the nearest warm-water port. Sixty years earlier, Russia had successfully challenged Sweden for supremacy on the Baltic. Now it looked as though Russia had a new challenge, control of central Europe.

Catherine became notorious in Europe for her sexual activities as well as her domestic and foreign policy. She herself later hinted that her husband had never been able to consummate their marriage, and her son's father was her first lover, a Russian nobleman. Another of her lovers was one of the chief supporters of her coup and of her early years on the throne. Still another, Gregory Potemkin, was the most talented of her administrators. Yet she never let her love affairs interfere with her government. She never chose men from among the great noble families, because they might gain too much influence, and she allowed ex-lovers to keep their governmental positions as long as they were valuable to the state. After she died lurid stories spread about the cause of her death, but in fact the truth is well-documented: she had a stroke early one morning while working at her desk and died peacefully in her bed two days later.

Partitions of Poland (1772, 1793, 1795)

In 1763, King Augustus III of Poland died. Both Russia and Prussia were instantly alert. "Do not laugh at me for jumping off my chair when I received the news of the death of the Polish king," Catherine II told her minister; "the King of Prussia jumped out from behind his desk when he heard it."[17] Both monarchs had been greedily eyeing Polish territory for some time, as had Maria Theresa. For Poland was vulnerable. In an age of increasing centralization and military buildup, Poland had stuck to its ancient constitution, whereby kings were elected and served only at the pleasure of the nobility. There was no standing army: instead, nobles were virtually feudal lords in their own territories, providing their king with troops at their pleasure. The Polish nobility were "independent and unaccountable for their conduct," wrote a British observer. "They have the power of life and death over their tenants, pay no taxes, are subject to none but the king, may choose who they will for their king, and lay him under what restraints they please."[18] Great nobles lived luxuriously, traveling with full retinue of servants, speaking French and importing the latest fashions, but this contrasted with the poverty of their serfs, living in villages that were no more than clusters of wood huts.

Frederick II had long contemplated taking territories away from Po- land "like artichokes, leaf by leaf." Whenever a Polish king died, the country's nobles were divided into factions. Frederick hoped to "profit by these and gain . . . sometimes a town, sometimes another district, until the whole has been eaten up."[19] Catherine II's plans were similar. She and Frederick together successfully imposed on the Polish election her own candidate, Count Stanislaus-Augustus Poniatowski (1732– 1798). He was her former lover and father of one of her daughters; he was also intelligent, enlightened, and a Polish patriot. Catherine clearly intended King Stanislaus-Augustus to run Poland as a puppet, favorable to Russia's interest. A British traveler noted that Russian troops were seen everywhere. The new king had his own vision, however. He saw his task as introducing Enlightenment ideas and promoting Polish unity, while paying attention to the political realities of a weak kingdom caught between three aggressive states.

Stanislaus's government did promote Enlightenment ideas and policies, and under his reign Polish intellectuals began to discuss constitutional reforms and a hereditary monarchy. Some nobles freed their serfs. The political realities eventually defeated them, however. Catherine II's military expansion south during the Turkish Wars made both Prussia and Austria nervous. Setting aside old differences, the three states concluded a secret treaty to divide Poland into three parts in 1772. Frederick took West Prussia, which enabled him to finally unite the two separate parts of his realm. This made Prussia second only to Austria in contiguous land area among the German states. Austria took the province of Galicia, important for salt mines, one of the most valuable sources of revenue for the state. Russia took northwestern provinces. "The provinces taken by Russia are the largest," noted a British observer, "by Austria the most populous, and by Prussia the most commercial."[20] Western European countries protested the dismemberment, but did nothing to prevent it. In 1788, when Russia was busy with its war against the Turks, Polish patriots began a reform movement designed to unite the country against the foreign powers which controlled it. On May 3, 1791, the Polish diet voted on a new constitution. Their best hope would have been an alliance with Prussia against Russia, but instead Catherine II made peace with the Turks and dictated a second partition of Poland. Thaddeus Kosciuszko, a hero of the American Revolution, led a Polish army against the Russians, but he was defeated. Russia, Prussia, and Austria carved up what remained of the country, and the ancient feudal kingdom of Poland-Lithuania ceased to exist.

Joseph II (1741–1790)

Enlightened ideals often suffered a setback when confronted with the realities of eighteenth-century government, and the ruler who suffered the most from the clash of ideal with reality was Joseph II of Austria, son of Maria Theresa. Ascending to the throne at the age of thirty-nine, he was the most striking example of the enlightened despot, determined to impose Enlightenment ideals of efficiency and rationality on his entire kingdom, whatever his subjects thought of it. He, like Frederick, called for legal and tax reform, so that laws and taxes would be uniform throughout the realm. He had roads built and went on personal inspection tours of farms and manufacturing districts. He abolished the legal status of serfdom because he believed the former serfs would be more productive if they were given the freedom to marry, to learn skills, and to improve their land. He instituted religious toleration for Christians, removed many of the restrictions on Jews, and tried to limit the power of the Catholic clergy, closing monasteries and making priests subordinate to state authority.

The result of these enlightened policies was a series of both noble and peasant rebellions. Roman Catholics hated the Edict of Toleration, which allowed private worship for Protestants, and Christians everywhere protested the improved position of Jews. The nobles, particularly in Hungary, were furious at his attack on their privileges, including the privilege to elect him as their king. In the Austrian Netherlands, Joseph's attack on both local privilege and on religious institutions led to armed revolt. Joseph's sister, Marie Christine, was the governor of the region, and she and her husband had to flee the country. Joseph had neither the army nor the government bureaucracy to impose his authority on his diverse kingdom, and in both Hungary and Belgium he had to back down. He died in 1790, after only ten years of rule. His brother, Leopold II (1747–1792) combined his brother's Enlightenment ideals with his mother's pragmatic approach to politics and was able to restore order. "I believe that the sovereign should rule only through the law," he wrote in a letter intended to mollify the leaders of the rebellion in the Netherlands. The sovereign occupied his special position in his state "in order that he may bring about its happiness and prosperity, not as he wills it, but as the people itself wills and feels it."[21] The letter achieved its purpose, but Leopold died in 1792. By that time, European ideas on government had taken a whole new turn.

Profile: Thaddeus Kosciuszko (1746–1817)

In 1776, a young Polish nobleman, Thaddeus Kosciuszko, presented his credentials to the Continental Congress meeting in Philadelphia. The American colonies had declared their independence from Great Britain, and the city of Philadelphia, like the rest of the region, was preparing for British attack. But the commander-in-chief of the American forces,

George Washington, faced a shortage of officers, for most of the officers who had led troops on American soil either were British or retained British sympathy. Kosciuszko was one of several foreign officers to volunteer to serve the American cause. He came from a well-respected, but poor noble family, that is, "poor" by noble standards. Though they had land and serfs and funds for young Thaddeus to travel in France, they had too little money for him to live peacefully on his estates. He would have sought service with the Polish army, but it was greatly reduced after the first partition, and officer's commissions were therefore very expensive. He, like other cash-poor nobles, looked to service abroad. His arrival in Philadelphia coincided with a serious need for engineers to supervise the creation of fortifications, and so Kosciuszko was appointed "an engineer in the service of the United States," with a pay of sixty dollars a month and the rank of colonel.[22]

Kosciuszko served the United States Army faithfully and well as a military engineer throughout the war, which lasted until 1783. He was especially commended for his efforts at the Battle of Saratoga in 1777, and his fortifications for the garrison at West Point "had the credit," according to an American general, "of giving to it a character of strength which deterred the enemy from any new attempt."[23] He missed his native land, however, and his greatest wish was "to be of use to his country at some future period and to repay her the benefits of his citizenship."[24] The years after his return to Poland in 1784 were quiet ones, but the Polish reform movement begun in 1788 called for an increase in the army. Kosciuszko's service in the American war was widely admired: "If he knew how to shed his blood for a foreign country, he undoubtedly will not spare it for his own."[25] Appointed major general, he immediately began reforming the army to turn it into an effective fighting force. He was one of the first to swear allegiance to the new constitution voted on May 3, 1791. "We must all unite for one purpose," he wrote, "to free our country from the domination of foreigners, from the abasement and destruction of the very name of Pole."[26] When Catherine II ordered Russian troops to invade, Kosciuszko's soldiers did their best to resist. King Stanislaus, alarmed by the prospect of complete devastation of his country, asked Kosciuszko to agree to stop fighting. He, together with several other patriotic Polish military leaders, resigned from the army.

After the second partition, Polish patriots everywhere looked to Kosciuszko to lead an uprising against the foreign invaders. He went on a European tour to drum up support, but though the French recognized him as a "defender of the people against despots," and the Americans called for "a union of all free countries to save Poland from the rapacious hands of all spoilers," no government would actually send aid. Kosciuszko tried to inspire his countrymen with the American experience: "Poles! Rise and you will win," he told them, just as the Americans had won against the British.[27] But this was to ignore political reality, for the American colonies had extensive resources, a powerful foreign ally, and an opponent 3,000 miles away. Polish patriots, in contrast, had lost control of most of the country's resources, had no foreign allies, and faced three powerful enemies just over the border. Largely owing to Kosciuszko's inspiring leadership and untiring efforts, the Polish army managed to hold off the combined Prussian and Russian armies for six months in 1794. It was finally defeated in October 1794. Kosciuszko was wounded and taken prisoner. He was kept for the next two years in prison in St. Petersburg and was only freed on the death of Catherine II. He spent the rest of his life in exile in the United States and in Switzerland.

Important Dates

1740	Death of Frederick William I of Prussia; Frederick II the Great becomes king; death of Holy Roman Emperor Charles VI; Maria Theresa becomes archduchess of Austria
1740–1748	War of the Austrian Succession
1756	Diplomatic Revolution
1756–1763	Seven Years' War
1760	Death of Czarina Elizabeth of Russia; Peter III becomes czar
1762	Coup d'etat against Peter III; Catherine the Great becomes czarina
1765	Joseph II becomes Holy Roman Emperor
1772	First Partition of Poland
1780	Death of Maria Theresa of Austria; Joseph II becomes sole ruler in Austria
1790	Death of Joseph II
1791	New Constitution promulgated in Poland
1793	Second Partition of Poland
1794	Defeat of Polish army under Kosciuszko by Prussia and Russia

1795   Third Partition of Poland; death of Frederick II the Great
1796   Death of Catherine the Great

Further Reading

John T. Alexander, *Catherine the Great: Life and Legend* (New York, 1989)
Robert B. Asprey, *Frederick the Great: The Magnificent Enigma* (New York, 1986)
Derek Beales, *Joseph II* (New York, 1987)
C.B.A. Behrens, *Society, Government, and the Enlightenment: The Experiences of Eighteenth Century France and Prussia* (New York1985)
Paul Bernard, *Jesuits and Jacobins: Enlightenment and Enlightened Despotism in Austria* (Urbana, IL, 1971)
Paul Bernard, *The Limits of Enlightenment: Joseph II and the Law* (Urbana, IL, 1979)
T.C.W. Blanning, *Joseph II and Enlightened Despotism* (New York, 1970)
T.C.W. Blanning, *Joseph II* (London, 1994)
Norman Davies, *God's Playground. A History of Poland*, 2 vols. (New York, 1984)
John Gagliardo, *Reich and Nation: The Holy Roman Empire as Idea and Reality, 1763–1806* (Bloomington, IN, 1980)
Miecislaus Haiman, *Kosciuszko in the American Revolution* (New York, 1975)
Miecislaus Haiman, *Kosciuszko: Leader and Exile* (New York, 1977)
R.W. Harris, *Absolutism and Enlightenment, 1660–1789* (New York, 1966)
Walter Hubatsch, *Frederick the Great of Prussia: Absolutism and Administration* (New Brunswick, 1975)
Charles Ingrao, *The Hessian Mercenary State: Ideas, Institutions, and Reform under Frederick II, 1760–1785* (Cambridge, 1987)
C.A. Macartney, ed., *The Habsburg and Hohenzollern Dynasties in the Seventeenth and Eighteenth Centuries* (New York, 1970)
Victor S. Mamatey, *Rise of the Habsburg Empire 1526–1815* (New York, 1971)
James Van Horn Melton, *Absolutism and the Eighteenth-Century Origins of Compulsory Schooling in Prussia and Austria* (Cambridge, 1988)
Marc Raeff, *The Well-Ordered Police State: Social and Institutional Change through Law in the Germanies and Russia, 1600–1800* (New Haven, 1983)
Hans Rosenberg, *Bureaucracy, Aristocracy, Autocracy: The Prussian Experience, 1600–1815* (Boston, 1958)
John L. Sutton, *The King's Honor and the King's Cardinal: The War of the Polish Succession* (Lexington, KY, 1980)
Franz A.J. Szabo, *Kaunitz and Enlightened Absolutism 1753–1780* (Cambridge, 1994)
Mack Walker, *Johann Jakob Moser and the Holy Roman Empire of the German Nation* (Chapel Hill, 1981)

Chapter Sixteen

A Consumer Society

Though the pace of change was slow, often even imperceptible, European society in the mid-eighteenth century was clearly somehow different from what it had been at the beginning of the seventeenth century. More wealth was accumulating in the hands of a wider band of urban and rural commoners, who were gaining a new self-confidence in their position. The pillars of the older economy, such as the guilds and communal control over agricultural production, began to give way to new, usually more entrepreneurial, organizations. The ratio of urban to rural inhabitants began to increase, though that was due more to a higher concentration of population in a few major cities than a general increase in the size of all towns. London and Paris in particular were now major cities with several hundred thousand inhabitants. Some towns that had been very important in the sixteenth and seventeenth centuries became economic backwaters, while new, virtually unknown towns grew dramatically. In the mid-eighteenth century, these slow changes began to accelerate into an entirely new phenomenon, known as the industrial revolution.

The industrial revolution can be viewed in two ways. On the one hand, it is a series of interrelated technological changes in a narrow range of industries (textiles, coal mining, iron) that introduced a dramatically new way of organizing production. On the other hand, it is the more fundamental transformation of first British, then European, society that allowed the changes in production to take hold and accelerate. Change in how things were made became change in how people lived. In this latter sense, the industrial revolution is intimately connected with several other major changes that have also sometimes been labeled "revolutions." The eighteenth century witnessed a "transportation revolution," an "agricultural revolution," and a "democratic revolution," as well as the more famous "industrial revolution." Historians dispute which of these changes should be viewed as cause and which as effect of the larger transformation.

Transportation Revolution

One of the prime characteristics of the traditional economy was that bulky products like foodstuffs, raw materials, and metal products could be sold only in a small circle around the site of production because of the difficulty of transport. Roads were generally terrible: muddy ruts that were impassable in bad weather and beset with highwaymen in the deserted forest stretches. It was simply uneconomic to use horse- or oxen-drawn wagons to move products over long distances unless they had high profit margins. Adam Smith observed, for example, that "six or eight men by the help of water carriage can bring back in the same time the same quantity of goods between London and Edinburgh as 50 broad-wheeled wagons attended by a hundred men and drawn by 400 horses."[1] The economic mastery of the Dutch came, in part, from the fact that it was much easier to move bulky items by ship than by land. Amsterdam bakers were supplied with their grain from distant Prussian estates, which were more accessible than peasant farms in nearby central Germany.

Rivers were the primary alternative to the roads in most of inland Europe. They had been the main pathways of trade since the Middle Ages. But, of course, they only benefited those communities that lay on or near them. In the late seventeenth century, several governments designed projects to extend access to remote areas in order to foster trade. The French took the lead in dredging rivers to enhance navigability and developing a canal network. The most famous project was the Canal de Deux Mers, in southern France, opened in 1691, which stretched for 150 miles between the Mediterranean and the Atlantic. But of greater economic importance was the series of canals linking the Loire to the Seine and the Seine to the Somme. This network, completed in 1734, proved essential for providing Paris with the supplies to fuel its growth.

France was not alone in developing an extensive canal network. The Dutch had always relied on river transport and continued to link the navigable arms of their rivers. But the most dramatic movement in dredging and canal building was in England. Between 1600 and 1760 the length of navigable water doubled to 1,400 miles. The Duke of Bridgewater's Canal, completed in 1761, set the stage for a new wave of canal building that eventually linked London with the industrializing Midlands and the Severn River.

Though roads were secondary to canals in fostering trade, they too were improved in the eighteenth century. The French established a system of royal roads that, according to its 1738 plan, was intended to cover 24,800 miles. Though the network was not completed as planned, most of the main routes were, thus connecting Paris with the rest of the country. The English tried a different approach from royal central planning to improve their roads. The Turnpike Act of 1662 gave permission to a syndicate to collect tolls on a stretch of road, provided that the syndicate upgraded the route and made all repairs. That initial experiment proved so successful that it became the general principle of road maintenance for the next century; on average, Parliament granted eight turnpike acts per year to the 1750s and more than twice as many thereafter. By 1750 there were thirteen main roads leading from London to different parts of the kingdom. In both France and England travel times between major cities (like Paris to Lyon or London to Liverpool) were cut in half as a result of the improvements.

Agricultural Revolution

The traditional three-field crop rotation system that predominated in northern Europe had been especially well suited for production for a limited regional market. In theory, self-sufficient peasant farmers produced just enough surplus to purchase manufactured goods from the local town, so that town and countryside were in a symbiotic relationship. The rapid growth of major cities like Paris and London demanded a new orientation of farming. Already in the seventeenth century, some farmers, especially the Dutch, had begun to specialize in more exotic produce to meet urban needs. Now farmers began to search for ways to increase productivity to create larger surpluses and make more efficient use of the land.

There are several elements to the agricultural revolution. First, in England especially, the process of creating larger farms that could be worked more efficiently by hired labor was extended. This process was known as enclosure. A large landowner would get approval to take over the common lands and wasteland of a village and to buy out all the small holders in a village. Some of the displaced small holders would then be available to work as laborers. Enclosure had been progressing in England for more than two centuries (it was even criticized by Sir Thomas More). By 1700, about half of the English farmland was enclosed, usually through private agreements between a large-scale farmer and the villagers. In the eighteenth century, that process accelerated because would-be enclosers began to get formal permission to enclose by act of Parliament. Before 1760, there had been just over one hundred parliamentary enclosure acts. Between 1760 and 1830 the number grew to more than 1,800, with 1.5 million acres being enclosed. In France and western Germany, it was harder to use the legal machinery to displace peasants with small plots, so villages continued to operate with open field, rather than enclosed farming. On the whole, large farms were more efficient than small ones, so the process of enclosure tended to increase productivity.

A second element of the agricultural revolution that could be enhanced by the concentration of farms into fewer hands was experimentation with new crop combinations. In the old three-field system, one third of the land had to remain fallow (i.e., empty) every year to ensure that the soil did not lose its nutrients. In the eighteenth century, farmers began experimenting with crops that could replenish those nutrients and thus make use of all the land. In general, the crops grown in the new phases of the rotation were fodder crops for the animals: turnips, rutabagas, clover, rapeseed, sainfoin, and lucerne. A typical crop rotation would now be first wheat, then turnips, then barley, and finally clover. The use of root crops was promoted after 1706 in England by Lord Townshend, who gained the nickname "Turnip" Townshend for his advocacy. An Austrian civil servant, Johann Christian Schubart, did even better by his enthusiasm for clover, eventually being knighted by Emperor Joseph II, with the title "von Kleefeld" (from the cloverfield). In general, it was easier for noble landlords and the owners of enclosed estates than for peasants to carry out the change to four-course crop rotation. They were not obligated to persuade everyone with a plot in the main field to change their planting habits in order to bring about the change. The association of nobles with "progressive" agriculture and the resistance of the peasantry led many observers to conclude that peasants were inherently opposed to new ideas.

The new crop that had the most dramatic impact was the potato. Potatoes were relatively rare in Europe before 1740. But a major crop failure of wheat and rye that year led many farmers to try any new product that could supply their hunger. People accustomed themselves to the different taste of potatoes and began to recognize their benefit, especially for a subsistence economy. Potatoes could generate about four times as many calories per acre as could grains. Especially for those peasants deprived of their lands through enclosures, potatoes represented a crop that they could cultivate in their own gardens. In regions where the majority of the population held very little land, such as Ireland, potatoes thus became the main part of the diet within a few decades.

As a result of all of these agricultural changes, Europe was producing significantly more food by the end of the eighteenth century than it had at the beginning. The improvements were not just in total volume produced, but also in productivity per acre. The increase in productivity also meant that a smaller percentage of the overall population of Europe had to be engaged in agriculture.

Demographic Revolution

Which came first, the chicken or the egg? This question is somewhat like the one historians ask about the relationship between the agricultural revolution and the demographic revolution. Did a larger population mean that more food had to be produced or did increases in food production mean that a larger population was possible? In either case, the population of Europe began to rise sharply in the eighteenth century. The population of England increased by more than 50 percent between 1750 and the first census in 1801, while the population of Ireland may have doubled in that same period. For Europe as a whole, it has been estimated that population grew by 18 percent between 1550 and 1680, but 62 percent between 1680 and 1820. It was essential that there be more food available to feed that increasing population.

In broad terms, the level of population in any society is shaped by two factors: fertility, the number of children being born, and mortality, the number of people dying. So the first thing to establish about the demographic revolution is whether it was caused primarily by an increase in the rate of births, a decrease in the rate of deaths, or some balance between the two.

For most of the early modern period, mortality tended to come in waves. Disease or famine would hit a region for a period of a few months, carrying away most of the weak (as well as some of the strong). The death rate would then go down to a steady state for a few years until the next wave of disease or famine hit. Historical demographers have even given this pattern a name: the "mortality crisis of the old type." There was little that individuals could do directly to control the death rate. Even in the eighteenth century, the effects of famine and pestilence were often viewed as "God's will," though the idea of inoculation was introduced from Turkey during the eighteenth century in an effort to overcome at least some of the randomness of mortality. Epidemic disease appears to have been less widespread in the later eighteenth century than before (for example, the last great outbreak of bubonic plague, which had been the most feared epidemic scourge in early modern Europe, was in 1731 in Marseilles), but historians now doubt that the rise in European population can be explained primarily by improvements in mortality rates.

By contrast, the birth rate was more directly susceptible to individual decisions. Traditionally, European villages and towns had tried to inhibit the growth of population by keeping the average age of first marriage high. Birth control within marriage was known, but imperfectly followed, so most couples would produce babies as long as husband and wife remained fertile. A late age at first marriage removed several years of fertility and thus reduced the total number of children. In the early eighteenth century, this traditional brake on childbearing began to break down. On the one hand, the average age at first marriage began to go down. It was becoming possible to establish one's independent household without waiting for an inheritance, which removed one hold that parents had over their children's choice of marriage partner. In England, where this process was most pronounced, the proportion of the population that never married was cut in half, from 15 percent to 7 percent, while the average age of first marriage for women decreased by two full years, from 26.5 to 23.5 years. More women were having babies, and, because they were marrying earlier, they had the chance to have more babies.

At the same time, the inhibitions against sexual contact outside of marriage also began to break down. The illegitimacy rate rose from 1.5 percent to 5 percent between 1680 and 1800. A Swiss pastor commented on the prevalence of "bundling" in the industrial regions of the Alps: "The young lad begins as soon as he is confirmed to steal after one or more girls. The girls, knowing that they cannot get a man any other way, open their chambers to these night boys and abandon themselves to the certain or uncertain hope that, in case of pregnancy, they will not be abandoned to shame."[2] And indeed in addition to an increasing proportion of children born out of wedlock, there was a dramatic increase in the number of children born less than nine months after marriage: from 15 percent of first children in 1680 to 35 percent of first children in 1800.

Contemporaries noted the dramatic increase in population from all this sexual activity. Whereas mercantilist theories of economy emphasized that it was good to have an increasing population, now some began to worry that population was increasing too rapidly to be sustained. The demographic analysis of Thomas Malthus in *An Essay on Population* (1792) set the standard for later interpretations of population. He argued that population would ordinarily increase geometrically (i.e., 2x2x2x2 . . .), while the underlying resources to support population would only increase arithmetically (i.e., 2+2+2+2 . . .). Eventually, population would outstrip resources and a "positive check," such as massive famine, would have to bring the population back into line with resources. Ironically, Malthus's system was much better at explaining how demographic patterns worked before the industrial revolution than it was at anticipating how population would behave during the industrial revolution. Demography had broken through the "Malthusian trap."

Protoindustry and Rural Labor

The increasing population of Europe created both a labor supply for manufacturing and a potential market for manufactured products. It became increasingly difficult for most villagers to rely exclusively, or even primarily, on agricultural production for their livelihoods. In regions where inheritances were divided among heirs, the plots of land became smaller and smaller until they could no longer support a family. In regions where inheritances were kept intact for one heir, there were a larger number of "castoffs" looking for alternate ways to support themselves. In some areas, enclosures also drove small farmers off their land and into the labor force. Even in those parts of Europe not affected by enclosure, rural society became more and more stratified, with a small group of peasant farmers in control of farms large enough to support their families and an increasing number of landless or land-poor neighbors. How were all of these people to make a living?

Some migrated to the big cities. There were jobs available for servants in noble and even bourgeois households. There were also innumerable odd jobs that had to be performed and a large sector of desperate men and women who made their livings as day laborers. For most who went to the urban centers, life was hard and dangerous. The annual death rate in London far exceeded the birth rate throughout the eighteenth century. The only way that London sustained its phenomenal growth was by massive immigration. Still others migrated continually as farmworkers and itinerant journeyman craftsmen. By the mid-eighteenth century, there was a regular seasonal traffic in workers from central Germany to the Netherlands.

But most of the displaced farmers continued to reside in the communities where they were born. They formed a significant new labor pool that began to take on various work that had traditionally been done in cities. Craft production became as essential to the village economy as agriculture. Most of the production could be carried out within the homes of villagers, so the intensification of rural craft production is sometimes known as "cottage industry." As Daniel Defoe commented on the Halifax district in England: "Neither indeed could one fifth part of the inhabitants be supported without manufactures for the land could not maintain them."[3] Rural artisans began to compete with urban craftspeople, much to the annoyance of guilds, who did what they could to enforce their traditional monopoly over production in their geographical area. Though almost any trade except the finest luxury goods could be done in the countryside, it was primarily in the production of textiles that rural industry took root.

The competition between the countryside and the town for manufacturing took on two forms. In many parts of Europe, rural crafts simply competed with urban manufactures within the same narrow geographical area. Instead of going to the town fairs to purchase a linen jacket, a peasant would turn to someone in the village who could do the same work. But at the same time, some urban merchants organized rural manufacturing to create a significant export business. The most entrepreneurial would lease spinning wheels and weaving looms to peasants in order to carry out the work of preparing cloth. They would then supply the peasants with raw materials and expect delivery of a fixed amount of finished product, which they could then bring to the international market. This general form of business was known as the "putting-out" system. In this manner, whole districts became committed to manufacturing, most often of linens or linen-cotton and linen-wool blends. Those regions where the putting-out system and cottage industry were particularly intensive are sometimes said to be "protoindustrial," because they show all the hallmarks of modern industrial production, except for the factories.

It is notable that many regions that adapted most fully to this new form of protoindustry did not take the next step of full industrialization. In fact, some of the areas that seemed most prosperous in the eighteenth century, such as Silesia, were to become synonymous with poverty and deprivation when forced to compete with factory industry from England in the nineteenth century.

At the same time that rural industry and the putting-out system began to threaten urban crafts, the urban craft system had to confront its own internal crisis. Population increases meant that there was a greater number of journeymen who had no prospects of achieving master status. Journeymen established their own culture within the guild, some of which was in conscious opposition to the culture of the master. Journeymen formed their own associations, which sometimes acted as the focus of strikes and work stoppages. There were other, more symbolic challenges to masters' authority too. One notable case is the reaction of the printers of Paris to a plague of alley cats. Journeymen and apprentices joined together to round up all of the wild cats, but also the pet cats of the master and his wife, which they proceeded to slaughter after a large mock trial. The master's wife immediately interpreted the trial as a veiled attack on the master: "These wicked men can't kill the masters so they have killed my pussy."[4] Journeymen were caught between opposition to the control that masters exercised within the guilds and fear that they would lose their work to rural artisans completely outside of the guild system. It is against this social backdrop that the industrial revolution unfolded.

The Industrial Revolution

The emblem of the industrial revolution was the steam engine. Before the eighteenth century, the main sources of power available for work were animals or some kind of mill. Animal power was limited by the number of animals that could be hooked up in any one space, while mills were restricted to those places with sufficient wind or water to drive them. Neither could be used for an increasingly important function: to drive the pumps necessary to get water out of coal and iron mines. A workable engine was first developed by Thomas Savery in England in 1698. Thomas Newcomen introduced a competing model in

1705, which went on to become the standard for the first half of the eighteenth century. Because the fuel for these engines was right at hand in the coal mines, there was little incentive to make the engines efficient. Nevertheless, they spread. By 1781, there were 360 Newcomen and Savery engines operating in English mines, and a handful of engines in mines on the Continent. It took a further refinement, James Watt's condensor and rotary motion in 1781, to make the steam engine a widespread commercially viable tool for manufacturing.

But development of the engine was a sign of an inventive spirit that was taking root, especially in England. Technology was not yet dependent on scientific training. Watt was unusual in having attended university lectures in chemistry. Savery and Newcomen were both artisans. Hundreds of master artisans and inspired amateurs gravitated toward trying to solve technical problems within a limited industry or geographical area. That inventive spirit began to transform another area of work: the production of cloth. In earlier centuries, the principal fabric for making clothing was wool. With the advent of protoindustrialization, linen, made from flax, became the fabric of choice for less expensive clothing. The first inventions in fabric production were designed to accelerate wool and flax production. In 1733, John Kay developed a flying shuttle, which made it easier to weave woolens. But Kay's shuttle reinforced a structural bottleneck in cloth production that eager inventors now tried to overcome: it took much less time to weave cloth than to spin the threads to be woven. Industrious artisans set about finding ways of improving on the spinning wheel that could be found in so many rural houses.

The key breakthrough came in 1766, when James Hargreaves perfected a multistranded spinning device known as the spinning jenny. In rapid succession this jenny was improved by several innovations: Arkwright's water frame in 1769 and Crompton's mule (so named because it combined features of the jenny and the water frame just as a mule combines features of a horse and a donkey) in 1779. These machines could not only produce several strands of thread simultaneously, they could also spin the thread to be much stronger than it would have been if spun by hand. This quality made it possible to use a new raw material to spin the thread: cotton. A new international trade pattern was about to develop.

Whereas even the spinning jenny could be operated by hand, the water frame and mule demanded an alternate source of power. Arkwright established his factory at Cromford, on the Derwent river, where it could rely on constant power from a water mill to drive the machines. Thus, the inventions of the textile industry dramatically boosted productivity and changed the nature of the workplace. Arkwright became a very wealthy man as a result. His mill in Cromford employed some 300 workers with several thousand spindles by 1779. In 1785, a mill near Nottingham began to apply steam engine power to the running of the machinery. It was no longer necessary to tie the location of a factory to a running stream. Rural spinners in putting-out systems, unable to compete with the expanding industry, abandoned their wheels to go to the factories. All of the conditions for the spread of factories were in place, and the driving force was now cotton. One manufacturer observed that "from the year 1770 to 1788 a complete change had gradually been effected in the spinning of yarns. That of wool had disappeared altogether and that of linen was also nearly gone: cotton, cotton, cotton was become the almost universal material for employment."[5] And, indeed, cotton cloth grew from less than 1 percent of industrial production in 1770 to more than 8 percent in 1815 in a period when all branches of industry were growing.

The full impact of that change would be felt in the early nineteenth century. But already in the eighteenth century, the industrial revolution was changing the lives of ordinary working people. Adam Smith noted in *Wealth of Nations* that not only had the staple, grain, become cheaper over the preceding fifty years, but also "many other things from which the industrious poor derive an agreeable and wholesome variety of food." The cost of potatoes had been cut in half; the cost of turnips, carrots, and cabbages had also gone down so much that they had become staples for the poor. Apples and onions had gone from luxuries to ordinary items of diet. "The great improvements in the coarser manufactures of both linen and woollen cloth," Smith went on, "furnish the laborers with cheaper and better clothing; and those in the manufactures of the coarser metals, with cheaper and better instruments of trade, as well as with many agreeable and convenient pieces of household furniture." Some of those in the "higher ranks" of society complained of this process, saying that the poor were living in too much luxury and that it made them unwilling to work. But Smith disagreed: "No society can surely be flourishing and happy, of which the far greater part of the members are poor and miserable." It was, in fact, absurd to think that people would be able to work more when subject to starvation and sickness than they would when healthy and prosperous. And "it is but equity," Smith concluded, "that they who food, clothe, and lodge the whole body of the people, should have such a share of the produce of their own labour as to be themselves tolerably well fed, clothed, and lodged."[6]

Conspicuous Consumption

If the increase in the production of consumer goods meant that the poor lived better, it also meant that the "middling classes" and the rich lived better still. In Britain, a servant in a responsible position, in charge of maintaining the buildings and supervising the harvest on an estate, might make £10, plus room, board, and "perks" (perquisites) including the master's cast-off clothes. The lady of the house might spend that same £10 in an afternoon's shopping for a new ball gown. A prosperous grocer might have an income of £40 per year; a gentry or prosperous physician's family might have an income of £400, and a wealthy nobleman or financier might have an income of £4,000. In Paris, a wealthy noble family had an income 500 times greater than that of a poor working family. The servants of the duke of Saulx-Tavanes were paid unusually well, with wages ranging from 400 to 900 *livres* (the most commonly used unit of French money). The duke's own family, though, spent over 20,000 livres on their own clothes, jewelry, and gifts. When the duke's son was married, the duke gave him wedding presents amounting to 25,000 livres. He spent 4,000 livres on new clothes, 700 livres on the actual wedding, and 96 livres for the poor. The Duc de Choiseul had a staff of fifty-four servants in his main house (only one of his residences); they were prepared to serve up to fifty guests daily, using 4,000 chickens and thirty sheep per year, and 300 pounds of bread per day. Guests could enjoy deer hunting in the duke's private forest, games such as billiards and chess, an excellent private library and collection of engravings, and formal gardens with a Chinese pagoda.

Such consumption was deliberate, ostentatious, and magnificent, and eighteenth-century observers were puzzled what to think of it. Was all this spending necessary for economic growth, because it kept merchants, craftsmen, and farmers employed? Or was it what old-fashioned moralists called luxury, or unnecessary abundance, one of the seven deadly sins? The English artist and engraver William Hogarth (1697–1764) criticized the excesses that consumption could lead to in his sets of engravings, *Marriage a La Mode* and *The Rake's Progress*. The first set tells

William Hogarth's *Marriage a la Mode* (*After the Marriage*) (Alinari/Art Resource, NY)

the story of a marriage "of convenience," that is, a marriage arranged for the benefit of the family, between the daughter of a wealthy merchant and a young nobleman. The marriage is contracted by their fathers, without the consent, or concern for the happiness, of the soon-to-be-newlyweds. After the marriage, the two lead separate lives in the fashionable London world, with separate amusements and separate lovers. The husband is eventually killed by the wife's lover, and the wife commits suicide. Each plate in the set of engravings depicts the details of fashionable life, from the ruffles on the dress, to the ornate ceilings and rows of portraits in the rooms, to the variety of liveried servants. The same is true of *The Rake's Progress*, in which a young man leaves his true love and honest life in the country and comes to London, where he lives a dissolute life until he goes mad and is confined to the lunatic asylum known as Bedlam (a corruption of its name, the Bethlehem Hospital). Hogarth's engravings imply that the endless pursuit of wealth, riches, and consumer goods, instead of virtue, have brought these young people to their tragic end.

Portraits of the Age

Other artists portrayed the wealth and tastes of polite society more sympathetically. Angelica Kauffmann (1741–1807) was a child prodigy whose talent was first recognized by her father, a Swiss artist. She was torn between painting and music, and her earliest self-portrait, at the age of thirteen, is a beautiful oil-painting showing her holding a musical score. She studied art in Italy with her father, where she received commissions to paint portraits for a number of wealthy Englishmen. They encouraged her to settle in England, where she became well-known as a painter and decorative artist.

In Britain, the core of the art market was always portraits. "Most men extend their ideas of painting no farther," complained one artist, "than to get their own portrait executed, and that of their favorite child."[7] Kauffmann's portraits were much sought after, and she had a set schedule of fees, whether for half-length portraits, full-length, or miniature full-length. She may even have kept a set of sketches to suggest poses for her sitters, just like a modern photographer. Her studio consisted of four rooms, "one in which I paint," she wrote, "the other where I set up my finished paintings . . . the people come into the house to sit—to visit me—or to see my work."[8] But despite the popularity of portraits, the highest form of painting was considered to be history painting, paintings of classical, allegorical, or historical subjects. Kauffmann was unusual for a woman artist in specializing in history painting, and she received a number of important commissions as a result. She also painted subjects from popular novels. Throughout, she looked for subjects in which women played important roles, such as *Penelope Awakened . . . with the News of Ulysses's Return* (1773) or *The Tender Eleanora Sucking the Venom out of the Wound [of] Edward I* (1776). She became the favorite painter of well-educated gentlewomen, who could see her paintings exhibited at the Royal Academy of Art in London. They could also buy engravings made from her paintings or screens and porcelain with her designs. Even a male reviewer wrote that she, "considering her sex, is certainly possessed of very great merit. She is endued with . . . bold and daring genius."[9]

The most famous portrait-painter of her day was the glamorous Elisabeth Louise Vigée-Le Brun (1755–1842). She, like Kauffmann, was the daughter of an artist, but he died when she was only twelve. She began to draw and sketch, she later wrote, as a distraction from her grief, and her mother took her to public art galleries and private collec-

Portrait of an English lady (ca. 1795) by Angelica Kauffmann (Tate Gallery, London/Art Resource, NY)

tions. "As soon as I entered these great galleries," she wrote, "I behaved just like a bee, gathering knowledge and ideas that I might apply to my own art." By the age of nineteen she began to receive commissions for portraits. A year later she married an artist and dealer, who helped her promote her career. Vigée-Le Brun held musical salons at her house, which were enormously popular. "I did not flatter myself," she wrote, "that . . . people came just to see me; as often happens when a place is considered 'open house,' people came to meet others and most came to enjoy some of the finest music in Paris." Beautiful and charming, she used her own self-portraits to attract clients, and she became the favored painter of the aristocracy, many of whom became friends. Her select

Portrait of Marie Antoinette and her children by Elisabeth Louise Vigée-LeBrun (Alinari/Art Resource, NY)

dinner parties became the talk of Paris, and much later she looked back on their "relaxed and easy good humor" and their "air of shared confidence and intimacy." The guests, who included writers, musicians, and actresses as well as aristocrats, discussed art and literature, listened to music, put on plays, danced, and sang. "We were happy and content," Vigée-Le Brun wrote; "the hours passed like minutes and people would not start to drift home until midnight."[10]

In painting her aristocratic clients, Vigée-Le Brun introduced a new, more natural style. Instead of the powdered wigs and elaborate costumes of earlier portraits, her sitters wore their own hair and loose, flowing drapery. She herself "wore only white gowns of muslin or lawn. . . . My hair cost me nothing. I styled it myself." This appearance of simplicity—though it sometimes took hours to achieve—became all the fashion in Paris. Though her clients seldom styled their own hair, they were painted to look as though they had. Her paintings, exhibited publicly, were "the most highly praised," wrote one critic; "when someone announces that he has just come from the Salon, the first thing he is asked is 'Have you seen Madame Le Brun? What do you think of Madame Le Brun?. . . Madame Le Brun, is she not astonishing?'"[11] When, in 1785, a Swedish artist painted a portrait of the queen, Marie Antoinette, that the French government found objectionable, they turned to Vigée-Le Brun for help. The Austrian princess Marie Antoinette had, by that time, a bad reputation in France, criticized for her foreign ways, her extravagance, and her supposedly scandalous life. Vigée-Le Brun created a group portrait of the queen and her young children that emphasized both her majesty and her motherly devotion. The portrait was exhibited at the Salon of 1787, but by then the pleasure-loving, aristocratic world that Vigée-Le Brun depicted so well was already under attack.

High Culture and Low Culture

The consumer culture that produced goods for every taste and budget affected the world of music and drama. A distinction emerged between "high culture," which attracted the connoisseur, the person of discerning taste, and "low culture," which appealed to a more general, less demanding audience. Throughout the eighteenth century, the true arbiter of "high culture" was aristocratic society, who set the tone and the style for the rest of the cultured world. "Low culture" was aimed at the "middling sorts" who flocked to theaters and pleasure gardens (parks, open to the public, with outdoor performances, fairs, and dances).

This distinction was especially clear in opera. *Opera seria* (serious opera) was the most prestigious form of musical entertainment and the most lucrative for composer, librettist, and performers. Virtually all serious opera was written in Italian, and it featured noble characters and a tragic plot. Often it incorporated ballet as well. It was associated with courts, patronized by royal and noble families. In order to provide a grand enough venue for "*Les Grands*" as they were known in France ("the Great" in English), new opera houses were commissioned in the early eighteenth century, with a central seating area for "the public" surrounded by tiers with boxed seats for noble families, anxious to see and be seen. Naples and Milan competed for the largest, but they were overshadowed by the magnificent theater built in Dresden, which could seat 2,000 spectators. In Prussia, the new opera house commissioned by Frederick II was even more elaborate, with a canal system and water-falls. The "season" for opera began in October and ended in May, be-cause nobles tended to spend the summer at their country estates rather than at court. Frequently kings and courts commissioned new operas to celebrate birthdays or other occasions. Since serious operas were so firmly attached to royal courts, they were seldom subjected to any cen-sorship, and in fact they hardly needed any, since they did not raise objectionable political or social issues. Two of the most prominent com-posers of the early eighteenth century, Alessandro Scarlatti (1660–1725) and George Frideric Handel (1685–1759), were known for their mag-nificent music, not their social commentary.

If social commentary did enter the musical stage, it was in comic operas, called *opera buffa*, traditionally associated with "low culture." In England, a new genre, called ballad opera, the ancestor of the modern musical, developed in the early eighteenth century. John Gay (1685–1732) initiated this form with *The Beggar's Opera*, first performed in 1728. It tells the story of the cutthroat robber Macheath and his mar-riage to Polly, the daughter of the King of the Beggars, the man who provides implements like realistic sores and wooden legs to the legion of beggars on the London streets. Instead of creating a whole musical score for the opera, Gay drew on popular tunes, ballads, and dances. *The Beggar's Opera* and its sequel, *Polly*, were openly satirical, poking fun at British society and government as well as at the conventions of seri-ous opera. So were other ballad operas written by Henry Fielding, the author of *Tom Jones*, in the 1730s. As writers and composers soon found, any story could be set to music, and by the later eighteenth century public taste leaned towards familiar stories, set to popular music. Samuel Richardson's novel *Pamela*, for example, a story of a virtuous servant who resists seduction by her gentleman-employer and ends up happily as his wife, was recast as a ballad opera with the title *The Maid of the Mill* (1765). It remained a hit with the public for many years.

Ballad operas were crowd-pleasers, but could comic opera ever be art? The composer who convinced the demanding operatic audience of central Europe that it could was Wolfgang Mozart. His opera *Don Giovanni* (1787), based on the Spanish story of Don Juan, took the disreputable subject of a noble rake and turned it into a musical masterpiece, performed before the emperor Joseph II. "In any spoken play such a caricature would be chased off the stage with oranges and nutshells and hissed into the wings," wrote one reviewer, "but in an opera he is found uncommonly entertaining, and as he is a personality on the musical stage, his infamies are considered delightful things, and provoke laughter and pleasure."[12] Mozart's last opera, *The Magic Flute* (1791), combined noble and heroic subjects with comic and popular ones. Written in German, not Italian, it was not well received by the Viennese court. However, it attracted large audiences when performed in public theaters and has continued to do so ever since.

Profile: Life in a Spa

Of all the conspicuous places for eighteenth-century consumption, the spa was the most remarkable. Spas were towns located on or near thermal springs whose waters were (and in some cases, still are) believed to have curative properties. Fashionable ladies and gentlemen and their families would spend a period of weeks or months at a spa, drinking the waters whose chemical properties had been very carefully analyzed. Medical men flocked to spas to supervise the treatment and sometimes even ran private rest-homes for their patients. Some patients were really ill, but many more came for rest and relaxation. Since so many well-off patients came for "the cure," the atmosphere in a spa-town was much like that in a modern beach or ski resort, with hotels, expensive shops, and opportunities for theater, music, and gambling.

In central Europe, the most fashionable spa was at Karlsbad, in Bohemia, long a favorite with the German nobility. Johann Sebastian Bach had played there to the guests of one of his noble patrons, and in 1786, the poet and novelist Johann Wolfgang Goethe (1749–1832) accompanied his own aristocratic friends to the spa. It was a small town, with half-timbered houses and elegant hotels with guests from Germany, Italy, Russia, and Poland. Each new arrival was saluted with trumpets in front of the city hall, and the two main streets were lined with shops. There were dances every evening, and gambling as well; guests at the spa took excursions in the mountains. Karlsbad had its own theater and concert halls, and there were Tyrolian singers, puppeteers, and ventriloquists. Local Bohemian glassmakers, catering to the tourists, produced high-quality glassware etched with views of Karlsbad, and local villagers collected stones from the thermal springs and polished them, selling them to visitors as souvenirs. Goethe was interested in geology and made a special study of the rocks around Karlsbad. "The waters agree with me," he wrote to Duke Karl August of Weimar; ". . . everything from the granite formations on and up the spiral of created things even unto women has contributed to make my stay agreeable and interesting."[13]

Goethe was in Karlsbad as the start of a vacation from the service of Duke Karl August in the small German principality of Weimar. Born to a wealthy family, Goethe had studied law but found it hopelessly boring. Instead, he turned to belles-lettres. His first published work, the play *Götz von Berlichingen* (1773), was a romantic story based on a German folk hero, and it was an immediate success. His next, the novel *The Sorrows of Young Werther* (1774), was even more popular. It is the story of Werther, a poet, who falls in love with a virtuous young woman who is engaged to a dull but respectable man. The plot mattered less than the emotionally charged style, which became known as *Sturm und Drang*, "storm and stress." Werther became the immediate symbol of the young poet and philosopher, alienated from the practical-minded world around him.

Though Goethe based *Werther* in part on his own experiences and temperament, he was not as impractical or melancholic as his fictional character. He was, instead, charming and intelligent, just the sort of young man the young Duke Karl August was looking for as a companion. Goethe went to Weimar first as the duke's guest, then later as his friend and, for many years, his senior civil servant. In that capacity, he had to wrestle with the many problems of consumption with limited resources. Weimar was poor, its peasantry living in scattered villages, and not even when Goethe imported an English agricultural expert could he produce an agricultural revolution in Weimar. Taxes were too high, Goethe thought, but if they were lowered, the duchy's revenues were decreased and the duke could not pay for his boar-hunting or his civil servants. The inhabitants of one small town, Ruhla, complained when they were required to pay part of their taxes "in kind," that is, in chickens and produce instead of money, and Goethe recommended their food not be taken away from them: "Where are the arrangements for giving them hopes and prospects? . . . At least leave them unmolested with what they have, their progress should not be hindered by weighting them down still further."[14] But Goethe's own income came from his inheritance from his wealthy grandfather; the paper on which he wrote his governmental reports was worth more than the whole tax assessment from Ruhla. With such unmanageable problems, no wonder he needed a vacation.

Goethe visited Karlsbad twelve times over the course of his long life, drinking the waters, entertaining friends, and flirting with women. In 1806, a new road was built to improve travel from the Habsburg court in Vienna to the spa, and by the 1820s there were special stagecoaches with frequent service between Vienna, Prague, and Karlsbad. Goethe kept track of the improvement in the city: new "promenades" for strolling around town, better food, more luxury items in the shops. Catering to an increasingly cosmopolitan clientele, consumption in Karlsbad in the nineteenth century became even more conspicuous.

Important Dates

1662	Turnpike Act in England
1691	Canal de Deux Mers opened
1698	Savery's steam engine introduced
1705	Newcomen's engine introduced
1720	Outbreak of bubonic plague in Marseilles; last reported outbreak in Europe
1728	Gay's *Beggar's Opera* performed
1733	Kay's flying shuttle introduced
1734	Completion of canal network around Paris
1759	Death of Handel
1761	Completion of Duke of Bridgewater's Canal
1766	Hargreaves's spinning jenny introduced
1769	Arkwright's water frame introduced
1773	Kauffmann's painting *Penelope Awakened* completed
1774	Publication of Goethe's *Sorrows of Young Werther*
1781	Watts's steam engine introduced
1785	First steam-powered textile factory
1787	Vigée-Le Brun's painting of Marie Antoinette exhibited; Mozart's opera *Don Giovanni* performed

1791   Mozart's opera *The Magic Flute* performed
1792   Publication of Malthus's *An Essay on Population*

Further Reading

Joseph Baillio, *Elisabeth Louise Vigée-Le Brun* (Fort Worth, 1982)

Geoffrey Beard, *Upholsterers and Interior Furnishing in England, 1530–1840* (New Haven, 1997)

Thomas Brennan, *Burgundy to Champagne: The Wine Trade in Early Modern France* (Baltimore, 1997)

John Brewer, *The Pleasures of the Imagination: English Culture in the Eighteenth Century* (New York, 1997)

John Brewer and Ann Bermingham, eds., *The Consumption of Culture 1600–1800* (London, 1996)

Linda Colley, *Britons: Forging the Nation, 1707–1837* (New Haven, 1992)

Penelope Jane Corfield, *Power and the Professions in Britain, 1700–1850* (London, 1995)

L.M. Cullen, *The Brandy Trade under the Ancien Régime: Regional Specialisation in the Charente* (Cambridge, 1997)

Madeleine Delpierre, *Dress in France in the Eighteenth Century* (New Haven, 1997)

Jan De Vries, *The Dutch Rural Economy in the Golden Age* (New Haven, 1980)

Jan De Vries, *The Economy of Europe in an Age of Crisis, 1600–1750* (Cambridge, 1976)

Robert DuPlessis, *Transitions to Capitalism in Early Modern Europe* (Cambridge, 1997)

Carl Estabrook, *Urbane and Rustic England: Cultural Ties and Social Spheres in the Provinces, 1660–1780* (Manchester, 1999)

Michael Flinn, *The European Demographic System, 1500–1800* (Baltimore, 1980)

Robert Forster, *The House of Saulx-Tavanes: Versailles and Burgundy, 1700–1830* (Baltimore, 1971)

Richard Friedenthal, *Goethe: His Life and Times* (New York, 1965)

Myron Gutmann, *Toward the Modern Economy* (New York, 1988)

Bridget Hill, *Servants: English Domestics in the Eighteenth Century* (Oxford, 1996)

Philip T. Hoffman, *Growth in a Traditional Economy: The French Countryside, 1450–1815* (Princeton, 1996)

Ludwig Lewisohn, *Goethe: The Story of a Man* 2 vols. (New York, 1949)

Lady Victoria Manners and G.C. Williamson, *Angelica Kauffmann, R.A.: Her Life and Her Works* (New York, 1976)

Terence McIntosh, *Urban Decline in Early Modern Germany: Schwabisch Hall and its Region, 1650–1750* (Chapel Hill, 1997)

Judith Miller, *Mastering the Market: The State and the Grain Trade in Northern France, 1700–1860* (Cambridge, 1998)

J.M. Neeson, *Commoners: Common Right, Enclosure and Social Change in England, 1700–1820* (Cambridge, 1993)

Sheilagh Ogilvie, *State Corporatism and Proto-Industry: The Wurttemberg Black Forest, 1580–1797* (Cambridge, 1997)

Sheilagh Ogilvie and Markus Cerman, eds., *European Proto-Industrialization* (Cambridge, 1996)

Mark Overton, *Agricultural Revolution in England: The Transformation of the Agrarian Economy 1500–1850* (Cambridge, 1996)

Roger Parker, ed., *The Oxford Illustrated History of Opera* (Oxford, 1994)

Marcia Pointon, *Strategies for Showing: Women, Possession, and Representation in English Visual Culture, 1665–1800* (Oxford, 1997)

Aileen Ribeiro, *The Art of Dress: Fashion in England and France, 1750–1820* (New Haven, 1995)

Daniel Roche, *The Culture of Clothing: Dress and Fashion in the Ancien Régime* trans. Jean Birrell (Cambridge, 1997)

Wendy Wassyng Roworth, ed., *Angelica Kauffmann: A Continental Artist in Georgian England* (London, 1992)

Carolyn Sargentson, *Merchants and Luxury: The Marchands Merciers of Eighteenth-Century Paris* (Oxford, 1996)

Katie Scott, *The Rococo Interior: Decoration and Social Spaces in Early Eighteenth-Century Paris* (New Haven, 1996)

John Smail, *The Origins of Middle Class Culture: Halifax, Yorkshire, 1660–1780* (Ithaca, 1994)

Michael Sonenscher, *The Hatters of Eighteenth-Century France* (Berkeley, 1987)

Michael Sonenscher, *Work and Wages: Natural Law, Politics, and the Eighteenth-Century French Trades* (Berkeley, 1989)

Cynthia Maria Truant, *The Rites of Labor: Brotherhoods of Compagnonnage in Old and New Regime France* (Ithaca, 1994)

Jenny Uglow, *Hogarth: A Life and a World* (New York, 1997)

Elisabeth Vigée-Le Brun, *The Memoirs of Elisabeth Vigée-Le Brun* trans. Siân Evans (Bloomington, 1989)

Kathleen Wilson, *The Sense of the People: Politics, Culture, and Imperialism in England, 1715–1785* (Cambridge, 1995)

E.A. Wrigley, R.S. Davies, J.E. Oeppen, and R.S. Schofield, *English Population History from Family Reconstitution 1580–1837* (Cambridge, 1997)

J.A. Yelling, *The Common Fields and Enclosure in England, 1450–1850* (Cambridge, 1977)

Part IV

ca. 1790–1815

Chapter Seventeen

The Reform of France

In the eighteenth century, the wealthiest, most populous, most glamorous country in Europe was France. No court was as magnificent, no countryside as fertile, no salons as brilliant. And yet by the 1770s, reformers saw room for improvement everywhere. France, home of the *philosophes*, was not enlightened. There was censorship, regulated by the clergy: the works even of French philosophes were published and smuggled into France, where their clandestine character ensured their rapid sale. Voltaire, symbol of the Enlightenment, adored by millions, had to spend much of his life in exile. Religious tolerance, equality before the law, representative government were all prevented by the absolutist policies of the French Crown. If the king, Louis XVI (1754–1793), had been as commanding an absolute ruler as his predecessor Louis XIV or his contemporary Frederick II of Prussia, there might have been fewer complaints. But Louis XVI, though conscientious and well-intentioned, was only 20 when he inherited the throne in 1775. Young and inexperienced, he quickly found himself surrounded by court intrigue, as factions of great nobles competed with each other for his favor and for government policies that would best support their particular interests. "Great and eminent superiority of talents," noted the British ambassador, might be enough to crush the intrigues, "but as there is no reason to believe [the king] possessed of that superiority, I think he will be a prey to them and find himself more and more entangled every day."[1]

The most superior of kings, though, might have found himself at a loss to deal with France's long-standing problems. For years, agricultural writers, imbued with Enlightenment ideas, had been calling for reforms. These writers, called *physiocrats*, were convinced that the wealth of a country rested on the productivity of its land, and they were well aware that the farmland of France was not nearly as productive as it could be. They called for the introduction of new agricultural techniques, largely based on English agriculture: removal of the many local tolls and tariffs, encouragement of free trade with no price controls on staples like bread, planting of nutrient-rich crops like clover and potatoes.

Yet these techniques were chiefly valuable to wealthy landowners who owned large tracts of land. They were largely irrelevant to the lives of peasants. The peasantry made up 80 percent of the 27 million persons usually estimated as the total population of France, but only a quarter of those (approximately 4 to 5 million) owned their own land, amounting to perhaps 25 percent of French farmland. To make matters worse, the land they did own was cut up into tiny parcels, barely able to support a single family. They were subject to taxation, which often amounted to 10 to 15 percent of the gross product; they were also subjected to *tithes*, taxes levied by the church, which might take an additional 8 percent. The peasants of each community were also subject to the *corvée*, forced labor for road and bridge maintenance; since the season for roadwork was also the season for planting and harvest, peasants were forced to leave their lands at the very time that their work in the fields would be most productive. And these were the fortunate peasants who owned some part of the land they farmed. Perhaps another quarter of the peasants (approximately 4 to 5 million) were tenants, farming land they rented from property technically designated as a *seigneurie* (belonging to a *seigneur*, or lord), though in fact the true owner might be a noble, a *bourgeois* (the word often given to any wealthy non-noble who owned land or businesses), or an institution like a church or town. In addition to paying rent, peasants who were tenants might have a host of duties, sometimes called feudal dues, to perform for the seigneurie, which often, again, interfered with their cultivation even of the land they rented. And contemporary observers agreed that at least half of the peasants (approximately 8 million people in good years, and as many as 10 or 11 million in bad years) did not have enough to live on, eking out an existence based on makeshifts: day laboring during the planting and harvesting seasons, migrating to towns or coasts for temporary work in construction or small industry, begging, robbing, or prostitution in the middle of winter when food and clothing were especially scarce. Poor relief, where it existed, came from church institutions, rather than the government. Even the wealthier peasants could be undone by a succession of bad harvests, and the rest could be ruined by a single bad harvest or the death of one wage-earner.

Under these conditions, the poor peasants could hardly be expected to undertake agricultural improvements, which physiocrat writers usually expected to come from above, imposed on the peasantry for its own good. Yet in 1774, when the physiocrat-turned-controller general (chief finance minister), Anne Robert Jacques Turgot (1727–1781), tried to put his principles into practice by allowing the free market to set the price of grain, the result was disaster. Bread was so important a staple that its price had long been regulated by both local and governmental policy. Everyone knew that when the price of bread rose too much, riots would break out. Although Turgot was aware that the bad harvest would drive up the price of grain, he thought the resulting free market would be ultimately better for the French economy. The result was that bread prices rose 50 percent, thousands starved, and the series of riots throughout northeastern France came to be called the "Flour War." It took the army, hundreds of arrests, and two public executions to bring the rioting to an end. Price controls were reimposed; but rural poverty continued.

Rural poverty was not the only target of reformers: so too was the institution of legal privileges, for economic as well as political reasons. In France, the clergy consisted of about 130,000 members by 1789, a tiny fraction of France's 27 million inhabitants. But the clergy controlled about 10 percent of the land; and though they paid regular "contributions" to the government, it was a small fraction of their yearly revenues. Moreover, the wealth of the church was concentrated in the hands of high church officials, such as bishops, in the monasteries and convents, and in the wealthier towns, with the parish priest only slightly better off than his village parishioners. The great church lords, such as the bishop of the city of Strasbourg, might have an income a hundred times greater than the parish priest's. In addition to religious practice, the church controlled education, poor relief, and hospitals. Moreover, church positions were highly sought after by nobles and bourgeois for their younger sons and daughters, who thus collectively acquired up to a quarter of the church revenues. So extensive an area of public wealth and influence, reformers felt, should contribute more to the upkeep of the government.

So too, many believed, should the nobility. There were anywhere from 120,000 to 350,000 nobles in France, but they owned between 25 and 30 percent of the land, and had feudal rights over most of the rest of it. Government ministers came from the nobility, and the most important government, military, and church offices were owned by them, bought and sold as their private property. Only the great nobles were allowed to influence the king's court, and they dominated high society in Paris. Yet despite their control over so much of the resources of France, they were not subject to tax on their personal wealth. For nobility continued to carry the privilege of exemption from most kinds of taxes, as it always had in France. That same privilege acted as a magnet for the nearly 2.75 million bourgeois, who controlled perhaps 25 percent of the land. They also controlled most French industry and commerce, including the lucrative sugar and coffee trade from the West Indies. In order to protect their wealth, they bought land and government offices that conveyed nobility; they married their sons and daughters into noble families to acquire nobility for their grandchildren. Thus no sooner did a bourgeois family acquire great taxable wealth than it transferred that wealth into tax-exempt status.

At the root of the problem was the system of legal privilege, as entrenched as property rights and bought and sold just as freely, by those who could afford to do so. Take away the noble privilege of tax-exemption, argued one of Turgot's political opponents within Louis XVI's ministry, and "you destroy the national character, and the nation ceasing to be warlike will soon be the prey of neighboring nations." That was ridiculous, Turgot responded; "the nations in which the nobility pays taxes are not less martial than ours," and the idea that nobles should be exempt was no more than "an antiquated pretension abandoned by all intelligent men, even in the order of nobility."[2] These views only made him more enemies. The last straw was his response to opposition to his policies from provincial *parlements* (law courts). Earlier in his life, Turgot had been sympathetic to the claims of parlements, made up of local officials and magistrates, that representative bodies should play a larger role in government. Now, as a government minister, he urged on Louis XVI the strongest absolutist policies against his opponents, including arbitrary arrest and confinement to the Bastille, a prison in Paris, to support his own views. Faced with faction within his government and greatly desiring to be popular, Louis backed down and dismissed Turgot in 1776.

This would have been no more than another incident in the continuing drama of court intrigue if it were not for the fact that the finances of France were indeed in bad shape. The costs of government, with its growing bureaucracy, and of being a world power, with colonies and garrisons throughout the world, increased greatly in the eighteenth century. The usual ways of raising money for the Crown were the sale of offices, increased taxation, and raising loans. But every governmental position that was sold obligated the government to pay a certain amount to the office holder; increased taxes could be levied only on the poorest part of the population; loans required the payment of yearly interest. Of the three, the latter seemed the easiest course, as long as loans could be obtained at a favorable rate. For that, the French government needed a good credit rating, and to obtain that credit rating, Louis appointed the financier Jacques Necker (1732–1804) as director-general of French finance. Necker was an outsider in French government circles: a Swiss, a commoner, a Protestant, he was widely hailed as a wonderworker who would be able to painlessly extract France from its financial predicament. He did his best to cut costs in the government bureaucracy, to balance expenditures and income, and to retain public credit to support his increased program of borrowing. In 1781 he published the first public account of the French monarchy's finances, usually regarded as a state secret. Public opinion was so much in his favor that he tried to use it to convince Louis XVI to admit him to the royal council. When other members of the council threatened to resign if he joined them, Necker was forced to resign as director-general instead. "One would have thought that there was a public calamity," remembered one observer; "people looked at each other in silent dismay and sadly pressed each other's hand as they passed."[3]

Turgot had warned of the dangers that the vast expenses of a new war would cause to the regime: "the first gunshot will drive the state to bankruptcy."[4] When Necker took over, war was already underway, for in 1776 the thirteen British colonies in North America had declared their independence. French public opinion was enthusiastically in favor of the American revolutionaries; the beau monde declared General George Washington their hero; and French foreign policy was inclined to favor any development that appeared to weaken the British empire. In 1777, France had pledged to support the Americans with arms and, eventually, with army and navy as well. The war, called in the new United States of America the War of Independence, ended in 1783 and was perceived in Europe as a clear victory for France. Through it, France gained a new, valuable trading partner in the newly independent country and the satisfaction of having weakened its international rival. Moreover, the success of the Americans in creating a new constitution out of Enlightenment principles only increased reformers' determination to bring about change in France. Unfortunately, the war also increased the amount of French indebtedness, which was perceived as rapidly tending towards the bankruptcy of the state. All countries in the eighteenth century financed their wars through loans. But Great Britain, France's rival, could borrow the money through the Bank of England. The loans could be repaid by instituting new taxes without political disruption, because raising taxes was the recognized function of Parliament. In France, the king had the option to use his authority to impose new taxes. The question was, could he do it without political upheaval?

The Assembly of Notables

In 1787, the young hero of the American War, the Marquis de Lafayette (1757–1834), took his place in a newly formed Assembly of Notables, a supposedly representative body of 144 great men of the realm, handpicked for their status and their adherence to the king. The Assembly of Notables had legal precedent in French history as a kind of royal task force, called in emergencies like the present fiscal crisis. By 1787, the French government had a deficit (payments exceeding income) of almost a quarter of expected income. In addition, short-term loans raised for carrying on the American war had come due. To meet the crisis, the king's new minister of finance, Charles Alexandre de Calonne (1734–1802), proposed a three-part plan: new taxes to pay debts coupled with administrative reform to limit government spending, new economic initiatives to increase the prosperity of the country, and new loans to fill the gap until the first two parts could have an effect. To raise more loans, Calonne told the king, he would have to raise public confidence in the government's credit. Calling the Assembly of Notables would show that the government was willing to listen to the French people, which would help its credit rating. Since all but ten of the delegates were from the nobility and clergy, the assembly could be expected to be favorable to any policy that the king or his ministers might propose.

But the plan backfired. The assembly had little confidence in Calonne, who had a reputation as ambitious and self-interested; in any reform scheme, they wanted protection for their privileges; instead of agreeing to Calonne's proposal, they called for independent auditors to investigate government finances. All Paris and, eventually, all France watched with bated breath to see the outcome of this three-month experiment in representative government, however limited the representation. When Louis XVI vetoed the assembly's proposals, the notables responded that they, in fact, had no authority to approve new taxes or loans. Only a truly representative body, like the English House of Commons or the new American Congress, could do that. "It seems to me," declared Lafayette, "that this is the moment for us to beseech His Majesty to fix, immediately . . . the convocation of a truly national assembly." "What Sir," responded the king's brother, "are you calling for the Estates General?" "Yes, my lord," replied Lafayette, "and even better than that."[5]

The Estates General

The Estates General, the French medieval equivalent of the English Parliament, had once possessed powers similar to the English Parliament before the seventeenth century, of expressing grievances when called by the Crown to administer new taxes. It had not been called since 1614, because French kings since Louis XIII had taken control of raising taxes on their own. But the repeated fiscal crises of the preceding twenty years had led many reform-minded Frenchmen, Lafayette among them, to imagine the Estates General becoming a truly representative body on the English and American model. Indeed, many went even beyond fiscal reform to envision the Estates General, as Lafayette put it, as a national assembly, the legislative branch of a government with the king as the executive, but retaining the power to approve taxation as well as the appointment of the king's ministers, foreign policy, and a host of other governmental prerogatives currently held by the French Crown.

The king tried to push a financial package designed to stave off bankruptcy through the *parlements*, the law courts that had the privilege of registering royal edicts, in Paris and the provinces. The parlements refused, and though the king ordered the members exiled, that did nothing to help government credit. A freak hailstorm followed by continued bad weather, poor harvests, and ever-rising grain prices led to riots: "The wretchedness of the poor people during this inclement season surpasses all description,"[6] wrote one noble observer. The shortages also ended all hope that the government could collect enough in taxes to make a dent in its deficit. In August 1788, the French government declared bankruptcy and the treasury suspended all payments. In desperation, King Louis XVI gave the order to call the Estates General. Necker, who still retained some luster as a wonderworker, was invited back to head off what appeared to be inevitable fiscal disaster.

The Grievances of France

France had not had elected representatives for 175 years and had never had them in the eighteenth-century sense of candidates running for contested seats, in full view of the public. At once, the election of representatives for each of the three estates, clergy, nobility, and commons, became the focus for an outpouring of both reform-minded patriotism and anger at what many saw as the abuses of the present government: absolutist policies, extravagant government ministers, exclusion of non-nobles from government. This anger, and hope of redress, was expressed in the thousands of *cahiers de doléances*, lists of grievances, prepared by French regions to be presented when the Estates General convened. They had certain points in common. They claimed that the Estates General should be the representative body of the nation, with elected delegates called on a regular basis. They asked for freedom of thought, speech, and assembly. On financial matters, they asked for a consolidation of debt, with open disclosure of government budgets. They also asked for abolition of the privilege of tax-exempt status: all were to be taxed equally.

The cahiers also show deep divisions in reform ideals. The poor, those dependent on buying grain and other commodities in order to survive, wanted price controls, while the bourgeois, usually sellers of grain and other commodities, called for the fashionable Enlightenment ideal of free trade, which included abolition of all price controls. The great nobles wanted greater voice in the king's ministry; the lesser nobles wanted higher positions in the government and military open to men of talent. The wealthy clergy wanted to protect the privileged position of the church; the parish priests wanted more voice in clerical policy. There were significant differences among regions, too, with the grievances of wealthier, urban areas in direct conflict with those of the poorer rural districts. And since they were prepared by a literate elite, the cahiers underrepresented the views of the poor, including most peasants and provincial artisans. The grievance process, therefore, still denied a voice to the poorest sections of the population, leaving them only their traditional means of expressing their political opinions—the riot.

These ideals of the representatives were mirrored by the general public and expressed in an outpouring of pamphlets. The Paris parlement, asked to set up rules for the Estates General, initially adhered to precedent and declared that the forms of the Estates General in 1614 must be followed, with each estate allowed 300 delegates and one vote per estate. That would mean that the nobility and clergy, representing perhaps 2 percent of the nation, would have 600 delegates, while the commons, representing the other 98 percent, would only have 300. Moreover, it would mean that the first two estates, each with one vote, could always work together to outvote the commons two to one. This was ridiculous, representatives of the third estate declared, and they demanded that their representation be doubled (to 600 delegates) and that voting be by head, not by estate. Their demands were echoed by the many pamphlets published in the early months of 1789. "What is the Third Estate," asked the Abbé Emmanuel Joseph Sieyès (1748–1836) in the most famous of these pamphlets. "Everything," he answered. "What has it been until now in the political order? Nothing. What does it want to become? Something." Noble and clerical privileges do not strengthen a country, he argued, but weaken it, because the nobility and clergy choose to live under special laws which apply only to them, contriving "to consume the best part of the product without having in any way helped to produce it." They should not even be considered part of the nation, but rather as a "malignant tumor that torments [a sick man] and drains his strength." A nation, in contrast, is "a body of associates living under *common* laws and represented by the same *legislative assembly*."[7] In part as a result of public outcry, the third estate won the right to double its representation to 600. Confident and hopeful, the delegates made their way toward Versailles. As the astronomer Sylvain Bailly, mayor of Paris and thus the head of the government of the most politically aware, and traditionally the most politically disruptive, city in France, put it: "It was truly a phenomenon to be something in the political order and by virtue alone of one's capacity as a citizen." The assembly that had elected him, he felt, "though an infinitely small fraction of the Nation, felt nonetheless part of the power and rights of the whole."[8]

When the delegates arrived in Versailles, however, the idealism of the third estate suffered a blow. The king and his court had wished to use traditional pomp and ceremony to bolster their authority, so the ceremony of 1614 had been retained. On opening day, May 5, 1789, the nobility and clergy arrived arrayed in their court dress and paraded into the grand hall to be presented to the king and queen. The third estate, however, were required to dress in black and enter through a rear door. At one point, the king took off his hat, then replaced it. The nobility, as was their privilege, likewise replaced their own hats. Some members of the third estate did the same, whereupon the queen, Marie Antoinette, became furious at this breach of court protocol; slowly, the offending delegates removed their hats; to cover the situation, the king took his own hat off. "So if the Ceremonial requires these manoeuvers," noted the American observer Gouverneur Morris, "the troops are not yet drilled."[9]

The anger over dress and protocol had deeper connotations. First, it made clear to all observers how opposed the queen was to all the proceedings: "She looks," noted Morris, "with contempt on the scene . . . and seems to say: for the present I submit but I shall have my turn."[10] This appeared ominous, for she was widely believed to have great influence with Louis XVI. Second, it reinforced the fear that the king would only approve voting by order, not by head. This fear turned out to be justified, as delegates for the first two estates went through the routine procedure of registering and having their credentials verified. In opposition, the third estate issued its own declaration: it would not register its own representatives unless all the delegates, from all three estates, agreed to be united in one body, with voting to be by head, not estate. The Abbé Sieyès was one of the leaders of this obstructionist policy; so was the dissolute, ambitious, and controversial Comte de Mirabeau (1749–1791), elected as a delegate for the third estate despite his noble birth and enormously popular with his constituency; so was the idealistic, incorruptible young lawyer Maximilien Robespierre (1758–1794). On June 10, Mirabeau (he refused to be called by his title after his election), interrupted the proceedings to allow the Abbé Sieyès to present the motion that the registration of delegates proceed by roll call. If the delegates from the other two orders failed to join, the third estate would proceed anyway. The motion was carried, by 493 to 41. By it, the third estate proclaimed themselves the only legitimate representative body in France. On June 12, after waiting one day to hear from the other estates, the roll call began. On June 13, three parish priests broke ranks with their estate and answered to the roll. During the next few days, they were joined by over a hundred, and eventually the first estate voted to join the third, amid enthusiastic applause. By June 19, Sieyès proposed that the old name "Estates General" no longer described the delegates or their authority, and a new name, "National Assembly," was adopted by 491 to 89. It was clear to everyone, whether inside or outside the hall, that the members of the National Assembly were proposing themselves as the true government of France, and "the spectacle of the representatives of twenty-five millions of people," wrote Arthur Young, an

English observer, "just emerging from the evils of two hundred years of arbitrary power and rising to the blessings of a freer constitution, assembled with open doors under the eye of the public," led him "to dwell with pleasure on the glorious idea of happiness to a great nation, of felicity to millions yet unborn."[11]

On June 20, however, when the representatives of the National Assembly convened, they found themselves shut out of their meeting hall. Three weeks earlier, the king's eldest son had died, and the king and his family had retreated from Versailles. Both the queen and the royal ministers, appalled at the turn of political events, urged Louis XVI to retake control of his government by declaring the actions of the delegates illegal. For that purpose, workmen had taken over the customary meeting hall of the delegates, to build the necessary ceremonial apparatus for the king's speech. Though messages had been sent to the three estates, they were not received in time, and the delegates found themselves standing in the rain, wet, angry, and fearful that this was only the first step in their dissolution as a body. All 600 retreated to a nearby indoor tennis court and swore what became known as the Tennis Court Oath, formulated by Bailly: "We swear never to separate ourselves from the National Assembly, and to reassemble wherever circumstances require, until the constitution of the realm is drawn up and fixed upon solid foundations."[12]

This was clear opposition to royal authority, and on June 23 Louis XVI moved to quell it. He addressed the delegates, promising reforms, but insisting on retaining the three estates. At the conclusion of his speech, he ordered delegates to withdraw. They refused to do so. To the fury of his ministers, Louis XVI backed down, saying "Oh well, let them stay."[13] Most of the remaining nobles then joined the National Assembly, and the king finally gave his explicit approval of that body. "The whole business now seems over," wrote Arthur Young, "and the revolution complete."[14]

The People of Paris

The reconciliation between the king and the National Assembly was greeted everywhere with cheers, but nowhere more enthusiastically than in Paris. Though Versailles was the home of the court, Paris was the recognized capital of France, the largest and, notoriously, the most turbulent, city in the country. Like many cities, it was divided into *faubourgs*, or neighborhoods, each with its own citizen-militia, part-time military companies made up of civilians, to defend the city against attack. There were between 600,000 and 700,000 permanent residents of Paris, excluding the nobles and wealthy bourgeois who might have a town house there in addition to their estates elsewhere. At the upper end of the social scale were the bourgeois, bankers, financiers, merchants, as well as the professional men such as lawyers, judges, and doctors. At the lower end, amounting to perhaps a third of the city's population, were poor migrants from the countryside, working as servants or unskilled laborers. In between were the shopkeepers, master craftsmen, "the workers in the ports and various industries," noted a police report, "journeymen, joiners, carpenters, plasterers, masons, locksmiths, leather-workers, binders, parchment-makers, tailors, tinsmiths. . . ."[15] These groups, who worked with their hands in skilled occupations or crafts and were able to pay taxes, considered themselves to be the true citizens (residents with specific political rights) of the city.

Upper-class writers, observing Paris, tended to lump this middle group together as *sans-culottes* (without trousers), because they did not wear the elegant knee-breeches fashionable in high society. Prior to 1789, they had virtually no influence on national politics. The calling of the Estates General, though, had allowed Parisian citizens to elect representatives, and the events of May and June in Versailles had been watched with close attention in Paris. Tension mounted by the end of June, as the king's recognition of the National Assembly coincided with the traditional period when rents became due. For of all the grievances prepared for the king in the spring of 1789, one had come to overwhelm all others in the city: the high price of bread. After several years of bad harvests and more governmental experimentation with removal of price controls, the price of grain was higher than it had been in years. "The people are very worried and fear dying of hunger," reported one delegate to the Estates General in April. "Are they concerned with us, Monsieur?" another was asked. "Are they thinking of lowering the price of bread? We haven't eaten anything for two days."[16] To the shortage was added anger at supposed hoarders, who were believed to be storing grain to sell later at even higher prices. There were even rumors that the grain shortage was a deliberate plot by high-placed nobles who wanted to starve the revolution out of existence. Serious riots over grain prices had already broken out in Paris and other cities, and it had become clear that the police force was not capable of maintaining order. There were regiments of the French army garrisoned in Paris, but would French soldiers, often sans-culottes themselves, fire on their own countrymen?

To this already explosive situation in the capital, Louis XVI added fresh provocation. By mid-June he had ordered troops stationed on the eastern borders of France to march toward Paris. Throughout early July, regiments assembled around the city and Versailles, many with German or Swiss soldiers. Both delegates within the National Assembly and the population of Paris feared that Louis XVI was playing a waiting game, pretending to go along with the proposed reforms only until his army was in place, when he would order the National Assembly dispersed by force if necessary. Mirabeau argued against the marshaling of troops from the floor of the Assembly, asking whether those responsible had "foreseen the consequences they entail for the safety of the throne? Have they studied in the history of all peoples, how revolutions begin?" The Assembly as a whole sent an address to the King, pointing out the danger incurred by the military buildup, "beyond all the calculations of human prudence. . . . The presence of troops will produce excitement and riot."[17]

Within the city, the sense of emergency began to heighten. On July 12, crowds began to gather, closing theaters and other public places. The Paris police force could do little to disperse the thousands of people who gathered, and the city government decided to call out the city militia, both to defend the city against the feared attacks of the king's troops and to keep looting and violence to a minimum. They used the traditional signal for the militia, the sounding of the *tocsin* (ringing church bells in a recognized pattern), firing cannons and beating drums. Over the course of the next day, the citizen army, approximately 48,000 men, assembled in the *faubourgs*. Since uniforms could not be provided on such short notice, they were asked to wear the colors of Paris, red and blue, as *cockades* (knots of ribbon) on their hats. Marching on the Paris garrisons, rapidly abandoned by the outnumbered troops of the regular army, they commandeered muskets and other weapons, including antique cannon. What they needed now was powder, widely believed to be kept in Bastille prison. Early in the morning of July 14, therefore, the crowd began to assemble around the Bastille.

Though the Bastille was notorious as a place where political prisoners were kept, by 1789 it was largely empty, used instead as a storehouse for munitions. The commander, Bernard-René de Launay, had few troops and no provisions for a siege. When, therefore, about 900 members from the newly assembled Paris army stood in the courtyard and asked him to surrender the fortress and hand over the powder kept there, he looked for a way to surrender with honor. But he delayed for most of the day, and in the meantime the crowd grew restless and frightened that foreign troops might, after all, return at any moment. Shots were fired, believed to be aimed at the crowd; the besiegers managed to open the drawbridge, incidentally killing one of their own number, and the Parisians swarmed in and captured the fortress. De Launay was taken prisoner, but he was killed by angry rioters as he was being led away; other defenders were also killed, their heads set on pikes and carried around the city.

The "storming of the Bastille" became a symbol of the power of "the people"—formerly voiceless masses, now politically active participants— to stand up against what was increasingly seen as a deceitful monarchy, scheming against its own subjects. The king's brother and other highly placed nobles contributed to this image by fleeing to Vienna, where they attempted to get foreign help to restore the power of the king. Louis XVI and his family remained, but the fall of the Bastille convinced him, at least for the moment, that the National Assembly must be allowed to meet undisturbed. In order to emphasize the commitment of the new government to its citizens—a word that replaced "subjects" everywhere in France—the Paris militia was renamed the National Guard. It was put under the command of Lafayette, who added royal white to the red and blue on their cockades to make the tricolor that became the emblem of the new France.

The People of France

The fall of the Bastille was greeted with cheers, and the old prison be- came a major tourist attraction. As a symbolic representation of the old absolutist government or *ancien régime* ("old regime," a term used by 1790 to describe France before the revolution), it was demolished and pieces of its walls sold as tourist souvenirs. In their spare time, del- egates of the National Assembly toured the former prison and observed its destruction. Their real work, however, was to develop a new consti- tution for France. As they saw it, it would be a mixed government, with the king as the executive (like the American president). In order to pre- vent any return of absolutism, the executive was deliberately keep weak. Real power would lie with the legislature, an elected body.

The National Assembly soon faced other urgent tasks. In cities throughout France, grain shortages continued, and riots broke out. Ci- vilian militia like those in Paris were quickly established to keep the rioting under control and protect the city in case of foreign attack. Fear of foreign armies invading France to end the revolution spread, despite the king's apparent participation in the new government. In the countryside, the fear became a panic, fueled by the belief that all the lords of France, noble and bourgeois, were in league with foreign kings to reinstate the ancien régime. No amount of reassurance from authorities worked. This mass panic, known as the "Great Fear," was particularly strong in the eastern regions closest to the border and therefore more vulnerable to attack. Some peasants, hearing rumors of marching troops, fled to the forests or hid in barns. Others, believing the reports, took picks and torches, broke into barns to repossess the grain they had paid in taxes, and attacked manors and castles. In nearly all cases, the targets were not the residents themselves, but the legal papers that symbolized seigneurial authority.

Reports of the destruction, leading to new waves of riots, reached the National Assembly. "By letters from every province," noted a delegate on August 3, "it appears that properties of whatever sort are falling prey to the most disgraceful brigandage; on all sides castles are being burned, monasteries destroyed, farms given up to pillage. Taxes, payments to lords, all are destroyed; the law is powerless, magistrates without authority, and justice is a mere phantom sought from the courts in vain."[18] The National Assembly had intended to consider the plight of the peasant in due course, but the peasants themselves forced the issue. On the night of August 4, in a tense, emotional meeting that went on until two in the morning, one nobleman after another rose and renounced his feudal privileges. Representatives of towns renounced their corporate privileges over the countryside; office-holders renounced their privileges of office; clergymen renounced church privileges from hunting rights to tithes. Men could still own property and collect rents on that property, but they could not collect feudal services or dues.

By the end of the session, feudalism had been abolished in France, and the result was duly noted in a resolution passed by the Assembly on August 11. It was made even more explicit in the *Declaration of the Rights of Man and Citizen*, promulgated by the National Assembly on August 26, 1789. "Men are born free and remain equal in rights," it proclaimed; the aim of governments was "the preservation of the natural and imprescriptible rights of man. These rights are liberty, property, security, and resistance to oppression." France no longer had "nobility, nor peerage, nor hereditary distinctions," there was "no longer sale or inheritance of any public office. . . . There is no longer for any part of the nation nor for any individual any privilege or exception to the law that is common to all Frenchmen."[19]

The King of the French

The Declaration, together with the falling price of bread at the end of the summer, calmed the countryside. But tensions rose again as the price of bread rose in late September. The price of bread was expected to fall in the early autumn, as the harvest brought a new supply of grain for the coming year. In fact, the price remained high due to natural causes, but once again rumors blamed hoarders and plotting "aristocrats," for the term "aristocrat" had become a term of abuse applied to anyone believed to oppose the revolution. Grain riots again broke out, despite the activity of Lafayette and the National Guard. Sans-culottes women, in particular, took action, stopping grain convoy and petitioning for price controls to bring down the cost of bread.

Once again the situation in the capital was becoming explosive, and once again Louis XVI's own actions made it worse. Again he recalled troops from the border; again he seemed to be wavering in his commitment to revolution, voicing reluctance to accept the resolution of August 11 or the Declaration of the Rights of Man and Citizen. When Parisians heard that the troops had been welcomed to Versailles with a sumptuous banquet while they starved, tensions mounted to boiling point. Once again the tocsin was sounded; this time, it was crowds of women who assembled in the streets. They marched to city hall, apparently looking for weapons; then the crowd, amounting to perhaps 7,000 women carrying brooms and kitchen implements, as well as some men, set off for Versailles in the pouring rain. They first confronted the National Assembly, disrupting its session and demanding to present a petition on the price of bread. They next asked to see the king, and though he promised to ensure that bread was provided for the city, the majority felt that was not enough. Delegates to the National Assembly seized their chance and managed to get Louis to agree to their resolutions.

That still left the women with their demands unsatisfied, and at that point Lafayette arrived with 20,000 of the National Guard to restore order. He informed the king that he was there at the behest of the citizens of Paris and asked that Louis allow the National Guard to "protect his sacred person," guarantee grain for the city, and agree to move his

Engraving *A Versailles*, march of the female army to Versailles, October 5, 1789 (Giraudon/Art Resource, NY)

residence to Paris. The king asked for time to think it over, but early the next morning a group of Parisians made their way into the royal apartments and were fired upon by the king's bodyguards. Thousands of men (though few women, by this time) were still camped outside the palace; hearing the shots, they attacked the royal bodyguards, killing two. They were stopped by National Guard units, and Lafayette placed the king, queen, and family under his personal protection, convincing them to stand on the balcony and address the crowd. Louis XVI informed the assembled populace that he would go to Paris, entrusting himself "to the love of my good and faithful subjects."[20] Even Marie Antoinette was cheered in the euphoria of the moment. Lafayette pinned a tricolor cockade on one of the bodyguards to symbolize that they, too, were citizens of France.

The next day, October 6, escorted by 60,000 Frenchmen, Louis XVI, Marie Antoinette, and their children moved to Paris to the Tuileries, the traditional royal residence in the city. They brought wagonloads of grain as a gesture of goodwill. A few days later the National Assembly moved to Paris as well, setting up the government in an abandoned riding school near the Tuileries. On October 7, the National Assembly voted to change Louis XVI's official title from "King of France and Navarre"—a feudal designation indicating his family's lands—to "King of the French," as befitted the head of government of a free citizenry. As bread prices fell in November and tensions eased, the National Assembly continued its task of giving that free citizenry a new constitution.

Profile: The Marriage of Figaro

Tuesday, April 27, 1784, at 6 pm: The newly-opened Odèon theater was already packed with spectators waiting to see one of the most controversial plays on the French stage, *The Marriage of Figaro*. Five thousand people had been waiting around the theater since early that morning and, by noon, the pressure of the crowd forced the gates to give way and the guards to retreat. Three people were crushed to death, but the crowds were packed too tight for their bodies to be removed. Inside the theater, every seat and all the standing room was taken by the noble, the wealthy, the beau monde of Paris. As the curtain rose, there was a general gasp of pleasure, and, as the play went on, the audience applauded every line. The play ran for sixty-eight performances. Its author, Pierre Augustin Caron de Beaumarchais (1732–1799), had already been famous; now he was rich as well.

The *Marriage of Figaro* is a comedy, but what made it controversial—and successful — were its political overtones. Beaumarchais had created its main character, Figaro, in an earlier play, *The Barber of Seville*. Figaro is the valet of a nobleman, Almoviva, and, in the first play, performs the time-honored function of servants in comedy, assisting his master in accomplishing his designs, in this case marrying the noblewoman Rosine. *The Marriage of Figaro* takes place some years later and had, according to Beaumarchais's own summary, "the most trifling of plots: a Spanish nobleman, in love with a girl whom he wishes to seduce; and the efforts that the girl, the man to whom she is betrothed and the nobleman's wife make together to thwart an absolute master whose rank, fortune and profligacy make him all-powerful. That's all, nothing more." Yet another way of describing that "trifling" plot is that Figaro, a mere valet, unites with Suzanne, his sweetheart, and Rosine, Almoviva's wife—still her husband's subordinate despite her own noble rank—to rise up against the despotic authority of Almoviva. It took no great imagination to see Almoviva as a symbol of French feudal custom or to read the play as an attack on privilege based on birth, especially when Beaumarchais came right out and denied that birth had anything to do with ability:

By the hazards of gestation,
One's a shepherd, the other's a king;
Chance alone caused this separation;
Wit alone can change everything.

Verses like those created the controversy surrounding the play's production at the Odéon theater and almost kept it from being performed at
all. Beaumarchais was no revolutionary, but rather a true product of the
ancien régime. Born Pierre-Augustin Caron, the son of a watchmaker,
he was a successful social climber who nonetheless retained his sense of
being an outsider. His own watch designs were so ingenious, and his
manners so engaging, that he, first, became watchmaker to the royal
family, then married a woman of property and social status and gave up
watchmaking altogether. By the 1780s he was a successful playwright
and an equally successful, if notorious, courtier, in and out of government favor and in and out of the law courts as well. He served as a kind
of special agent in London during the American revolution, and there is
evidence that his support for the American cause may have influenced
the French government. He considered himself a loyal subject of King
Louis XVI, and the king, for his part, genuinely liked Beaumarchais.
Yet Beaumarchais insisted, all his life, that he had to be free to state his
own opinions, whatever anyone else—even the king—may have thought
of them.

It was that insistence that led to the controversy surrounding *The
Marriage of Figaro*. All plays, like books, were subject to censorship,
and when Louis XVI read Beaumarchais's manuscript, submitted in 1782,
he declared, "We should have to destroy the Bastille if a performance of
this play was not to be a serious blunder. This man mocks everything
that must be respected in a government." Government censors agreed.
Yet censoring materials, throughout the eighteenth century, only made
the public more avid to read them, and Beaumarchais was a nationally
known figure, with many noble supporters eager to see his latest production. His most prominent fans took to arranging their own readings
and performances, whatever the censors might say: "Every day," wrote
Queen Marie Antoinette's secretary, "you could hear people say, I have
been to or am going to a reading of Beaumarchais's play." Catherine I of
Russia let it be known that she would be delighted to produce the play in
St. Petersburg; Beaumarchais received offers from the London stage.
Under pressure, Louis XVI finally agreed to have a private performance,

by invitation only, in June 1783, but he changed his mind and ordered it canceled only ten minutes before the sold-out performance was to begin. This led to outcries of "oppression" and "tyranny" from the assembled audience, courtiers all, who had been waiting hours for the main event. Finally, public opinion, inside and outside the court, grew to such a pitch that the king gave in and allowed the play to be performed.[21] The result was theater history, and eventually opera history as well, as the composers Wolfgang Amadeus Mozart and Gioacchino Antonio Rossini (1792–1868) each took up the stories of Figaro, Almoviva, Suzanne, and Rosine.

Important Dates

1774	Ministry of Turgot
1775	Death of Louis XV of France; Louis XVI becomes king of France
1776	Dismissal of Turgot
1776–1783	American War of Independence
1781	Necker becomes director-general of French finance
1784	First performance of Beaumarchais's *The Marriage of Figaro*
1787	Assembly of Notables to advise king on financial crisis
1788	French declaration of bankruptcy
1789	May 5, Convocation of Estates General
1789	June 19, Conversion of Estates General into National Assembly
1789	June 20, Tennis Court Oath
1789	June 23, King agrees to National Assembly
1789	July 14, Storming of the Bastille
1789	July and August, "Great Fear" in the countryside
1789	August 4, Renunciation of feudalism by National Assembly
1789	August 26, Declaration of the Rights of Man and Citizen
1789	October 6, Louis XVI forced by Parisian crowds to return to Paris from Versailles

Further Reading

Ken Alder, *Engineering the Revolution: Arms and Enlightenment in France, 1763–1815* (Princeton, 1997)

Keith M. Baker, *Inventing the French Revolution* (Cambridge, 1990)

Lenard Berlanstein, *The Barristers of Toulouse in the Eighteenth Century* (Baltimore, 1975)

Roger Chartier, *The Cultural Origins of the French Revolution trans. Lydia Cochrane* (Durham, NC, 1991)

William Doyle, *Origins of the French Revolution* (Oxford, 1980)

William Doyle, *The Oxford History of the French Revolution* (Oxford, 1989)

William Doyle, *The Parlement of Bordeaux and the End of the Old Regime, 1771–1790* (New York, 1974)

William Doyle, *Venality: The Sale of Offices in Eighteenth Century France* (Oxford, 1997)

Arlette Farge, *Fragile Lives: Violence, Power and Solidarity in Eighteenth-Century Paris trans.* Carol Shelton (Cambridge, MA, 1993)

Nina Gelbart, *The King's Midwife: A History and Mystery of Madame du Coudray* (Berkeley, 1998)

Frederic Grendel, *Beaumarchais: The Man Who Was Figaro trans. Roger Greaves* (New York, 1977)

Lynn Hunt, *Revolution and Urban Politics in Provincial France: Troyes and Reims, 1786–1790* (Stanford, 1978)

Jeremy Popkin, *A Short History of the French Revolution* (Upper Saddle River, NJ, 1995)

Munro Price, *Preserving the Monarchy: The Comte de Vergennes, 1774–1787* (Cambridge, 1995)

Daniel Roche, *The People of Paris: An Essay in Popular Culture in the Eighteenth Century trans.* Marie Evans (Berkeley, 1987)

John Rogister, *Louis XV and the Parlement of Paris, 1737–1755* (Cambridge, 1995)

William Sewell, *A Rhetoric of Bourgeois Revolution: The Abbé Sieyès and What Is the Third Estate?* (Durham, NC, 1994)

Bailey Stone, *The Parlement of Paris, 1774–1789* (Chapel Hill, NC, 1981)

Donald Sutherland, *France 1789–1815: Revolution and Counter-Revolution* (Oxford, 1985)

Julian Swann, *Politics and the Parlement of Paris under Louis XV, 1754–1774* (Cambridge, 1995)

Dale K. Van Kley, *The Religious Origins of the French Revolution: From Calvin to the Civil Constitution, 1560–1791* (New Haven, 1996)

John D. Woodbridge, *Revolt in Pre-Revolutionary France: The Prince de Conti's Conspiracy against Louis XV, 1755–1757* (Baltimore, 1994)

Chapter Eighteen

Turns of Fortune's Wheel: France, 1789–1795

Constitutional Monarchy

The first year of the French Revolution was called the "happy year" in France, in which the whole country seemed to join together to work for a new government. Men and women addressed each other as "Citizen" and "Citizeness" instead of "Monsieur" (my lord) and "Madame" (my lady). Parisian ladies donated their jewels to help pay France's debts, wearing jewelry made out of fragments of the Bastille instead. The words "aristocrat" and "feudal" became terms of abuse, applied to everyone and everything that seemed to oppose the enlightened progress of the revolution.

This change in social interaction spurred the revolution's leaders to create a centralized political system that would conform to reason. The National Assembly, now formally called the Constituent Assembly, set about its work of creating a new, written constitution for the constitutional monarchy France had become. It consolidated the decisions of 1789. It swept away the local tolls, special laws, and regional privileges that, members believed, had impeded France's economic growth. The old complicated system of tax-exemption and privilege was replaced with a uniform tax structure, applicable to all citizens. The old citizen's militia was replaced by branches of the new National Guard, with its tricolor—red, white, and blue—uniform. Even price controls on grain were removed: from now on free trade would flourish in a newly free country.

But the urge to centralize and rationalize went even further. It was not enough to institute reforms and extend the right to vote. It was also necessary to create more rational districts in which voting would take place. Cities were divided into electoral districts. Traditional provinces such as Gascony and Burgundy were eliminated, replaced by eighty-three departments of about equal size. Historic names of regions were abandoned, as each department was named after its most prominent geographical feature (for example, the wine country of historic Guyenne, near Bordeaux, was divided into five departments, Gironde, Dordogne, Correze, Lot, and Lot-et-Garonne, named for the largest rivers in each department).

The euphoria of the moment soon passed. By July 1790, the first anniversary of the fall of the Bastille, serious disagreements over the future of the new government had surfaced. According to the proposed constitution, only *active citizens*, defined as adult males over twenty-five who paid taxes equivalent to three days' wages per year (about 60 percent of the adult male population), could vote in local and national elections. Furthermore, they could not vote directly for representatives, but for a slate of electors, who had an even stricter wealth qualification. Only about 50,000 Frenchmen were eligible to be electors. Members of the assembly, acting on the Enlightenment idea of the right of citizens to consent to their government, also acted on the Enlightenment fear of the uneducated mob taking over the government, leading to anarchy or the eventual despotism of a tyrant. The attack on the Bastille had aided their cause, but it had also frightened them: if the *sans-culottes* could help overthrow one government, they could help overthrow another.

The implicit message of the rights of suffrage was clear to the politically active sans-culottes in Paris as they met in the political clubs and read the political newspapers now legal under the Declaration of the Rights of Man. The most radical of these clubs, and the one that made its reputation as the voice of the Paris citizen, was the Society of the Friends of the Constitution, better known as the *Jacobin* Club (from its meeting place in the former convent of St. James—"Jacob" in Latin). By July 1790, it included 200 deputies from the assembly, and over 1,000 politically active members from the Paris neighborhoods. Citizens came to express their views to the deputies in the assembly; deputies came to debate issues before their constituency and to sway public opinion. Like business headquarters with branch offices, the Paris Jacobins formed associations with other Jacobin clubs throughout the country, spreading information and opinions.

Newspapers, too, sought both to debate issues and sway public opinion, and the radical journalist Camille Desmoulins (1760–1794) was vehement in his opposition to suffrage based on wealth requirements. "It has turned France into an aristocratic government," he wrote, drawing on the power of the new, negative buzzword. "But what is this much repeated word *active citizen* supposed to mean? The active citizens are the ones who took the Bastille."[1] His fellow-member of the Jacobin club, Robespierre, made the same point more formally in the assembly debate over suffrage. "Is a nation sovereign," he asked, "when the greater part of the persons composing it is deprived of the political rights from which sovereignty derives its essence?" No, he answered; instead, the nation becomes an aristocracy, "for aristocracy is that state in which one part of the citizens is sovereign and the rest is subject. And what kind of aristocracy? The most intolerable of all: an aristocracy of the rich." The rich "thought it natural to degrade the greater part of the human species by the use of terms such as canaille [scum] and populace [mob]"; they have "told the world that there were men without birth, as if any living man had not been born; that some men were nothing, and others men of respectability and distinction."[2] Robespierre, like Desmoulins, presented those in favor of the wealth requirement as opposed to the revolution itself. Deputies who favored the wealth requirement responded in kind. Accusing political opponents of opposition to the revolution—of reactionary, or counterrevolutionary, ideas or policies—soon became a favored tactic in political journalism, political clubs, and assembly debates on all issues.

There were other tensions. The new government of France was faced with the same fiscal crisis as the old one: mounting debt and insufficient revenue. Its tax base was, in fact, even smaller, for the new government abolished a host of hated taxes, direct and indirect, together with the *ancien régime* tax farm, the bureaucracy responsible for collecting them. The assembly believed that, since the lists of grievances had called for tax reform, citizens would be pleased to pay taxes once the structure was reformed. They quickly found that was not true: country- and urban-dwellers alike interpreted "revolution" as meaning the end of all hated taxes, not the substitution of one form of taxation for another. Moreover, the removal of price controls on bread as well as other goods led to high prices as well as hoarding and, subsequently, grain riots, just like during the ancien régime. The attempt of the newly elected local governments to collect taxes while maintaining order began to alienate local populations from the new government before the constitution was even completed.

The most serious threat to the new constitution, though, came with its policy on the clergy. Faced with the need to raise revenue and to maintain its credit rating in the eyes of foreign investors, the assembly voted to take over the land held by the former first estate. All clergymen, from bishops to parish priests, would become state officials, with their salaries paid by the government. The remaining lands not needed for payment of the government's debts would be sold. The certificates of sale issued by the government, called *assignats*, became a form of paper money. Since it was issued by the new French government, willingness to accept it as a medium of exchange for goods and services became a test of a citizen's loyalty to the new régime.

The Civil Constitution of the Clergy, as the new policy was called, was immediately controversial. The French clergy itself was split, and that split widened when Pope Pius VI condemned both the Civil Constitution and the Declaration of the Rights of Man. To many French men and women, that meant having to choose between loyalty to the revolution and loyalty to the Catholic Church. Conservative newspapers, as legal under the Declaration as their radical counterparts, denounced the Civil Constitution. After intense debate, the assembly decided to force the issue. They required all priests to swear their allegiance to the constitution and the new government or to be removed from their parishes. In Paris, virtually all the priests agreed to swear the oath. In the countryside, however, about half of all priests refused to swear. The assembly removed all those who refused from their parishes and appointed new priests, but many parishes were attached to their "old" priests and viewed their removal as merely an additional example of arbitrary government. In provincial towns and villages, especially in the north and east, murmurings grew even louder against the new government, murmurings that were often caught and recorded with alarm by the local Jacobin Clubs, who interpreted them as signs of counterrevolution.

To observers in the capital, the pope's condemnation of the Civil Constitution of the Clergy had a more important impact: it made Louis's participation in the new government even less likely. Though he eventually agreed to the Civil Constitution, he made it clear that he opposed it, just as he had opposed so many of measures of the new government. Many had observed that he seemed far from committed to the constitutional monarchy he was supposed to be leading; there were fears both within the assembly and on the Paris streets that he was merely waiting for an opportunity to repudiate the revolution. On June 20, 1791, Louis and his family confirmed that fear by attempting to escape from their palace in Paris, leaving a letter behind explaining their actions. Their destination was the Austrian border, but they were recognized by a postmaster in the town of Varennes, miles outside Paris, and forced to stop. They were brought back to Paris, and though the assembly quickly issued a denial that the king had really tried to escape, no one believed it. Louis's own letter made it impossible to believe in his cooperation, for it criticized, in the name of France, nearly all the goals and achievements of the assembly: as he put it, "The king does not think it possible to govern a kingdom of such great extent and importance as France by the means established by the National Assembly."[3]

After the "flight to Varennes," as the escape attempt was called, it was clear to everyone that the king was a prisoner of his own government. Many of the former aristocrats chose to emigrate, including over half the officers in the army (approximately 6,000 officers). To make matters worse, Marie Antoinette's brother, Emperor Leopold, issued the Declaration of Pillnitz on August 27, 1791, inviting foreign powers to employ "the most effectual means . . . to put the king of France in a state to strengthen . . . the bases of a monarchical government."[4] To Leopold, this was a mild statement, intending to uphold family honor while not committing him to any serious action. But it was received in France as a direct threat against the new government, strengthening the fears that émigrés (emigrant) aristocrats and army officers who had fled to Austria, Prussia, and Britain might join with counterrevolutionaries within France to restore absolute monarchy.

Amidst continuing fiscal crisis, religious tensions dividing the country, and the fear of foreign armies arriving to support the king, the Constituent Assembly prepared to finish its work. Elections were held during the summer of 1791 according to the new constitution, and delegates to the new Legislative Assembly—from which all member of the former Constituent Assembly were excluded—took their seats. As the British ambassador observed, "The present constitution has no friends and cannot last."[5]

Radicalization of the Revolution

The newly elected representatives of the French nation who arrived in Paris by October 1, 1791, were primarily lawyers and landowners, whose political experience came from their involvement in the local reforms of the past few years. This was their chance, they felt, to shape the revolution, to deal with the resistance to clerical reform, to ensure the cooperation of the king. The first step in this, politically ambitious representatives knew, was to form alliances with other members of the Legislative Assembly, in order to get enough votes to promote their policies. According to the new French constitution, the alliance which could marshal the most votes would form a ministry, a central coordinating unit like the American cabinet, with the king. In Britain, a similar system had led to the development of generally recognized political parties, Whig and Tory, but outside of Britain, the system of formal parties was looked on with great suspicion. Many political writers associated political parties with special interests, rather than the interests of the nation as a whole.

New representatives, therefore, faced a difficult task. They had to act like a "party" to gain votes within the assembly, but in doing so they were liable to be accused of acting for special interests, not for their nation. "Law is the expression of the general will," stated the Declaration of the Rights of Man, echoing the ideas of the *philosophe* Jean Jacques Rousseau: "the source of all sovereignty resides essentially in the nation." The modern idea of a pluralistic society with many competing interests—that is, of "the nation" and the "general will" itself being naturally and normally divided—was highly suspect. Moreover, the new French constitution did not provide for any way of calling for new elections if the representatives lost the confidence of the country and no longer seemed to be speaking for the "general will." After Emperor Leopold's Declaration of Pillnitz, accusers had no doubt of whose "special interests" might be undermining the assembly: the interests of foreign powers, of émigrés, of aristocrats, that is, of counterrevolutionaries.

This was the climate of opinion that dominated the capital as Manon Roland (1754–1793), wife of a representative from the new electoral district of the Gironde, entered the capital in the fall of 1791. Her husband, Jean Marie Roland (1734–1793), was not very ambitious himself, but urged on by his wife and the other *Girondins* (as representatives from the district came to be called), he became part of the ministry in 1792. The Girondins were the most effective force in rallying support in the new assembly, and Manon Roland's salon became their meeting ground. Fascinated by political ideas and discussion, she nonetheless had the political acumen to realize that many men accepted Rousseau's ideas about women as about politics, and Rousseau's *Emile* had made it very clear that women were to be guardians of the home, excluded from public life. A select group of representatives came to her house four times a week, and "There," she wrote, "were examined the state of affairs: that which the assembly convened to do, how one could propose it, the people's interests, court happenings, individual tactics." She loved these conferences, "and so as not to miss them," she wrote, "I never deviated from the role appropriate to my sex. Seated near the window, before a small table on which were books, study aids, and dainty handiwork, I plied the needle or wrote letters while they talked." Most of the men believed her to be completely absorbed in her own work while they talked, but instead she listened intently, saying nothing. She was very proud of her resolve: "To hold one's tongue when one is alone is not an amazing feat, but to steadfastly remain silent in the middle of men who speak of matters which interest you, to repress flashes of insight when you notice a contradiction . . . to measure like that the logic of each one while always controlling oneself, is a great means of acquiring penetration and rectitude."[6]

Under the lead of the Girondins, the assembly took the momentous step of declaring war on Austria on April 20, 1792. The goal was to act offensively to prevent what many believed would be the inevitable attack from Austria and Prussia, egged on by émigrés; many representatives also believed that it would unite "the people"—already a buzzword meaning "patriotic Frenchmen"—behind the faltering government. War-fever, indeed, spread throughout France. An infantry captain stationed in Alsace, on the eastern border near the Rhine river, wrote the "War Song for the Army of the Rhine," better known by the name the "Marseillaise." It became the marching-song of the French armies (now the French national anthem), inspiring soldiers with its fierce nationalism:

> Forward, children of the homeland!
> The day of glory is upon us;
> Against us, the bloody standard
> Of tyranny is raised.
> Do you hear these ferocious soldiers
> Bellowing in the fields?
> They come into your very midst
> To slaughter your sons, your wives!
> To arms, citizens, form your battalions,
> March on, march on, that impure
> Blood will water our furrows.[7]

Yet despite the rhetoric, the war was disastrous. The French army had few officers left, and the troops were demoralized and undisciplined. Battle after battle was lost, and the atmosphere in Paris became more and more tense. The Girondins, looking for a scapegoat, publicly accused the king of bad faith. The radical newspapers as well as the Jacobin clubs in Paris and elsewhere denounced the king and queen; more and more openly, they began calling for a republic, a government without a king. The calls became even more strident in the late spring and early summer of 1792, as the provisioning for the army began to cause food shortages throughout France. Robespierre, now elected to a municipal office in Paris and the most influential member of the Jacobin club, began to side more and more with the republicans, like the influential Paris politician Georges Jacques Danton (1759–1794), who called for the deposition of the king. Robespierre "is cool, measured, and resolved," wrote one English observer. "He is a stern man, rigid in his principles, plain, unaffected in his manners, no foppery in his dress, certainly above corruption, despising wealth. . . . He is *in his heart* Republican, honestly so, not to pay court to the multitude, but from an opinion that it is the very best, if not the only, form of government which men ought to admit."[8]

On June 13, 1792, Prussia declared war on France, intensifying the fears of foreign invasion as well as counterrevolutionary activity from within. To make matters worse, the duke of Brunswick, who commanded the Austrian and Prussian troops, issued the *Brunswick Manifesto* on July 25, threatening France and, especially, Paris with invasion and "an exemplary and ever-memorable vengeance" consisting of "military execution and complete ruin" if any harm came to the French royal family.[9] Throughout France it was assumed that the royal family supported this threat. The Paris electoral districts responded to it by petitioning the assembly to suspend the king on August 3, 1792. Seven days later, the city districts took matters into their own hands by staging another uprising. Sounding the tocsin, the Paris neighborhoods once again formed their militia and marched to the palace, in an attack against both the king and the assembly. The last remaining royal garrison in Paris fell, and the confidence of the constitutional government with it. Many representatives fled, and those that remained virtually surrendered power to the revolutionary government now in control of Paris. All vestiges of royal authority, or royal sympathies, were destroyed; anyone suspected of sympathy with the king and "aristocrats" was arrested. Louis and his family were now real, not virtual, prisoners, charged with crimes against the state.

The Republic

The aftermath of August 10 left France, and the world, shaken. The remnants of the assembly soon faced a new emergency. On September 2, 1792, word reached Paris that the fortress of Verdun had fallen, the last fortress between the Prussian troops and Paris. Panic gripped the city. Once again the tocsin rang, and once again the citizens assembled. This time, however, they did not attack garrisons. Instead, fearing that the invading troops, as part of their system of "exemplary vengeance" threatened by the duke of Brunswick, would release and arm prisoners, groups of sans-culottes attacked the prisons, in a series of massacres that neither the assembly nor the Paris municipal government did anything to stop. "Like everyone else," later wrote one Parisian woman, "I was shaking with fear lest these royalists be allowed to escape from their prison and come and kill me because I had no holy pictures to show them. . . . While shuddering with horror, we looked upon the action as almost justified."[10] Between 1,100 and 1,400 people were tortured and killed, and though some were well-known friends of the king, the rest were simply ordinary criminals, men, women, and children.

The prison massacres made it clear to all that the existing government was no longer in control. Those representatives who remained in Paris called for a new National Convention to develop a new constitution for a republic "to assure the sovereignty of the people and the reign of liberty and equality."[11] New elections were quickly held. Of the 749 deputies who were returned to the convention, 200 had been in the just-terminated Legislative Assembly. An additional eighty-three had served in the Constituent Assembly, including Robespierre, now a deputy from Paris.

The first act of the new body was to decide what to do with the king. Like Charles I in 1649, Louis was generally distrusted, and there were few objections when the monarchy was formally abolished, and France declared a republic, on September 21, 1792. But as in England, the trial of a king was a delicate matter. Louis, unlike Charles, was allowed defense counsel; like Charles, he behaved with unexpected dignity. And like Charles, his execution was a foregone conclusion. On Monday, January 21, 1793, Louis XVI was executed. The instrument used was a new invention, developed as a more humane method of carrying out capital punishment than decapitation by sword: the guillotine. Proven in political executions since the preceding April, it was to be used many more times in the years to come.

Year One

The prison massacres of September 2, 1792, had been horrible, but they seem to have reassured the Paris sans-culottes that their families were safe. In the succeeding weeks, 20,000 men of Paris volunteered for the army to fight against the Prussians and Austrians. On September 20, 1792, the French army had its first decisive victory at the town of Valmy, to the east of Paris. Foreign armies, stopped in their tracks, opened negotiations for a truce. Amidst general rejoicing, the new National Convention set about its formal task: legislating a whole new France, free from tainted monarchical trappings of the ancien régime.

The National Convention resumed the rationalization process of 1790 with a vengeance. Now, it was not just geography, but time, that could be molded to reason. The old system for numbering years was abolished, and a new numbering system instituted to commemorate the revolution. September 22, 1792, now became the first day of Year One of the Republic. The old names for months of the year, with their references to imperial Rome, were also changed, replaced with names that reflected seasons of the year or agricultural tasks: Thermidor for the heat of August, Brumaire for the fog of November. Feudal coinage, weights and measures, and the religious calendar were all to conform to reason: a national decimal coinage, the metric system, and a ten-day week, with a new day, Décadi, replacing Sunday as the day of rest, were all introduced. Catholicism itself was outlawed as contrary to reason and republican virtue.

The National Convention also drafted another new constitution, this time for a republic with universal manhood suffrage, not a constitutional monarchy. It was ready by the summer of 1793. Technically, the National Convention could have dissolved itself at that time and called for new elections based on the new constitution. But Year One had been disastrous for the country. After the victory at Valmy, the French had moved north and east into Dutch and German territories, proclaiming the revolution wherever they went; Britain entered the war in February 1793 and, with Prussia, Austria, Russia, and Spain, constituted an encircling European alliance against the French. When the government tried to raise more troops, by conscription when volunteers were not forth-coming, it met with massive evasion. The removal of price controls on bread and other goods had led to high prices and grain shortages, lead-ing to bread riots and making it near-impossible to provision the army.

In the east, in the region known as the *Vendée*, civil war broke out as 10,000 locally organized troops, wearing the royalist white, rebelled against the new government. "Long live the king and our good priests," they proclaimed; "We want our king, our priests, and the old regime."[12] To gain support from the rest of France, leaders of the rebellion pub-lished an open appeal to the country: "Heaven has declared for the holi-est and most just of causes. . . . Patriots, our enemies, you accuse us of overturning our homeland by rebellion but it is you, who, subverting all the principles of the religious and political order, were the first to pro-claim that insurrection is the most sacred of duties. You have introduced atheism in the place of religion, anarchy in the place of laws, men who are tyrants in place of the King who was our father."[13] Lyons, the second largest city in France, also broke out in insurrection. The fate of France and the revolution, people feared, hung in the balance, and members of the new government voted to postpone instituting the new constitution until the crisis was passed. The revolutionary government run by the National Convention, members agreed, would remain in effect until the revolution was over and France was at peace.

In Paris, the representatives from the Gironde, who were associated most closely with the king, tried to remain in control of the government even after his death in January 1793. Though they disagreed among themselves on many points, they were united in their hatred of the Jacobins, whom they derisively called the "Mountain" because they sat in seats high up in the hall. The Jacobins responded by attacking the "Girondins," their own derisive name for Roland and his associates. The uncommitted delegates in the middle, known as the "Plain," watched uneasily as every issue became colored by personal animosities, and as "Girondin" and "Mountain" became increasingly bitter terms of abuse. The Girondins received credit for the military successes of General Charles François Dumouriez (1739–1824), by then France's leading general, but they received equal blame when he defected to the Austri-ans. Foreign spies and traitors were everywhere, radical Paris newspa-pers proclaimed, perhaps even within the convention itself. The Girondins responded by attacking the twenty-four Jacobin deputies from Paris within the convention. In April 1793, the Girondins proposed that the seat of the government be moved from Paris to Versailles. They also proposed, and passed, the abolition of immunity from arrest granted to National Convention deputies, in order to arrest the bloodthirsty extremist Jean Paul Marat (1743–1793), distrusted for his unstable violence even among his political allies. It was a bad mistake. Marat was acquitted and paraded in triumph by sans-culottes. And the Mountain, fearing Girondins policies were keeping the convention in perpetual political gridlock, responded by attacking twenty-two of the Girondin deputies, calling for their arrest as counterrevolutionaries. Many were arrested; others fled to their home territory.

Once rounded up, the conviction and execution of leading Girondins was virtually guaranteed, for the Paris sections once again threatened to rise in revolt if the "traitors who conspired against the Republic"[14] were not executed. Any last doubt was removed when, on June 13, 1793, Charlotte Corday, a young woman from the Gironde, assassinated Marat in his bath. Corday had studied Roman history and believed herself to be acting for her country: she blamed Marat both for turning away from the original principles of the 1789 revolution and for the current plight of the Girondins. Marat instantly became a martyr, and Corday was widely rumored to be the agent of a Girondin plot. She was executed on July 17, 1793 (and quickly became an anti-Jacobin martyr in turn). Twenty-one Girondins, including Madame Roland, were guillotined on October 31, 1793; her husband, in hiding near Bordeaux, committed suicide when he heard of her death. "It must be feared that the revolution, like Saturn, successively devouring its own children, will engender, finally, only despotism with the calamities that accompany it," the Girondin representative, Pierre Victurnien Vergniaud (1753–1793), told the Convention; he went to the guillotine singing the "Marseillaise."[15]

The Reign of Terror

The execution of the Girondins, as well as the former queen Marie Antoinette (on October 16, 1793), ushered in the period known as the Reign of Terror, which lasted until the death of its most prominent political figure, Robespierre, on July 28, 1794. In a period of ten months, approximately 16,000 people were tried for treason and, in an atmosphere of patriotic hysteria precluding any fair trial or examination of evidence, found guilty and executed. Historians estimate that an 14,000 died in prison or in the provincial counterrevolutiona ings. Only a small percentage were aristocratic in origin: most former nobles had the means to emigrate until the situation calmed down. Instead, the overwhelming majority were sans-culottes or small proprietors, as towns and villages became locked in political upheavals beyond their control.

These numbers must be put in perspective. The 1790s were a bloody period in European history. In November 1794 in Warsaw, 20,000 people were killed in a single day during the Polish uprising against Russian occupation following the second partition. In 1798, 30,000 people died over a period of three months during the Irish rebellion against the British government. In both those cases, a powerful government resting on claims of traditional legitimacy was fighting against revolutionary threats to the established order: while repressive measures might evoke protest, they did not evoke surprise. But the French revolutionary government, in contrast, had come to power amidst calls for the civil rights of men and citizens, for freedom from oppression, for "Liberty, Equality, and Fraternity." How, people have asked from its own time to the present, could it turn on its own people with such ferocity? How could it justify its call for "Terror" as an instrument of government? How could it state, as Robespierre did state, "To good citizens revolutionary government owes the full protection of the state; to the enemies of the people it owes only death"?[16] How could a revolution launched with such ideals lead to the dictum that "the republic consists in the extermination of everything that opposes it"?[17]

If there is an answer, it comes from the need of the National Convention to take control of a country rapidly spinning into anarchy. Again in Robespierre's words, "The revolutionary government has to summon extraordinary activity to its aid precisely because it is at war,"[18] a war against foreign governments, internal civil war, and more passive, but equally dangerous, refusal to pay taxes or join the army. Time and time again, throughout Year One (September 1792–September 1793), the convention had shown itself incapable of taking executive action. In order to remedy this, a new Committee of Public Safety had been created on April 6, 1793, to act as an executive body to implement government business. Its members were to be elected each month from among representatives to the convention, but eventually came to consist of twelve men reelected regularly. Robespierre was one of the most influential of the twelve, but in fact the committee acted in concert, meeting every day, often far into the night, to transact government business and reporting to the convention on a regular basis. The Committee of Public Safety also controlled the Revolutionary Tribunal, a special court set up in Paris to try those accused of political crimes.

First and foremost among committee business was to deal with the military crisis: both army and navy were underprovisioned, undisciplined, and lacking competent leadership, since so many officers had emigrated. In August 1793, Lazare Carnot (1753–1824) took over responsibility for improving the army. He seriously searched among the officers still loyal to France for the most competent men who could be promoted quickly. He also implemented the committee's new national mobilization of troops, the *levée en masse*. According to Carnot's decree of August 23, "all Frenchmen are permanently requisitioned for the service of the armies."[19] This created the modern notion of a citizen's obligation to fight for the country. The levée en masse created armies not only of unprecedented size, but also of unprecedented fervor: for the first time, soldiers truly felt that they were fighting for their country. In addition, under committee direction, the National Convention passed price controls on grain and set a minimum wage, which reduced the economic crisis of the sans-culottes and reinforced loyalty to the army. By mid-1793, the French armies were able to go on the offensive, and the European coalition was beaten back.

French government forces were also able to put down the rebellions in the Vendée and in Lyons, by deploying troops and by setting up special courts to try those accused of being "enemies of the people." This gave effective control of the country back to the government in Paris, though with chilling effect, for the worst excesses of the Terror—the most widespread arrests and most brutal executions—came in areas that had rebelled against the republican revolution.

For the Committee of Public Safety increasingly came to see itself as the sole, pure force of the revolution, with the mission of bringing the entire country under its centralized authority. Special representatives were sent out from Paris to provincial districts, especially those which seemed to be disaffected, with power to bring the local, elected governments into line with the committee's policies. Robespierre, in particular, believed that the task of government was not just to make laws, but to create a whole new republican world view. "Revolution is the war waged by liberty against its enemies," he wrote; "it is the function of government to guide the moral and physical energies of the nation toward the purposes for which it was established."[20] That purpose was civic virtue, a "tender, imperious, irresistible passion," leading to "profound horror of tyranny . . . [and] compassionate zeal for the oppressed. It exists, this generous ambition to found on earth the first Republic of the world; this self-assertion of free men who find a pure pleasure in the calm of a clear conscience and in the delectable vision of public happiness."[21] The short-term goal of the committee was to restore authority to the French government, but its higher, long-term goal was to create a whole country of 29 million zealous republicans.

Yet its policies were highly unpopular. Draft-dodging and tax-evasion continued throughout the French countryside, and so did attachment to Catholicism. The new day of rest, Décadi, was especially unpopular among countrywomen, because while men could still go to the tavern, women no longer had the traditional social events organized around Sunday mass. Price controls were popular in towns among grain-buyers, but detested in the countryside among grain-sellers, who had enjoyed the high prices of previous years. Murmurings against the new regime and longings for the "good old days" had been heard since the tumultuous days of 1789, but by 1793, in the wake of foreign war and internal rebellion, they were taken as symptomatic of a conspiracy. Provincial Jacobins governments, facing opposition from their communities, called for revolutionary justice and arrested those they believed to be conspirators; the Terror, so employed, became as ruthless an instrument of government repression as that employed by any king.

Even within Paris, the Committee of Public Safety moved to take control of the revolution, to move it in the direction consonant with virtue and, more importantly, government control. In October 1793, it moved to close the club of Revolutionary Republican Women, a group of politically active Parisian women with sans-culottes sympathies. In October 1789, the women who had marched on Versailles had helped propel the revolution forward, but now the National Convention declared that women should not be politically active at all: "Morality and nature itself have assigned her functions to her: to begin the education of men, to prepare the minds and hearts of children for the exercise of public virtues, to direct them early in life towards the good, to elevate their souls, to educate them in the cult of liberty."[22] Their entry into politics could bring only disorder and intrigue. Henceforth any gathering of women was banned.

Among the women caught up in the political turmoil of the revolution was Olympe de Gouges (1748–1793), an actress, courtesan, and would-be playwright who had been a fervent supporter of the early revolution. She made it her cause to argue for true universal suffrage, for women as well as men, and in September 1791 had published the *Declaration of the Rights of Woman and Citizen.* "Mothers, daughters, sisters, representatives of the Nation, demand to be constituted into a national assembly," de Gouges wrote; "woman is born free and lives equal to man in her rights. . . . The purpose of any political association is the conservation of the natural and imprescriptible rights of woman and man."[23] De Gouges addressed the *Declaration* to Marie Antoinette, still an acceptable, if ill-judged, dedication in 1791. Two years later, the combination of the dedication to the hated queen, radical ideas on women, and de Gouges's continued outspoken writings on political issues led to her arrest. She was executed in November 1793, like others facing her death with unexpected courage: "Citizens," she cried when seeing the guillotine, "you will avenge my death."[24]

The Committee of Public Safety faced an even more significant break with past supporters with the divisions that began to emerge between influential Jacobins. The most radical of the Paris newspapers was closed for criticizing government policies, and its editor, Camille Desmoulins, long a Jacobin supporter, was arrested and executed on April 5, 1794. So was Georges Danton, for many years one of Robespierre's closest friends. Danton was very popular, and his execution shook the convention, for he was accused of no real crime beyond somehow not living in a manner befitting a virtuous republican. Almost anyone, delegates outside the Committee of Public Safety began to fear, might be in danger from revolutionary justice, no matter their past political track record. And some delegates had good reason to be worried: not as "uncorruptible" as Robespierre, they had used their government positions to enrich themselves.

After April 1794, the number of executions in the provinces went down, as the Committee of Public Safety acted again to centralize authority by closing down the provincial revolutionary courts. All political cases from then on were to be tried at the Revolutionary Tribunal in Paris. The Paris prisons soon became overcrowded, and on June 10, 1794 (22 Prairial in the new calendar), the convention passed a law, largely drafted by Robespierre, that eliminated due process for those arrested under suspicion of treason. Anyone arrested was automatically assumed to be guilty. From June, the number of executions in Paris rose sharply, and a much higher proportion of those executed were from the former nobility, clergy, and wealthy bourgeoisie. Nearly anyone who had prospered under the ancien régime was liable to be considered tainted with "impurity," to be accused of counterrevolution, not for what they had done, but simply for who they were.

Many convention delegates were now convinced that Robespierre intended to make himself dictator. The Festival of The Supreme Being, held on June 8, 1794, created by the committee to replace outlawed Catholic religious festivals with Republican ones, only confirmed their fears, for Robespierre himself rode in the center of the procession. "Look at the bugger," muttered one delegate; "it's not enough for him to be master, he has to be God."[25] On July 27, 1794 (9 Thermidor in the new calendar), Robespierre was denounced on the floor of the convention as an enemy of the people. The denunciation was orchestrated, as had been done so many times before, so that he had no opportunity to reply to the charges. That night, Robespierre, his brother, and eighty-two other "Robespierrists" were arrested by the National Convention. Initially they may have believed that the city of Paris would come to their defense, and some of the Paris districts did give orders that the prisoners were not to be held. But though the tocsin was sounded, the city did not rise in revolt against the convention as it had against the king and assembly in 1792. The most politically active sans-culottes were fighting with the armies at the front, or had been executed, or had lost interest in political activity, or had been intimidated into silence through the relentless arrests of the Terror. Robespierre and his associates were executed the next day. On August 1, 1794, the law of 22 Prairial was rescinded, and the remaining prisoners released, as many as 500 in a single week. The Committee of Public Safety was dismantled. The Reign of Terror was over.

Thermidorian Reaction

Throughout France, the end of the Terror brought an outpouring of relief. Within the National Convention, it brought the men who took over leadership a host of new problems. Primarily from the "Plain," they were still, of necessity, pledged to support the revolution, the republic, and the war, but they had no intention of allowing the "lower orders"— whether Parisian or provincial sans-culottes or rural peasants—to continue to have any voice in shaping government policies. The independent political clout of the sans-culottes had been successfully undermined by the centralizing efforts of the Committee of Public Safety. Now, with Robespierre and the committee gone, the Paris sans-culottes lost their political allies within the convention. It became politically suspect to be a Jacobin. Gangs of young men, known in Paris as Gilded Youth, claiming to have been imprisoned during the Terror or to have relatives who had been imprisoned, dressed in a deliberately aristocratic style and went around beating up known Jacobins. On November 12, 1794, hundreds stormed the Jacobin Club in Paris, beating up everyone found inside. Instead of punishing the attackers, the convention ordered the Jacobin Club closed, claiming it was an incitement to public disorder, just as it had once ordered the closure of the club of Revolutionary Republican Women. And just as men and women had once been suspect merely for looking like an aristocrat, now it was "enough simply to have the look of a Jacobin to be called after, insulted and even beaten up."[26]

Within the convention itself, those delegates most associated with the Terror were now brought before the Revolutionary Tribunal; some were executed, while others were deported to Guiana on the coast of South America, later known as "Devil's Island." In the countryside, particularly those areas where civil war had raged against the republic and had been severely suppressed, reprisals against the Jacobins were savage. In April 1795, the convention passed a law authorizing the disarmament and, if necessary, arrest of all those suspected of Jacobin sympathies. Perhaps 80,000 were arrested throughout the country during the summer of 1795, and though most were released unharmed, an estimated 2,000 were killed in prison massacres and lynch mobs.

Throughout France, and especially in Paris, ancien régime society seemed to have been reborn. Special balls were held to which only those who had lost a relative in the Terror were invited. Yet while high society seemed to flourish, France was undergoing its worst economic crisis since 1789. The grain harvest of 1794 had been only adequate, and the winter of 1794–1795 was the coldest in the entire eighteenth century. In December 1794, the convention abolished price controls on food. The price of grain skyrocketed; so did the prices of meat and butter. The poor froze in the streets; the suicide rate went up in Paris as well as other cities in northern France. Though the weather improved during early spring, the grain supply did not, and the city was reduced to rationing bread. By April Parisians were down to a daily ration of a quarter of a pound of bread each—"Never has Paris found itself in such distress," noted a diarist,[27]—but by May the ration was reduced to two ounces of bread.

On May 20, 1795, the Paris districts began another uprising, with a crowd of approximately 20,000 surrounding the National Convention, shouting the slogan "Bread and the Constitution of 1793!" The convention responded by calling out the National Guard, amounting to perhaps 40,000 troops. This time, though, there were no massacres: the convention declared that it would accept a petition, which the leaders of the uprising presented. The crowd then dispersed. In the weeks that followed, the convention arrested the most visible leaders of the uprising. Thirty-six of them were executed, and an additional thirty-seven sentenced to prison or deportation; fourteen deputies from within the convention were also arrested, and six were executed. Within the Paris districts, approximately 3,000 of those suspected of instigating the uprising were arrested, and an additional 3,000 were ordered disarmed. The Paris sans-culottes ceased to be a political force for another 50 years.

By 1795, many of those who had been most active in the revolution had died or were imprisoned. Lafayette had surrendered himself to the Austrians following the execution of the king, but since he refused to betray French military secrets, he was kept in prison by the Austrian government. Mirabeau had died of disease in 1790. The philosophe Condorcet, the chemist Lavoisier, and the astronomer Bailly all died in the Terror. When asked years later what he had done in the revolution, the Abbé Sieyès replied, "I survived."

Foreign Political Opinion

In 1790, as the Constituent Assembly met in Paris to determine the new constitution and political clubs debated issues all over France, reform-minded Englishmen formed their own political societies to consider the French revolution and the example it might set for their own country. Dissenters, especially, wanted to see parliamentary reform that would remove their exclusion from public life on religious grounds; others wanted to change the voting requirements to allow for wider suffrage. An especially vocal spokesperson for reform was Richard Price (1723–1791), a minister and influential member of Joseph Johnson's publishing circle. In a speech on the anniversary of the birth of William III, he compared the French Revolution to the English Glorious Revolution of 1688, which, he said, gave Englishmen three rights: to choose their governors, to remove them for misconduct, and to frame their own government. The recent revolution showed that the French had taken the same rights for themselves; he thanked God that "I have lived to see thirty millions of people, indignant and resolute, spurning at slavery, and demanding liberty with an irresistible voice."[28]

Price's sermon, widely applauded in his own "Revolution Society" as well as other reforming societies throughout Britain, led to one of the most influential published attacks on the revolution, *The Reflections on the Revolution in France* (1790) by Edmund Burke, a former member of Parliament and influential Whig politician. Burke had supported the American Revolution, but he was horrified by the French attack on the king and queen, clergy, and nobility, and his horror only deepened as the revolution continued and became more radical. He was particularly outraged by proponents, in France and Britain, of the abstract rights of man as the foundation of government. "Government," he retorted, "is a contrivance of human wisdom to provide for human *wants*," and the foremost right men possess is that "these wants should be provided for by this wisdom. Among these wants is to be reckoned the want, out of civil society, of a sufficient restraint upon their passions."[29] It was just that restraint that was so evidently lacking in France. Burke was especially angry that British reformers should claim that all Englishmen would agree with the French. "We are not the converts of Rousseau; we are not the disciples of Voltaire. . . . We have not been drawn and trussed, in order that we may be filled, like stuffed birds in a museum, with chaff and rags, and paltry, blurred shreds of paper about the rights of man."[30] Instead, Burke argued, the British had a natural, and inalienable, affection and respect for their own traditional government, and that traditional government was the best guarantor of British rights and social and political stability.

Burke's *Reflections* was a bestseller in Britain and abroad, and many agreed with this connection he had made between the dangerous ideas of the philosophes and the outbreak of revolution. In Austria and the German states, governments responded to the French revolution by instituting repressive measures against any and all proponents of Enlightenment ideals. "The empire of ignorance and superstition was moving closer and closer towards its collapse," complained one Catholic journal noted for its Enlightenment views; "the light of the *Aufklärung* made more and more progress. . . . Then the disorders in France erupted," and opponents "reared again their empty heads and screeched at the tops of their voices: 'Look there at the shocking results of the *Aufklärung*! Look there at the philosophes, the preachers of sedition!' Everyone seized this magnificent opportunity to spray their poison at the supporters of the *Aufklärung*."[31]

In Britain, anti-French feeling also ran strong. "'From liberty, equality and the rights of man,' wailed one writer, 'good Lord deliver *us*!'" and the British newspaper *Anti-Jacobin* satirized revolutionary principles as "Reason, Philosophy, 'fiddledum, diddledum' Peace and Fraternity, higgledy, piggledy."[32] More ominously, rioters in the manufacturing center of Birmingham attacked and burned down the houses of well-known radical Dissenters, while government officials did nothing to stop them. Yet Britain, with its comparative freedom of the press, was also the location for the most stirring defense of both the French revolution and of revolutionary change in government, Thomas Paine's *The Rights of Man* (1791). Paine (1737–1809) had been one of the most influential writers for the American Revolution, and he dedicated this new book to George Washington. Burke's idea that a traditional government should be retained simply because it was traditional, Paine argued, was nonsense, a self-serving argument made by a privileged member of that government. "There never did, there never will, and there never can exist a parliament, or any description of men, or any generation of men, in any country, possessed of the right or the power . . . of commanding forever how the world shall be governed, or who shall govern it," Paine wrote.[33] "We now see all over Europe, and particularly in England, the curious phenomenon of a nation looking one way, and the Government the other—the one forward and the other backward."[34] To Paine, it seemed obvious that the forward-looking nation must prevail. It seemed obvious to his readers, too, for sales of the *Rights of Man* reached 200,000 in 1791. Fearful of the impact of the book, particularly in Ireland, the British government suspended freedom of the press and prosecuted radical writers, publishers, and printers for sedition. Paine, faced with arrest, crossed the Channel to France. His outspoken political views led to his arrest under the Terror, but he was subsequently released and returned to the United States.

Paine was not the only writer in Britain to attack Burke's *Reflections*: in December 1790, Mary Wollstonecraft (1759–1797), writer and critic, rushed to the defense of the revolution with *A Vindication of the Rights of Men*. Wollstonecraft's childhood with an unstable, improvident father had left her with a strong desire to leave home, and she had first tried to earn her living in the ways open to an intelligent woman, first by operating a school for girls and then by becoming a governess in an aristocratic household. Neither situation worked out well, but she had the good fortune to come into contact with Richard Price and other Dissenting reformers, who had put her in touch with the publisher Joseph

Johnson. She settled in London and worked as a staff writer for Johnson's journal, the *Analytic Review*. Through Johnson and her own work she came in contact with leading radicals, including Thomas Paine. She was outraged at Burke's attack on Price as well as on the French Revolution.

Wollstonecraft's *Vindication of the Rights of Man* was a kind of political pamphlet, an immediate response to a felt provocation. More enduring was her *Vindication of the Rights of Woman*, written in about six weeks and published in 1791. Unlike the rest of the literature on the rights of men and women, including Olympe de Gouges's *Declaration of the Rights of Woman and Citizen*, Wollstonecraft's *Vindication* did not discuss civil rights. Instead, she concentrated on what she considered the fundamental principles of human society, that "the perfection of our nature and capability of happiness, must be estimated by the degree of reason, virtue and knowledge, that distinguish the individual, and direct the laws which bind society."[35] Reason was the key element, because virtue and knowledge come directly from reason, and Wollstonecraft argued that women were just as capable of exercising their reason as men. With the authority of a former teacher, she set out the defects in the current system of education that led women as well as men to believe that it was to their advantage to be ignorant and frivolous instead of rational and virtuous. "Make women rational creatures, and free citizens" she concluded, "and they will quickly become good wives and mothers; that is — if men do not neglect the duties of husbands and fathers."[36] In its emphasis on reason, virtue, and education, the *Vindication* reaffirmed the philosophe ideals attacked by Burke and other conservative writers.

Profile: Toussaint L'Ouverture (1744?–1803)

In 1789, the most important of all French overseas possessions was Saint Domingue, the western half of the tiny island of Hispaniola, noted principally for sugar and coffee and accounting for two-thirds of French imports and exports. To the nearly 1 million Africans who had been imported to work there as slaves, it was hell on earth. Though their treatment by their owners was, in theory, constrained by law, in practice no constraints operated. Flogging was commonplace, as were other examples of extraordinary brutality, because it had been found most profitable to pay off the cost of slaves in installments over a seven-year period and to work them to exhaustion during that time. Slave owners also widely believed that brutal treatment would frighten slaves from attempting to revolt. The result was that the death rate among slaves was appallingly high, estimated at 11 percent per year. Even free blacks, which included mulattoes, were treated badly and denied access to civil and political rights, though they might own slaves themselves.

When the French Revolution began, even the delegates to the National Assembly were reluctant to consider the rights of mulattoes and slaves, for the island contributed a substantial part of French revenue. In 1789, however, deputies from Saint Domingue to the National Assembly raised the question of the political rights of the mulatto population, and in 1791, civil rights were granted to mulattoes born of two free parents. But by that time events on the island had far outdistanced the French government. In October 1790, as the assembly moved from discussion of the colonies to other issues, the mulattoes rose in rebellion against the plantation owners, a rebellion that was repressed with ferocity. In August 1791, the far more numerous slaves rebelled, escaping by the thousands to the hills.

Toussaint L'Ouverture, a former household slave, joined the rebellion and soon was noted for his insistence on discipline and training, becoming the most powerful general in the rebellion. At first he allied himself with the Spanish, who controlled the other half of the island and who hoped to take advantage of the situation to take over the whole territory. The French representative from the National Convention who arrived in 1793 to enforce the new laws found himself hated by the plantation owners who wanted a return of their old slave-owning society. He appealed to Toussaint to come fight for the French Republic against the Spanish and British, promising freedom: "It is with the natives of the country, that is, the Africans, that we will save Saint Domingue for France."[37] In February 1794, the National Convention abolished slavery in all French colonies, declaring that all former slaves were now citizens.

With Toussaint at their head, the armies of former slaves defeated the Spanish, leading them to cede the entire island to the French. "He disappears—he has flown—as if by magic. . . . One never knows where his army is, what it subsists on, how he manages to recruit it. . . . He, on the other hand, seems perfectly informed concerning everything that goes on in the enemy camp."[38] His armies also held off British forces, sent to support the white slave-owners and to ensure that slave uprisings did not spread to their own island possessions, for three years until they were forced to withdraw in 1798. Widely admired, Toussaint was considered invincible by his own troops and became the de facto ruler of Saint

Domingue, though remaining loyal to France. When Napoleon took power, however, he was determined to remove so formidable a local figure, and Toussaint was captured, brought to France, and imprisoned until his death. The reimposition of slavery in French colonies in 1802 was too much for the Black troops remaining in Saint Domingue, and after an additional two years of brutal fighting, marked by atrocities on both sides, the Republic of Haiti was declared on the island of Hispaniola on January 1, 1804.

Important Dates

1790	Publication of Burke's Reflections on the Revolution in France
1790	July promulgation of the Civil Constitution of the Clergy
1791	Publication of Paine's Rights of Man; publication of Wollstonecraft's Vindication of the Rights of Woman
1791	June 20, Louis XVI's flight to Varennes
1791	August, Beginning of slave rebellion in Saint Domingue
1791	August 27, Declaration of Pillnitz
1791	September, Publication of Olympe de Gouges's Declaration of the Rights of Woman and Citizen
1792	April 20, French declaration of war on Austria
1792	June 13, Prussian declaration of war on France
1792	August 10, Paris uprising makes Louis XVI prisoner
1792	September 2, Paris prison massacres
1792	September 20, Cannonade at Valmy defeats Prussians and Austrians
1792	September 21, France formally proclaimed a republic— Year I
1793	January 21, Execution of Louis XVI
1793	March, Beginning of Vendée rebellion
1793	April 6, Formation of Committee of Public Safety
1793	June 13, Assassination of Marat by Charlotte Corday
1793	August 23, Promulgation of levée en masse
1793	October, Beginning of Reign of Terror
1794	February, Abolition of slavery in French colonies
1794	April 5, Executions of Danton and Desmoulins
1794	June 10, Law of 22 Prairial, formally revoking due process for treason suspects
1794	July 28, Execution of Robespierre

1794	August 1, Law of 22 Prairial rescinded
1794	November 12, Crowd attacks Jacobin Club of Paris
1794	December, Price controls on bread ended
1795	May 20, Last sans-culottes uprising in Paris
1803	Death of Toussaint L'Ouverture

Further Reading

David Andress, *French Society in Revolution, 1789–1799* (Manchester, 1999)

Howard G. Brown, *War, Revolution, and the Bureaucratic State: Politics and Army Administration in France, 1791–1799* (Oxford, 1995)

Jack Censer, *Prelude to Power: The Parisian Radical Press, 1789–1791* (Baltimore, 1976)

Richard C. Cobb, *The Police and the People: French Popular Protest, 1789–1820* (Oxford, 1970)

Alfred Cobban, *The Social Interpretation of the French Revolution* (Cambridge, 1964)

Malcolm Crook, *Elections in the French Revolution: An Apprenticeship in Democracy, 1789–1799* (Cambridge, 1996)

Thomas Crow, *Emulation: Making Artists for Revolutionary France* (New Haven, 1994)

Philip Dawson, *Provincial Magistrates and Revolutionary Politics in France, 1789–1795* (Cambridge, MA, 1972)

Suzanne Desan, *Reclaiming the Sacred: Lay Religion and Popular Politics in Revolutionary France* (Ithaca, NY, 1990)

Carolyn E. Fick, *The Making of Haiti: The Saint Domingue Revolution from Below* (Knoxville, TN, 1990)

Michael P. Fitzsimmons, *The Remaking of France: The National Assembly and the Constitution of 1791* (Cambridge, 1994)

Alan Forrest, *Conscripts and Deserters: The Army and French Society During the Revolution and Empire* (Oxford, 1989)

Alan Forrest, *The Revolution in Provincial France: Aquitaine, 1789–1799* (Oxford, 1996)

Alan Forrest, *Society and Politics in Revolutionary Bordeaux* (Oxford, 1975)

Alan Forrest, *Soldiers of the French Revolution* (Durham, NC, 1990)

Francois Furet, *Interpreting the French Revolution* trans. Elborg Forster (Cambridge, 1981)

Francois Furet, *The French Revolution, 1770–1814* trans. Antonia Nevill (Oxford, 1996)

Jacques Godechot, *The Counter-Revolution: Doctrine and Action, 1789–1804* trans. Salvator Attansio (New York, 1971)

Dominique Godineau, *The Women of Paris and Their French Revolution* trans. Katherine Streip (Berkeley, 1998)

Jean-Pierre Gross, *Fair Shares for All: Jacobin Egalitarianism in Practice* (Cambridge, 1997)

John Hardman, *Louis XVI* (New Haven, 1992)

Carla Hesse, *Publishing and Cultural Politics in Revolutionary Paris, 1789–1810* (Berkeley, 1991)

Patrice Higonnet, *Class, Ideology, and the Rights of Nobles during the French Revolution* (Oxford, 1981)

Patrice Higonnet, *Goodness beyond Virtue: Jacobins during the French Revolution* (Cambridge, MA, 1999)

Olwen Hufton, *Women and the Limits of Citizenship in the French Revolution* (Toronto, 1992)

Lynn Hunt, *The Family Romance of the French Revolution* (Berkeley, 1992)

Lynn Hunt, *Politics, Culture, and Class in the French Revolution* (Berkeley, 1984)

C.R.L. James, *The Black Jacobins: Toussaint L'Ouverture and the San Domingo Revolution* (London, 1980)

P.M. Jones, *Reform and Revolution in France, 1774–1791: An Essay in the Politics of Transition* (Cambridge, 1995)

Peter Jones, *The Peasantry in the French Revolution* (Cambridge, 1988)

David P. Jordan, *The King's Trial: The French Revolution vs. Louis XVI* (Berkeley, 1979)

David P. Jordan, *The Revolutionary Career of Maximilien Robespierre* (Chicago, 1989)

Michael L. Kennedy, *The Jacobin Club of Marseilles, 1790–1794* (Ithaca, NY, 1973)

Michael L. Kennedy, *The Jacobin Clubs in the French Revolution: The First Years* (Princeton, 1981)

Joan Landes, *Women and the Public Sphere in the Age of the French Revolution* (Ithaca, NY, 1988)

Gwynne Lewis, *The Second Vendée: The Continuity of Counterrevolution in the Department of Gard, 1789–1815* (Oxford, 1978)

Colin Lucas, *The Structure of the Terror: The Example of Javogues and the Loire* (Oxford, 1973)

John Lynn, *The Bayonets of the Republic: Motivation and Tactics in the Army of Revolutionary France, 1790–1794* (Urbana, IL, 1984)

John Markoff, *The Abolition of Feudalism: Peasants, Lords, and Legislators in the French Revolution* (University Park, PA, 1996)

Alison Patrick, *The Men of the First French Republic: Political Alignments in the National Convention of 1792* (Baltimore, 1972)

Jeremy Popkin, *The Right-Wing Press in France, 1792–1800* (Chapel Hill, NC, 1980)

Clay Ramsay, *The Ideology of the Great Fear: The Soissonnais in 1789* (Baltimore, 1992)

Joan Wallach Scott, *Only Paradoxes to Offer: French Feminists and the Rights of Man* (Cambridge, MA, 1996)

Albert Soboul, *The French Revolution 1781–1799: From the Storming of the Bastille to Napoleon* trans. Alan Forrest and Colin Jones (New York, 1974)

Donald Sutherland, *The Chouans: The Social Origins of Popular Counter-Revolution in Upper Brittany, 1770–1796* (Oxford, 1982)

Timothy Tackett, *Becoming a Revolutionary: The Deputies of the French National Assembly and the Emergence of a Revolutionary Culture (1789–1790)* (Princeton, 1996)

Timothy Tackett, *Religion, Revolution, and Regional Culture in Eighteenth Century France: The Ecclesiastical Oath of 1791* (Princeton, 1986)

Charles Tilly, *The Vendée* (Cambridge, MA, 1964)

Chapter Nineteen

Napoleon and the Export of the French Revolution

Though the government that emerged in France during the Thermidorian reaction was not as radical as that of the Reign of Terror, it remained an activist revolutionary government. The new regime was called the Directory, so named because executive power was placed in the hands of five directors, who were chosen by the legislative councils. The directors themselves changed several times during the five years that the Directory existed, but there was one constant in their policy: France aggressively exported its revolution to neighboring lands. Indeed, this phase of the French revolution was characterized by a stark contrast between the ineffectualness and instability of internal politics in France and the rapid success of the extension of French dominance over its neighbors.

The Directory was unable to maintain internal stability, both because the people who became directors lacked the stature of the first revolutionaries and because it faced an impossible balancing act. As committed revolutionaries, supporters of the Directory could not afford a restoration of the monarchy. The return of a king would mean, at best, exile and, at worst, execution for the leaders. At the same time, the violence of the Thermidorian reaction meant that supporters of the Directory were equally threatened by any reemergence of Jacobinism and the sans-culottes. Radical Jacobins would certainly exact their revenge for the fate of Robespierre and his lieutenants. And there were plenty of both Royalists and Jacobins for the supporters of the Directory to worry about. For all five years of its existence, the Directory was caught between those who wished to return France to the radical egalitarianism of the Terror and those who wished a return to the monarchy. Conspiracies were everywhere. No sooner did the directors fend off an assault from the one side than they had to contend with the other.

Indeed, the Directory faced massive demonstrations even before it took effect. In order to ensure that supporters of the new regime had a controlling position in the new legislature, Directory members decreed in the new constitution that two-thirds of the people elected to it had to already be in it. This would ensure that no more than one-third of the legislature would be Royalist or Jacobin, no matter how popular either position was among the voters. In 1795, Parisians rioted against the proposed constitution, but were subdued by troops loyal to the Directory under the command of a young artillery general by the name of Napoleon Bonaparte. The "whiff of grapeshot" from his cannons left more than a thousand dead and broke the back of the resistance. Napoleon's presence at the founding of the Directory is highly symbolic. The Directory depended on the army as the basis of the legitimacy of its government, and as time went on, the army became the instrument for Napoleon's personal quest for power. From that time onward, the fate of the French Revolution was directly linked to Napoleon's ambitions.

The Origins of Napoleon Bonaparte

Napoleon Bonaparte (1769–1821) was born on the island of Corsica in the Mediterranean. Corsica had only become "French" in 1768, the year before Napoleon's birth, when France purchased it from the Italian city-state of Genoa. Genoa was probably happy to be rid of the island, since it had been agitating for independence for most of the previous decade and had effectively thrown off Genoese control in 1760. There was widespread hostility to the new French regime, which was all the greater because the native language of the island was Italian, not French. The guerrilla independence movement, led by Pasquale Paoli, continued for the first two years of French occupation. Among the captains supporting Paoli was one Carlo Buonoparte, Napoleon's father.

But, in 1770, when the French finally drove the guerrilla movement from the island and Paoli into exile, Carlo Buonoparte remained on the island and reconciled himself to the French regime. Napoleon's father was from a minor noble family on the island and was, therefore, able to secure an administrative position appropriate to his status. At the age of nine, Napoleon was sent to France to attend one of the leading new military schools at Brienne. He did not return to Corsica for eight years.

Napoleon was a very good student, especially in mathematics, but he had difficulty with his fellow students because of his heavy Italian accent and his ardent Corsican patriotism (at one point he wrote to General Paoli, "You left the island, and the hope of happiness went with you; slavery was the price of our submission").[1] At the elite *École Militaire* (Military School) in Paris, to which he transferred in 1784, he suffered a great deal from the disdain of the high nobility who set the tone at the school. Like many of his generation, he was an avid reader of Rousseau, which, combined with his passion for Corsican liberation, made him something of a radical among his army compatriots. Nevertheless, he continued to find supporters and won a commission as a second lieutenant in the artillery regiment at Valence in 1785, at the age of sixteen.

Napoleon was still a second lieutenant when the revolution broke out in 1789. By temperament, Napoleon was supportive of the revolutionary ideas. Though not humiliated as much as Voltaire had been a half century earlier, Napoleon's contact with the true upper-crust nobility left him with a sense of grievance against the social order. His younger brother Lucien (1775–1840) was an even more committed revolutionary, joining the Jacobin Club of Toulon and backing Robespierre's Terror. But equally importantly, Napoleon recognized the pragmatic advantages of backing the revolution. His career was made possible by the French Revolution. The social conventions of the old regime would have slowed his rise to a position of genuine authority, because he did not belong to the right networks or have the financial resources to buy his way to the top. Bright, ambitious sons of the lower nobility were concentrated in the artillery in part because it lacked the aristocratic glamour of the cavalry or infantry. It is thus a sign of Napoleon's own foresight that he observed to a fellow officer in 1789, "Revolutions are ideal times for soldiers with a bit of wit and the courage to act."[2] He immediately accepted an appointment in the revolutionary army, helping in late 1793 to recapture the city of Toulon from an English force that had taken it in 1792. He was rewarded for his work with a promotion to brigadier general.

Napoleon's career was in limbo several times over the next two years, as he negotiated the tricky transition from Robespierre's terror to the Thermidorian reaction. Not long after the triumph of Toulon, Napoleon's commanding officer dismissed him from his commission because he was too closely associated with the Jacobins. But he survived the first wave of retribution against Robespierre's supporters. His presence in Paris in 1795, where he suppressed the rioters against the Directory, was partly a happy accident of his demotion.

The Expansion of France under the Directory

Napoleon's presence in Paris at the beginning of the Directory proved very beneficial for securing even greater patronage from the new regime. While there, he was able to present his plans for an invasion of northern Italy to the minister of war, Lazare Carnot (1753–1823). The plans impressed Carnot enough that he appointed Napoleon major general and named him commander of the Army of Italy in Savoy in 1796. Napoleon had the opportunity he had been waiting for. Now he took full advantage of it.

France had been fighting Austria in northern Italy since 1792. The French could count on widespread support of pro-Enlightenment, anticlerical people in much of the area, but by 1795, the military initiative seemed to be with the Austrians. Napoleon rapidly changed all that. The next twelve months were the beginning of the legend of Napoleon as a military genius. He first separated Austria's Piedmontese allies and defeated them; then he launched rapid-fire movements resulting in battles that destroyed four successive Austrian armies. By March 1797, he crossed over into Austrian territory, coming within a hundred miles of Vienna. Meanwhile, the riches of Italy flowed into the coffers of the French state: not just gold and silver, but art, too, became part of the French plunder. The Austrians were forced to seek an armistice, the Treaty of Campo Formio, that left France in control of most of Northern Italy. Napoleon returned to France a national hero.

Napoleon's victory in Italy consolidated revolutionary control over almost all of the territories bordering on France. Already in 1795, Belgium had been annexed outright to France. Austria, its former ruler, recognized that annexation at Campo Formio. Others territories were given new constitutions as satellite states, completely subservient to Paris. The Batavian Republic, consisting of the old Netherlands, was proclaimed in 1795; the Cis-Rhenan (Across the Rhine) Republic, consisting of several small states in the western part of Germany, was created in 1797; the Helvetic Republic, consisting of Switzerland, was proclaimed in 1798; and the Cis-Alpine (Across the Alps) Republic was created out of the territories conquered by Napoleon in 1798. This combination of annexation and creation of satellite puppet regimes directly extended the impact of the French Revolution throughout Europe.

Buoyed by his success in Italy, Napoleon strove to find ways to extend France's power and thwart the commercial advantages of the English. He decided to conquer Egypt from the Ottoman Turks. He reasoned that a direct invasion of England was impossible because of English naval superiority, but the conquest of Egypt would give France a stranglehold on the Mediterranean, ensuring a profitable position in trade with India, despite the English presence there. Upon landing in Egypt, Napoleon demonstrated his continued mastery of battle, routing the Turkish forces at the Battle of the Pyramids, but he seriously misjudged the overall strategic situation. While his army was winning, the naval fleet sent to support him was destroyed at Aboukir Bay by the English under Admiral Horatio Nelson (1758–1805). Now, both Napoleon and his army were completely cut off from France. Napoleon abandoned his army, sneaking past the English fleet in a single ship, and returned to France. To his surprise, the news of his victories had arrived in France, but not the news of the disaster to his fleet. In his absence, the situation in Italy had once again become threatening. He was, therefore, once again greeted as a hero as he made his way from Provence to Paris. Meanwhile, the army remaining in Egypt gradually disintegrated. The final remnants of it surrendered to the British in 1801. But by then, Napoleon was on to bigger things.

The Coup d'Etat of Eighteenth Brumaire

Partly because of the striking contrast between the expansion of French power in Europe and the muddle-headedness of French internal policies, some people within the Directory became convinced that a more authoritarian central executive was necessary. Ironically, one of the most persistent conspirators against the new regime was the Abbé Sieyès, who had managed to survive all of the different phases of the revolution and now served as one of the Directors. He forged an alliance with two important ministers who had up to that point been personal enemies, Charles-Maurice de Talleyrand (1754–1838), the foreign minister, and Joseph Fouché (1759–1820), the minister of police. The three realized that any successful coup would have to be supported by the army, so they sought a like-minded army officer who had support both within the army and among the populace. The recent return of Napoleon from Egypt fit their plans perfectly.

In a discussion on November 1, 1799, Napoleon agreed to join Sieyès in deposing the "Ancients" and "Five Hundred," the two legislative bodies of the Directory, and appointing themselves, along with Pierre Roger-Ducos, as three consuls who would be responsible for creating a new constitution. The moment to strike soon came. On November 9 (or 18 Brumaire according to the revolutionary calendar still in effect in France), the conspirators made their move. They forced a meeting of the two assemblies, proclaiming a state of emergency. The next day, when members of the Five Hundred began to balk at the proposals, Napoleon harangued them: "I am marching with the gods of victory and war on my side. . . . He who loves me, will follow me."[3] The Jacobins in the assembly shouted him down: "Down with the dictator! the sanctuary of the nation's laws has been violated. Down with the tyrant! Down with this Cromwell! Outlaw him! Long live the Constitution." But Napoleon's brother Lucien acted quickly, inciting the guardsmen that Napoleon had brought together outside the assembly to act. They fixed bayonets and charged into the chamber, dispersing the Five Hundred in all directions. Some even crawled out of windows to escape. Shortly thereafter, the rump of Napoleon's supporters met and proclaimed the provisional Consulate regime of Sieyès, Roger-Ducos, and Napoleon. The consuls produced a new constitution three weeks later, which they announced with the claim, "The Revolution is established upon the principles which began it: it is ended."[4]

Napoleon's Glory Days: Internal Transformation of France

However cynical Napoleon's grab for power may have been, he did have a clear sense of the defects of the Directory regime and a plan for overcoming them. He easily outsmarted Sieyès, getting himself named First Consul and taking the initiative in proposing administrative changes. His earliest pronouncements as First Consul demonstrate his confidence in his own abilities: "The art of governing involves nothing more that the application of common sense when dealing with important political matters."[5] With incredible energy and guile he set about demonstrating just how much common sense he possessed. The real triad of power in the regime rapidly became not the three consuls, but Napoleon, flanked by Talleyrand and Fouché. The first five years of Napoleon's regime are notable for triumphs in both foreign and domestic policy that earned him admiration from many parts of Europe.

The first internal step that Napoleon took was to defuse one of the most potent opposition groups in France, the "refractory clergy" and the large numbers of peasants and workers who were repelled by the anticlericalism of the revolution. He pulled the rug out from under that resistance by negotiating a deal, known as the Concordat of 1801, with Pope Pius VII. After drawn-out negotiations, Napoleon agreed to recognize Catholicism as the religion of the majority of French people, but not as the state religion. Both the old clergy who had been ousted by the revolution but who still claimed their parishes and the new clergy instituted by the revolution were dismissed and their replacements were chosen by mutual agreement between Napoleon and French bishops chosen by the papacy. The clergy would now be paid a state salary, rather than the local tithe. Church lands confiscated during the revolution would not be returned (most had been sold and could not be bought back). Catholic religious practices would not be interfered with. On the whole, the agreement was highly beneficial to Napoleon: he undercut one of his main sources of opposition in exchange for some platitudes. His reasons for the deal were entirely pragmatic, even cynical. They certainly did not come from any personal religious feelings of his own, but instead from his own sense of reason. He wrote: "In religion, I do not see the mystery of the Incarnation, but the mystery of the social order. Society is impossible without inequality, inequality intolerable without a code of morality, and a code of morality unacceptable without religion."[6] Karl Marx (1818–1883) would express the same idea more pointedly nearly fifty years later with the phrase "religion is the opiate of the masses."

Napoleon's second major internal task was to create new social morals more in tune with his own values. In 1802, he announced the creation of a new honor to be bestowed on those who provided the greatest service to France (and by extension himself): the Legion of Honor. This move aroused greater resistance among his supporters in the Tribunate than did his Concordat with the pope because it seemed to indicate a return to the pomp and ceremony of the monarchy. The structure of the Legion consciously evoked that of the army, but also the old regime, with the highest honors going to "grand officers," "commanders," and "knights." The large cross-shaped decoration new members received reinforced the military and aristocratic image. Napoleon himself was to act as the head of the council that chose new members. In that way, he would be able to offer incentives to all citizens to excel for the good of the state, while binding those who were most successful to himself. His motto was "A career open to all talents, without distinction of birth."[7] During Napoleon's rule, about 48,000 members were nominated, the vast majority of whom served in the military. Some criticized the Legion of Honor as nothing more than a scheme to give special rewards to Napoleon's supporters. As one Italian satirical newspaper quipped:

> In fierce old times they balanced loss
> By hanging thieves upon a cross.
> But our humaner age believes
> In hanging crosses on the thieves.[8]

Cynics like that Italian satirist had good reason to question how much "serving France" really meant serving Napoleon and self-interest. Many of Napoleon's internal innovations were transparent devices for protecting his own power. Napoleon invented a new technique for creating an aura of popular support for his policies: the *plebiscite*. A plebiscite was a national referendum on some issue: much like a ballot initiative in many U.S. states. Voters could either vote for or against it, but they were not given the opportunity to debate the issues involved. Napoleon first used the plebiscite to gain approval for the new Constitution of the Year VIII, which set up the consulship and eliminated the Directory. Like dictators to this day, Napoleon could not entrust such an important decision to the unguided opinions of the voters, so he made sure that the votes would be counted by his loyal agents to ensure that the results came out as he desired. His brother, Lucien, was minister of the interior and when he finished counting the ballots, 3,011,007 people had voted for the new constitution and only 1,562 against. This result undoubtedly pleased Napoleon much better than the real balloting would have, since the measure probably actually lost by a 2 to 1 margin. But the promulgated results were the official ones, and the minister of police, Joseph Fouché, promptly suppressed any criticism. Fouché proved very adept at squashing threats to the regime until he was dismissed in 1810. The combination of a ruthless police state and rigged elections became a staple of populist dictatorial regimes to the present. Subsequent plebiscites, on whether Napoleon should become First Consul for Life in 1802, or emperor in 1804, met with the same overwhelming support.

The Civil Code

The final pillar of Napoleon's internal policy is the one that he pointed to later in life as his greatest accomplishment: the Civil Code, promulgated in 1804 and renamed the Code Napoleon in 1807. Work on a comprehensive legal code had actually begun early in the revolutionary era. But it proved much harder to come up with rational laws than to rationalize the days of the week, months of the year, and weights and measures. The purpose of the Code was to bring uniformity to all forms of legal practice. Local customs were superseded by written statutes that owed much to the ideas of Roman law as well as to the Enlightenment. The first attempts at a legal code were deeply affected by the spirit of the first phase of the revolution. When work continued under Napoleon, the code moved in a more traditionalist direction. Nevertheless, one of the key merits of the Code was that it was now possible for any literate person to look up any point of law. That in itself was an important step in the direction of the rule of laws, not arbitrary justice. As the Napoleonic Empire expanded, the Civil Code spread too, so that it became the basis of the law not only in France but in Italy and western Germany as well.

However much the Civil Code rationalized the administration of justice according to Enlightenment principles, it also embodied the prejudices of Napoleon himself. Napoleon was particularly concerned about the authority of fathers in relation to children and wives. In the Civil Code, the legal position of women was much more restricted than it had been under the earlier revolutionary codes. For example, adulterous wives could be imprisoned at the will of their husbands, while wives could only divorce adulterous husbands if they brought their mistresses into the household. This provision embodied both Napoleon's dislike of female power and autonomy and his fears of dynastic legitimacy (perhaps heightened by the fact that he had not managed to conceive a son with his wife Josephine). In evaluating the relations between husbands and wives he observed, "the husband must possess the absolute power and right to say to his wife: 'Madam, you shall not go out, you shall not go to the theater, you shall not receive such and such a person: for the children you bear will be mine.'"[9] He saw little need for learning or reason among women. He claimed, "What we ask of education is not that girls should think, but that they should believe. . . . Care must be taken not to let them see any Latin, or other foreign languages."[10]

Napoleon's Glory Days: Victory in Battle

It is a sign of Napoleon's incredible energy that at the same time that he was restructuring the internal administration of France, he was also renewing the expansion of the French state in Europe. Napoleon's victory in Italy in 1797 had virtually guaranteed French control of Belgium and the Netherlands, the Rhineland, Switzerland, and the western half of northern Italy. Yet, when Napoleon became First Consul in 1799, France continued to face two quite different rivals, England and Austria, united in the Second Coalition. (The First Coalition had been made up of all of the countries allied against France in 1792. It unraveled by 1795 when the Prussians withdrew from it and formally ended with Austria's surrender at Campo Formio.) On strictly ideological grounds, one would expect that the rivalry between France and Austria would be the fiercest. But, in fact, the English proved to be the most consistent foe of the French throughout the revolutionary and Napoleonic era. The rivalry between France and England shows that the wars of the revolutionary era were not just about liberty vs. absolutism, but also about the balance of power between the two most prosperous states in Europe.

Almost immediately upon assuming power, Napoleon set about destroying the Second Coalition. An aggressive campaign in Italy reprised his successes of 1797. His victories at Marengo (June 1800) and Hohenlinden (December 1800) forced the Austrians to once again sue for peace. Marengo was particularly important because it solidified wavering support for Napoleon in France.

At the Treaty of Lunéville (1801), Austria confirmed French control over northern Italy, Belgium, and the Netherlands and had to tolerate the deposition of a Habsburg duke of Tuscany and his replacement with a supporter of France. With Austria eliminated, the English also sought peace. At the Treaty of Amiens (1802), France was forced to abandon its claims to Egypt and Malta, but otherwise was left in possession of its continental holdings.

By 1802, Napoleon could claim to have brought not only internal stability to France through the Concordat of 1801, but external peace as well. At the peak of his success, he used the opportunity for personal aggrandizement. When the legislative of the Consulate proposed extending Napoleon's consulship for an additional ten years (sort of like offering a successful football coach a contract extension), Napoleon quickly trumped them by proposing that he be granted lifetime tenure as First Consul. That accomplished, he rewrote the constitution to make himself the only person who could choose his deputies and his successor. Finally, he rewrote the constitution yet again to establish that the position of First Consul would now be known as Emperor of the French,

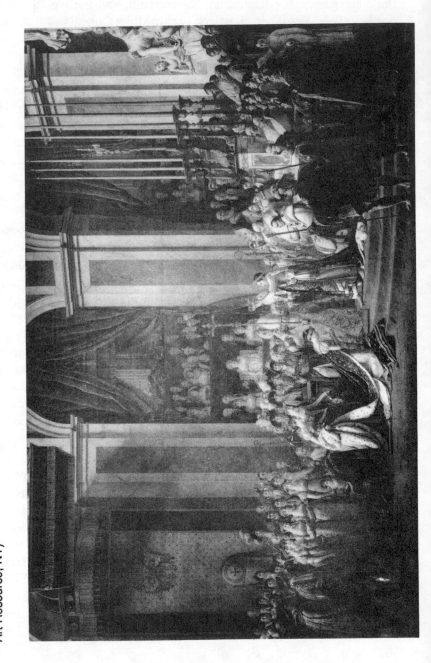

Jacques Louis David's painting of Emperor Napoleon crowning Empress Josephine in Notre-Dame, Paris (Giraudon/Art Resource, NY)

and it would be hereditary. On December 1, 1804, a great coronation ceremony was held in Paris. Pope Pius VII came personally to consecrate and officiate at the ceremony. But, at the moment of coronation, Napoleon deviated from the traditional royal coronation. He did not allow the pope to place the crown on his head, but instead picked the crown up from the cushion himself and placed it on his own head. It was as if he meant to say: I don't need any pope to verify that I am emperor, I did it all by myself!

As Emperor of the French, Napoleon shared many of the same ambitions as Louis XIV, king of France in the seventeenth century. The moment of international peace was now past. Napoleon was ready to extend France's and his own glory through war. Already in 1803, the peace with England had unraveled. All the while when he was planning his coronation as emperor, Napoleon was also preparing to launch an invasion of the island. He gathered a large invasion force and hundreds of transport boats on the French shore, but never could challenge the might of the British navy. When the main French fleet finally did confront the English at the Battle of Trafalgar (off the coast of Spain) in 1805, it suffered an overwhelming defeat. From that point on, Britain ruled the seas and there was nothing Napoleon could do about it.

So Napoleon tried a different tack. He rapidly marched his invasion force from the coast to confront a new Austrian army and a Russian army that had joined the British in the Third Coalition. Again, Napoleon demonstrated his brilliance as a military strategist. Victories at Ulm and Austerlitz (1805) once again ruined the Austrians and forced the Russians to retreat far into Poland. Now, a worried Prussia abandoned the neutrality it had followed for the past decade and tried to confront Napoleon's advance. At the Battles of Jena and Auerstädt (1806), the Prussians, too, were defeated, simultaneously shattering the last bastion of resistance to Napoleon in western Europe and the reputation of Prussian military superiority that had been fostered since the days of Frederick the Great.

In just a year's time, Napoleon had transformed the continent once again. The only continental power left to keep Napoleon from dictating terms to the entire continent was Russia. After an indecisive battle at Eylau and a major French victory at Friedland (both in 1807), the Russian czar, Alexander I (1777–1825), was willing to negotiate an armistice. During the negotiations, Alexander came under Napoleon's personal spell. At the Treaties of Tilsit (1807) he agreed to a much more sweeping settlement of the continental conflict than he had at first envisioned. Napoleon convinced him to divide the continent into two spheres of influence, leaving Alexander free to expand in the directions of Scandinavia and Turkey if he so desired, but giving France preeminence in Prussia and Austria, as well as Italy and the west. Alexander agreed to join Napoleon in opposing the English at all opportunities. Through sheer military genius, Napoleon had managed to impose his imperial vision on almost all of Europe. But then things started to go very wrong.

The Territorial Settlement

How would Napoleon take advantage of the opportunities victory had presented? Austria and Prussia were too big for Napoleon simply to incorporate into his system of satellite states, but both were coerced into becoming his formal "allies" and following his dictates in foreign policy. They had to tolerate the ways in which he redrew the maps of Germany and Italy. The most conspicuous changes were in Germany. Already in 1803, an "Imperial Recess" had reorganized the internal structure of the Holy Roman Empire, eliminating or secularizing virtually all of the states ruled by abbots, bishops, and archbishops and reducing the number of Free Imperial Cities to six. In all, 112 "countries" had disappeared, most of them going to the two largest German states, Prussia and Bavaria. Neither Prussia nor Austria had much lamented these changes.

Now, in 1806, the very existence of the Holy Roman Empire was in question. Most of the new states in western Germany were joined into the Confederation of the Rhine, completely dependent on Napoleon's dictates. The formation of the Confederation of the Rhine made the old structures of the Holy Roman Empire irrelevant. Responding to the inevitable, Francis II (1768–1835), Holy Roman Emperor, formally relinquished the title of emperor on August 9, 1806. After more than a millennium, the formal political framework that had governed Germany disappeared with hardly a whimper.

The second step Napoleon took in redrawing the map of Europe was to reintroduce hereditary monarchy into a number of conquered regions, but with a twist: the new countries would now be ruled by his friends and relatives. Prussian territories in northwest Germany were combined with a few other principalities into the Kingdom of Westphalia, which would be ruled by Napoleon's youngest brother Jerome (1784–1860). In Italy, various northern territories, including those that had made up the Cis-Alpine Republic, were joined into the Kingdom of Italy and given over to Napoleon's stepson Eugene (1781–1824). Meanwhile, the southern territories were consolidated into the Kingdom of Naples and given over to his oldest brother Joseph (1767–1844) in 1806. Nowhere were these imposed monarchs greeted with local enthusiasm, but the simple fact that they became subject to Napoleonic administration stripped away vestiges of the old order and made it impossible for a complete restoration after the carpetbagging monarchs left.

The Continental System and the "Spanish Ulcer"

The one part of the map of Europe that Napoleon could not affect was Britain. Britain occupied the same place in Napoleon's world as the Dutch Republic had in Louis XIV's: a nation of "shopkeepers" who dared to stand up to his greatness. Napoleon decided that the only way to deal with British naval superiority was to hit England in its pocketbook, by sealing off the Continent to all British trade. He imposed this continent-wide blockade, known as the Continental System, on the territories he had conquered and even convinced Alexander I to bring Russia into the system. "I intend to conquer the sea by the land," he claimed, and conjured an image of Britain's "vessels laden with useless wealth wandering around the high seas . . . seeking in vain from the Sound to the Hellespont for a port to open and receive them."[11]

But the system could never be as airtight as Napoleon envisioned. The Continental System put pressure on the British economy, but it also heightened economic problems on the Continent. Smugglers operated everywhere, including France, bringing in British materials that people considered essential for their lifestyles. Russia quickly abandoned its commitment to the system, but the greatest hole in the system was Spain and Portugal, which were soon to cause an even greater hole in Napoleon's entire imperial system.

In November 1807, a French army invaded Portugal in order to try to deprive England of its longest-standing trading partner in Europe. The king was forced to flee to Brazil and French troops occupied the country. In 1808, however, the British landed a small army of their own in Portugal, where they found support among the locals. They consolidated their position, while French troops reacted listlessly to their presence. While skirmishes were beginning in Portugal, Napoleon maneuvered a clever ploy to depose the king of Spain and have

Napoleon's brother Joseph installed as the new king. Spanish patriots began to resist the usurpation. French military governors were assassinated and groups of partisan fighters harassed French troops throughout the kingdom. When two French divisions were captured by Spanish troops supported by guerrillas at the town of Beilin in 1808, Napoleon received his first decisive setback in his continental war. What Napoleon had viewed as merely a sidelight to his main theaters of operations began to soak up more and more French troops. The British army in Portugal grew slowly and began to threaten the French directly, though initially fighting was confined to Portugal and the immediate Spanish border. By 1813, the French were driven across the Pyrenees back into France.

The implications of what people called Napoleon's "Spanish ulcer" were quickly recognized by other countries subjected to his rule. The Austrian minister Friedrich Gentz observed in 1808, "It is clear that luck is leaving Bonaparte and that his frightful career has reached its Zenith. Europe can be saved through Spain, if Europe still has the courage and determination to save itself."[12] At Gentz's urging, the Austrians launched yet another ill-fated attempt to defeat Napoleon and overthrow his system. At the Battle of Wagram (1809), the Austrians lost for the fourth straight time to Napoleon's military genius and had to accept another humiliating peace treaty. The only observable result of Austria's efforts was that the old set of ministers was fired and a new chief minister put in place, Clemens von Metternich (1773–1859).

Napoleon's Fall

By this time, Napoleon had to rely on his police state to keep order in France. The general mood of the people of France was for peace at almost any cost. France was in deep economic difficulties from the drain of continuing warfare, not to mention the psychological and demographic toll of so many sons of France dying on the battlefields of Europe. But Napoleon was hatching even more grandiose plans for his empire. Unable to strike at England, he decided that he must conquer the one remaining power that could threaten him on the Continent: Russia. He assembled an army of unprecedented size, 600,000 men. On June 25, 1812, he marched this Grand Army into Russia. This time, Napoleon's genius for military victory deserted him. He advanced rapidly, but was unable to destroy the smaller Russian army that confronted him. When he arrived at Moscow on September 14, he did not cause Russia's surrender, as he had hoped, but instead encountered a series of fires that had been deliberately set and destroyed the city. Winter was approaching and it was not clear where the French army could go. Russian forces harassed the French army as it retreated through devastated countryside back to the Polish border, where it could find food and shelter. Most did not make it. Of the 600,000 who set out in June, less than 40,000 regrouped in Polish territory by the end of December. The crisis of the Napoleonic Empire was at hand.

Napoleon rushed back to Paris ahead of his army. There were threats of a coup and he had to act quickly to forestall the spread of the bad news and recruit a new army. Suddenly, the forces of opposition to Napoleon began to surge together. For the first time Russia, Austria, and Prussia joined together into a coalition against France. They finally defeated him in battle at the Battle of Leipzig (1813) and now pushed the war effort onto French soil. This time, there was no patriotic uprising against the invading armies. The British general Wellington reported from southern France that "all except the officials are sick of Bonaparte, because there is no prospect of peace with him."[13] The Coalition armies occupied Paris and Napoleon was sent into exile on the island of Elba in the Mediterranean.

But even before the allies could decide how to deal with conquered France, Napoleon was back. Again, he was greeted with patriotic enthusiasm by the people in the regions he passed through. He was able to assemble yet another army. This time, however, the coalition remained steadfast. At the Battle of Waterloo, 1815, Napoleon met his Waterloo. This time, the allies made sure that Napoleon could cause no more trouble. They exiled him to a nearly deserted island in the South Atlantic, where he remained, writing his memoirs, until he died in 1821.

The International Impact of Napoleon

It is easy to view Napoleon's authoritarian streak and compulsion to conquer as a rejection of the principles of the French Revolution, yet Napoleon was also part of the process by which the French Revolution became a worldwide phenomenon. As dramatic as the events of the French Revolution were in the first five years, their European-wide impact was rather restricted. It was business as usual in those regions far removed from the French border. For instance, the period between the formation of the National Assembly and the end of the Thermidorian

Reaction, 1792 to 1795, is exactly the period when Austria, Prussia, and Russia twice sat around negotiating tables and decided how they wanted to carve up Poland. Napoleon changed all that. He harnessed the evangelical spirit of the revolutionaries, their desire to change the world, and turned it into a genuine threat to the existence of the old order. The German philosopher George William Hegel (1770–1831) called Napoleon "history on horseback" to describe how profoundly he changed the rules by which politics and society operated.

The only way that the traditional powers of Europe could compete with Napoleon's power was to make adjustments within their own societies that would enable them to tap the same sources of success. Certain features of the French regime had to be emulated in order to avoid becoming mere subjects of the French. The first feature of the French that people tried to harness was the patriotic nationalism that had mobilized thousands to fight and die for the idea of France. The French revolutionary anthem, the "Marseillaise," began with the line "Forward, children of the homeland," because the French army was a citizen army, not an army recruited from the rootless and unemployed of the country. Perhaps the children of other homelands could be mobilized too, as seemed to be happening in Spain.

The most conspicuous patriotic response to Napoleon's successes came from the educated civil servants of Germany. The collapse of Prussia unleashed feelings of anger and shame, which were perfectly captured in a series of lectures by the philosophy professor Johann Gottlieb Fichte (1762–1815) in 1807. The title of the lectures emphasized the new thinking now in existence in Germany; it was *Addresses to the German Nation.* In the *Addresses,* he claimed, "we are conquered, the clash of weapons is ended. If we will it, a new struggle of principles, of morals, of character now begins."[14] According to German patriots, who listened avidly to Fichte, the only way to liberate Germany from French dominance was through a complete overhaul of society and personal moral rejuvenation. The most aggressive anti-Napoleon agitators organized themselves into a *Tugendbund* (Virtue League) and a *Turnverein* (Gymnastics Association) as part of the project of rebuilding German strength through moral regeneration.

The explicit loyalty of these German patriots was to the abstract notion of "Germany," which did not exist in any real political sense. So, pragmatically, most focused on regenerating Prussia, traditionally the strongest and most cosmopolitan German-speaking state. The notions of reform spread widely within Prussian administration, most notably under the minister Heinrich Freiherr zu Stein (1757–1831). He thoroughly reorganized the Prussian bureaucracy in order to rationalize the arbitrary authority of local nobles and officials. Above all, he realized that if Prussia were to compete with France, it would have to follow the French lead and abolish feudalism, in the form of hereditary serfdom, which was done in an edict in 1807. Napoleon himself became concerned enough about Stein's reorganization of Prussia that he strong-armed the Prussian King Frederick William III into dismissing him in 1808. Meanwhile, the army was also restructured along modern principles under the guidance of two of Stein's supporters, Neidthardt von Gneisenau and Gerhard von Scharnhorst. Though the reforms had not had much time to take root before the uprising against Napoleon in 1813, the foundation for the revival of Prussian military power was laid, on principles that more closely resembled Napoleon's than Frederick the Great's.

There were other, though less dramatic, outpourings of patriotic sentiments in other parts of Europe. In Italy, the *Carbonari* (Good Cousins) emerged as an anti-Napoleonic, prodemocratic secret society in 1806. Even Austria began to mobilize its people to resist Napoleon. It established a national militia, called the *Landwehr*, designed to supplement the regular army with a citizen army like the French. Since the Habsburgs could no longer call themselves Holy Roman Emperors, they focused on unifying their disparate territories into a single state. Already in 1804, Francis II had declared himself "hereditary Emperor of Austria," which he intended to include all of the traditional Habsburg domains. Schoolbooks and official propaganda now began to emphasize the collective history of these regions, though with limited success. Aside from the destruction of the countryside in 1812, Russia remained untouched by the revolutionary tide and underwent no internal changes. Yet Napoleon's conquests changed the ideological equation of Europe by making Russia a permanent participant in European politics.

The Congress of Vienna and the End of the Napoleonic Era

With the defeat of Napoleon, the shape of Europe was not supposed to be determined by the will of the people, but by old-fashioned diplomacy of favorite ministers and kings. The Congress of Vienna convened in

1815 to work out the details. Despite, or probably because of, the fear of Napoleon, the victors did not want to impose too punitive a settlement on France and so they allowed France to remain within its pre-1790 boundaries. Their main goal was to ensure a restoration of the Bourbon family as kings. Louis XVII, son of Louis XVI and Marie Antoinette, had died in prison in 1795. His uncle Louis XVIII (1755–1824) had already been recognized as king during the interim between Napoleon's exile to Elba and his return to Waterloo.

Though all of the powers participated in creating a settlement, three personalities dominated: the French foreign minister Talleyrand, who had adeptly transferred his allegiance from Napoleon and had, in fact, been the main instigator for the restoration of Louis XVIII; the czar of Russia, Alexander I; and the chief minister of Austria, Metternich. Talleyrand's goals were entirely pragmatic: to get the most advantageous deal for France that he could, given that France had lost. Alexander's goals were idealistic and impractical. He directed his energy toward getting the major powers to agree to base all diplomatic relations on Christian principles of charity and justice. All major European powers except England eventually signed this "Holy Alliance," though their motives for doing so varied. The third main protagonist of the Congress of Vienna, Metternich, was more ideological than Talleyrand, but more practical than Alexander. His goal was to make Europe safe for aristocrats and monarchs given the dramatic changes wrought by the French Revolution. For the next generation, his name was indelibly associated with "reaction," the effort to stamp out constitutional reforms in any form.

In the long run, the Congress of Vienna failed to eradicate the ideas of the French Revolution from European soil. The transformations wrought by the twin revolutions, the industrial and the French, made change irresistible. But in its more limited horizon, the settlement of the Napoleonic threat proved a great success. Almost four decades would pass before there was another war between the major European powers. Nineteenth-century Europe was a society confident of its abilities and prepared to harness the advantages that a rational world had given it.

Profile: Beethoven and the Arts in the Napoleonic Era

One of the greatest transitions in European cultural history and one of the notable stories of the relationship between art and politics center

Europe after the Congress of Vienna (Copyright: Hammond World Atlas Corporation, NJ, Lic. No. 12504) around a single piece of music: Ludwig van Beethoven's Symphony No. 3 in E-flat Major. In European cultural history, Beethoven's Third Symphony marks the moment when the full expressive power of the sonata form for orchestras was worked out. The modern idea of the symphony was born. A number of impressive symphonies had been written in the classical style by masters such as Joseph Haydn (1732–1809) and Wolfgang Amadeus Mozart (1756–1791), but none had managed to achieve the sheer emotional impact that Beethoven was able to create. The period between the creation of Beethoven's Third and Seventh Symphonies, roughly from 1803 to 1812, was the heyday of Beethoven's "heroic style," so called because of the emotional content of so many of his works but also because of the larger scale and lasting quality of that body of work.

Today, the Third Symphony has the nickname "Eroica," a sign of how it introduced the heroic style. But, when first conceived, Beethoven gave it a different name: "Bonaparte." According to legend, Beethoven had inscribed the work to Napoleon. But when he heard that Napoleon had had himself proclaimed emperor, he flew into a rage and exclaimed, "Is he then, too, nothing more than an ordinary human being? Now he, too, will trample on all the rights of man and indulge only his ambition. He will exalt himself above all others, become a tyrant!"[15] With that, he ripped out the dedication and became an implacable foe of Napoleon. Thus, the great artist and the great military man seemed briefly to be thinking along the same lines about the future of humanity, only to veer off in entirely different directions.

It is indeed true that Beethoven initially dedicated his Third Symphony to Napoleon. Beethoven felt himself to be a kindred spirit of the young Napoleon in his own field. He had the same overwhelming confidence in his own genius that he was ready to break the bounds that restricted ordinary mortals. Later in life, when he had turned against Napoleon, he was to claim, "It's a pity that I do not understand the art of war as well as I do the art of music or I would conquer him!"[16]—suggesting that his own musical genius was even greater than Napoleon's military genius. The kindred spirit extended to the fact that both achieved their standing by transcending their rather ordinary background. They were both examples of the career achieved by talent.

Like Mozart, Beethoven came from a musical family. He was the grandson of a *Kapellmeister* at the court of the Elector of Cologne in Bonn. His father had also tried to attain the status of Kapellmeister, but only managed to eke out a living as a music teacher and singer. Beethoven showed early talent as a pianist, but his father, through either incompetence or an unconscious need to remain superior to his son, did not develop his son's talents as an improviser as Mozart's father had. Once, when he found Beethoven playing without a musical score in front of him, he exclaimed, "What silly trash are you scraping away at now? You know that I can't bear that; scrape according to the notes; otherwise your scraping won't be of much use."[17]

When Beethoven went in 1792 from provincial Bonn to Vienna, the music capital of Europe, he was determined to make his mark on the musical world on his own terms. Though Beethoven quickly won respect from aristocratic patrons for his virtuosity on the piano and his early compositions, he also developed a reputation for being arrogant. His moodiness was no doubt increased by the fact that he was slowly losing his hearing. He became aware of the condition by 1801, though total deafness did not take hold until 1815.

As Beethoven developed his revolutionary heroic style, traditional musicians balked at it. Some contemporaries viewed the Third Symphony as "too long, elaborate, incomprehensible, and much too noisy."[18] A music reviewer divided listeners into three groups: those who were outraged by "an untamed and unsuccessful striving after singularity"; those who found many beautiful passages, but did not think the symphony measured up to Beethoven's previous two because it was simply too long; and a small group of Beethoven's "particular friends" who argued that "this is the true style for high-class music, and if it does not please now, it is because the public is not cultured enough artistically to grasp all these lofty beauties; after a few thousand years have passed it will not fail of its effect."[19] The third group eventually won out. It did not take a few thousand, but just a couple of years before the heroic style equaled the classical style of Mozart and Haydn in popularity. When Beethoven conducted his Seventh Symphony, which was in much the same style as the Third, in 1813, it was frequently interrupted by spontaneous ovations from the audience. The case of Beethoven once again seemed to confirm the image of the artistic genius, misunderstood by contemporaries, who eventually triumphs over the ignorance of critics.

Important Dates

1768	French acquisition of Corsica
1793	Napoleon participates in capture of Toulon

1795	Napoleon helps suppress Paris uprising; annexation of Belgium to France
1796–1797	Napoleon's campaign in Italy dislodges Austrians
1798	Napoleon's campaign in Egypt
1799	Coup d'état of 18 Brumaire
1800	Napoleon's second campaign in Italy
1801	Concordat with Pope; peace of Luneville ends Second Coalition
1802	Creation of Legion of Honor; Napoleon named First Consul for Life
1803	War with Britain renewed; Imperial Recess in Germany; Beethoven composes his Third Symphony, initially dedicated to Napoleon
1804	Napoleon proclaimed Emperor of the French; promulgation of Civil Code
1805	Battle of Trafalgar; battle of Austerlitz
1806	Battles of Jena and Auerstädt; formation of Confederation of the Rhine; dissolution of the Holy Roman Empire; foundation of *Carbonari* in Italy
1807	Treaties of Tilsit; beginning of Continental System; beginning of campaigns in Spain; Fichte presents *Addresses to the German Nation*; Stein's ministry in Prussia
1808	Dismissal of Stein in Prussia
1812	French invasion of Russia
1813	Battle of Leipzig
1815	Napoleon finally defeated at Waterloo; Congress of Vienna

Further Reading

Louis Bergeron, *France under Napoleon* trans. R.R. Palmer (Princeton, 1981)

Jeremy Black, *British Foreign Policy in an Age of Revolutions, 1783–1793* (Cambridge, 1994)

T.C.W. Blanning, *Reform and Revolution in Mainz* (Cambridge, 1974)

T.C.W. Blanning, *The French Revolution in Germany: Occupation and Resistance in the Rhineland, 1792–1802* (Oxford, 1983)

Norman Hampson, *The Perfidy of Albion: French Perceptions of England During the Revolution* (New York, 1998)

David Wyn Jones, *The Life of Beethoven* (Cambridge, 1998)

Georges Lefebvre, *Napoleon* trans. J.E. Anderson and Henry F. Stockhold (New York, 1969)

Martyn Lyons, *France under the Directory* (Cambridge, 1975)

Martyn Lyons, *Napoleon Bonaparte and the Legacy of the French Revolution* (New York, 1994)

Felix Markham, *Napoleon* (New York, 1966)

Rory Muir, *Britain and the Defeat of Napoleon, 1807–1815* (New Haven, 1996)

Rory Muir, *Tactics and Experience of Battle in the Age of Napoleon* (New Haven, 1998)

Marilyn Morris, *The British Monarchy and the French Revolution* (New Haven, 1998)

Brendan Simms, *The Impact of Napoleon: Prussian High Politics, Foreign Policy and the Crisis of the Executive, 1797–1806* (Cambridge, 1997)

Isser Woloch, *Jacobin Legacy: The Democratic Movement under the Directory* (Princeton, 1970)

Glossary

The following are terms that appear in this text. They are included in this glossary either because they are based on foreign words or because they mean something different in the early modern period than they do today. For information on specific people, places, events, or themes (e.g. Versailles, War of the Austrian Succession, or Baroque), use the index to locate the passages in the text that cover the topic.

Absolutism. This term was coined by historians to describe the efforts of early modern kings to exert influence over all aspects of their states. The most striking example of an *absolutist king* was Louis XIV of France. He and his ministers assumed that the king literally embodied the whole of the state. His example was followed by Peter I of Russia, among many others. One difference between an early modern *absolutist government* and a twentieth-century dictatorship is that *absolutist kings* were recognized as legitimate authority by their subjects. Another difference is that they did not possess the resources to completely dominate their countries.

Bourgeois/Bourgeoisie. In the early modern era, the term *bourgeois* designated those people who possessed full citizenship in an urban community. Sometimes the term was used in an even more restrictive way, to designate the most prominent financiers and merchants in a city. Since wealthy townsmen often owned agricultural land worked by peasants, mines, or factories, the term *bourgeois* was used by the beginning of the nineteenth century as a synonym for *capitalist* or *middle class*.

Citizen. For most of the early modern era, this term designated legally privileged residents of a *town* or *city* who were subject to and protected by that town's laws. During the course of the eighteenth century, the term *citizen* was more broadly applied in political writings to refer to legally privileged residents of a country or nation. In the course of the French Revolution, the word *citizen* was used to denote anyone belonging to the nation, to replace the words *lord* and *subject*.

Community/Commune. This term referred primarily to the legally constituted governing body of a town, village, or parish. It was the equivalent of local government. It did not acquire its modern sense of *neighborhood* until the nineteenth century.

Dynastic succession. The principle of *dynastic succession* determined who would become the ruler of a territory upon the death of the current ruler. There was broad agreement in Europe that succession should go to the oldest son of the current ruler if possible. In the absence of a son, different territories had different rules for determining who came first in line, either an eldest daughter or a brother of the current ruler.

Estate/Order/Stand. These terms describe the main social groupings in early modern society. Instead of basing social categories primarily on wealth, social commentators grouped people by public functions and defined legal privileges and immunities. The *first estate* was the clergy, the *second estate*, the nobility, and the *third estate*, the commons. The *third estate* comprised the bulk of the population.

Family/Household/Kin. These interrelated terms refer to different ways of conceiving the key relationships for most individuals in the early modern era. *Kinship* is the primary link between people with common ancestors. *Household* is the primary unit of shared production and consumption, which often coincided with the nuclear family, but sometimes also included servants or apprentices and additional *kin*. *Family* is an in-between term that captures the degree of emotional attachment between members of the group.

Feudalism. This term was first used as a legal term to describe the economic relationship between lords who owned and governed land and the peasants who were their tenants and subjects. By the end of the eighteenth century, *feudalism* came to refer to the entire system of privileges and noble dominance in society. *Feudalism* gained currency as a social definition when it was "abolished" in the first year of the French Revolution.

Guild. *Guilds* were the legal corporations that regulated most industries in the towns for much of the early modern era. Members of a *guild* had a legal monopoly on the production and sale of specific goods within a town, and membership was carefully controlled. *Guilds* acted both as political representatives of the members and as economic regulators of the market.

Junkers. This is the name given to the distinctive noblemen of eastern Germany, especially in Brandenburg-Prussia. The *Junkers* supported their territorial rulers in exchange for a particularly exploitative seigneurial relationship with the peasants who were their tenants and subjects. This was the basis of their economic and political position.

Lord. This is the generic term for the actual owner of property in the seigneurial system or a specific right in the system of privilege. Though most *lords* were noble, the actual basis of *lordship* could come from ownership of distinct pieces of property, so church institutions and even towns sometimes acted as *lords*.

Natural Philosophy. This was the term used for the study of natural phenomena. The term *natural philosophy* was replaced by the modern term *natural science* in the nineteenth century. Experts in *natural philosophy* were known as *virtuosi* or *savants*, the forerunners of modern scientists.

Nobility/Aristocracy. The *nobility*, or *aristocracy*, was the ruling class in most of early modern Europe. *Nobility* was a legal status possessing numerous privileges, passed on through inheritance. It carried with it the obligations to *live nobly*, by collecting rents from landholdings and spending a great deal on lavish display. Almost all European nobles depended on their seigneurial control over the land for economic and social dominance.

Parlement. The *parlements* were law courts in the major cities and provinces of France, composed of judges from important local families. They were responsible for registering laws that had been promulgated by the king and his ministers. They also had the privilege of remonstrating with the king if new laws went against earlier legal precedent. Throughout the early modern period, the most powerful *parlements*, like the one in Paris, tried to influence legislation by remonstrating with the king if they disapproved of new laws.

Parliament/Estates General/Diet. These terms designated the official gathering of the principal stakeholders in a territory designed to advise the ruler how to deal with some pressing issue. The composition of these official bodies varied from one territory to another, but most included representatives from the three *estates*. Some bodies, like the English *Parliament*, were able to exert a great deal of practical influence over policy by retaining for themselves the right to grant and collect taxes. Others, like the Brandenburg *Diet*, simply agreed to whatever the ruler asked.

Peasant. *Peasants* were farmers in an early modern rural community. In contrast to modern farmers, *peasant households* usually tried to produce enough of a variety of products for family subsistence before committing produce to the open market. *Peasants* lived in rural villages, and decisions on crops, land use, and allocation of resources were often regulated by local village government.

Plebiscite. This term denotes a system for voting yes or no on a proposition in order to determine if it should become law. It was used by Napoleon Bonaparte as a political strategy to allow him to claim that the people of France supported his policies.

Principality. This is the generic name for the different kinds of territories ruled by individuals in the early modern era. The term is derived from *prince*, meaning a noble ruler rather than the son of the king. The term *principality* implied that the primary cohesiveness of the territory comes from its ruler, the *prince*; in contrast, the modern words *country* and *nation* imply that the primary cohesiveness of a territory come from the people who live there.

Privilege. A *privilege* is something that an individual or corporation could lay claim to as a result of social status or ownership of property. Exemption from taxation was a *privilege* that went with noble status in many countries; control over the marketing of cloth was a *privilege* owned by guilds in many towns. *Privileges* remained in force as long as people exercised them, so people were generally careful to be sure that their own *privileges* were not infringed by others and to seek redress if they were.

Public and Private Spheres. At the beginning of the early modern era, the distinction between *public* and *private* was between different estates or orders. The clergy and nobility had *public* roles; only they could formulate government policy, so only they had a role in *public opinion*. The third estate was involved strictly in *private* business. In the course of the early modern era, the range of people responsible for *public opinion* broadened. At the same time, business in its modern sense became a *public* affair too. The *private sphere* no longer referred to work, but rather to the home where the domestic tranquility of the family prevailed.

Republic. For most of the early modern era, a *republic* was an unusual form of government, based on ancient Greek ideals, in which some number of the inhabitants of the territory made and enforced the laws for the territory. The city-state of Venice was one well-known example of a *republic*. Republics were not modern democracies, because the circle of people who could make laws and take part in government was usually limited.

Right. Initially in the early modern era, *rights* were the exercise of privileges. A lord had the *right* to collect taxes; a town had the *right* to levy a toll on travelers who passed through its gates. By the eighteenth century, *rights* came to be viewed as inherent possessions of individuals resident in a territory, such as the *right* to freedom of speech. These *rights* could not be transgressed by the government of that territory.

Sans-culottes. This term referred to French workers "without knee-breeches." It became a politically charged term during the French Revolution, when it denoted the artisans and ordinary working people of Paris who were politically active.

Seigneur/Seigneurie/Seigneurialism. *Seigneurialism* is the system of ownership over the land in the early modern era. The unit of land in which *seigneurial* control was exercised was called the *seigneurie* (in some areas called the *estate* or *domain*). The person who owned the *seigneurie* was called the *seigneur* (in some areas called the *lord*). Most *seigneurs* were nobles, but any privileged individual or corporation, such as a parish or town, could be a *seigneur*.

State. The *state* is a term that became increasingly common beginning in the sixteenth century to describe the territorial basis of rulership. It was based on the idea that rule over a territory meant having sovereign (unchallenged) authority within that territory. The concept of the *state* made it possible to think of diplomatic relations as relations between *countries*, not just of disputes between two kings.

Taille. This was the principal tax levied in France to support the king's policies. Because of the system of privilege, nobles and the church were exempt from the *taille*.

Notes

Notes to Chapter One:

1. Cited in C.V. Wedgwood, *A Coffin for King Charles* (New York: Time Life Books, 1966), pp. 151, 181.

2. Cited in Wedgwood, p. 2.

3. Wedgwood, p. 2.

Notes to Chapter Two:

1. Michel de Montaigne, *The Complete Essays of Montaigne*, trans. Donald Frame (Stanford: Stanford University Press, 1965), p. 615.

2. Famianus Strada, *De Bello Belgico. The History of the Low-Country Warres*, trans. Robert Stapylton (London: Humphrey Moseley, 1650), p. 4.

3. Montaigne, *The Complete Essays of Montaigne*, p. 324.

4. Fynes Moryson, *Shakespeare's Europe: A Survey of the Condition of Europe at the End of the 16th Century*, ed. Charles Hughes (New York: Benjamin Blom, 1967), p. 477.

5. Fynes Moryson, *The Itinerary of Fynes Moryson*, 4 vols. (Glasgow: University Press, 1907), vol. 4, pp. 136–137.

6. Moryson, *Shakespeare's Europe*, pp. 421, 119.

7. Moryson, *Itinerary*, 4:56.

8. Moryson, *Shakespeare's Europe*, p. 275.

9. Ibid., p. 270.

10. Ibid., p. 358.

11. Cited in Thomas A. Brady, *Turning Swiss: Cities and Empire 1450–1550* (Cambridge: Cambridge University Press, 1985), p. 35.

12. Moryson, *Shakespeare's Europe*, p. 175.

13. Ibid., p. 79.

14. Cited in Norman Davies, *God's Playground: A History of Poland*, vol. 1 (New York: Columbia University Press, 1984), p. 321.

15. Moryson, *Shakespeare's Europe*, p. 394.

16. Cited in Davies, p. 160.

17. Moryson, *Shakespeare's Europe*, pp. 10–12.

Notes to Chapter Three

1. Cited in Roland Mousnier, *The Institutions of France under the Absolute Monarchy, 1598–1789* (Chicago: University of Chicago Press, 1979), pp. 5–6.

2. Cited in John Theibault, *German Villages in Crisis: Rural Life in Hesse-Kassel and the Thirty Years War, 1580–1720* (Atlantic Highlands, NJ: Humanities Press, 1995), p. 101.

3. Cited in Theibault, p. 94.

4. Cited in Richard Bonney, *The European Dynastic State, 1494–1660* (Oxford: Oxford University Press, 1991), p. 361.

5. Cited in Bonny, p. 362.

6. Cited in Henry Kamen, *The Iron Century, 1550–1650* (New York: Praeger Publishers, 1971), p. 140.

7. Cited in W.H. Bruford, *Germany in the Eighteenth Century: The Social Background of the Literary Revival* (Cambridge: Cambridge University Press, 1971), p. 121.

8. Cited in Mack Walker, *German Home Towns: Community, State, and General Estate, 1648–1871* (Ithaca: Cornell University Press, 1971), p. 106.

9. Cited in Benedict Anderson, *Imagined Communities* (New York: Verso Press, 1991), p. 20.

Notes to Chapter Four

1. René Descartes, *Discourse on Method, Optics, Geometry, and Meteorology*, trans. Paul Olscamp (Indianapolis: Bobbs-Merrill, 1965), p. 4.

2. Cited in Hiram Haydn, ed., *The Portable Elizabethan Reader* (New York: Penguin Books, 1981), p. 136.

3. Cited in E.M.W. Tillyard, *The Elizabethan World Picture* (New York: Vintage Books, 1967), p. 9.

4. Cited in Keith Thomas, *Religion and the Decline of Magic* (New York: Charles Scribner's Sons, 1971), p. 331.

5. Ibid., p. 325.

6. Cited in Haydn, p. 133.

7. John Donne, *The Complete Poetry and Selected Prose of John Donne*, ed. Charles Coffin (New York: Modern Library, 1952), p. 417.

8. Cited in Olwen Hufton, *The Prospect Before Her: A History of Women in Western Europe* (New York: Knopf, 1996), p. 39.

9. Cited in Hufton, pp. 32–33.

10. Martin Luther, *Small Catechism* (Philadelphia, 1919), p. 29.

11. Desiderius Erasmus and Martin Luther, *Discourse on Free Will*, ed. Ernst Winter (New York: Frederick Ungar, 1980), p. 22.

12. Michel de Montaigne *The Complete Essays of Montaigne* trans. Donald M. Frame (Stanford, CA: Stanford University Press, 1965), p. 69.

13. Luther, p. 29.

14. Michel de Montaigne, "On Repentence," cited in Haydn, p. 159.

15. Erasmus and Luther, p. 22.

16. Luther, p. 19.

17. Jean Calvin, *On God and Political Duty*, ed. John McNeil (Indianapolis: Bobbs-Merrill, 1956), p. 7.

18. Cited in Paul Seaver, *Wallington's World: A Puritan Artisan in Seventeenth-Century London* (Stanford: Stanford University Press, 1985), p. 17.

19. Teresa of Avila, *The Life of Saint Teresa of Avila by Herself*, trans. J.M. Cohen (New York: Penguin Books, 1957), pp. 33–34.

20. Cited in Seaver, p. 20.

21. Christopher Marlowe, *Doctor Faustus* (New York: New American Library, 1969), p. 26.

22. Cited in Thomas, p. 520.

23. Ibid., pp. 535–546.

24. Cited in Donne, p. 428.

25. Cited in Marie Boas Hall, *The Scientific Renaissance, 1450–1630* (New York: Harper and Row, 1962), p. 330.

26. Cited in John Carey, ed., *Eyewitness to Science* (Cambridge: Harvard University Press, 1995), pp. 17–21.

Notes to Chapter Five

1. Cited in Geoffrey Parker, *The Thirty Years' War* (London: Routledge and Kegan Paul, 1984), p. 55.

2. Cited in A. Lloyd Moote, *Louis XIII: The Just* (Berkeley: University of California Press, 1989) p. 177.

3. Cited in Moote, p. 180.

4. Cited in John Theibault, "The Rhetoric of Death and Destruction in the Thirty Years' War," *Journal of Social History* 27:2 (1993): 271.

5. Cited in Theibault, p. 281.

6. Cited in Georges Pages, *The Thirty Years War, 1618–1648*, trans. David Maland and John Hooper (New York: Harper and Row, 1970), p. 108.

Notes to Chapter Six

1. James VI and I, *Political Writings*, ed. Johann Sommerville (Cambridge: Cambridge University Press, 1994), p. 1.

2. James VI and I, pp. 21–22.

3. Cited in Christopher Hill, *Oliver Cromwell and the English Revolution* (New York: Dial Press, 1970), p. 43.

4. Cited in Maurish Ashley, *England in the Seventeenth Century* (Middlesex: Penguin Books, 1967), p. 71.

5. Cited in Ashley, p. 75.

6. Cited in Ashley, p. 77.

7. Cited in Christopher Hibbert, *Charles I* (New York: Harper and Row, 1968), p. 181.

8. Cited in Ashley, p. 81.

9. Cited in Hibbert, p. 185.

10. Cited in C.V. Wedgwood, *A Coffin for King Charles* (New York: Time Life Books, 1966), pp. 68, 214.

11. Cited in Hibbert, p. 203.

12. Cited in Hibbert, p. 252.

13. Cited in Wedgwood, p. 127.

14. Cited in Ashley, p. 99.

15. Cited in Phyllis Mack, *Visionary Women: Ecstatic Prophecy in Seventeenth-Century England* (Berkeley: University of California Press, 1992), pp. 127–128.

16. Cited in Mack, p. 132.

17. Cited in A.N. Wilson, *The Life of John Milton* (New York: Oxford University Press, 1984), p. 125.

18. John Milton, *Areopagitica and Of Education*, ed. George Sabine (Arlington Heights, TX: Harlan Davidson, 1951), p. 6.

19. Cited in Wilson, p. 162.

20. John Milton, "Paradise Lost, " Book 1, in *Paradise Lost and Other Poems*, ed. Maurice Kelley (New York: Walter J. Black, 1943), p. 109.

21. Thomas Hobbes, *Leviathan* (New York: Penguin Books, 1980), p. 229.

22. Cited in Ashley, p. 107.

23. Cited in Wilson, p. 222.

Notes to Chapter Seven

1. Cited in Philippe Erlanger, *Louis XIV*, trans. Stephen Cox (London: Weidenfeld and Nicolson, 1970), p. 65.

2. Cited in Pierre Goubert, *Louis XIV and Twenty Million Frenchmen*, trans. Anne Carter (New York: Vintage Books, 1970), p. 63.

3. Cited in Goubert, p. 64.

4. Cited in Erlanger, pp. 141, 151.

5. Cited in Erlanger, p. 147.

6. Cited in Erlanger, p. 153.

7. Cited in Goubert, pp. 65–66.

8. Cited in Erlanger, p. 162.

9. Cited in Goubert, p. 63.

10. Cited in Goubert, p. 68.

11. Cited in Goubert, p. 87.

12. Cited in W.H. Lewis, *The Splendid Century: Life in the France of Louis XIV* (New York: Morrow Quill Paperbacks, 1978), p. 30.

13. Cited in Inès Murat, *Colbert*, trans. Robert Francis Cook and Jeannie Van Asselt (Charlottesville: University Press of Virginia, 1984), p. 109.

14. Cited in Murat, pp. 89–90.

15. Cited in Guy Walton, *Louis XIV's Versailles* (Chicago: University of Chicago Press, 1986), p. 60.

16. Cited in Walton, p. 53.

17. Cited in Walton, p. 43.

18. Cited in Nicole Aronson, *Mademoiselle de Scudéry* (Boston: Twayne, 1978), pp. 109, 50.

19. Cited in Stirling Haig, *Madame de Lafayette* (New York: Twayne, 1970), pp. 46, 50.

20. Cited in Claude Abraham, *Pierre Corneille* (New York: Twayne), pp. 30–31.

21. Cited in Geoffrey Brereton, *Jean Racine* (London: Cassell, 1951), p. 143.

22. Cited in Erlanger, p. 143.

23. Cited in Henry Trollope, *The Life of Molière* (London: Archibald Constable, 1905), p. 491.

24. Cited in Erlanger, p. 168.

25. Cited in Jeanne A. Ojala and William T. Ojala, *Madame de Sévigné: A Seventeenth-Century Life* (New York: Berg, 1990), p. 58.

26. Cited in Walton, p. 181.

27. Cited in Walton, p. 214.

Notes to Chapter Eight

1. Cited in José Antonio Maravall, *Culture of the Baroque: Analysis of a Historical Structure*, trans. Terry Cochran (Minneapolis: University of Minnesota Press, 1983), p. 71.

2. Ibid., p. 119.

3. Cited in Jonathan Brown and J.H. Elliott, *A Palace for a King: The Buen Retiro and the Court of Philip IV* (New Haven: Yale University Press, 1986), p. 7.

4. Cited in Walter Starkie, Introduction to Miguel de Cervantes Saavedra, *Don Quixote of La Mancha*, trans. Walter Starkie (New York: New American Library, 1979), p. 22.

5. Cited in Margaret Wilson, *Spanish Drama of the Golden Age* (Oxford: Pergamon Press, 1969), p. 20.

6. Cited in Starkie, p. 26.

7. Miguel de Cervantes Saavedra, *Don Quixote of La Mancha*, trans. Walter Starkie (New York: New American Library, 1979), p. 59.

8. Ibid., p. 173.

9. Cited in Starkie, p. 27.

10. Cited in Starkie, p. 33.

11. Cited in Wilson, p. 39.

12. Cited in Wilson, p. 31.

13. Lope de Vega, "Fuenteovejuna, " in Angel Flores, ed., *Masterpieces of the Spanish Golden Age* (New York: Rinehart, 1957), pp. 235–286.

14. Cited in Christopher White, *Rubens and His World* (New York: Viking Press, 1968), pp. 67, 81. Emphasis added.

15. Cited in White, p. 47.

16. Cited in Simon Schama, *The Embarrassment of Riches: An Interpretation of Dutch Culture in the Golden Age* (Berkeley: University of California Press, 1988), p. 303.

17. Tirso de Molina, *The Trickster of Seville and the Guest of Stone*, in Flores, pp. 287–367.

Notes to Chapter Nine

1. Cited in Phillippe Erlanger, *Louis XIV*, trans. Stephen Cox (London: Weidenfeld and Nicolson, 1970), pp. 204, 205, 207.

2. Cited in Simon Schama, *The Embarassment of Riches: An Interpretation of Dutch Culture in the Golden Age* (Berkeley: University of California Press, 1988), p. 234.

3. Cited in Perry Anderson, *Lineages of the Absolutist State* (London: NLB, 1974), p. 36.

4. Cited in Erlanger, p. 285.

5. Maurice Ashley, *England in the Seventeenth Century* (New York: Penguin, 1962), p. 150.

6. John Locke, *Two Treatises on Government* (New York: Macmillan, 1974), p. 89.

7. Ibid., pp. 122–123.

8. Ibid., p. 163.

9. Ibid., pp. 229–230.

10. Ibid., p. 247.

11. Cited in Sven Stolpe, *Christina of Sweden* (New York: Macmillan, 1966), p. 90.

12. Cited in Raymond Birn, *Crisis, Absolutism, Revolution: Europe, 1648–1789* (New York: Harcourt Brace Jovanovich, 1992), p. 128.

13. Cited in John Spielman, *Leopold I of Austria* (New Brunswick: Rutgers University Press, 1977), p. 140.

14. Cited in Lindsey Hughes, *Russia in the Age of Peter the Great* (New Haven: Yale University Press, 1998), p. 24.

Notes to Chapter Ten

1. Cited in Alfred W. Crosby, *Ecological Imperialism: The Biological Expansion of Europe, 900–1900* (Cambridge: Cambridge University Press, 1986), p. 202.

2. Cited in Simon Schama, *The Embarassment of Riches: An Interpretation of Dutch Culture in the Golden Age* (Berkeley: University of California Press, 1988), p. 198.

3. Cited in Janice Thomson, *Mercenaries, Pirates, and Sovereigns* (Princeton: Princeton University Press, 1994), p. 32.

4. J.H. Parry, *The Age of Reconnaissance: Discovery, Exploration and Settlement, 1450 to1650* (Berkeley: University of California Press, 1981), p. 186.

5. Cited in Parry, p. 223.

6. Cited in Roger Anstey, *The Atlantic Slave Trade and British Abolition, 1760–1830* (Atlantic Highlands, NJ: Humanities Press, 1975), p. 103.

7. Cited in Johannes M. Postma, *The Dutch in the Atlantic Slave Trade, 1600–1815* (Cambridge: Cambridge University Press, 1990), p. 36.

8. Cited in Robert C. Ritchie, *Captain Kidd and the War Against the Pirates* (Cambridge: Harvard University Press, 1986), p. 63.

9. Cited in Frank Sherry, *Raiders and Rebels: The Golden Age of Piracy* (New York: Hearst Marine Books, 1986), p. 270.

Notes to Chapter Eleven

1. Francis Bacon, *Essays and New Atlantis* (New York: Walter J. Black, 1942), p. 4.

2. Francis Bacon, *The New Organon*, ed. Fulton Anderson (Indianapolis: Bobbs-Merrill, 1960), p. 72.

3. René Descartes, *Discourse on Method, Optics, Geometry, and Meteorology*, trans. Paul Olscamp (Indianapolis: Bobbs-Merrill, 1961), pp. 3–19.

4. Bernard le Bovier de Fontenelle, *Conversations on the Plurality of Worlds*, trans. H.A. Hargreaves (Berkeley: University of California Press, 1990), p. 11.

5. Cited in Paul Hazard, *The European Mind, 1680–1715* (New York: World Publishing Company, 1967), p. 132.

6. Cited in Roger Hahn, *The Anatomy of a Scientific Institution: The Paris Academy of Sciences, 1666–1803* (Berkeley: University of California Press, 1971), p. 26.

7. Cited in John Carey, ed., *Eyewitness to Science* (Cambridge: Harvard University Press, 1995), p. 30.

8. Blaise Pascal, *Pensées. The Provincial Letters* (New York: Modern Library, 1941), section III, Number 187, p. 64.

9. Cited in Hazard, p. 105.

10. Cited in Hazard, p. 157.

11. Cited in Hazard, pp. 89–90.

12. François Poullain de la Barre, *The Woman as Good as the Man. Or, The Equality of Both Sexes*, ed. Gerald M. MacLean (Detroit: Wayne State University Press, 1988), p. 64.

13. Cited in Simon Schama, *The Embarassment of Riches: An Interpretation of Dutch Culture in the Seventeenth Century* (Berkeley: University of California Press, 1988), p. 412.

14. Poullain de la Barre, p. 87.

15. Cited in Hazard, p. 377.

16. Poullain de la Barre, pp. 77–78.

Notes to Chapter Twelve

1. Cited in Roy Porter, *English Society in the Eighteenth Century* (Middlesex, England: Penguin Books, 1983), p. 252.

2. Cited in Paula Backscheider, *Daniel Defoe: His Life* (Baltimore: Johns Hopkins University Press, 1989), p. 103.

3. Cited in Backscheider, p. 122.

4. Journal of Anna Larpent, cited in John Brewer, *The Pleasures of the Imagination: English Culture in the Eighteenth Century* (New York: Farrar Straus Giroux, 1997), p. 196.

5. Cited in J.H. Plumb, *England in the Eighteenth Century* (Middlesex, England: Penguin Books, 1972), p. 31.

6. Cited in Porter, p. 253.

7. Cited in Olwen Hufton, *The Prospect Before Her: A History of Women in Western Europe. Volume1, 1500–1800* (New York: Alfred A. Knopf, 1996), pp. 435–436.

8. Cited in John Middleton Murry, *Jonathan Swift: A Critical Biography* (New York: Farrar, Straus and Giroux, 1967), p. 429.

9. Cited in Porter, p. 252.

10. Cited in Ioan Williams, ed., *Novel and Romance 1700–1800: A Documentary Record* (New York: Barnes and Noble, 1970), p. 370.

11. Cited in Williams, p. 275.

12. Cited in Williams, p. 126.

13. Cited in Susan Ferrier, *Memoir and Correspondence of Susan Ferrier1782–1854*, ed. John Doyle (New York: AMC Press, 1970), p. 128.

14. Cited in Richard Altick, *The English Common Reader: A Social History of the Mass Reading Public, 1800–1900* (Chicago: University of Chicago Press, 1957), p. 39.

15. Cited in Bill Henderson, ed., *Rotten Reviews: A Literary Companion* (New York: Pushcart Press, 1986), p. 42.

16. Oliver Goldsmith, *The Vicar of Wakefield and Other Writings*, ed. Frank Hilles (New York: Modern Library, 1955), p. 63.

17. Cited in Thomas E. Crow, *Painters and Public Life in Eighteenth-Century Paris* (New Haven: Yale University Press, 1985), p. 6.

18. Cited in Crow, p. 10.

19. Cited in Crow, p. 19.

20. Cited in Hans David and Arthur Mendel, eds., *The New Bach Reader: A Life of Johann Sebastian Bach in Letters and Documents*, revised by Christoph Wolff (New York: W.W. Norton, 1998), pp. 21, 325, 338.

21. Cited in Otto Erich Deutsch, *Mozart: A Documentary Biography*, trans. Eric Blom, Peter Branscombe, and Jeremy Noble (Stanford: Stanford University Press, 1966), pp. 21, 44, 69.

22. Cited in Deutsch, pp. 214–215.

23. Cited in Peter Quennell, *The Profane Virtues: Four Studies of the Eighteenth Century* (New York: Viking Press, 1945), p. 181.

24. Cited in Quennell, p. 194.

25. Cited in Quennell, p. 190.

Notes to Chapter Thirteen

1. Cited in Peter Gay, ed., *The Enlightenment: A Comprehensive Anthology* (New York: Simon and Schuster, 1973), p. 384.

2. Cited in Gay, p. 14.

3. Cited in Theodore Besterman, *Voltaire* (New York: Harcourt, Brace and World, 1969), p. 236.

4. Cited in Gay, pp. 162–163.

5. Cited in Gay, pp. 242, 241.

6. Cited in Gay, p. 804.

7. Cited in Richard Holmes, "Voltaire's Grin," *New York Review of Books*, November 30, 1995, p. 51.

8. Voltaire, *Voltaire's Alphabet of Wit*, ed. Paul McPharlin (New York: Peter Pauper Press, 1955), s.v. "Justice."

9. As translated by Holmes, p. 54.

10. Cited in J. Robert Loy, *Montesquieu* (New York: Twayne, 1968), p. 51.

11. Cited in Loy, p. 132.

12. Cited in Loy, p. 26.

13. Cited in Gay, p. 288.

14. Cited in Arthur Wilson, *Diderot* (New York: Oxford University Press, 1972), p. 28.

15. Cited in Wilson, p. 98.

16. Jean Jacques Rousseau, *The Confessions*, trans. J.M. Cohen (New York: Penguin Books, 1953), p. 17.

17. Jean Jacques Rousseau, *The Social Contract* (New York: Hafner, 1947), p. 16.

18. Cited in Gay, p. 304.

19. Antoine Lavoisier, *Elements of Chemistry*, trans. Robert Kerr (New York: Dover, 1965), pp. xiv–xv.

20. Cited in P.N. Furbank, *Diderot: A Critical Biography* (New York: Alfred A. Knopf, 1992), p. 190.

21. Cited in Jean-Pierre Poirier, *Lavoisier: Chemist, Biologist, Economist*, trans. Rebecca Balinski (Philadelphia: University of Pennsylvania Press, 1996), p. 96.

22. Jean-Antoine-Nicolas de Caritat, Marquis de Condorcet, *Condorcet: Selected Writings*, ed. Keith Baker (Indianapolis: Bobbs-Merrill, 1976), p. 145.

Notes to Chapter Fourteen

1. Adam Smith, *The Wealth of Nations*, ed. Andrew Skinner (New York: Penguin Books, 1979), pp. 120–121.

2. Cited in E.C. Mossner, *The Life of David Hume* (Oxford: Clarendon Press, 1970), p. 65.

3. Cited in Peter Gay, ed., *The Enlightenment: A Comprehensive Anthology* (New York: Simon and Schuster, 1973), p. 486.

4. David Hume, "The Life of David Hume, Esq. Written by Himself," in *Dialogues Concerning Natural Religion*, ed. Norman Kemp Smith (Indianapolis: Bobbs-Merrill), p. 234.

5. Cited in Mossner, p. 225.

6. Hume, p. 169.

7. Cited in Mossner, p. 245.

8. Cited in Carl Van Doren, *Benjamin Franklin* (New York: Viking Press, 1964), p. 139.

9. Cited in Van Doren, p. 165.

10. Cited in Claire Tomalin, *The Life and Death of Mary Wollstonecraft* (London: Weidenfeld and Nicolson, 1974), p. 76.

11. Cited in Londa Schiebinger, *The Mind Has No Sex? Women in the Origins of Modern Science* (Cambridge: Harvard University Press, 1989), p. 14.

12. Cited in Cesare Beccaria, *On Crimes and Punishments* (Indianapolis: Bobbs-Merrill, 1961), pp. x, xiv.

13. Cited in Alexander Altmann, *Moses Mendelssohn: A Biographical Study* (University, AL: University of Alabama Press, 1973), p. 31.

14. Cited in Altmann, p. 39.

15. Cited in Altmann, p. 221.

16. Cited in Hannah Arendt, *Rahel Varnhagen: The Life of a Jewess*, ed. Liliane Weissberg (Baltimore: Johns Hopkins University Press, 1997), p. 126.

17. Cited in Ernst Cassirer, *Kant's Life and Thought*, trans. James Haden (Yale: Yale University Press, 1981), p. 77.

18. Cited in Cassirer, p. 140.

19. Cited in Cassirer, p. 40.

20. Cited in Cassirer, p. 121.

21. Cited in Simon Schama, "The Enlightenment in the Netherlands," in Roy Porter and Mikuláš Teich, eds., *The Enlightenment in National Context* (Cambridge: Cambridge University Press, 1981), p. 56.

22. Cited in Schama, p. 61.

23. Maaike Meijer, ed., *The Defiant Muse: Dutch and Flemish Feminist Poems from the Middle Ages to the Present* (New York: Feminist Press of the City University of New York, 1998), pp. 65–67.

24. Cited in David Daiches, *Robert Burns* (New York: Macmillan, 1966), p. 104.

Notes to Chapter Fifteen

1. Cited in R.W. Harris, *Absolutism and Enlightenment, 1660–1789* (New York: Harper and Row, 1966), p. 173.

2. Cited in C.A. Macartney, ed., *The Habsburg and Hohenzollern Dynasties in the Seventeenth and Eighteenth Centuries* (New York: Harper and Row, 1970), p. 323.

3. Cited in Harris, p. 172.

4. Cited in Macartney, p. 328.

5. Cited in Macartney, p. 97.

6. Cited in Harris, p. 287.

7. Cited in Robert Pick, *Empress Maria Theresa* (New York: Harper and Row, 1966), p. 263.

8. Cited in Robert B. Asprey, *Frederick the Great: The Magnificent Enigma* (New York: Ticknor and Fields, 1986), p. 286.

9. Cited in Macartney, p. 334.

10. Cited in Macartney, pp. 114–115.

11. Cited in Pick, p. 205.

12. Cited in Walter Dorn, *Competition for Empire, 1740–1763* (New York: Harper and Row, 1963), p. 139.

13. William Guthrie, *A New Geographical, Historical, and Commercial Grammar and Present State of the Several Kingdoms of the World* (London, 1788), p. 557.

14. Cited in John T. Alexander, *Catherine the Great: Life and Legend* (New York: Oxford University Press, 1989), p. 14.

15. Cited in Alexander, p. 78.

16. Cited in Alexander, p. 101.

17. Cited in Alexander, p. 125.

18. Cited in Guthrie, p. 548.

19. Cited in Macartney, p. 343.

20. Guthrie, p. 539.

21. Cited in Macartney, p. 206.

22. Cited in Miecislaus Haiman, *Kosciuszko in the American Revolution* (New York: The Kosciuszko Foundation, 1975), p. 9.

23. Cited in Haiman, *American Revolution*, p. 96.

24. Cited in Haiman, *American Revolution*, p. 4.

25. Cited in Miecislaus Haiman, *Kosciuszko: Leader and Exile* (New York: The Kosciuszko Foundation, 1977), p. 6.

26. Cited in Haiman, *Leader and Exile*, p. 9.

27. Cited in Haiman, *Leader and Exile*, pp. 12, 17.

Notes to Chapter Sixteen

1. Cited in Phyllis Dean, *The First Industrial Revolution* (Cambridge: Cambridge University Press, 1965), p. 74.

2. Cited in Myron Gutmann, *Toward the Modern Economy: Early Industry in Europe, 1500–1800* (New York: Alfred A. Knopf, 1988), p. 128.

3. Cited in Peter Mathias, *The First Industrial Nation: An Economic History of Britain, 1700–1914*, 2nd ed. (London: Methuen Press, 1983), p. 171.

4. Cited in Robert Darnton, *The Great Cat Massacre and Other Episodes in French Cultural History* (New York: Vintage Books, 1985), p. 104.

5. Cited in Dean, p. 87.

6. Adam Smith, *The Wealth of Nations*, ed. Andrew Skinner (Middlesex, England: Penguin Books, 1979), p. 181.

7. Cited in Wendy Wassyng Roworth, ed., *Angelica Kauffmann: A Continental Artist in Georgian England* (London: Reaktion Books, 1992) p. 24.

8. Cited in John Brewer, *The Pleasures of the Imagination: English Culture in the Eighteenth Century* (New York: Farrar Straus Giroux, 1997), p. 224.

9. Cited in Roworth, p. 84.

10. Elisabeth Vigée-Le Brun, *The Memoirs of Elisabeth Vigée-Le Brun*, trans. Siân Evans (Bloomington: Indiana University Press, 1989), pp. 16, 39, 41.

11. Cited in Joseph Baillio, *Elisabeth Louise Vigée Le Brun* (Fort Worth, TX: Kimbell Art Museum, 1982), pp. 46–48.

12. Cited in Otto Erich Deutsch, *Mozart: A Documentary Biography* (Stanford: Stanford University Press, 1966), p. 354.

13. Cited in Ludwig Lewisohn, *Goethe: The Story of a Man* 2 vols. (New York: Farrar, Straus, 1949), vol. 1, p. 298.

14. Cited in Richard Friedenthal, *Goethe: His Life and Times* (New York: World Publishing Company, 1965), p. 200.

Notes to Chapter Seventeen

1. Cited in William Doyle, *The Oxford History of the French Revolution* (Oxford: Clarendon Press, 1989), p. 43.

2. Cited in Simon Schama, *Citizens: A Chronicle of the French Revolution* (New York: Alfred A. Knopf, 1989), p. 86.

3. Cited in Schama, p. 95.

4. Cited in Schama, p. 87.

5. Cited in Doyle, p. 74.

6. Cited in Doyle, p. 87.

7. Cited in Laura Mason and Tracey Rizzo, eds., *The French Revolution: A Document Collection* (NewYork: Houghton Mifflin, 1999), pp. 51–54.

8. Cited in Schama, p. 331.

9. Gouverneur Morris, *A Diary of the French Revolution*, ed. Beatrix Cary Davenport, 2 vols. (Boston: Houghton Mifflin, 1939), p. 69.

10. Morris, p. 66.

11. Cited in Schama, p. 356.

12. Cited in Mason and Rizzo, p. 61.

13. Cited in Schama, p. 364.

14. Cited in Doyle, p. 108

15. Cited in Daniel Roche, *The People of Paris: An Essay in Popular Culture in the Eighteenth Century* (Berkeley: University of California Press, 1987), p. 58.

16. Cited in Schama, pp. 333, 331.

17. Cited in Schama, p. 176.

18. Cited in Doyle, p. 115.

19. Cited in Mason and Rizzo, p. 104.

20. Cited in Schama, p. 468.

21. Cited in Frédéric Grendel, *Beaumarchais: The Man Who Was Figaro*, trans. Robert Greaves (New York: Thomas Y. Crowell, 1977), pp. 212–222.

Notes to Chapter Eighteen

1. Cited in William Doyle, *The Oxford History of the French Revolution* (Oxford: Clarendon Press, 1989), p. 124.

2. Cited in George Rudé, ed., *Robespierre* (Englewood Cliffs, NJ: Prentice-Hall, 1967), pp. 18–21.

3. Cited by Laura Mason and Tracey Rizzo, eds., *The French Revolution: A Document Collection* (New York: Houghton Mifflin, 1999), p. 153.

4. Cited in Doyle, p. 156.

5. Cited in Doyle, p. 158.

6. Cited in Mason and Rizzo, p. 158.

7. Cited in Mason and Rizzo, p. 166.

8. Cited in Rudé, p. 87.

9. Cited in Mason and Rizzo, p. 170.

10. Cited in Christopher Hibbert, *The Days of the French Revolution* (New York: Morrow Quill Paperbacks, 1981), p. 178.

11. Cited in Doyle, p. 193.

12. Cited in Doyle, p. 226.

13. Cited in Simon Schama, *Citizens: A Chronicle of the French Revolution* (New York: Alfred A. Knopf, 1989), p. 705.

14. Cited in Doyle, p. 233.

15. Cited in Schama, p. 714.

16. Cited in Rudé, p. 59.

17. Cited in Schama, p. 787.

18. Cited in Rudé, p. 59.

19. Cited in Doyle, p. 205.

20. Cited in Rudé, p. 59.

21. Cited in Rudé, p. 76.

22. Cited in Linda Kelly, *Women of the French Revolution* (London: Hamish Hamilton, 1987), p. 127.

23. Cited in Mason and Rizzo, p. 111.

24. Cited in Kelly, p. 122.

25. Cited in Doyle, p. 277.

26. Cited in Doyle, p. 284.

27. Cited in Doyle, p. 293.

28. Cited in Doyle, p. 167.

29. Edmund Burke, *Reflections on the Revolution in France* (New York: Doubleday, 1989), pp. 72–73.

30. Ibid. , pp. 99–100.

31. Cited in T.C. Blanning, "The Enlightenment in Catholic Germany," in Roy Porter and Mikuláš Teich, eds., *The Enlightenment in National Context* (Cambridge: Cambridge University Press, 1981), p. 126.

32. Roy Porter, "The Enlightenment in England," in Porter and Teich, p. 17.

33. Thomas Paine, *The Rights of Man* (New York: Doubleday, 1989), p. 277.

34. Ibid., p. 433.

35. Mary Wollstonecraft, *Political Writings*, ed. Janet Todd (Toronto: University of Toronto Press, 1993), p. 81.

36. Wollstonecraft, p. 276.

37. Cited in Doyle, p. 412.

38. Cited in Ralph Korngold, *Citizen Toussaint* (New York: Hill and Wang, 1944). p. 111.

Notes to Chapter Nineteen

1. Cited in Felix Markham, *Napoleon* (New York: Mentor Books, 1966), p. 21.

2. Cited in Alan Schom, *Napoleon Bonaparte* (New York: Harper-Collins, 1997) p. 12.

3. Cited in Schom, p. 219.

4. Cited in George Rudé, *Revolutionary Europe, 1783–1815* (New York: Harper and Row, 1975) p. 177.

5. Cited in Schom, p. 290.

6. Cited in Rudé, p. 237.

7. Cited in Markham, p. 95.

8. Cited in Markham, p. 95.

9. Cited in Markham, p. 97.

10. Cited in Rudé, p. 235.

11. Cited in Markham, p. 155.

12. Cited in Markham, p. 180.

13. Cited in Markham, p. 210.

14. Cited in Friedrich Meinecke, *The Age of German Liberation, 1795–1815* (Berkeley: University of California Press, 1977), p. 44.

15. Cited in Maynard Solomon, *Beethoven* (New York: Schirmer Books, 1977) p. 132.

16. Cited in Solomon, p. 138.

17. Cited in Solomon, p. 17.

18. Cited in Solomon, p. 127.

19. Cited in J.N. Burk, *The Life and Works of Beethoven* (New York, 1943), p. 91.

Index

About the Authors

Lisa Rosner is currently Professor of History at Richard Stockton College of New Jersey. Her previous books include *Medical Education in the Age of Improvement: Edinburgh Students and Apprentices 1760–1826* (1991) and *The Most Beautiful Man in Existence: The Scandalous Life of Alexander Lesassier* (1999).

John Theibault has taught at the University of Oregon, Princeton University, and Loyola College of Maryland. He is the author of *German Villages in Crisis: Rural Life in Hesse-Kassel and the Thirty Years' War, 1580–1720* (1995).